People on the Move

This book is part of the European Science Foundation (ESF) programme 'Occupation in Europe: The Impact of National Socialist and Fascist Rule'.
ISSN: 1753–7894

SETTING SCIENCE AGENDAS FOR EUROPE

The ESF is an independent, non-governmental organization of national research organizations.

Our strength lies in the membership and in our ability to bring together the different domains of European science in order to meet the scientific challenges of the future. The ESF's membership currently includes seventy-seven influential national funding agencies, research-performing agencies and academies from thirty nations as its contributing members.

Since its establishment in 1974, the ESF, which has its headquarters in Strasbourg with offices in Brussels and Ostend, has assembled a host of research organizations that span all disciplines of science in Europe, to create a common platform for cross-border cooperation.

We are dedicated to supporting our members in promoting science, scientific research and science policy across Europe. Through its activities and instruments ESF has made major contributions to science in a global context. The ESF covers the following scientific domains:

- Humanities
- Life, Earth and Environmental Sciences
- Medical Sciences
- Physical and Engineering Sciences
- Social Sciences
- Marine Sciences
- Nuclear Physics
- Polar Sciences
- Radio Astronomy Frequencies
- Space Sciences

This series includes:

Vol. 1
Surviving Hitler and Mussolini: Daily Life in Occupied Europe
Edited by Robert Gildea, Olivier Wieviorka and Anette Warring

Vol. 2
The War for Legitimacy in Politics and Culture, 1936–1946
Edited by Martin Conway and Peter Romijn

Vol. 3
People on the Move: Forced Population Movements in Europe in the Second World War and its Aftermath
Pertti Ahonen, Gustavo Corni, Jerzy Kochanowski, Rainer Schulze, Tamás Stark and Barbara Stelzl-Marx

People on the Move

Forced Population Movements in Europe in the Second
World War and Its Aftermath

Pertti Ahonen, Gustavo Corni, Jerzy Kochanowski,
Rainer Schulze, Tamás Stark and Barbara Stelzl-Marx

Oxford • New York

English Edition
First published in 2008 by
Berg
Editorial offices:
1st Floor, Angel Court, 81 St Clements Street, Oxford, OX4 1AW, UK
175 Fifth Avenue, New York, NY 10010, USA

Berg is the imprint of Oxford International Publishers Ltd.

Library of Congress Cataloguing-in-Publication Data
People on the move : forced population movements in Europe in the
Second World War and its aftermath / Pertti Ahonen ... [et al.]. — English
ed.
   p. cm.
  Includes bibliographical references and index.
  ISBN-13: 978-1-84520-480-8 (cloth)
  ISBN-10: 1-84520-480-8 (cloth)
  ISBN-13: 978-1-84520-824-0 (pbk.)
  ISBN-10: 1-84520-824-2 (pbk.)
  1. Population transfers—History—20th century. 2. World War, 1939-
1945—Deportations. 3. Forced migration—Europe—History—20th
century. I. Ahonen, Pertti.

  D820.P7P46 2008
  940.53'1—dc22   2008023634

British Library Cataloguing-in-Publication Data
A catalogue record for this book is available from the British Library.

ISBN 978 1 84520 480 8 (Cloth)
     978 1 84520 824 0 (Paper)

Typeset by Avocet Typeset, Chilton, Aylesbury, Bucks
Printed in the United Kingdom by Biddles Ltd, King's Lynn

www.bergpublishers.com

Contents

Authors

Pertti Ahonen is Senior Lecturer in Modern European History in the School of History, Classics and Archaeology at the University of Edinburgh. He received his PhD in modern European history from Yale University and taught for several years at the University of Sheffield before moving to Edinburgh in 2005. He is the author of *After the Expulsion: West Germany and Eastern Europe, 1945–1990* (Oxford, 2003) and of a range of articles and book chapters on twentieth century European history. He is currently writing a book entitled *Victims of the Berlin Wall: Political Legitimation and Identity Building in Cold War Germany* for Oxford University Press.

Gustavo Corni has taught at the universities of Bologna, Venice, Chieti and Trieste, and since 2001 has been full Professor of Contemporary History at the University of Trento. He was 1992 and 2008 fellow of the Alexander von Humboldt Foundation, in 1995 visiting professor in Vienna, 1999/2000 fellow at the Oxford Centre for Hebrew and Jewish Studies, and is permanent fellow at the Institute for Contemporary History, Munich. He specializes in German history in the twentieth century and the comparative social history of wars. His main publications are: *Hitler's Ghettos: Voices from a Beleaguered Society 1939–1944* (London, 2002), *Il sogno del grande spazio: Le politiche d'occupazione nell'Europa nazista* (Rome, 2005) and *Hitler* (Bologna, 2007).

Jerzy Kochanowski graduated in 1984 from Warsaw University and since 2005 has been a professor at Warsaw University. From 2000 to 2005 he was a fellow at the German Historical Institute in Warsaw and in 2007 visiting professor at the University of Mainz. Since 2006 he has been coordinator of the international research project 'Hidden paths: unofficial contacts in socialist societies 1956–1989'. His main areas of interest are: Polish social history since 1945, forced migrations, and the German minority in Poland. His publications include *In polnischer Gefangenschaft: Deutsche Kriegsgefangene in Polen 1945–1950* (Osnabrück, 2004).

Rainer Schulze taught Modern European History at the University of Bochum, Birkbeck College London and Roehampton University, before joining the

University of Essex in 1995, where he is currently Head of the Department of History. He has specialized in twentieth-century German history, German collective memory and identity, the history of Bergen-Belsen and the history of forced migrations after the Second World War, and published widely in these areas. His publications include the edited volumes *Zwischen Heimat und Zuhause: Deutsche Flüchtlinge und Vertriebene in (West-)Deutschland 1945–2000* (Osnabrück, 2001) and *AugenZeugen: Fotos, Filme und Zeitzeugenbericht in der neuen Dauerausstellung der Gedenkstätte Bergen-Belsen – Hintergrund und Kontext* (Hannover, 2007). He contributed as one of the project leaders to the development of the new permanent exhibition at the Gedenkstätte Bergen-Belsen and, in 2005, was appointed a member of the International Experts' Commission for the Redevelopment of the Gedenkstätte Bergen-Belsen. He is currently preparing a monograph on the history and memory of Bergen-Belsen concentration camp.

Tamás Stark received his PhD from the University of Budapest in 1993. From 1983 he was a researcher at the Institute of History of the Hungarian Academy of Sciences, and in 2000 he was appointed a senior research fellow. Since 2003 he has worked at the Museum of the House of Terror in Budapest. His specialization is forced population movement in East-Central Europe in the period 1938–56, with special regard to the history of the Holocaust, the fate of prisoners of war and civilian internees, and the post-war migrations. His main publications include *Hungary's Human Losses in World War II* (Uppsala, 1995), *Hungarian Jews during the Holocaust and after the Second World War, 1939–1949: A Statistical Review* (Boulder, CO, 2000) and *Magyarok szoviet fogszgbar* (Budapest, 2006) on the fate of the Hungarian prisoners under Soviet control.

Barbara Stelzl-Marx is deputy director at the Ludwig Boltzmann Institute for Research on War Consequences (BIK), Graz–Vienna–Klagenfurt, and lecturer at the University of Graz. Since October 2005 she has been APART-scholar of the Austrian Academy of Sciences. She has been a student at the universities of Graz, Oxford, Volgograd, Moscow and Stamford. The focus of her research is the Soviet occupation of Austria 1945–55, the Cold War, and Second World War prisoners of war in the Third Reich and in the USSR. Her publications include: *Zwischen Fiktion und Zeitzeugenschaft: Amerikanische und sowjetische Kriegsgefangene im Stalag XVII B Krems-Gneixendorf* (Tübingen, 2000); ed. with Stefan Karner and Alexander Tschubarjan, *Die Rote Armee in Österreich: Sowjetische Besatzung 1945–1955. Dokumente*, 2 vols (Graz–Vienna–Munich, 2005); ed. with Günter Bischof and Stefan Karner, *Kriegsgefangene des Zweiten Weltkrieges: Gefangennahme – Lagerleben – Rückkehr. Zehn Jahre Ludwig Boltzmann-Institut für Kriegsfolgen-Forschung* (Vienna and Munich, 2005).

Abbreviations

AAN	Archiwum Akt Nowych (Archive of Modern Records, Warsaw)
AdBIK	Archiv des Ludwig Boltzmann Instituts für Kriegsfolgen-Forschung (Archive of the Ludwig Boltzmann Institute for Research on War Consequences, Graz–Vienna–Klagenfurt)
AO	Auslandsorganisation (NSDAP Foreign Organization)
APART	Austrian Programme for Advanced Research and Technology
APW	Archiwum Państwowe m.st. Warszawy (Warsaw Regional State Archive)
AVNOJ	Antifašističko vijeće narodnog oslobođenja Jugoslavije (Anti-Fascist Council of the People's Liberation of Yugoslavia)
BdV	Bund der Vertriebenen (German League of Expellees)
BGBl	*Bundesgesetzblatt*
BHE	Bund der Heimatvertriebenen und Entrechteten (German League of Expellees and Disenfranchised)
BVFK	Bundesministerium für Vertriebene, Flüchtlinge und Kriegsgeschädigte (German Federal Ministry of Expellees, Refugees and War Victims)
CAUR	Comitati d'azione per l'universalità di Roma (Action Committees for the Universality of Rome)
CIS	Commonwealth of Independent States (original Russian: Sodruzhestvo Nezavisimych Gosudarstv, SNG)
CPSU	Communist Party of the Soviet Union (original Russian: Kommunističeskaja Partija Sovetskogo Sojuza, KPSS)
CUP	Committee of Union and Progress (original Turkish: Ittihad ve Terakki Cemiyeti)
DP	Displaced person
DVL	*Deutsche Volksliste* (List of Ethnic Germans)
FRG	Federal Republic of Germany
GARF	Gosudarstvennyi Archiv Rossiiskoi Federacii (State Archive of the Russian Federation, Moscow)
GDR	German Democratic Republic
GG	Generalgouvernement (German General Government in Polish Occupied Territories)

GPO	Generalplan Ost (German General Plan for the East)
GPRR	Główny Pełnomocnik Rzadu do spraw Repatriacji (Polish Main Plenipotentiary Administration for Repatriation)
GULAG	Glavnoe Upravlenie Lagerei (Soviet Main Administration of the Camps)
GUPVI	Glavnoe Upravlenie po delam voennoplennykh i internirovannykh (Main Administration for the Affairs of Prisoners of War and Internees)
ILO	International Labour Organization
IMI	Italian Military Internees
KOR	Komitet Obrony Robotnikow (Committee for the Defence of the Workers)
KSH Levéltár	Központi Statisztikai Hivatal Levéltára (Archives of Hungarian Central Statistical Office, Budapest)
MGB	Ministerstvo Gosudarstvennoi Bezopasnosti (Soviet Ministry of State Security)
MIP	Ministerstwo Informacji i Propagandy (Ministry for Information and Propaganda)
MVD	Ministerstvo Vnutrennich Del (Soviet Ministry of Internal Affairs)
NKGB	Narodnyi Komissariat Gosudarstvennoi Bezopastnosti (Soviet People's Commissariat for State Security)
NKVD	Narodnyi Komissariat Vnutrennich Del (Soviet People's Commissariat for Internal Affairs)
NSDAP	Nationalsozialistische Deutsche Arbeiterpartei (National Socialist German Workers' Party)
Oflag	*Offizierslager* (Officers' Camp)
OZNA	Odeljenje za zaštitu naroda (Yugoslav Department for the Protection of the People)
PCI	Partito Comunista Italiano (Italian Communist Party)
PFL	Proverochno-Fil'tracionnye Lageria (Soviet Screening-filtration Camps)
PFP	Proverochno-Fil'tracionnye Punkty (Soviet Screening-filtration Points)
POW	Prisoner of war
PRL	Polska Rzeczpospolita Ludowa (Polish People's Republic)
PUR	Państwowy Urząd Repatriacyjny (State Bureau for Repatriations)
RAD	Reichsarbeitsdienst (Reich Labour Service)
RF-SS	Reichsführer der Schutzstaffel
RGASPI	Rossiiskii Gosudarstvennij Archiv Social'no-Političeskoj Istorii (Russian State Archive for Social-Political History, Moscow)
RGBl	*Reichsgesetzblatt* (Reich Law Gazette)

RKFDV	Reichskommissariat für die Festigung des deutschen Volkstums (Reich Commissariat for the Strengthening of Germandom)
RSHA	Reichssicherheitshauptamt (Reich Security Main Office)
RuSHA	Rasse- und Siedlungshauptamt (Race and Settlement Main Office of the SS)
SA	Sturmabteilung (NSDAP Storm Department)
SD	Sicherheitsdienst (German Security Service)
SED	Sozialistische Einheitspartei Deutschland (Socialist Unity Party of Germany)
SMERSH	Smert' šhpionam (Soviet Counterintelligence, literally 'Death to the Spies')
SNK	Sovet Narodnich Komissarov (Soviet Council of the People's Commissars)
SS	Schutzstaffel (NSDAP Protective Squadron)
Stalag	*Stammlager* (Regular POW Camp)
UPA	Ukrajins'ka Povstans'ka Armija (Ukrainian Insurgent Army)
UPVI	Upravlenie Voennoplennych i Internirovannych (Soviet Administration for the Affairs of Prisoners of War and Internees of the Soviet Commissariat of the Interior)
USHMM	United States Holocaust Memorial Museum
UWZ	Umwandererzentralstelle (German Relocation Headquarters)
VKP(b)	Vsesoiuznaia Kommunisticheskaia Partija (bolshevikov) (All-Union Communist Party – Bolshevik)
VoMi	Volksdeutsche Mittelstelle (Liaison Office for Ethnic Germans)
WVHA	Wirtschafts- und Verwaltungshauptamt (SS Economic and Administrative Main Office)

Foreword

This book is the result of a collaborative venture which involved six authors from different cultural backgrounds, languages and historiographical traditions from all over Europe. As such, it presented a notable challenge for all involved – a challenge of which the authors were aware from the very beginning of the project. In addition, the topic itself presented a major challenge. Forced movements of populations are arguably one of the most dramatic and significant events during and after the Second World War, but the authors of this book realized during their research that the subject has been treated very unevenly so far. Some aspects of the subject were well defined; in other cases, however, the historiography was 'peripheral' insofar as it was in languages that are not widely read. Moreover, some aspects of the subject had not been dealt with by historians at all.

The book is the result of seven years of work on the question of 'The Migration of the Masses' within a larger research project, 'The Impact of National Socialist and Fascist Occupation in Europe, 1938–1950', funded by the European Science Foundation (ESF) and directed by Wolfgang Benz (Berlin) and Hans Blom (Amsterdam). This ambitious project consisted of six research teams and brought together historians from all over Europe. For the first time since the fall of communism this project provided an opportunity to exchange ideas within a profession that had been divided by the ideological split between West and East since 1945.

After an inaugural meeting in Trento, Italy, in December 2000, there were two more joint meetings of all teams, in September 2003 in Jachranka/Warsaw, Poland, and in April 2005 in Amsterdam, Netherlands.

In addition to the three joint meetings, the research team on 'The Migration of the Masses' held three specialized workshops: Budapest, Hungary, September 2001, Villa Vigoni, Italy, October 2002, Jachranka/Warsaw, Poland, September 2003.[1] Many scholars who were not part of the core team gave papers at these seminars and offered numerous important observations and comments. These papers were an indispensable part of the preparation of this book, and all authors express their gratitude to the contributors of these essays and to the institutions that hosted us.

It quickly transpired that the greatest challenge for this team was to go beyond specializations of its members, widening the research in order to produce a volume which was as balanced as possible and which would be able to highlight all aspects of the question. This book concentrates upon the policies of deportation and forced movements of populations planned and partially enacted by Nazi Germany and its Axis allies between 1939 and 1945, as well as those which were implemented in the wake, and as a consequence, of the Second World War.

Right from the start, it was agreed that looking at Nazi Germany's plans in isolation would be inadequate. It was therefore decided to take a wider view and include, for example, an analysis of how ethnic resettlements have been remembered up to the present day. The nineteenth century needed to be referred to at least briefly, as this was the period when the various radical ethno-nationalisms started to proliferate. The First World War brought about the first attempt by sovereign nations to achieve ethnic homogeneity through the exchange of entire populations, manifested in the Greek–Turkish population transfers sanctioned by the Treaty of Lausanne of 1923.

Obviously, it was necessary to go beyond the end of the Second World War and analyse the redrawing of the ethno-geographical map of Europe at the end of the war with the forced migration of millions of people, the largest group of them the 12–14 million ethnic Germans, in central, eastern and south-eastern Europe. We only refer to the forced population movements carried out by the Soviet Union during and at the end of the war insofar as they played a role for the main theme of the research project.

The extermination of the European Jews is not included in this book, even though it affected Jews in all of Nazi-occupied Europe and, at least in its ideological planning phase, can be regarded as the forced movement of an entire people. This decision was obligatory since another of the six research teams worked specifically on this theme. However, one chapter deals with the millions of men and women deported to the German Reich from the occupied territories and satellite states to work as forced labourers, as these deportations form part of the forced population movements of this period.

The process of producing this book has been very complex. At meetings in Graz, Austria, in September 2004, and Trento, Italy, in July 2006, we jointly decided upon the structure of the book and divided up the work, giving each member of the team responsibility for writing the first drafts of particular chapters (or sub-chapters). In a second and even more complex phase, we exchanged the chapters and made suggestions, corrections and criticisms. This intense process of collective writing led to the present volume. It can justly be described as a good example of cross-European work. We could not have done it without the modern means of communication, especially email.

Nevertheless, some responsibility for individual chapters and sub-chapters can be attributed. Each main chapter had one or two coordinators:

Chapter 1 – Corni, Stark
Chapter 2 – Corni, Stark

Chapter 3 – Corni, Stark
Chapter 4 – Corni, Stark
Chapter 5 – Ahonen, Kochanowski
Chapter 6 – Schulze
Chapter 7 – Stelzl-Marx

The overall coordinator for the volume was Gustavo Corni. The final texts were written by:

Chapter 1 – Stark (1.1), Corni (1.2) and Schulze (1.3)
Chapter 2 – Corni (2.1, 2.2, 2.3, 2.5), and Corni and Kochanowski (2.4, 2.6, 2.7)
Chapter 3 – Corni (3.1) and Stark (3.2, 3.3)
Chapter 4 – Stark (4.1, 4.2), Ahonen and Schulze (4.3), Kochanowski (4.4) and Corni (4.5)
Chapter 5 – Ahonen and Kochanowski
Chapter 6 – Corni (6.1), Schulze (6.2) and Kochanowski (6.3)
Chapter 7 – Stelzl-Marx

The chapters written by Corni, Kochanowski, Stark and Stelzl-Marx were translated by Irene Diamond, Jacek Soszyński, Ildiko Hortobágyi and Alexj Kay, respectively. Their precious contributions made the successive critical interaction between all six authors possible and the authors' most sincere thanks go to them. Ahonen undertook an initial edit of the completed English-language manuscript. We would also like to thank Niccolò Pianciola, who edited the footnotes and compiled the bibliography and the index, Fintan Power and Ken Bruce, who contributed to the editing, Nirvana Martinelli for helping to draw the maps and finally Carla Manca, who designed a striking cover for the book. We wish to thank Wolfgang Benz and J.C.H. Blom, the project directors, and Johannes Houwink Ten Cate and Conny Kristel, who successively held the post of overall project coordinators. Madelise Blumenroeder from the European Science Foundation and her staff in Strasbourg handled all administrative and financial questions smoothly and expertly.

Pertti Ahonen, Edinburgh, UK
Gustavo Corni, Trento, Italy
Jerzy Kochanowski, Warsaw, Poland
Rainer Schulze, London/Colchester, UK
Tamás Stark, Budapest, Hungary
Barbara Stelzl-Marx, Graz, Austria

–1–

Introduction

1.1 The Rise of the Modern Idea of a Nation

Transfers of populations, whether partial or total, are a modern phenomenon of the 1900s. In many cases, but not all, they have been part of policies of ethnic cleansing. This remark appears appropriate, even though we may assume that transfers of people who are part of a community, and which have involved some level of violence, have occurred throughout history. But organized, large-scale population transfers are nevertheless a modern occurrence, connected to the emergence of a strong idea of nation during the 1800s, which played an essential role in legitimizing political systems on the way to democratization.

The rationalizing activity of absolute monarchies and the ideology of the Enlightenment were the two most important factors that led to the birth of nationalism. In order to improve the general efficiency of the state, absolute monarchs tried to mould the territories under their authority into one economic and administrative unit. From the seventeenth century on, the more and more rapidly developing modern state extended and strengthened its power over the population. The modern state is the offspring of the absolute monarchy, but the new conditions that it created contributed to the elimination of absolutism. With the rise of the modern state the system of relationships between rulers and the ruled slowly changed. Civil society accepted the state's centralizing ambitions but demanded greater control over its taxing and enforcing monopolies. The idea of a nation was born during the fight for a redistribution of power.

In the period preceding the modern state the idea of a nation was restricted to the nobility. During the struggle for the redistribution of power the bourgeoisie proclaimed that by the establishment of a unified state each citizen should take his share of power, that each citizen (although excluding women) should be a member of the nation. This process was carried out in the clearest way in France, where – after the victory of the revolution of 1789 – all inhabitants of the country were declared to be citizens of the state and members of the French nation. At the end of the eighteenth century nationalism gained its force from the fact that it was connected to ideas of freedom and equality.

When during the nineteenth century the doctrine of nationalism reached the central and eastern parts of Europe, which were ruled by the multinational empires of Tsarist Russia, the Ottomans and Austria-Hungary, its contents gradually changed. The communities living in the central and peripheral parts of Europe started to reorganize themselves on a cultural basis. The notion of a culture-nation arose in German philosophy and literature (from Herder to Fichte) before the united German Reich was born. Elsewhere in Central and Eastern Europe the new nations that were about to be born could not connect their existence to the idea of citizenship because they lacked an independent state; so they defined themselves with the help of their culture and language. Thus, reading and writing became the main constituents in the process of building a nation. Language was an applicable criterion to define a nation. If a community has its own language, its members must be a nation, and as a nation they have the right to form their own state. The mixing of the two main schemes of nation-building – the French, in which the state is an offspring of the nation, and the German, in which the state takes priority over the nation – had wide-ranging consequences, especially in the new nation states aiming to establish their identities in Central and Eastern Europe.[1]

In that part of the continent the evolving nationalism assumed an increasingly ethnic character. During the nineteenth century the concept of the nation as *demos*, i.e. as a community of people who live on the same territory, was increasingly pervaded by a concept based on *ethnos*, i.e. an ethnic-cultural community. In some instances – especially in Central and Eastern Europe – the idea of a 'homogeneous' nation based on an organic vision of the people, the *Volk*, began to gain strength. These contexts, which differ radically from those of stratified nations – stratified along class lines, for example – provide the conditions for policies of ethnic cleansing, according to the British sociologist Michael Mann.[2] The new ties that were formed on a cultural and ethnic basis proved to be much stronger than loyalty to an empire, in the name of which the rulers wanted to homogenize their culturally and linguistically diverse subjects.

After 1918 the main force driving the course of events in Central and Eastern Europe was the kind of nationalism that set the formation of an ethnically homogeneous state as its target. Ethnic minorities were regarded as foreign bodies and their elimination and forced assimilation as an obligation for the nation. Fearing disintegration, the young 'successor states' of the region attempted to weaken ethnic minorities with the means and tools put at their disposal by the complex international post-war situation, and according to their own political structures.

Tomáš Masaryk's 1917 study *New Europe* summed up the guidelines for restructuring Europe – or, more precisely, Central and Eastern Europe – as follows: 'Today all European nations struggle for liberation and political unity, for the political organization of Europe on the basis of nationality. The intrinsic historical connection of democracy with nationality [and socialism] explains why the democratic states: France, England, Italy, and so on, and now revolutionary Russia, declare solemnly in favor of the right of all nations to self-determination.'[3]

The peace settlement that ended the First World War attempted to divide the region's empires into nation states on the basis of the principle of self-determination. But the principle, although widely propagated, was so subordinated to other – political, economic and strategic – considerations and so undermined by fears of the Bolshevik menace that the new state system of Central and Eastern Europe hardly matched national-ethnic principles. Moreover, the relationships among nationalities within the new states were characterized mostly by conditions of inferiority versus superiority. The new post-1918 borders in Western Prussia, the Western Ukraine, the Sudetenland, Southern Slovakia, Subcarpathia, Transylvania, the Banat, Bessarabia and Voivodina were determined by the victors with almost complete disregard for the ethnic-linguistic conditions on the ground. East-Central Europe was portrayed by the former Austrian Minister of Foreign Affairs Gusztáv Gratz in the following way: 'The principle of nationality has a strong suggestive influence on the masses even today and maybe more than ever. People are willing to make such sacrifices for it, which they would be reluctant to do for anything else. There were times when people threw life away, went into exile or to the stake because of their religious belief. These days, the principle of nation rules over the minds with an equal might.'[4]

All states in the region applied forceful assimilation policies. Even Czechoslovakia – the most accommodating country to have signed the Paris peace treaties – was far from realizing a federal Swiss-like model, although this had been announced by the government itself. Any sort of territorially based settlement of the various ethnic questions was thwarted by a series of reforms introduced in public administration, and in the field of education a discriminatory attitude was maintained from the primary to the tertiary levels. Even in Hungary, which had practically been reduced to a nation state as a result of the peace treaty, assimilationist tendencies towards minorities survived. This political attitude did not change even when it became obvious that it might discredit the actions that Budapest sought to undertake to defend Hungarian minorities abroad within the framework of the League of Nation's minority protection system.

1.2 The Paris Peace Conference and Its Consequences

According to the plans of United States President Woodrow Wilson, the Paris Peace Conference, which began in January 1919, was to provide the opportunity to solve the national and ethnic problems that had helped to spark off the Great War.[5]

Although the numbers were lower than they would be in 1945, even at the end of the First World War there were several million European refugees without a homeland, expelled by military authorities from areas of battle – especially in the western provinces of the Russian empire – or forced to move by the new borders laid down by the outcome of the battles even before the peace treaty. Such a fate befell in particular German citizens who moved from the territories that the Reich had lost – including Alsace and Lorraine, Schleswig and especially the eastern provinces – or who were the object of contention between opposing nationalisms. However, the same also holds true for the Magyars who fled from Romanian rule in Transylvania.[6] Finally, there was the problem of the people without a homeland par excellence, i.e. the Jews, who had to flee in their hundreds of thousands because of the war, the redrawing of borders and the Russian Revolution and resulting Russian Civil War.

On the other hand, the break-up of three empires with strong super-national characteristics, particularly that of Austria-Hungary, seemed to make an organic settlement on a national basis feasible. The victors cherished the hope of being able to define the characteristics and territories of all minority groups. Hopes ran very high of drawing up a political map of Europe that was as close as possible to the distribution of the nationalities.

Among all the ideas brought to Europe by Wilson, the concept of self-determination was the most obscure and most ill defined, even for the president himself. This concept was variously interpreted as 'self-development' or as the 'rights and freedoms of the small nations' by the experts who accompanied him to Paris. In the text of the Fourteen Points, the 'freest opportunity of autonomous development' was explicitly mentioned, but only with reference to the population of the Austro-Hungarian Empire.[7]

Wilson himself voiced various, and sometimes contradictory, opinions on this topic; for a long time the US diplomatic corps shared the opinion that it would be appropriate to keep the Habsburg Empire standing, but with suitable reforms, and it is well known that the president was hostile to the Irish independence movement. Wilson spoke of independence exclusively for Poland, but not for other parts of the Habsburg Empire, let alone for other areas of mixed nationalities. What exactly did Wilson mean when he talked about a 'nation'?

It should not be forgotten that Wilson's cultural and political background was 'parochial'.[8] For him, self-determination was rooted in the Anglo-American tradition of civic nationalism; it coincided almost completely with the right of communities to self-government. An ethnic conception of the nation was totally alien to him; for this reason, what he said in the crucial phase of 1918/19 was sometimes interpreted in Europe, and especially in East-Central Europe, very differently from what the American president actually intended in his statements. Neither Wilson nor his collaborators had developed a serious plan; his commitment to the principle of self-determination in fact reflected an attitude, a creed, rather than a policy or a programme. On the other hand, Wilson was a politician who was extremely concerned about the strategic interests of the United States, and this priority was also reflected in his viewpoints. As a matter of fact, in the design of 'self-determination' expounded by the American president there was a peculiar mixture of democratic and nationalistic visions of the state.

At the end of 1919, speaking in Congress, Wilson admitted that when he had proclaimed the principle of self-determination, he had done so 'without the knowledge that nationalities existed, which are coming to us day after day'.[9] It can be said that 'Wilson's commitment to national self-determination suffered from significant conceptual, empirical and geopolitical limitations'.[10] Moreover, his principle was applied only very partially.

Although the political map of post-war Europe did at first sight meet national expectations – the Polish and Czech-Slovak cases being the most significant examples – in reality it raised new possibilities for tensions and conflicts. It has been estimated that in the so-called 'successor states' that had come into existence – or had come into existence again, or been extended, or been reduced – as a result of the break-up of the empires of East-Central Europe, between 10 and 37 per cent of the population belonged to a national minority. Only in some cases, such as Upper Silesia, Eastern Prussia and Carinthia, was it possible to abide by the wishes of the majority of the population by calling plebiscites of an ethnic nature. Elsewhere, the coexistence of majorities and minorities became an open political problem after 1919.[11] This was especially so in the case of the so-called 'frontier minorities', i.e. those minorities that had on the other side of the frontier a state dominated by their ethnic brethren willing to support their protests and, if necessary, their desire for secessionism. This was a particular problem for the defeated and revisionist state par excellence, Germany.

The Jewish communities scattered through East-Central Europe formed a peculiar case, lacking any state to which they could refer. From the outbreak of the war, international Jewish associations, such as the American Jewish Congress, had pushed for a settlement of the rights of Jewish communities at the end of the war. Various projects were laid out, based on the recognition of the Jews as national minorities.

To address the problem of the territorial dispersal of the various national communities in East-Central Europe, the victors introduced into the peace agreements clauses for the cultural and economic protection of the minority groups. The clauses were approved only after intense discussion and protests by many of the states that hosted the minorities; these states were opposed to any interference with their sovereignty. In response, Wilson was forced to threaten the most hostile ones with exclusion from the peace treaties about to be completed. Later on, a League of Nations commission was set up to tackle and peacefully solve conflicts between majority and minority ethnic groups. However, the League of Nations proved unable to play a very major role in this delicate area in the years that followed.[12] The commission did not have any effective tools of intervention and soon became a forum for circulating propagandistic points; for example, it was used by the Germans to justify requests for a reassessment of the decisions taken by the victorious powers in 1919.[13] The other measure introduced by the victors was no more successful. It foresaw the possibility of all citizens individually opting for a country different from that in which they were living, with the ensuing obligation for the chosen state to accommodate them and grant them full citizenship rights. The only positive example was Estonia, which guaranteed extensive cultural autonomy to the German and Russian minorities.

What was the ethnic distribution within the new borders drawn up by the peace conference? Censuses, which usually underestimate the numbers of ethnic and linguistic minorities, reveal that ethnic Poles never made up more than two thirds of the population of Poland; that ethnic Romanians constituted less than three quarters of the citizens of Romania; and that the Baltic Republics had a minority presence of 12–15 per cent of the population.[14] Throughout post-war East-Central Europe, resentment smouldered among repressed minorities, while the dominant nationalities managed to impose their hegemonic claims only by way of militaristic-authoritarian regimes. There were particularly significant Jewish[15] and German minorities. The Germans enjoyed the backing of a state that tried to look after them, while the Jewish communities were at the mercy of their 'hosts'.[16]

In concrete terms, Wilson's principle could only have been put into practice by creating state borders which corresponded to ethnic dividing lines, or by moving large groups of people in order to give birth to 'pure' nations. Both solutions would have imposed high human costs. However, even the 'democratic' solution of plebiscites, applied, for example, in the eastern provinces of the German Reich during the immediate post-war years in the process of establishing Poland's borders, involved majority and minority groups and hence mutual tension.[17] So, an exchange of populations appeared to be the inevitable solution when, immediately after the war, a bloody war broke out between Greece and Turkey.

1.3 The Compulsory Greek–Turkish Population Exchange

The Paris Peace conference attempted to protect from oppression the sizeable ethnic minorities which remained in all states in Central, Eastern and Southeastern Europe by including minority clauses in each of the peace agreements. However, it became clear very quickly that this approach was not a sufficient safeguard as ethnic antagonisms grew in the post-war period.

In the Aegean region, ethnic conflict reached such a point that radical measures seemed the only solution, and for the first time an organized compulsory transfer of minority populations was internationally negotiated and implemented. The background to this outcome was the progressive disintegration of the multi-ethnic Ottoman Empire during the nineteenth century. This had led to the formation of a number of successor states on its crumbling Balkan fringes in the name of national self-determination. Ethnic nationalism continued to gather pace in this region towards the end of the nineteenth century. Armed conflict, driven by the pursuit of national territorial claims, broke out in 1912 with the Balkan Wars and continued beyond the end of the First World War.[18]

In the Ottoman Empire, the 'Committee of Union and Progress' (CUP), also known as the 'Young Turks' movement, had seized power in 1908 and increasingly adopted a policy of Turkification and strong centralized government. The most notorious manifestation was the uprooting of the Christian Armenian population from eastern Anatolia, which culminated in massacres and mass deportations during the First World War. This caused the death of approximately one million Armenians and the flight and displacement of up to another million. Officially, these acts were justified by the fact that the Armenians were suspected of aligning themselves with the Entente powers to secure their own independent state.[19]

During the same period in Greece, the leader of the Liberal Party and long-time prime minister, Eleftherios Venizelos, was an ardent exponent of the 'Megali Idea', the nationalist aspiration to establish a 'Greater Greece' that would incorporate all territories in the Aegean region inhabited by ethnic Greeks that had remained 'unredeemed' when the Greek state was established in 1830.[20] The First World War seemed to offer a chance to fulfil these territorial dreams. The Ottoman Empire was in an alliance with the Central Powers, and in 1917, under Venizelos' leadership, Greece entered the war on the side of the Entente. The peace treaties, and in particular the Treaty of Sèvres of 10 August 1920 between the Ottoman Empire and the Entente powers, can be regarded as having yielded 'the triumphal climax of the "Megali Idea" and the realization of a five-century old hellenic dream'.[21] Greece gained Eastern Thrace and several Aegean islands, and parts of the western coastal region of Anatolia, including the important port of Smyrna (Izmir), were placed under Greek administration. The permanent status of this area was to be decided through a plebiscite, but there was little doubt about the outcome, as almost 60 per cent of the population was Greek.

Taking advantage of the collapse of the Ottoman armies, and under the pretext of having to protect the Greek population against Turkish massacres, Greek troops had landed in Smyrna in May 1919, while the peace negotiations in Paris were still ongoing. Their military campaign in Anatolia only came to a halt in August 1921, some 50 miles west of Ankara, when the Greek army was defeated by Turkish forces under the command of the leader of the military resistance, Mustafa Kemal (later Atatürk). The following summer, Kemalist troops launched an offensive and successfully retook Smyrna in September 1922.

During the course of the war both sides used large-scale violence against the civilian population in the areas under their control, causing the extensive flight and forced displacement of minority groups. The worst outrages in this campaign were committed after the recapture of Smyrna by Kemalist troops. The Greek army had retreated in disarray and, in a mixture of a desire for revenge for earlier Greek atrocities against Muslims and a deliberate attempt to drive out the non-Muslim, non-Turkish populations, the victorious Kemalist soldiers went on a rampage of looting, rape and killing. Large parts of Smyrna, in particular the Greek and Armenian quarters, were set ablaze. This prompted frantic evacuations and mass flight across the Aegean Sea.[22] After the armistice of 11 October 1922, Eastern Thrace reverted to Turkey, and most of the Greek population fled from this territory as well. Many adult Greek males who remained in Turkey were interned or sent to labour battalions, and a large number of them perished. The League of Nations and international aid agencies tried to intervene and provide emergency assistance, but with limited success.

By the time peace talks began in Lausanne on 30 November 1922, the Greek state had experienced an influx of over one million refugees. This added to the pressure to find a comprehensive, long-term solution to the conflict, and very quickly all parties settled on an official exchange of populations between Greece and Turkey. Limited (voluntary) exchanges had already been agreed in principle after the end of the Balkan Wars but not implemented because of the outbreak of the First World War.[23] At Lausanne, the Turkish side supported the principle of a compulsory exchange of minorities because of its desire to prevent the return of Greek refugees. The Greek side also favoured such a plan, as most of the Greek population had already fled Turkey and, by removing the Turkish minority from Greece, Athens hoped to facilitate the settlement of the Greek refugees. The four Great Powers present at Lausanne – Great Britain, France, Italy and Japan – believed 'that to unmix the populations in the Near East will tend to secure the true pacification of the Near East'.[24]

The 'Convention concerning the Exchange of Greek and Turkish Populations', signed at Lausanne on 30 January 1923, six months before the Lausanne peace treaty between Greece and Turkey was concluded, provided for 'a compulsory exchange of Turkish nationals of the Greek Orthodox religion established in Turkish territory, and of Greek nationals of the Muslim religion established in Greek territory'.[25] This applied to all those who had fled their homes since the outbreak of the First Balkan War on 18 October 1912 and to those left behind who were now to be removed. This meant that altogether more than 1.5 million people were affected by the Lausanne Convention, some 1.2 million Greeks and about 365,000 Turks. The Convention also prescribed that no one was allowed to 'return to live in Turkey or Greece, respectively, without the authorization of the Turkish Government or the Greek Government, respectively',[26] making the resettlement permanent and irreversible. The only exclusions from the forced transfer were the Greek inhabitants of Constantinople (Istanbul) and the Turkish population of Western Thrace.[27] 'Greek' and 'Turkish' were defined by religion rather than linguistically or culturally. Refugees were to be allowed to take their property with them where possible and to receive compensation for what they had to leave behind. A 'Mixed Commission', consisting of four representatives each from Greece and Turkey and three neutral members, was set up to supervise the population transfer and to adjudicate in all disputes.

From 1923 the 'Mixed Commission' oversaw the transfer of around 1,100,000 Greeks to Greece and 355,000 Turks to Turkey.[28] The Ankara Convention, signed on 10 June 1930, formally marked the completion of the compulsory population exchange between the two countries. Despite the imbalance in the numbers of those transferred, the treaty declared the accounts to be settled, and Greece received no further compensation from Turkey for the property which the expelled Greeks had left behind.[29]

Greece's refugee problem was compounded by the fact that in 1923–4 it also conducted an exchange of populations with Bulgaria. This transfer had already been agreed between the two countries in a 'Convention concerning reciprocal emigration of national minorities' signed at Neuilly-sur-Seine on the same day, 27 November 1919, as the Neuilly peace treaty between the Entente powers and Bulgaria. The Greek–Bulgarian population exchange was nominally voluntary and – with just under 200,000 people in total – the numbers involved were much smaller than those in the Greek–Turkish exchange. However, this exchange caused similar human suffering and added to the generally chaotic situation in the region.[30]

The human, economic and social costs of the mass flight and the subsequent compulsory population transfers were immense, with Greece having to bear a much greater share of the burden. Turkey experienced an overall loss of population and, in Anatolia, many villages remained deserted. By contrast, the population of Greece increased by 25 per cent in less than two years, with some urban conurbations, such as Athens and Salonika, doubling in size. Most refugees were in a state of complete destitution, having saved little more than their lives. They came to a country that was politically divided and demoralized and economically exhausted after war and defeat. The result was severe overcrowding, inadequate provision of the most basic goods, high unemployment and high mortality rates among the refugees.

Prompted by the League of Nations, the Greek government set up an independent Refugee Settlement Commission to formulate and implement a long-term plan for the permanent absorption of the refugees into the Greek economy and society. The Commission raised large international loans and spearheaded a programme of economic reforms, which included land redistribution, a modernization of agricultural production, the establishment of new industries, and improvements in infrastructure and public health.[31] As a result of these measures, many of the most urgent needs of the refugees could be addressed, and for most the situation improved noticeably. However, when the Commission was absorbed into the Ministry of Social Welfare in 1930, more than 30,000 families in urban areas and more than 15,000 families in rural areas were still waiting for permanent housing.[32] In addition, the sense of displacement and the longing for the lost homelands lingered for decades and, even though this never expressed itself as a major force in Greek politics, most refugees kept a distinct sense of separate identity and passed this down to the second and third generations.[33]

The Lausanne Convention was the first internationally sanctioned compulsory transfer of populations. War and violence played a central role in bringing it about, and the agreement ratified a transfer which, to a large extent, had already taken place. The result was a radical and permanent restructuring of the demographic map of the Aegean region, separating ethnic groups from each other and greatly accelerating the process of ethnic homogenization in both Greece and Turkey. Both sides used the exchange to rid themselves of other unwanted ethnic minorities and to pursue policies of Turkification and Hellenization of their respective countries. The Turkish authorities expelled groups of Armenians as well as some Serbs, Russians and Sinti and Roma together with the remaining Greek population; the Greek government used the resettlement of Greek refugees in Macedonia and Western Thrace to establish Greek majorities in these two provinces, thereby safeguarding them against any outside territorial claims based on national self-determination.

The implementation of the exchange meant the abrupt end of Hellenic settlements and Hellenic entrepreneurial and cultural activity in Anatolia after a period of some 3,000 years. For the Greeks, this still represents 'the Asia Minor Catastrophe', whereas for the Turks it marks victory in their 'War of Independence', leading to the birth of the modern Turkish Republic. Just as the collective and individual memories of the events differ sharply, so do assessments of the Lausanne Convention itself. Some praise it as an impressive landmark, hailing its swiftness and comprehensiveness and regard it as a model for solving other conflicts,[34] whereas others are critical of the fact that individual human rights and ethical and moral considerations were subordinated to state interests.[35] The Lausanne Convention has remained controversial, and the only point of agreement is that it set a precedent for international conflict resolution in the twentieth century.[36]

−2−

Forced Migration Plans and Policies of Nazi Germany

2.1 Hitler's Ideology

The preceding pages have shown that the matter of national 'purity', i.e. of an ethnically homogeneous state territory, was not at all peculiar to National Socialism, but was to be found in other cultural and political contexts. Nevertheless, we have now to focus on Germany.

Hitler's vision of the world[1] was based on a belief in an eternal struggle among peoples for the soil, the 'vital space' (*Lebensraum*), and on the assumption that the laws of history reward the strongest. The future dictator wrote in *Mein Kampf*: 'Nature as such has not reserved this soil for the future possession of a particular nation or race; on the contrary, this soil exists for the people which possesses the force to take it.'[2] In 1942 Hitler declared: 'The soil is like a mug which goes from one table guest to another, and tends to finish up in the hands of the strongest. This has been happening for thousands of years.'[3] In Hitler's thought, this rough social Darwinism, drawn from currents of Viennese and Central European culture of the late 1800s and early 1900s, merged with the theories of the geographical school of geopolitics, whose chief exponent was Friedrich Ratzel.[4]

According to Hitler, the need for more living space (*Lebensraum*) was the result of two factors: the imbalance between demographic growth and internal resources, especially food, which could lead to a severe crisis, and the superior racial quality of the Germanic population. Its *Lebensraum* was decidedly insufficient, especially in comparison with the other great colonial powers, Great Britain and France. However, to achieve the goal of more vital space, it would be necessary to fight against many enemies, the foremost of which was 'international Judaism', the real target of Hitler's *Weltanschauung* in this initial phase.

Thus, according to Hitler's 'programmatic' writings of the 1920s, the main objective of Germany's ruler would be to give to the Germanic people the vital space that they needed and rightfully deserved. War would be the means to attain this objective: 'The foreign policy of a *völkisch* State must first of all bear in mind the obligation to secure the existence of the race incorporated in this State.'[5]

In what direction would Germany have to push its expansionism? The restoration of the Reich's 1914 borders was not sufficient, nor was Hitler attracted by the prospect of rebuilding a colonial empire. In this sense, his rough vision went well beyond the claims of the Alldeutscher Verband, the Pan-German League, which had been active before 1914. The aims of the League had been confined to the social, economic and demographic reinforcement of the eastern provinces of the Reich in which a considerable Polish minority lived.[6] The aims of the National Socialist regime were much more ambitious. The vital space could only be extended towards the East: 'Today, if we talk about new territories in Europe, then we can firstly only think of Russia and of the marginal states which are subject to it.' He proposed 'taking up where we left off six hundred years before. We are putting an end to the perpetual German march towards the South and West of Europe and turning our eyes towards the land in the East.'[7] In these immense spaces endowed with apparently infinite resources, which Hitler, in his rough vision, regarded as almost empty, National Socialist Germany would find a decisive outlet: 'What India was for England, the territories of Russia will be for us.' The Soviet communist regime would be easily destroyed because of the presumed predominance of the Jewish element within it: 'The colossal empire is ripe for dissolution,' Hitler believed.[8]

In Hitler's ideological programme, already laid out in *Mein Kampf*, the projected expansionism on the European continent was a response to the vital needs of the Germanic people. This aim, which implied eliminating the restrictions imposed by the Versailles Treaty, contributed to the growing popularity of the National Socialist Party in the critical phase of the Weimar Republic between 1930 and 1933, thereby helping to pave Hitler's way to power. One should not forget the popular resonance of arguments about the alleged shortage of space and the need to attain more *Lebensraum* for the German people, as testified by the great success of Hans Grimm's 1926 novel *Volk ohne Raum* (People without space). These concerns and expectations were also prevalent among important segments of the ruling classes (civilian and military), which were dissatisfied with the policies of the Republican governments and interested in an expansionism that would give Germany new political, military and economic power. These groups, which supported Hitler's rise to power in 1932/3 and tagged along with the victorious regime, rejected the laws of the liberal market economy since they regarded them as a swindle devised by those who wanted to perpetuate Germany's economic weakness. In the business world and among economists, visions and plans of a 'great Germanic economic space' at the centre of the continent had spread well before 1933. A particularly interesting example was the Mitteleuropäischer Wirtschaftstag, a powerful lobby that would play an important role during the Nazi regime as well, especially in the expansion towards the Danube-Balkan area. Economists and technocrats, supporters of the National Socialist regime, reasoned in terms of 'huge economic blocs' competing against one another. Only by establishing itself in this way would Germany be able to reclaim its role as a great power. This was the direction in which the Minister of Economics, Hjalmar

Schacht, moved between 1933 and 1937; his aim was to build close commercial and political relations with the countries of the Danube-Balkan area.

The issue of the German-speaking minorities scattered throughout Europe, especially in the East, played quite a marginal role in Hitler's writings, as testified by the way in which he addressed the issue of the German speakers living south of the Alps in areas assigned to Italy in the post-First World War peace settlement. From the early 1920s, the future Führer claimed to have no intention of restoring the German minority of South Tyrol to the *Volksgemeinschaft*, so as not to upset relations with fascist Italy. This caused widespread discontent in *völkisch* circles and even in his party. As a result, during the summer of 1928 Hitler wrote an unpublished manuscript, his so-called 'Second Book', which was specifically devoted to problems of foreign policy.[9] He stressed again the points that he had already made years before: the right of the Germanic people to attain their own vital space in the East, and ruthlessly brushing aside all enemies, above all the Jews. The book offered nothing new as such; indeed, according to Ian Kershaw: 'Long before the dictation of the *Second Book* Hitler was a fixated ideologue.'[10]

After 1918 wide sectors of the German scholarly community, particularly in social science disciplines (history, anthropology, linguistics, economics, demography) worked to justify Germany's alleged need for territorial and economic expansion. After Hitler's rise to power, the regime used this research to legitimate Germany's presumed right to a hegemonic position in Eastern Europe. The legitimization was based mostly on the assumption that German culture had left enduring signs of its supremacy during a millennium of eastward expansion. Subsequent Slavic domination had merely hidden the traces of German cultural supremacy, which the Third Reich intended to rediscover.

There were many reasons that drove a great number of academics – especially, although not exclusively, of the younger generations – to identify with the cause of German expansion. Although many of these researchers boasted about their scientific neutrality – and would do so even more after 1945 – they were spurred on by an ideological affinity to a regime that promised to restore Germany to the ranks of great powers. However, there were also many opportunists, above all those attracted by funds and opportunities for research. Perhaps only a minority of the researchers approved fully of the racial ideology of the regime. Nevertheless, they usually ended up caving in to the 'magnetic force' of that ideology.[11]

A network of public and private research centres with huge financial means worked to support the expansionist cause. Some had been established during the Weimar period, showing that political and cultural interest in the East was a long-time force in Germany that had emerged well before 30 January 1933. Six research societies (*Forschungsgesellschaften*) were set up between 1931 and 1934 to coordinate the financing of research projects on different areas of Europe.[12]

The dense network of research produced during the years preceding the outbreak of the war, as well as in the first years of the conflict, was directed towards different, partly divergent political aims. They included legitimizing border revisions to undermine the decisions taken by the victors at Versailles and providing support for expansionist policies, including planning the forced transfers of population groups that might hinder the reorganization of the eastern territories under German domination. Contrary to Hitler's opinions, according to which the East was a sort of semi-empty space open to German colonization, much of this research reached the conclusion that these territories were overpopulated in relation to the available space. Hence, it was necessary to reorganize and replan the space in which Germany could and should exert its hegemony.[13] Thus, this research, perhaps in some cases inadvertently, provided the theoretical and practical-operational basis for policies of large-scale expulsion and elimination.[14] We can conclude that before the outbreak of the war scientists and the experts of the Rasse- und Siedlungshauptamt of the SS (RuSHA) had already produced the ideological background and even the technical tools for a policy of racial selection in the East .

2.2 Germans outside the Reich: From Protection to 'Heim ins Reich'

Before the Second World War, German minorities were to be found in all the states of East-Central Europe, right to the banks of the Volga. In most cases, they had settled in these areas during the preceding centuries. The German – or German-speaking – communities consisted mainly of peasants, but their ranks also included various other socioeconomic groups, including workers, craftsmen, merchants and members of the bourgeoisie and the nobility, such as wealthy Baltic landowners. Although the communities often enjoyed better economic conditions than other ethnic groups around them, they remained relatively poor and culturally backward by contemporary German standards. However, popular tradition had for some time ennobled the German communities in the East with an aura of heroism, performing a civilizing mission towards the supposedly inferior indigenous populations.[15]

Although the most distant communities had few contacts with Germany, the question of how to protect them assumed growing importance after the defeat of 1918.[16] The prevailing vision of the nation was from now on increasingly dominated by the concept of *Volk*. 'In all German political fields there was an analytic re-reading of the concepts of nation and people. Starting from here, German speakers spread throughout Europe for the first time began to see themselves as a community that shared experiences, sufferings and responsibilities.'[17] The Verein für das Deutschtum im Ausland, founded at the end of the nineteenth century, became a mass organization, with more than two million members, and the youth organizations of all parties – from the right to the left (the Communists excluded) – devoted their efforts to getting to know the German communities beyond the Reich's borders.[18]

Right-wing groups of all shades in particular kept declaring in their programmes that this precious component of the Germanic people had to be protected. But specific policies proved difficult to develop. The Republican governments were intent on implementing a policy of support for the minority groups, not least because the minority issue was a useful propaganda tool for a revision of the peace treaties. Not including the Austrians and the German Swiss, who totalled some ten million, the following estimates of German minorities were produced: 3.2 million in Czechoslovakia, 1.7 million in France, about 1 million in Poland, between 1 and 1.5 million in the Soviet Union, 786,000 in Romania, 623,000 in Hungary, more than half a million in Yugoslavia.[19] After January 1933, the number of *Volksdeutsche* living beyond Germany's state borders was inflated to approximately 30 million.[20]

With the rise to power of National Socialism, the theme of the Germanic diaspora became more relevant. Hitler proclaimed the principle that the groups dispersed beyond Germany's eastern borders had to be reincorporated into the Reich at all costs. Even in the Nazi party programme of February 1920, one of the stated objectives was the 'reunion of all the Germans on the basis of the right of the people to self-determination'.[21] In Hitler's opinion, this would strengthen a great people, who did not possess adequate space.

A special Nazi Party organization, the Auslandsorganisation (AO), was set up in 1931 to deal with relations with the German communities abroad, especially through assistance and propaganda. Gauleiter Ernst W. Bohle, son-in-law of Rudolph Hess, was put in charge of the organization. Bohle implemented an ambitious policy that conflicted with the strategy of the Foreign Ministry. Similar functions were also entrusted to the Verein für das Deutschtum im Ausland; it was forced to conform to the rules of the regime and placed under the control of the SS. The AO pursued a policy of organizational and propagandistic support for the German communities; this support was aimed at integrating their organizations, such as the Sudetendeutsche Partei in Czechoslovakia, or the Arbeitsgemeinschaft der Optanten für Deutschland in South Tyrol, into the regime's plans: 'Whether they wanted to or not, the Germans abroad became a tool of the nationalsocialist foreign policy.'[22] It is plausible to conclude that the regime's propaganda met with some success. It is not by chance that statistical surveys of the social origins of the perpetrators of National Socialist crimes reveal an overrepresentation of people who came from 'border regions that were threatened or lost'.[23]

The mixture of revisionism and expansionism by Germany paved the way for the Second World War. Notoriously, the attack on Poland on 1 September 1939 was justified with nationalistic arguments, i.e. the need to free the Germans living in Danzig from the grasp of the Poles. Hitler's intentions towards Poland were revealed at a conference with senior Wehrmacht commanders on 22 August 1939, when he announced that German settlers would be introduced into the conquered

lands. The Danzig NSDAP organization also discussed enforced population movements before the outbreak of the Second World War.[24]

In a meeting with the High Command on 23 May 1939, the Führer highlighted the
link between two different levels of his foreign policy strategy: the revisionist and
the expansionist: 'It is not Danzig that is at stake here. For us it is a matter of
expanding our living space in the East, making food supplies secure and also
solving the problems of the Baltic states.'[25] During the months preceding the
attack on Poland, the regime's propaganda accentuated pre-existing disputes over
acts of violence allegedly carried out by Poles against the German minority: it was
claimed that there had been 50,000 German victims. Thus, the German attack was
justified as a defence of the sacred rights of the *Volksdeutsche*.[26]

Hitler's previous foreign policy moves, from the annexation of Austria in March
1938 to the occupation of the Sudetenland in March 1939, had been presented as
steps on the way to the establishment of a Greater German Reich, which would
incorporate all the German minorities. An exception was made with regard to the
German-speaking population of South Tyrol; from the 1920s Hitler had stated that
he would press no claims against Italy. This example shows that Hitler did not view
the ethnic principle as an absolute, but as something secondary to matters of
greater importance, i.e. in this case building up good relations with fascist Italy.[27]

The conquest of Poland at the start of the war opened the way to a new phase in
Hitler's policy towards ethnic Germans. In the decree that established the
Commissioner for the Strengthening of the Germanic People (Reichskommissariat
für die Festigung des deutschen Volkstums, RKFDV), dated 7 October 1939, Hitler
wrote that the consequences of the Versailles Treaty had been obliterated. Now that
the war had begun, it was possible to welcome back into the Reich those 'Germans
who had had to live far away until then'. Moreover, the Führer stated that in the
future clear-cut dividers would be established between racial groups, to avoid conflict. Commissioner Himmler was given the generic task of 'eliminating harmful,
alien elements from the German Volk and its living space'; he received *carte
blanche*.[28]

However, this 'historic' turn in the policy of the German state towards the
German-speaking communities beyond its borders was subject to strict conditions,
which were laid out in the guidelines published by the RKFDV in 1940: 'Those
Germans who return will be required to adapt themselves organically to the discipline and order of the Greater German Reich … The concept of Baltic, Volhynian
and Bessarabian Germans must, on the contrary, be eliminated as soon as possible.'[29]

The regime pursued a policy of concluding agreements with countries that were
happy to get rid of their *Volksdeutsche*. Between 1939 and 1940 such treaties were
signed with the Reich's allies Italy and Romania and with the Soviet Union. In the
latter case, there was mutual interest. Hitler was counting on the propaganda effect
of bringing hundreds of thousands of Germans into the Reich and on the

possibility of benefiting from potential settlers. A large influx of newcomers was also a potential boon to the German economy, which was in dire need of low-cost labour. Stalin was following a policy of neutralizing national groups regarded as dangerous for the USSR. In the case of the 'options' for the German-speaking residents in the province of Bolzano, Mussolini's goal was clear: to get rid of a population that had resisted the denationalization policies attempted until then.

The agreement signed with the Soviet government in September 1939 envisaged the 'repatriation' of the *Volksdeutsche* living in east Volhynia and Galicia, as well as in the three Baltic countries 'liberated' by the Red Army, on the basis of the agreements concluded by Molotov and Ribbentrop on 23 August 1939. A follow-up treaty was signed in January 1941. The 'repatriation' was supposed to occur on a voluntary basis, but the percentage of people who signed up was very high, especially in cases where the technical details were settled so quickly that there was no time for second thoughts.

Initially, the 'repatriation' of the *Volksdeutsche* from the Baltic states was depicted in the propaganda as a 'rescue operation' from the Bolshevik danger, which had become concrete after the Soviet occupation of those territories. However, with the Führer's speech of 6 October 1939, in which he emphasized that the *Volksdeutsche*, once returned to the homeland, should become a positive factor in the stabilization of international relations, the tone of the propaganda changed. The emphasis was placed on the need for the Baltic *Volksdeutsche* to take part in creating a great, ethnically homogeneous German Reich. In this way it would be possible to guarantee peace in the whole region. The operation was handed over to Himmler and the SS.[30]

The SS squads were greeted enthusiastically by the inhabitants of the German villages. Applicants streamed to the registration points to plead their case for resettlement. The primary motivation to resettle was previous experience of Soviet rule. It should also be remembered that, in the bilateral agreements reached with the Baltic governments still formally in power, Germans no longer had minority status. The undecided stood with their backs to the wall: if they stayed, they would be left without any protection. Nazi propaganda also conjured up a big threat: all those who dropped out now would be excluded from the *Volksgemeinschaft* forever.[31] The main incentive that drove such a high percentage of Germans to accept resettlement was a fear of communism rather than nationalistic fervour, contrary to what the regime's propaganda proclaimed. One should not forget that a considerable number of *Volksdeutsche* were peasants frightened by the spectre of forced collectivization, while bourgeois elements in the no-longer-independent Baltic countries feared the arrival of a communist regime. Young people seemed to respond with much more enthusiasm than the elderly.

Those who decided to 'return' to the Reich could only take a minimum amount of baggage with them; the promise was that in the homeland they would be fully compensated.[32] Technical agreements signed between the governments involved envisaged that the property left by the *Volksdeutsche* would be repaid by the import of goods from the Reich. The expatriation was completed in just a few weeks in late 1939 and early 1940; it was a major logistical feat. The journey to the Reich was long and difficult, in some cases troubled by robbery. Images of the cart convoys were skilfully exploited by Himmler as a propaganda resource.[33]

According to official statistics, about 65 per cent of the *Volksdeutsche* of Estonia agreed to be 'repatriated', as did 80 per cent of those of Latvia, a country in which the National Socialist authorities had launched a major propaganda campaign. Following a smaller resettlement wave in 1941, a total of some 84,000 ethnic Germans had emigrated from Latvia and Estonia. The extant German minority in the two Baltic countries was reduced to perhaps 2,000.[34]

'The transfer policy planned and carried out by the Third Reich was, by far, the most extensive and best organised of all transfers of population.'[35] The National-Socialist government had created an apparatus that was to take care of the reset-tlers' reception, selection and direction towards specific areas of the Reich with a view to permanent settlement. The incoming people were accommodated within the new eastern borders of the Reich in temporary reception camps. Łódź, the second city of Poland, renamed Litzmannstadt, was the seat of the main govern-mental organ responsible for receiving, selecting and distributing the newcomers, the Central Immigration Office (Einwandererzentralstelle). Each family under-went political, occupational, physical and racial examinations. The latter involved an evaluation of twenty-one different physical characteristics, fifteen of which referred to the head. But many examiners, most of whom were badly trained SS officers ineligible for front-line duties, included in their final assessment personal and psychological impressions.[36] The political examination was handled by the intelligence service of the SS, the Sicherheitsdienst (SD), whereas the selection procedures were run by the machinery of the RuSHA in the Einwanderer-zentralstelle in Łódź and in its regional branches.

The interrogations conducted by the bureaucrats of the RuSHA were to be deci-sive for the fate of the immigrant families.[37] Resettlers now discovered that all members of the *Volk* were not equal. Families with farming backgrounds and positive racial and political evaluations were classified as O-cases (*Ost*), the elite of the resettlers, and assigned to the annexed Warthegau as farmers. A-cases were designated to work inside the *Altreich*, while a smaller group – the so-called S-cases (*Sonderfälle*) – were deemed racially unsatisfactory and targeted for deportation to their areas of origin or to the General Government in occupied Poland. Whereas most A-cases left Łódź relatively quickly for the Reich, the O-cases had to await their final placement.[38]

The National Socialist authorities exerted less pressure for resettlement on the Germans residing in Lithuania. In fact, the German community in the westernmost Baltic state was seen as a bridgehead for the subsequent expansion of Germandom. The same happened with the ethnic Germans living within the borders of pre-war

Romania, whom Hitler also intended to leave *in loco* as an ethnic outpost. On the other hand, a considerable number of those who joined the 'repatriation' to the Reich did not belong to German ethnic groups at all but for various other reasons wanted to leave areas that had fallen into communist hands. These people took advantage of the fact that religion was one of the selection criteria: all Lutheran families were allowed to be 'repatriated'.

In September 1940 the German government signed an agreement with Moscow aimed at bringing into the Reich the German community which had resided in Bukovina and Bessarabia for centuries. The Soviet Union had wrested these two regions from Romania a few months before, under the threat of attack. About 150,000 people, mostly peasants, were potentially affected. A month later, an agreement was also reached with the Romanian government for the 'repatriation' of the Germans residing in southern Bukovina and Dobrogea. In this case, too, many complied because they were afraid of falling into the hands of the Soviets: 215,000 people were transported in just a few weeks. Again, the resettlers could take only a few belongings with them.

Within just over a year, the National Socialist regime had achieved notable results, which strengthened the aura of a great statesman that Hitler had already built for himself. There were about 180,000 'repatriates' from Volhynia and Galicia, almost 150,000 from Bukovina and Bessarabia, some 113,000 from the three Baltic countries, 215,000 from Romania, and around 60,000 from South Tyrol. Thus, more than half a million people were repatriated into the heart of the German Reich, thanks to a well-oiled logistical organization. In the years that followed, there were further repatriations, from both the Soviet Union and Yugoslavia, which contributed to an official overall total of 770,000 'repatriates'. However, in these two cases the context was different since the Soviet Union and Yugoslavia were militarily occupied by Germany and its allies at the time. Although the exact percentages of those who complied in each German community are not easy to calculate, we can assume that in all cases it was the majority, and sometimes there was almost unanimous compliance.

In this climate of overwhelming compliance, the main exception was the German-speaking community in the Italian province of Bolzano, together with small linguistic islands in neighbouring Trentino. The people involved numbered about 300,000. The fascist regime had carried out a harsh denationalizing policy in the region, forbidding the use of the German language in schools and in public. The Italianization programme had been facilitated further, especially in Bolzano, by the building of an industrial area with more than 7,000 Italian workers. Thanks to these policies, the number of Italians in the area had increased from a few thousand in 1919 to about 100,000 by the outbreak of the war. However, it had proved impossible to undermine the linguistic and cultural cohesion of the local population. The National Socialists had been trying for some time to intensify their presence in the region, even though the Führer's desire was not to make territorial claims that could spoil relations with Mussolini. In the end, the two dictators reached an agreement whereby the German-speaking people of South Tyrol could choose to move to the Reich: the so-called 'option'. These bilateral agreements, reached between June and October 1939, presented the population with an uncertain future. Within a framework of conflicting propagandistic manipulations – for example, a rumour spread that those who did not opt for the Reich would be 'deported' to Sicily, or to Abyssinia – and deep uncertainty, the local community grew divided.

It can be estimated that between 69 and 93 per cent of those having the right to the option decided for the Reich. The wide discrepancy in the estimates reflects the difficulty of quantifying this category, a problem exacerbated by different Italian and German figures. Many – the so-called *Dableiber* – opted to stay, while others refused to choose, for various reasons: attachment to their birthplace, fear of the unknown, concern that they would not be adequately compensated for their lost assets. The presence of clergy and other active Catholics among the *Dableiber* was significant. A conspicuous part of the local ruling class, consisting of tradesmen, landowners, professionals and priests, openly opposed the option. It should be noted that for the people of South Tyrol the area had been their 'homeland' for centuries. By contrast, the other ethnic German communities of East-Central Europe typically lived in isolation, often in hostile surroundings and with less well-established local roots.

The options in South Tyrol were of great social impact and left long-lasting tensions within the German-speaking community. Bewilderment and uncertainty about the future were widespread, as a recent publication of letters illustrates.[39] The fate of those who opted to go was unclear. In fact, the declared desire of the National Socialist authorities was to move them en masse to a specific territory, but the aim vanished because of the war. The 'repatriations' were slowed down by external factors (the war itself), by difficulties caused by the respective bureaucracies,[40] and especially by increasing hesitation among the 'opters', many of whom preferred not to move and wait to see what would happen. In total, the 'repatriates' numbered about 85,000 – scarcely a third of the German-speaking population in the region – and among them at least 20,000 migrated because, as citizens of the Reich, they had been called to arms. Most of them belonged to the lower classes. The example of the options in South Tyrol shows that economic and social factors could have a significant influence on the decisions of the Germans scattered around Europe.[41]

2.3 Nazi Germany's Plans for Occupied Poland

The campaign in Poland was not yet over when Joachim von Ribbentrop and Vjačeslav Molotov met in Moscow on 28 September 1939 to sign a treaty concerning the 'borders and friendship' between Soviet Russia and the Third Reich. This treaty was a natural consequence of the forceful invasion of Poland by the Red Army eleven days earlier and the ensuing Soviet occupation of Poland's eastern provinces. With the fighting drawing to an end, the time to divide the spoils had arrived: Nazi Germany took 49 per cent and the USSR 51 per cent of the Polish territories. On 22 October 1939 the Soviet authorities staged 'elections' to so-called popular assemblies, which then issued appeals to incorporate 'Western Belarus' and 'Western Ukraine' into the respective Soviet republics. Hitler did not care to play such games to mask his true motives: on 26 October two acts, originally decreed on 10 and 12 October, were put into effect. The first incorporated western and northern Polish territories directly into the Third Reich, while the other created the so-called General Government (Generalgouvernement, GG) out of the other Polish areas under German occupation.

The reorganization of the captured territories began immediately on both sides of the river Bug, which now became the Soviet–German border. Mass movements of people turned out to be one of the fundamentals of this 'reorganization'. But before we go on to discuss internal relocations within the German and Soviet spheres, we must first deal with the 'exchange' of populations between the new allies.

Starting on 1 September 1939, simultaneously with the outbreak of hostilities between Germany and Poland, a huge wave of fugitives began to move towards the Polish eastern provinces, which were considered safe. After 17 September some 300,000 fugitives, mainly Jews, found themselves in the territories captured by the Red Army, and intensive migratory flows continued in both directions during the autumn of 1939, before the new frontier was sealed off tightly. At the same time, considerable numbers of Ukrainians and Belorussians who were now supposed to be 'united' with the Soviet republics remained under German occupation. The possibility of moving them to the USSR was foreseen in the protocol of the treaty signed on 28 September. In November 1939 another agreement was negotiated between the Third Reich and the USSR. It provided that the Germans who dwelt in the lands occupied by the Soviets and the Polish refugees whose permanent residence lay west of the river Bug could cross the frontier westwards. The agreement also decreed that about 15,000 Belorussians and Ukrainians were to be moved from the General Government into the USSR. This exchange of populations peaked between April and June 1940, when 66,600 refugees from Poland crossed the border towards the west, and approximately 35,000 Ukrainians and Belorussians proceeded eastwards. It is difficult to establish to what degree the latter movement was voluntary.[42]

The Germans from Volhynia and Eastern Galicia who were moved westwards had previously been Polish citizens and constituted a considerably larger group. The transfer of the ethnic Germans to the Reich was integrally linked to Germany's general policy towards the inhabitants of the occupied Polish territories, as we shall see. On 29 September 1939, during a meeting with Alfred Rosenberg, Hitler outlined his plans for moving all Jews – including the German Jews – to the territories between the rivers Vistula and Bug. Ethnic Germans from all over the world, however, were to be settled in the lands integrated into the Reich.[43] In Berlin's view, transforming the ethnic situation in the newly acquired lands as radically as possible became an urgent priority. The fact that the Germans had annexed 919,000 square kilometres, nearly twice as much as Prussia had acquired during the partition of Poland in the eighteenth century, only aggravated the problem. It meant that within Germany proper there now lived an enormous number of 'racial enemies': Poles made up 8.9 million of the 10,138,000 inhabitants in the incorporated lands, while Germans constituted a minority group of some 600,000.

The western Polish provinces were to be subjected to brutal 'Germanization'. At first, the measures undertaken by the occupiers were directed not at the people but at the territories. This was due to the fact that, as previously indicated, the inhabitants were identified as racially 'alien'. The basic assumption was that all the Poles and Jews were to be replaced by Germans, relocated either from the Reich or from areas of ethnic German settlement in the East.[44] The removal and dispossession of the Poles and the Jews were supposed to create an economic basis for the incoming Germans. The exclusion of the racially 'less valuable elements' was to be carried out by a variety of methods, which ranged from forced migrations and mass terror aimed at the Polish ruling classes – with executions starting as early as September 1939 – to the extermination of the Jews.

The Nazis planned to remove several million ethnic Poles and Jews from the territories incorporated in the autumn of 1939. But these goals were soon thwarted by reality. Adolf Eichmann's plans for deporting the Jews from the Reich to the south-eastern parts of the GG ended in complete fiasco.[45] The plans drawn up in early November, which envisaged the forced movement of approximately one million Poles and Jews, proved impossible to execute because of logistical problems, the need for labour in the annexed lands, and the refusal of the authorities of the GG to receive the deportees. The plans were based on ideological considerations that disregarded reality, and they were obstructed by other Nazi elites. Göring, for instance, underscored the need to keep war production going, while Hans Frank objected to the chaotic and ill-organized influx of Poles and Jews into his GG. These protests frequently proved effective, in particular if the migrations coincided with major developments on the military front. Accordingly, the deportations were suspended before the spring offensive of 1940 and ultimately abandoned for good in the period directly preceding the attack on Russia.

The views of individual Gauleiter on the internal situation within their territories proved an important influence on the migration plans and their implementation. While Arthur Greiser, the Gauleiter of the Warthegau, was in favour of strict Germanization, the administrators of other provinces that had absorbed Polish territories advocated mass enrolment of Poles onto the so-called German *Volksliste* instead – as we shall see later in this chapter.

2.4 Soviet Population Policy in Poland

What plans did the Soviets have for the occupied Polish provinces and their inhabitants, and how did they differ from the German ones?[46] Answering this question is difficult. There is little doubt that both Soviet Russia and Nazi Germany regarded Poland and its territories in the context of wider projects for boosting their position as world powers. Did Stalin's plans foresee the relocation of the Poles? The answer remains unclear. On the one hand, Stalin was much less a far-sighted strategist than a clever tactician who skilfully exploited his current options. But, on the other hand, forced mass migrations within the USSR were a recognized method by which the Soviet elite sought to solve internal problems.[47] The Kremlin had extensive experience in the targeted use of mass deportations, which had started with the forced transports of more than half a million families labelled as kulaks in 1929/30. The deportations of the kulaks, who were taken to remote territories, must be regarded as essentially class-driven. However, a certain ethnic undercurrent cannot be ignored, as the worst-hit population group comprised the Ukrainians, whose rooted nationalism was unwelcome to Stalin.[48]

The Soviet dictator pursued his repressive policies from a nationalistic and Russian-centred viewpoint, particularly during the war. The mass deportations of the ethnic minorities who lived along the borders of the vast Soviet Empire are evidence of this: from the Koreans, whose deportations had begun as early as 1937/8, to the Ingush, from the Chechens to the Tartars of Crimea. In these cases, military considerations played an important role: under attack from Germany, Stalin intended to sweep away all the population groups that he considered untrustworthy. This was the case in particular with the *Volksdeutsche* living in the Soviet Union. In the first weeks of the war, more than one million of them – about 80 per cent of the entire ethnic German minority in the USSR – were deported eastwards. The long-standing tendency of the Russian Empire to eliminate the perceived danger from Turkish populations also seems to have had its influence on Stalin's decisions. Between three and five million people of this background were affected by deportations that continued until the end of the war.[49]

The Poles in the USSR were one of the first ethnic groups to experience the fury of forced migrations.[50] In 1935–7 perhaps as many as 130,000 Poles from the Ukraine and Belarus were exiled to Kazakhstan.[51] One must pose the question: could these relocations have influenced the situation of the Poles inhabiting the eastern territories of pre-war Poland in the 1940s? Obviously, there was no direct causal link. One can surmise, however, that the Soviets had mustered plenty of practical experience, in a way that the Germans had not. All that, combined with the unlimited territories at the Soviet leaders' disposal, facilitated the deportations of Poles. In retrospect, these forced transportations seem almost inevitable: the political, economic, ethnic and social conditions in the eastern territories of Poland contrasted far too starkly with Soviet ideals.[52]

Forced relocations of people from the provinces incorporated into the Reich and the USSR constituted an attempt to remove all traces of Polish statehood, primarily by removing the educated classes, 'carriers' of national traditions. While the Germans justified their actions with ideological and ethnic arguments, the Russians emphasized the class struggle. Another, more general difference can be found if we compare the deaths caused by Soviet and German deportations. Experts tend to think that high mortality rates in the Soviet case were caused primarily by hasty implementation and organizational flaws, whereas in the National Socialist case – as in ethnic-national mass deportation projects more generally – the high death rates were more intentional. National Socialist policies were therefore more genuinely ideological and aimed at thorough 'ethnic cleansing'. However, these differences were only relative because political and ethnic-racial considerations did intermingle in Nazi projects, too, as we shall see.

As early as 5 October 1939, NKVD units started to compile lists of the most 'untrustworthy' inhabitants of the newly occupied Polish lands; they were to be arrested and deported. The rules governing the first deportations were established in December by the Politburo and the Council of the People's Commissars of the USSR (SNK). It was decided that particular groups were to be relocated first: Polish army settlers who had acquired farms in the region after the war of 1919–20, foresters, and their families.[53] The plan decreed what was to be done with the possessions of the deportees, regulated the logistics of the transfers, and dictated their destinations as well as the measures to be undertaken to prepare for the arrival of the deportees.[54] To oversee the preparation of the relocations Lavrentij Berija created a special commission, headed by the Deputy Commissioner for Interior Affairs Vsevolod Merkulov. Territorial units of the NKVD were charged with compiling lists of the deportees and implementing the transfers themselves. The operations began in early January 1940. The deportees were resettled chiefly in colonies in the Archangel, Sverdlovsk, Irkutsk and Molotovsk regions. They were assigned the status of so-called 'special deportees' under strict NKVD supervision.[55]

The relocations from areas under Soviet occupation were not aimed at transforming the ethnic make-up of the region. They were directed at the ruling political, social and economic elites instead. A new bureaucratic elite replaced the deportees in local government, the judiciary, the army, the police and the economy.[56] The threat of underground organizations was another key consideration for the Soviets; pre-emptive arrests or deportations of potential resistance activists therefore seemed prudent. It was no wonder, then, that among the first to be relocated were officers, army settlers, policemen, foresters, state and local self-government officials of all ranks, and wealthier peasants. The next to go were the families of those already deported and the refugees from central and western Poland who were unwilling to move to areas now occupied by the Germans.

Between February 1940 and June 1941, the Soviets deported over 300,000 people; the relocations were executed in four waves. In keeping with the principle of collective responsibility, the second wave consisted of the families of previously deported persons, as well as of prisoners-of-war and individuals who had been arrested and sent to prisons or concentration camps. The Politburo of the Soviet Communist Party decided on these deportations on 2 March 1940. The actual expulsions were carried out on 13 April 1940 and encompassed some 61,000 people, who were relocated to Kazakhstan. The fate of the so-called 'beżency', i.e. refugees from the territories conquered by the Germans, was also sealed in March. But the implementation of the decision to deport them was postponed until the end of the mutual 'population exchange' with the Germans. At the end of this 'exchange' in June 1940, another wave of deportations started on 28/9 June, comprising 76,000–79,000 people.[57]

In mid-1940, when the Germans conquered France, relations between Berlin and Moscow suddenly cooled, and the Soviet Union's policy towards the Poles grew temporarily less hostile. The executions of Polish officers in concentration camps were stopped; expulsions from the eastern regions of Poland were suspended for nearly a year; and the lives of those already deported were made somewhat easier.[58] The international political situation then caused the deportations to resume in the spring of 1941. By removing all remaining 'untrustworthy elements' from the territories captured in 1939–40, the Soviets wanted to 'cleanse' their hinterland before the expected conflict with Germany. This time the deportations were to encompass the former ruling classes and people connected to the Polish governmental and administrative system: landowners, merchants, office clerks, army officers, policemen. The deportations started on 22 May 1941 in the Western Ukraine, and by the outbreak of the Soviet–German war had come to cover all the territories captured since September 1939, from Estonia to Moldavia. An estimated 86,000 to 91,000 people were relocated, at least 34,000 to 44,000 of whom were Polish citizens, although some authors put this figure as high as 52,000. The deportees were directed chiefly to the Novosibirsk region, Altai, the Krasnojarsk territories, and Kazakhstan.[59]

Poles were not the only victims of these operations. The ethnic scope of the deportations depended not so much on general orders as on the incidental circumstances of each individual action. Of the people deported in February 1940, 81.7 per cent were Poles, 8.8 per cent Ukrainians, and 8.1 per cent Belorussians. But the third deportation of June 1940, encompassing chiefly refugees from central Poland, consisted of 84.6 per cent Jews, 11 per cent Poles, and 2.3 per cent Ukrainians.[60] The aggregate statistics of those deported in 1940 reveal that about 59 per cent were Poles – a much larger percentage than the number of Poles inhabiting the region before the war – while approximately 25 per cent were Jews, as compared with 9 per cent of Jews in the region's pre-war population.

The Soviet occupation of Poland between September 1939 and June/July 1941 was too short-lived to reveal much about Stalin's ultimate plans for Poland's eastern provinces and their inhabitants. It is possible that – if the German–Soviet war had not broken out – ethnic homogenization of the region, with mass relocations of Poles, would have been the USSR's next move. But that is counter-factual history. The real course of events was determined by the German invasion of the Soviet Union on 22 June 1941.

The impact of the forced migrations conducted between 1939 and 1941 on the territories occupied by the Soviets was gruesome: 309,000–327,000 people were deported eastwards in four consecutive waves. One third of the approximately 110,000 Polish citizens arrested in this period were taken to gulags, deep inside the USSR.[61] Some 45,000 soldiers, officers and policemen, captured by the Red Army in September 1939, found themselves in prisoner-of-war camps.[62] It is estimated that during the years 1939–41 around 100,000 Polish citizens were drafted into the Soviet Army and about 50,000 were sent to forced labour camps, chiefly in the Donbas mines.[63] Considerable numbers of Polish citizens were also relocated to Soviet republics neighbouring Poland.[64] Overall, the various forms of forced migrations in the territories conquered by the Soviets between 1939 and 1941 affected a total of some 700,000 people.

2.5 The Implementation of the German Plans in the Occupied Eastern Territories

The 'repatriation' of the *Volksdeutsche* had been a seemingly impressive demonstration of German efficiency. However, once the phase of festive welcome ceremonies for the newcomers was over, numerous problems emerged. Where could these people be settled? How could they be integrated? Would they be promptly compensated? In some cases, the resettlers were moved to temporary camps situated within the Reich, in the hope of a prompt permanent settlement. But the reactions of the local population were not always friendly. Compensation was slow to arrive; tens of thousands of *Volksdeutsche* were still living in precarious conditions even years after their entry into the Reich. According to an overall statistic of January 1944, 278,000 of the 770,000 repatriates were still in transit camps, awaiting permanent settlement. The Nazi authorities decided not to build homogeneous communities of *Volksdeutsche* within the Reich, a policy aimed at reducing tendencies for separatism and isolation among the newcomers. But this only increased discontent among them.[65] Another negative factor was the fact that, following the Wehrmacht's conquest of areas from which some of the ethnic Germans came, their pressing requests to be allowed to return were usually rejected. In fact, the RKFDV wanted to maintain a free hand in the reorganization of the conquered territories.

However, the most critical point was lack of space. The gradual realization that *Lebensraum* in the East was in fact relatively scarce caused a major radicalization of the ideological anti-Slavism within the Nazi regime. The same can be said about the attitude towards the presence of the Jews in these territories, as they became the primary group targeted for elimination in an effort to make room for new colonizers. The policy of settling *Volksdeutsche* in the eastern territories of the Reich was intended to establish a 'wall of hearts and bodies' against the presumed threat posed by the Slavic population in general and the Poles in particular. This policy ended up clashing with the simultaneously pursued goal of 'Germanizing' those components of the population of occupied Poland that were regarded as possessing Germanic roots.

On numerous occasions, the Führer expressed his contempt for the Polish population. The ruling class was to be eliminated. 'It may sound cruel, but basically it is just a law of life,' Hitler stated in a conversation with Bormann.[66] The Polish people would be forced to provide a low-cost work force for heavy labour and especially for agriculture.[67] However, the aim of making the conquered territories Germanic in the ethnic-racial sense clashed with that of establishing a convenient supply of labour.

Initially, the administration of the occupied Polish territories was entrusted to the military, but soon Hitler changed his mind. He probably became convinced that the military would not be up to 'the tough *Volkstumskampf*' that was expected in the area,[68] particularly as some high military commanders felt that it was opportune to keep some form of Polish state alive.[69] Hitler, by contrast, opposed any form of stabilization of the political institutions in the occupied territories: 'Polish muddle must not be allowed to flourish,' he declared to General Keitel in October 1939.[70] At the end of the month, the four areas of military occupation were dissolved and the conflict with the civilian authorities resolved in favour of the latter. The western territories were annexed to the Reich and given new names: the area corresponding to the former Prussian province of Pomerania, with Posen (Poznań) as capital, was allocated to Arthur Greiser as Gau Wartheland, or Warthegau, named after the river that flows through it. Danzig and Western Prussia – jointly labelled Gau Danzig-Westpreussen – were entrusted to another old guard Nazi, Albert Forster, who was already Gauleiter of Danzig. The territory of Zichenau (Ciechanów) was annexed to the Reich province of Eastern Prussia. After the invasion of the Soviet Union in June 1941, the same fate befell the district of Białystok. Forster and Greiser received the title of *Reichsstatthalter*. They served directly under the authority of Hitler, tied to him by the peculiar relationship that existed within the party between the Führer and his 'old fighters'. Hence, they were free from the normal rules of governmental hierarchy. This autonomy created considerable problems in administrative procedures. The region of Katowice (Kattowitz)

in Upper Silesia, particularly important for its coal mines and iron and steel industries, was also annexed as a Reich province. Here as well Hitler chose an old party
comrade, Josef Wagner, to govern the region. However, Wagner's relative moderation vis-à-vis the population, as well as the fact that he had protested against widespread corruption, made him unpopular, and he was replaced in June 1940 by the
'tough' Fritz Brache. Brache was given extraordinary powers to turn occupied
Silesia into a sort of 'Eastern Ruhr' by exploiting the available resources.

The annexation implied that these territories, regarded as part of the German
Reich, would have to undergo rigid ethnic screening. Right from the start, Greiser
in particular pursued a very strict policy towards the numerically predominant
Polish population. All of its political and civil rights were removed. It was deprived
of its culture, its associational network, and its ruling class was targeted for elimination. The area not annexed to the Reich became a region of peculiar status: the
General Government. This territory, defined in Berlin circles as 'the rest of Poland'
and dubbed 'the work of the devil' by Hitler, was officially considered 'neighbouring territory' (*Nebenland*) of the German Reich. In fact, it was a sort of
colony, where the occupiers could exert their absolute power. Hans Frank, a lawyer
extremely loyal to Hitler, was put in charge of the GG.

Just as in the Protectorate of Bohemia and Moravia, the great importance
assigned to repressive and inquisitorial policies in the General Government
allowed the police machinery, led by high-ranking officer of the SS Friedrich
Wilhelm Krüger, to assume strong political power vis-à-vis Frank. The dualism
between civilian and police powers was strengthened by the fact that Himmler, as
mentioned above, viewed the GG as the preferred destination for the streams of
Poles and Jews who had been expelled from more western areas. This dualism led
Frank to compete with the cruelty of the SS. All forms of cultural and political
association were forbidden; many prominent members of the ruling classes, especially intellectuals and members of the clergy, were imprisoned, deported to
Auschwitz, or killed. Of the 10,000 or so secular clergy present in Poland in 1939,
almost 2,000 were missing at the end of the war, excluding those who had died of
natural causes.[71] There was an attempt to wipe out Polish culture by minimizing
the standards of school teaching. Museums and archives were closed and pillaged.[72] The formula used for carrying out reprisals for killings of Germans was
in many cases 200 or even 400 Poles or Jews for every German. The scope of
capital crimes, punishable by death, was extended to any action – even if only
planned – aimed to obstruct the German cause in the GG.[73]

Other atrocities were prepared. There was speculation, for example, about large-
scale sterilization, aimed at 'naturally' reducing the fertility and hence the overall
population of the Poles.[74] But these plans were not implemented. When in May
1942 Greiser, the most ferocious champion of denationalization policy, proposed
the physical elimination of 35,000 people suffering from tuberculosis, Himmler
objected, saying that the moment was not right for such drastic action.[75]

2.5.1 Relocations and Expulsions

As already explained, Nazi plans for the annexed provinces envisaged the massive expulsion of Poles and Jews in order to create an almost pure Germanic settlement there. Only the Poles essential as farm labourers and unskilled workers would be allowed to stay. The undesired masses would be expelled to the General Government, destined to become a sort of 'ethnic rubbish dump'.[76] In mid-1940 the Nazi authorities decided that the GG was not suitable for German settlement; the *Herrenvolk*, it was observed, would always remain a minority there, subject to pressure from the Polish majority.

As early as late October 1939, Reichskommissar Himmler had given orders for massive expulsions, scheduled for the month of February 1940: the annexed territories were to be expunged of all Jews and so-called Congress Poles – those residing in territories that had belonged to the Russian Empire prior to 1918 – as well as all other Poles considered 'hostile'. This order corresponded to those issued by Heydrich around the same time, which aimed to lock up Jews in ghettos. In both cases, the conquerors' desires ultimately clashed with insurmountable practical problems.[77] Preparations for mass relocations had begun in mid-October 1939, spurred by the arrival of ethnic Germans from the Baltic states. In November a Special Headquarters for the Relocation of Poles and Jews (Sonderstab für die Aussiedlung von Polen und Juden) was established, which was later renamed Relocation Headquarters (Umwandererzentralstelle, UWZ). The UWZ and its local branches[78] were charged with managing all migration-related problems in the territories incorporated into the Reich. These ranged from planning the operations to controlling camps, organizing transports, tracking down those in hiding, and confiscating and managing the possessions of the deportees.

Nazi plans set ambitious targets for the population removals from the incorporated territories: 80,000 people in December 1939; 600,000 in 1940; and over 800,000 in 1941.[79] The deportations proceeded on target until the spring of 1940, at which point they were suspended because of preparations for the military campaign in the West. The euphoria triggered by the victory over France brought about new changes, including the resurfacing of plans for moving European Jews to Madagascar. Such ideas brought relocations in the East to a temporary halt.[80] In the second half of 1940 the deportations of Poles accelerated again, only to be slowed down a few months later and then practically stopped in March 1941. This, in turn, was due primarily to the preparations for the war with the USSR. Another complicating factor was the continued opposition of Hans Frank, who was reluctant to admit multitudes of Jews and Poles from the Reich into his 'domain'. The governor opposed these grandiose plans on the grounds that to squeeze millions of destitute people into an already heavily burdened territory like the GG could cause serious sanitary and social problems.[81]

The first phase of the relocations proper – the so called 'First Short-term Plan' (*1. Nahplan*) – was executed between early November and 17 December 1939 and encompassed 87,765 persons. Phase two, the so-called 'Interim Plan' (*Zwischenplan*), started on 10 February and finished on 15 March 1940; it uprooted 40,128 people, chiefly urban residents, and was intended to make room for German settlers from the Baltic states. In mid-1940 the 'Second Short-term Plan' was launched, which lasted until January 1941. Under this scheme, 133,506 people, predominantly peasants, were relocated to free up land for ethnic Germans from Volhynia, Eastern Galicia, and the Lublin province. By the spring of 1941, the number of those violently expelled from the incorporated provinces had reached about 365,000.

As mentioned above, the deportations to the GG were suspended in March 1941 and never resumed on a similar scale, although several tens of thousands of people were relocated after that date. Short-range displacements (*Verdrängungen*) and internal relocations (*Umquartierungen*) affected them in large numbers. These forced migrations, initiated in May 1941, reached their peak in 1942. Most of the victims were peasants who, after being deprived of their property, were relocated to other quarters within the same district. Some of the migrants were expelled to the less fertile eastern part of Warthegau, where the Germans created so-called Polish reservations (*Polenreservate*), which were subject to strict police control. The 'reservations' were intended to provide labour reserves. By the end of 1942, a total of 686,054 peasant estates, with a total land area of almost six million hectares, had been expropriated, with the goal of handing them over to German colonizers.[82] Sometimes Poles were allowed to remain on their former farms as forced labourers. The last phase of the expulsions and deportations came in 1944, as some 66,000 Poles were taken to Germany proper for forced labour there.

Table 2.1 indicates the total numbers involved in forced movements to the GG. Taking into account unorganized flight and early, largely improvised deportations – such as the 'wild' expulsions from Gdynia at the end of October 1939 – carried

Table 2.1 The total numbers involved in forced movements to the General Government

Territory	Relocated prior to 15 March 1941	'Displacements' and internal relocations	Total
Warthegau	280,609	345,022	625,631
Danzig-West Prussia	41,262	70,000	111,262
Upper Silesia	22,148	59,191	81,399
Ciechanów	20,646	–	20,646
Total	364,665	474,213	838,878

Note: Isabel Heinemann gives a lower figure of a total of 780,000 people relocated and expelled in various ways; see her '*Rasse, Siedlung, deutsches Blut': Das Rasse- und Siedlungshauptamt der SS und die rassenpolitische Neuordnung Europas* (Göttingen, Wallstein, 2002), p. 230.

Source: Maria Rutowska, *Wysiedlenia ludności polskiej z Kraju Warty do Generalnego Gubernatorstwa 1939–1941* (Poznań, Instytut Zachodni, 2003), p. 37.

out before the organized, large-scale operations began, the number of people moved to the GG should probably be put even higher than 364,665, at some 400,000 people. It is difficult to establish the number of Jews among the escapees and the relocated. Estimates range between 70,000 and 100,000. However, we do know that at least 30,800 Jews were moved to the Lublin region from the territories incorporated into the Reich during the years 1939–41.[83]

The forced transport of Jews into ghettos can be interpreted, in part, as a step in the preparation of the Reich's eastern territories for German colonization by removing from them a population group classified as particularly undesirable. In a later phase, the ghettoization was linked to the further deportations and genocidal mass killing that ensued. Although a lack of documentation makes it difficult to reconstruct precise links between the forced transfers of Polish Jews and their subsequent mass murder, many factors point in that direction.[84] The initial plans to remove Jews from western and central Poland could not be implemented; the establishment of ghettos brought such unforeseen consequences – including problems with food provision and disease – that the radical solution of mass killing was eventually adopted.[85]

2.5.2 In Search of 'Good Blood'

Despite the extensive expropriations of property, the expulsion of Poles from areas absorbed into the Reich satisfied the expectations of neither National Socialist ideologues, nor the specialists – agronomists, demographers, economists, sociologists, historians – who had produced ambitious blueprints for ethnic-demographic engineering. One possible way out of the contradiction between too little space for colonization and too many undesired people was the policy of 'Germanization' (*Eindeutschung*) or 're-Germanization' (*Wiedereindeutschung*). Nazi experts believed that the Germanic sub-stratum in Poland had only been weakened by ethnic mixing.[86] Thus, it was necessary to recover the Germanic elements obscured by Slavic traits. This operation was to be carried out by tracking down those individuals or groups that were worthy of 're-Germanization'. However, key underlying questions remained unresolved. Were the Polish territories a sort of uncivilized 'Wild East' that should be dominated and subdued? Or had its population been so deeply imprinted by an age-old Germanic presence as to belong to the same stock as the population of the Reich? The presence of both of these contradictory assumptions in the regime's proclamations underscores the difficulties the Nazis faced in drawing up ethnic-racial policies for the conquered East.

One key objective of the SS, which Hitler had trusted with the implementation of racial policy, was to put an end to racial mixing;[87] according to Himmler, it was necessary to separate different ethnic groups and, in particular, to separate the ethnic Germans, or those that could be 'Germanized', from the rest of the population.[88] He envisaged a two-pronged approach: extracting from the Polish population those with a high level of Germanic blood – also because this elite was supposed to be particularly dangerous for the conquerors – and keeping the rest at a minimal level, so as to exploit their potential as slave labourers. However, to do this it was necessary to create space by expelling as many undesired Jews and Poles as possible.[89] As we have seen, on this point Himmler faced firm resistance from Frank, and also Göring, who thought that it would be better for German interests to allow the economy of the GG to function undisturbed.

Himmler rejected the policy of 'Germanization' that had been carried out by Prussia until 1914. He wrote: 'Our task is not to Germanize the East in the old sense, i.e. teaching those living there to speak German and to obey German laws, but to ensure that the East will be inhabited only by people of genuine German blood.' The logical consequence of this approach was that the ethnic policy of the Third Reich would first have to create space for German settlers. The policy aimed at recovering 'good blood' in the East was not abandoned, however. In 1942 Hitler declared: 'Wherever in the world there is German blood, we must make it ours, provided that it's good.'[90] In his table talks the Führer also pointed out that 'this question of the Germanization of certain peoples must not be examined in the light of abstract ideas and theory. We must examine each particular case.'[91] Moreover, even at the end of 1942 one expert at an RKFDV conference in Salzburg argued that the problems posed by the presence of different ethnic groups in the East could not be solved with drastic measures, such as expulsion or physical elimination, because of the simple fact that there were at least 70 million people in the German-occupied areas of Eastern Europe – excluding occupied Russian territories.[92]

The fact that the selection procedures were described by the German term *Fahndung*, meaning 'hunt', highlights the eagerness of the National Socialist authorities to recover 'good blood' at all costs.[93] A report by an officer in the field, the RSHA leader in Breslau, stressed a further contradiction between the policy of selecting 'good blood' and that of 'de-Polonization'. According to the officer, the Poles who could be selected belonged to the national elite; for this reason they were potentially dangerous. This fact made it necessary to carry out a careful check of the chosen people.[94] For this reason, the occupying authorities regarded it as essential that the 'Germanized' people should not be concentrated in sizeable groups but should be mixed with the *Volksdeutsche*.[95]

Hence it was decided to estimate the percentage of potential 'Germanness' present in the different populations. But the selection criteria were ambiguous: physiological components, which the experts thought could be measured with precision, were mixed with historical and cultural factors. According to the most optimistic calculations, between three and seven million Polish people were of 'Germanic descent' and therefore eligible for 'Germanization'.

In the context of the already existing 'Lebensborn', organized by a special office of the SS, Polish women, chosen because of their racial characteristics, were to be taken away from their families, locked up in special centres and used for procreation with SS men, with the goal of producing top-quality offspring. Another initiative, carried out not only in Poland but also in other countries occupied by Germany, involved kidnapping children from their families as well as from orphanages and educational centres.[96] These children, chosen on the basis of their racial characteristics, were brought to Germany and entrusted to German families. According to Polish estimates, 150,000 to 200,000 children suffered this fate. Both of these initiatives bear witness not only to the cynicism of the SS but also to the vagueness of their racial criteria.

The most important instrument of 'positive' racial selection applied in occupied Poland, however, was the so-called 'List of Ethnic Germans' – *Deutsche Volksliste* (DVL; March 1941) – which was meant to evaluate the inhabitants of the areas incorporated into the Reich.[97] The list contained four categories that – on a decreasing scale – ranked each individual's suitability for inclusion in the German *Volksgemeinschaft*, based on both ethnic-racial characteristics and behavioural/political attitudes. The people included in the third category of the *Volksliste*, those eligible for German citizenship 'with the possibility of annulment', were subjected to restrictions on their movement and employment, and they were to be settled within the pre-war Reich to be re-educated.[98] Underpinning the decision to carry out this ethnic screening was the principle that not even one drop of German blood should go wasted. But the DVL also reflected how difficult it was for the authorities to find people that they could trust with the grandiose tasks of colonization.

The selection was carried out differently from area to area, reflecting the leeway for local discretion left by the vaguely defined selection criteria. Predictably, therefore, the interpretations applied in the Warthegau, under its hardline leader Arthur Greiser, proved much stricter than those used in West Prussia, for example.[99] Greiser's attitude provoked a good deal of criticism. Himmler himself wrote in November 1941: 'I do not wish the Gauleiter of the Eastern Gaus to enter into a competition … Instead, I wish to have a population which is racially impeccable and am content if a Gauleiter can report it in ten years' time.'[100] Albert Forster, Gauleiter of Danzig-West Prussia and a major rival of Greiser, adopted a more pragmatic approach. 'He apparently believed that the majority of the people were not Polish at all … and were therefore detachable from the body of the Polish nation by political means.'[101]

Overall, the population of the incorporated areas was slightly more than ten million; 2.8 million of them were enrolled on the DVL: 437,000 in the first class and almost two million in the following two classes, with fewer possibilities for *Eindeutschung*.[102] In the GG, by contrast, just 130,000 people out of a total population of some 17 million were regarded as having Germanic qualities that could be recovered.[103] Many reports drawn up by personnel responsible for preparing and instructing the people considered *wiedereindeutschungsfähig* (capable of re-Germanization) show such great disappointment at their cultural level as to cast doubt on the possibility of turning them into 'good Germans'.[104]

After replacing Konstantin von Neurath as Reichsprotektor for occupied Bohemia and Moravia in September 1941, Reinhard Heydrich expressed similar assimilationist sentiments towards that region, too. According to him, between 40 and 60 per cent of the population could be 'Germanized' through a process of indoctrination, which would also involve forced transfers within the Reich. In the absence of objective ethnic-physiological criteria, Heydrich was inclined to privilege voluntariness; all those who expressed a desire to be Germanized could be accepted. Heydrich regarded *Gesinnung*, i.e. attitude, as a decisive factor. The most dangerous elements were those who, despite coming from 'good stock', harboured 'a negative attitude' towards the occupiers. However, it would have been equally harmful if most of the people who asked to be Germanized were 'of bad stock'. For the period after Germany's anticipated victory in the war, Heydrich envisaged a deportation further eastwards for Czechs deemed not to be 'Germanizable'; the experts of the RuSHA in Prague talked explicitly about the 'final solution of the Czech question'.[105] Heydrich's plans were never fulfilled.

Poland, meanwhile, presented the additional problem of population groups such as the Masurians and the Kassubians whose ethnic status was unclear.[106] After intense discussion among anthropologists, ethnologists and linguists, it was decided to define these groups as non-Slavs;[107] they were judged to be descendants of the oldest Germanic colonizers. A particular policy was to be implemented towards them, with more favourable treatment than that reserved for the Poles.[108]

In areas where the selection of 'Germanizable' elements was carried out with relative generosity, such as Gau Danzig-West Prussia, there was less space available for the incoming ethnic German colonizers than in regions such as the Warthegau that applied a much stricter ethnic-filtering policy. The results were predictable. By June 1944, 421,780 ethnic Germans had been resettled in the Warthegau on farms and other properties seized from their legitimate Polish owners, whereas only 53,258 settlers had been taken into Gau Danzig-West Prussia, according to official statistics.[109] Even so, Greiser's claim of March 1944 that he had completely Germanized the territory under his control did not respond to the facts.

2.6 The Generalplan Ost

The ethnic-demographic engineering projects envisaged by the officials of the RKFDV were not confined to selecting Germanic elements out of subject populations or resettling 'repatriated' ethnic Germans on Reich territory. They reached much further, as testified by the Generalplan Ost (GPO – 'General Plan East') formulated between 1940 and 1942.[110] Although drawn up in several stages by different bodies, the plan constituted a uniquely ambitious, global blueprint for demographic reorganization. The idea was to set up Germanic-rooted settlements far into the East, with concomitant expulsion of the mass of local Slavic and Jewish populations. The planners satisfied their whims in this supposedly vast and empty space, imagining a 'perfect' society with equilibrium between town and country and among social classes. The first version of the plan, which was drawn up in January 1940 by an office entrusted to the agronomist Konrad Meyer – director of the Institute of Agrarian Policy at the University of Berlin and head of the planning section of the RKFDV – and submitted directly to Himmler, dealt with the annexed territories only. It envisaged the expulsion of half a million Jews and at least three million Poles.[111] The Germanic colonists were supposed to increase from one to five million. Around the already existing ethnic German islands, regarded as 'points of crystallization', a belt of rural colonies entrusted to the Germans was to be built as a 'protective wall'. The regular colonizers were to be given farms large enough to support a family; bigger farms of up to 200 hectares would be given to the so-called *Wehrbauern* ('warrior farmers'). Poles would have to serve as labourers on the farms owned by the Germanic colonists.[112]

Meyer believed that space could be created for four million rural colonists.[113] The Führer was even more optimistic. In October 1941 he talked with his close collaborators of 'at least ten million colonists'.[114] The domestic ambitions of the plans were just as important as the external ones; the social engineering in the East was supposed to reduce internal contradictions within German society, where the *Blut und Boden* slogans had proved largely impossible to implement.[115] In the plans of the experts, great attention was paid to the so-called *Gestaltung der Landschaft* – 'shaping of the landscape' – in the territories to be colonized. This denoted a general reorganization of the productive and social texture of the territory, so as to create a balanced mixture of small, medium and large-scale farms, together with a suitable number of tradesmen, public-service workers and industrial manufacturers. The basic goal was to build a new *Heimat* for the colonists. Only in this way could the planned colonization take root and contribute to 'strengthening' the Germanic people.[116]

The colonists were to build a defensive wall against the Slavs. What characteristics were the new colonists expected to have? Their racial and political-ideological qualities were to be unobjectionable. There was confusion among the experts over the deployment of the 'repatriated' *Volksdeutsche*, who were considered unsuitable for colonizing roles; their re-education within the Reich was expected to take a long time. A blatant contradiction emerged between propaganda that had exalted the *Volksdeutsche* as the guardians of the most ancient Germanic virtues and policy-makers' actual evaluation of them. The military wanted to reward soldiers and officers with farmsteads in the Germanized East at the end of the war and therefore tried to slow down the process of settlement. At the same time, Alfred Rosenberg and his ministry for the occupied eastern territories hoped to recruit potential colonists from other Germanic population groups as well, including the Dutch, the Flemish and the Scandinavians. Of course, the search for colonists who were not even German in any strict sense also underscored the difficulty of finding a sufficient number of suitable candidates from within the Reich. In the words of one scholar: 'The greatest difficulty was simply to find colonists … Experiences during the war did not inspire confidence in the practicability of settling many tens of millions in an area inhabited by over 100 million people. Only a few hundred thousand "Germans" were found for the rather limited task of settling Western Poland.'[117]

The confidence that victory against the Soviet Union was at hand lasted until the summer of 1942; thus the planners of the RKFDV were persuaded to expand their horizons. A second version of the Generalplan Ost was presented to Himmler in June 1942. Areas of Germanic colonization were to be created deep within Russia, specifically in the regions of Leningrad, the Crimea and Memel-Narev, to be renamed with bizarre names that drew on Germanic traditions. Even in the Ukraine a belt of militarized colonies – shaped like a 'ring of pearls' – was to be created to connect the Reich to its outposts.[118] The majority of the local population – some forty-five to fifty million, excluding the Jews, whose elimination was taken for granted – would be expelled towards the East and left to their fate. The remaining 'primitive and passive' mass would be used as slave labour. The timescale envisaged for the completion of the plan was twenty-five years, but Himmler urged both accelerated implementation and extension of the areas to be completely Germanized.[119] The plan foresaw the resettlement of five to six million Germans, coming mostly from the Reich. The *Volksdeutsche* who had recently been brought to Germany were also regarded as potential colonists, whereas the possibility of 'Germanizing' some of the Slavic population, especially Ukrainians and Belorussians, through a laborious process of education remained vague.

The main objective of these plans was to stabilize German hegemony in territories that possessed abundant raw materials. But there was also a second objective, related to 'social engineering'. It aimed to solve existing problems in German society, ranging from congestion in urban centres to the weakness of agriculture, thereby offering the chance of social ascent to millions of inhabitants.[120]

At the end of 1942, RKFDV experts drew up a 'General Plan of Settlement' (*Generalsiedlungsplan*) that addressed not only the eastern areas that had just been conquered but western regions as well. The plan was conceived for a territory of more than 700,000 square kilometres inhabited by about 45 million people, covering Luxembourg, Alsace and Lorraine, the Protectorate of Bohemia and Moravia, the Baltic area, as well as the territories of Poland that had been occupied in 1939 and from which this apparently relentless trend of demographic-ethnic planning had started. The planners assumed that the existing population could be partially 'Germanized' – about 50 per cent of the French, Slovenians, Czechs and Estonians, but only some 15 per cent of the Lithuanians and 5 per cent of the Poles. The plan foresaw the resettlement of more than twelve million colonists in these areas over a twenty-year period, about two-thirds of whom would be employed in services and industry. Within the same span of time, the process of Germanizing the local population was to be completed. People considered unsuitable for Germanization were to be expelled or otherwise removed; they simply disappeared from the plan's elaborate tables and projections for the future. Their destiny was not stated on paper. The cost of implementing the plan was estimated at over 35 billion marks.

These astonishing planning scenarios were being drafted in the same weeks during which the German Sixth Army, surrounded at Stalingrad, was undergoing a defeat that would transform the course of the war.[121] However, the head of the SS did not balk at even more grandiose dreams; in a talk a few months later he outlined a plan which over the next four to five centuries would lead to the establishment of Germanic colonies all over Eastern Europe, stretching to the Ural Mountains and giving rise to an unbeatable population of at least 500 million.[122] Everything seemed possible to the planners of the SS.[123] However, the defeat at Stalingrad was a turning point also for the projected reorganization of the East. In early February 1943 the head of the Reich Chancellery, Heinrich Lammers, issued an order that officially put an end to any form of planning because of the priorities of the war.

2.7 Generalplan Ost: Implementation and Failure

How much of the plan was actually implemented? As we have already seen, about one and a half million Poles were dispossessed and expelled from the regions annexed. The people slated for deportation tried their best to evade that fate; since open rebellion was difficult, the most common method was to hide. This slowed the operations down and meant that the quotas set in Berlin were never reached on time.[124] Moreover, during the first phase of the expulsions, the bureaucratic apparatus in the GG continuously reacted with boycotts, which made the plans extremely difficult to implement.[125] However, forced deportations were also slowed down during the spring of 1941 by the request of the military to concentrate all available railway stock for the preparation of the impending attack against the Soviet Union.[126]

The colonists were driven by a variety of motives, such as ideological adhesion to Germany's presumed civilizing mission and hopes of social advancement, although for many the key factor was 'adventure and a change from routine'.[127] But the policy of colonization was plagued by internal contradictions. One was the clash between the pressing need to find agricultural land for the colonists, most of whom were farmers and peasants, and the fact that the deportations frequently targeted people deemed to be politically dangerous – many of whom were urban residents. A further contradiction derived from the propaganda about the supposed racial superiority of the Germanic colonists over the local population. Many colonists assumed that their privileged position entitled them not only to mistreat their Slavic farm labourers but also to put in little effort of their own. Press campaigns had to stress that colonizing was a personal commitment for the colonist and his family, full of hard work in difficult conditions. The tendency of the new colonists to keep to themselves because they considered themselves superior to the surrounding population was indirectly criticized by Odilo Globocnik, who, as we shall see later, had been assigned the task of colonizing the Polish district of Zamość. Given that the number of Germanic colonists was inadequate, he observed that disdainful attitudes on the part of the colonists would undermine the goal of Germanizing those locals regarded as suitable.[128]

The conditions in which the new colonists found themselves caused serious economic difficulties. Particularly in the countryside, the general structural difficulties of the war economy made it very difficult to give the future *Wehrbauern* what they needed and what official propaganda claimed was rightfully theirs. The farms on which they were settled were inadequately supplied with agricultural tools; the land was often poorly tilled. Tools, machines, seeds and chemical fertilizers were badly needed, but all of these were in short supply within the Reich as well.[129] After a couple of years many of the colonies remained unproductive, with their holders on the verge of failure.[130]

Carrying out Himmler's ambitious plans in regions further east proved even more difficult. The only example of attempted colonization there was the district of Zamość, south of Lublin. According to the Generalplan Ost, this region – today on the border between Poland and Belarus – was geographically crucial: 'to link the Baltic countries which are Nordic or German with Transylvania, which has also been settled with Germans, via the district of Lublin'.[131] Moreover, the head of the RKFDV was particularly fond of this ancient town, built in 1580 following Renaissance models; he fancied renaming it Himmlerstadt. In the summer of 1941 Himmler ordered planning for the expulsion of undesirable elements from the area – inhabited by over 400,000 Poles and Jews as well as smaller numbers of Belorussians and Ukrainians – and their replacement with German or 'Germanizable' colonists. In the end, this operation – which was opposed by Frank because he was convinced that a large-scale colonization could only be undertaken after the war had been won[132] – did not get under way until November of the following year. Globocnik operated brutally. Over a hundred thousand Poles were expropriated, expelled eastwards or deported into the Reich as forced labourers. Women and children were transported to remote villages whose inhabitants had previously been forcibly removed; thousands of children were taken from their families and assigned for forced 'Germanization'.[133] Much of the population tried to escape, destroyed the harvest or joined the partisans.

According to Himmler's wishes, German peasant families from Transnistria were to be settled in the Zamość district right away: 'As there are already some villages in the district whose inhabitants are certainly of German origin, a German bastion could in this way be made in the district.'[134] According to the plans, more than a hundred thousand Germanic colonists were to be settled within a year. Globocnik managed to bring into the Zamość region only 13,000 settlers. Although a specially built belt of Ukrainian villages divided the settlers from Polish society, the colonists were nevertheless harassed by the Polish underground. Their survival in a deeply hostile environment was assured only by the protection of the SS.[135]

The deportations from the region, carried out with extraordinary brutality, caused great unrest among the Poles. The memories of the fate of the Jewish population were still very fresh, and the Zamość scheme was considered a prelude to the 'final solution of the Polish problem'. The resistance of the civilian population became so determined as to pose serious difficulty for the German security forces.

Governor Frank grabbed the opportunity offered by the unsatisfactory progress of colonization in the district to reassert his basic criticisms of the RKFDV's policies. The Zamość operation had to be stopped immediately, he argued, because of the security situation and its implications for the supply of agricultural produce to the Reich.[136] Himmler tried to retaliate by proposing a change of policy that included, together with an even tougher crackdown on the partisan groups, the granting of farms to Poles and Ukrainians.[137] However, the situation was now out of control.[138]

In effect, the so-called 'Zamość operation' failed miserably: the colonization was superficial and the remaining Polish population fuelled the partisan movement. This fact, as the Governor of the district, Ernst Zörner, was forced to admit, seriously damaged the Reich's war economy, which needed 'every tonne of foodstuffs'.[139] In August 1943 the operation was officially suspended. Nothing remained of Himmler's dream of turning the area into a brilliant example of his 'ethnic policy'.

The attempt to colonize the vast Soviet territories under German occupation also ended in dismal failure. The only concrete result achieved was the systematic slaughter of the Jewish population.[140] German civilian and military authorities proceeded with a policy of forced transfers of civilians, especially during the first phase of the war, with different goals in mind. To weaken the rising partisan movement and to isolate it from the support that the countryside could provide, the populations of entire regions were compelled to move elsewhere. At the same time, massive expulsions were carried out from the towns to the surrounding rural areas in order to alleviate food shortages. In many urban centres, such as Minsk, all inhabitants not regarded as actively productive were expelled. The cities were also seen as dangerous hotbeds of Bolshevism. According to Hitler: 'The destruction of the major Russian cities is a prerequisite for the permanence of our power in Russia.'[141]

German authorities were not particularly worried about what would happen to the expellees. Forced transfers affected whole villages and districts, whose able-bodied inhabitants were seized and shipped for forced labour within the Reich. Even in the final phase of the war, the retreating Germans typically operated a scorched-earth policy, in many cases forcing the civilians who were fit to work to follow them. But it was not possible to pursue a policy of mere destruction, even against the despised Russian population. Some Nazi leaders pointed out that it was necessary to allow concessions to at least a certain segment of the occupied population, on the basis of loyalty or ability. This was simply 'because we would never have enough people to even come close to replacing these 70 million'.[142]

Nor should we forget the massive population movements, some of them partly voluntary, caused by the Reich's need to recruit labour at all costs. 'By June 1943, one million people had been displaced from the Reichskommissariat Ukraine in this campaign.'[143] These frantic demographic displacements, with their terrible burden of suffering, are still not well known. In the case of Belarus it has been estimated that about two million civilians were involved in these forced transfers.[144] The topic will be specifically addressed in the last chapter of this book.

Himmler and the RKFDV machinery pressed for expedited ethnic screening of the population even in the occupied Russian territories; as early as the summer of 1941 the Reichsführer-SS ordered Globocnik to organize 'a geological and geographical survey of the Eastern territories as far as the Ural Mountains, to plan police strongholds scattered throughout the vast area, to construct model farms ... to study ancient national costumes to be worn by German immigrants'.[145]

According to the Germans, there were about 150,000 *Volksdeutsche* in the Reichskommissariat Ukraine at the moment of conquest. During the following year, Himmler planned to bring them together into cities at the intersection of highways and railroads. The plan was partly implemented in the autumn of 1942. However, only one major tangible result was achieved: the establishment of a compact German colony, called Hegewald, with about 8,000 inhabitants, in the Ukrainian region of Vinnitsa, where Hitler and Himmler had their headquarters. The rural colonies established in the Crimean area and Hegewald together could host no more than 30,000 colonists, badly housed and under incessant pressure from partisans.[146]

Among the obstacles that the RKFDV planners encountered, the problem of determining who could be considered 'German' or 'Germanizable' became prominent in this region, too. Nazi ideology expected *Volksdeutsche* to be easily identifiable, but in practice the process was rife with ambiguities. Serious differences emerged between the inflexible line adopted by the SS and the greater flexibility advocated by Erich Koch, the chief of the Reichskommissariat Ukraine, according to whom a favourable attitude towards Germany was a sufficient qualification for inclusion on the *Deutsche Volksliste*. Hitler had also convinced himself that Ukrainians retained traces of Germanic blood, brought to the region by the ancient Goths. Many did, in fact, want to register in the hope of concrete advantages. As a result, the authorities, and the SS in particular, often had to act on a pragmatic basis, and the decisions taken by the screening commissions of the Rasse- und Siedlungshauptamt mixed political and racial criteria.

Because of the failed colonization efforts in the region, many German officials came to view the *Volksdeutsche* there 'as more of a welfare burden than a racial asset'.[147] The treatment of the ethnic Germans often reflected the perception that they were at best second-rate Germans. The relevant documents contain frequent complaints by the authorities about the poor work morale and censurable conduct of the *Volksdeutsche*, in particular their irresponsible sexual behaviour. The occupation authorities had to acknowledge that many ethnic Germans were 'ideologically heterogeneous and on the whole destitute'.[148] The end result was that they ended up performing auxiliary functions for the German authorities, often staining their hands with blood in the extermination of Ukrainian Jews.[149]

When the military situation began to worsen and the Wehrmacht started its retreat from the East, the situation of the *Volksdeutsche* deteriorated, as they became ever more uncertain about their future. Those who lived in the occupied territories were preferred targets for partisan attacks. This persuaded many to obey the orders of the authorities to withdraw from the area. But in the Banat region of Yugoslavia, for example, a considerable number of *Volksdeutsche* decided to stay, egged on by their community leaders and convinced that Germany would eventually win the war. Many chose to cling to their German identity at the decisive moment. There was a mixture of opportunism and inertia, with much variation between regions.

If the ethnic Germans fled to Germany too soon, they risked being stigmatized and punished as defeatists. If they stayed too long, they faced the wrath of the ethnic majority populations. In the end, many decided to desert the cause of the Third Reich because they were convinced that the war was lost. There were desertions, attempts to be struck off the lists of the *Volksdeutsche*, and fraternization with the Slavic population. The German authorities' trust in the *Volksdeutsche* began to crumble. The years 1944–5 can be considered a 'time of immense confusion'.[150]

The Third Reich did not remain inactive in its ethnic policy towards the West either, although the scope of the plans cannot be compared with those aimed at the East. Local authorities started to implement circumscribed plans of cultural, linguistic and economic Germanization, particularly in regions that were supposedly characterized by a major Germanic presence, particularly Alsace and Lorraine but also Luxembourg. These plans also envisaged forced population transfers; however, political factors ended up colliding with racial criteria in the western border area. Just as in the East, the RKFDV advocated a hardline policy that foresaw westward expulsion for those elements defined as undesirable. But Himmler had to reckon with the ambitions of two of Hitler's plenipotentiaries, respectively Adolf Wagner (in Alsace) and Josef Bürckel (Lorraine), who did not want to have complications within their 'fiefdoms'. This sparked off extended bureaucratic infighting that delayed the implementation of the plans.[151]

The forced deportations therefore mostly affected leading political activists, associations and parties that the National Socialists considered hostile. In Luxembourg, Gauleiter Simon and the SS tried to get rid of the 'hotheads' who opposed the idea of the Grand Duchy's incorporation into the Reich. The resulting expulsions were less sweeping than the plans, although still tragic for the victims; just over 7,000 of the 35,000 people originally slated for expulsion were in fact dispossessed and deported to the nearby rural region of Hunsrück. Moreover, attempts to assess the ethnic identity of the population on the basis of a census carried out in October 1941 showed that 95 per cent of the Grand Duchy's citizens declared themselves to be 'Luxembourgers', thereby refusing the call of Nazi racial ideology.[152]

The policy of denationalization put into action in the French territories close to the border with the Reich had many sides. People who donned the beret, a typical symbol of French nationalism, were punished with a fine. There was also a plan to expel everyone considered politically and/or racially untrustworthy, so as to favour a total integration of these territories into the Reich. From the beginning of 1940 about 140,000 people from Alsace and some 100,000 from Lorraine were expelled en masse towards non-occupied Vichy territory, mainly Jews, gypsies, aliens, criminals, so-called 'anti-socials', the mentally ill, and various individuals considered nationally French. But much more ambitious plans were discussed. According to Hitler, 250,000 people should have been expelled from Alsace alone. The lack of time, the war priorities and also the stubborn opposition of much of society undermined the expulsion and denationalization plans. Their implementation was also sabotaged by local Nazi leaders, who were primarily interested in political power.[153]

By August 1944 Reichskommissar Himmler was forced to draw conclusions from the poor progress of the colonization projects and the grim military situation. He issued an order suspending the implementation of all colonization plans in the East 'because they are not of decisive relevance to the war'.[154]

—3—

The Population Policies of the 'Axis' Allies

3.1 Fascist Italy and the 'Mediterranean Empire'

Italy at the beginning of the 1900s was experiencing social and economic modernization, reflected in nationalistic projects promoted primarily by the bourgeoisie, as exemplified by the founding of the Associazione Nazionalista Italiana (Italian Nationalist Association) in 1910.[1] According to the nationalists, it was necessary to renew the national idea by imbuing Italian society with an imperialist spirit that would enable the country to fight for international supremacy. The heroic imperial past was recalled not in a nostalgic way, but as a reference point for the future. A nationalist journal proclaimed: 'Past glories, Roman power, the science and art of the Renaissance, the value of the *Risorgimento* give much honour to the nation that produced them and make others envy them; however, they should help us mainly as an admonition and a source of encouragement.'[2]

Imperialist nationalism pervaded Italy's new culture: it was anti-democratic, anti-socialist and authoritarian, and it drew on race. War was a crucial element in this new ideological construct. It had been anticipated for a long time, and when it appeared on the horizon, the nationalists emerged as the most fervent supporters of the 'healthy blood-letting' that was supposed to mould a new nation.[3]

The myth of the nation was also central to fascism right from the beginning, and the alliance with the nationalists was fundamental in establishing the regime. However, there was a contradiction between the way in which the nationalists and the way in which the fascists exalted the nation. For the former, the nation was an end in itself, while for the latter it was subordinate to the main goal, i.e. fascism. Fascism possessed a totalitarian motivation. The nation was a myth, useful for creating the fascist political religion, a myth which, although anchored in the spirit of Rome, looked towards the future. As early as 1922 Mussolini wrote: 'Certainly the Rome that we honour but in particular the Rome that we long for and that we are preparing is different: it is not a matter of famous stones, but of living souls … a tough preparation for the future.'[4]

When the fascists rose to power, they accentuated their revolutionary view of the nation. In reality, however, the regime's totalitarian ambition was held in check by structural restraints which the Duce could not override. These included the rigidity of the bureaucratic apparatus, the sectional interests of the economic forces, and the Church. The supremacy of the state over the nation was stressed in the regime's main ideological documents, from the entry 'Fascism' in the *Enciclopedia Italiana*, written by the philosopher Giovanni Gentile, to the *Dizionario di Politica*. Carlo Costamagna wrote: 'It is precisely the state, as promoter of war, that generates the nations and the nationalities.'[5]

The fascist state aspired to an anthropological revolution aimed at creating soldier-citizens who would be ready for everything. But with the passing of time Mussolini was forced to acknowledge that his anthropological revolution had not even begun. The result was the launching of the 'anti-bourgeois' campaign in 1938, which singled out the bourgeoisie as *the* enemy of the regime. In the opinion of many young fascists, 'fascist universalism seemed … the only and, for some, even the last possibility that the regime had to renew and re-cleanse itself from the compromises and the conventionalities collected during its last ten years in power'.[6]

Although the race factor appeared in the regime's ideological pronouncements, it was eclipsed by a spiritualistic vision of the nation, which was a particular construct of the fascist state. This interpretation opened the way to the expansion of the myth of the nation, but not primarily in the sense of a 'transfer of mass from one territory to another', as the historian Delio Cantimori wrote, criticizing National Socialist ideology. The expansion was rather to have a predominantly cultural character, drawing on universalistic traditions: the Empire, the papacy, the Renaissance. Thus, the imperial destiny of the Italian nation envisaged by the fascist regime had a cultural connotation. Some concrete political initiatives emerged from this vision, such as the CAUR (Comitati d'azione per l'universalità di Roma or Action Committees for the Universality of Rome), founded in 1933.

In fact, the fascist regime's nationalist perspective gradually shifted towards a European one in competition with the National Socialists. During the war, fascist political culture began to focus on discussions of a New Europe, starting from the thesis that the principle of nationality was on the decline. As a result, concepts such as 'vital space', 'great space' and 'continental policy' became common in the regime's publications. As one prominent interpreter of Mussolini's thought wrote in 1942: 'There will not be a new Europe without universal revolution, i.e. without a new civilisation … Either the revolution is universal or it is not revolution.'[7]

Fascist ideologists adapted to the new atmosphere created by Nazi Germany's military triumphs. In the envisaged New Europe, fascist Italy was to assume a dominant cultural and spiritual role. The continent was to be reorganized in a hierarchy that would yield supremacy to the great nations. The key question was whether the position of predominance would be held by Italy or Germany. Fascist intellectuals conceded to Germany 'a material and moral impulse that is more evident and more decisive than ours', while claiming an 'even more precious' role for fascist Italy.[8]

Racist arguments gained ground in Italy, both in the circulation of ideas and in legislation, particularly after 1938.[9] But the regime's intellectuals took care to accentuate the differences from Germany. Thus, in the *Dizionario di Politica*, Cantimori wrote that the German movement conceived the nation as a 'political and natural unity that has its bond in the biological community of blood and lineage', while fascism viewed the nation as a 'political, historical, and cultural unity'.[10] In the fascist view, race was more a 'sentiment' and a 'myth' than a 'biological' fact. During the war Gentile himself reassessed the concept of the nation and stressed the necessity of 'brotherly collaboration among the different races, none of which was born to serve'.[11]

The final stages of fascism may be analysed through the prism of *Primato*, the journal founded in the spring of 1940 by Giuseppe Bottai, one of the main architects of the regime's cultural policy.[12] He wrote: 'Mussolini's prophecy has come true: today, Europe is fighting the war prepared by fascism, through its devastating and constructive criticism, through its audacity that has already been tested in Africa and Spain.'[13] The presumed primogeniture of fascism was thus strongly stressed by the journal, which reasserted fascist Italy's claim to a predominant role in the building of the 'new European order', thanks to its cultural prowess. One article claimed that 'it could just be the war that assigns to a strong, national-minded Italy the task of teaching the people, perplexed by so many doctrines and deafened by so many words'.[14] An unsigned editorial of August 1942 stated: 'it would be a purely barbarous and reactionary idea that the New Order should consist only in the domination of one race over another'.[15]

Italy's room for manoeuvre was becoming narrower, however, and external reality began to prevail over illusions. Bottai repeatedly stressed the need for the fascists to stop congratulating themselves on being 'pure champions of the spirit, in a Europe filled with arms and labour'.[16] In February 1941 Giaime Pintor, a leading figure at the journal, wrote: 'But as long as success accompanies the grey armies of the Reich, and the white and red flag waves over the conquered cities, there can be no room in Europe for another contrasting idea'.[17] The desertion of the Italian intellectuals that Bottai had tried to convince to take part in the conference of European writers held in Weimar in October 1942 mirrored the failure of plans to preserve Italy's cultural supremacy. The collapse of fascism was at hand.

Was fascist imperialism 'first of all an idea' based on 'spiritual dominion in the world'?[18] Or did it also build on political-military practice? Historiography has avoided this question for a long time, but some recent studies have placed it in the foreground.[19] Behind the ideological and propagandistic language, there was a second level of thinking which addressed the practicalities of how the 'imperial dream' should come true. The reasoning of Fascist theoreticians was influenced by the experience of governing the African colonies on the one hand,[20] and by the mythical appeal of imperial Rome on the other. They speculated about varying levels of subordination in different territories that would not suffocate national peculiarities. The empire was to be a flexible system. The *imperium* would be run 'with the methods that ... the degree of civilisation of the conquered peoples suggested'.[21] This implied that the exploitation of the colonial populations of Africa would be more severe than that foreseen for other areas. Mussolini established deadlines for the conquest of the desired 'vital space', starting with Tunisia, Corsica and Albania. Yugoslavia, Greece, Turkey and Egypt were to follow later, completing the sphere of Italian domination.

The fascist leadership developed its views about vital space in competition – and partial cooperation – with Nazi plans. Mussolini's 1936 alliance with Hitler proved irrevocable, and parallels between the expansionist projects of fascist Italy and those of Nazi Germany were also evident on an ideological level. At the root of both projects lay a view of history as a conflict among populations, based on a rigorous hierarchy. A shared racist component was thus indisputable.[22] Rodogno concludes that 'the relationship between the two ideologies is close indeed'.[23] However, the plans diverged in their contents: the racism of the Italian planners was inclusive, and it was based on the presumed civilizing superiority of the Italian race; the other races would have to submit, but it was possible for them to be integrated. This contrasted with the exclusionist views of the Nazis. Within this framework, the openly racist statements of the Italian anthropologist Guido Lantra were atypical.[24]

The course of the war posed insurmountable obstacles even to a partial realization of the fascist 'imperial dream'. In the spring of 1941 Mussolini's plans for a 'parallel war' had to be abandoned because of poor military preparation as well as mistakes in conducting the war.[25]

Fascism was particularly sensitive to nationalistic appeals along its eastern border, both because a Slovenian minority lived there and because the post-First World War peace treaty had not satisfied patriotic expectations. The regime planned or implemented a series of measures in the area, ranging from the closure of Slovenian and Croatian schools, completed in 1928/9, to the forced Italianization of personal and place names, and to repressive police control.[26] Mussolini also tried to destabilize the fragile Yugoslav state by abetting Croatian separatist terrorism, represented by Ante Pavelić's *Ustaša*. Their most sensational act was undoubtedly the October 1934 assassination of King Alexander Karageorgevic during an official visit to France.[27]

The situation worsened during the war. Germany and Italy, victorious in a brief campaign against Yugoslavia and Greece, subjected the area to a process of radical 'Balkanization', with the aim of stirring up national tensions and thereby reducing the risk of resistance. Ex-Yugoslavia was divided among the Axis countries in an attempt to satisfy their respective expansionist and nationalist ambitions. Mussolini had control over the so-called province of Ljubljana, encompassing central and southern Slovenia, the Dalmatian coast and Montenegro. Germany annexed some regions of central Slovenia – Carniola and Lower Styria – inhabited by a mixed Austrian and Slovenian population. The Banat, a region populated by an ethnic German minority, was likewise annexed. Berlin also imposed direct administration on Serbia, whereas in Croatia a satellite state was set up, entrusted to the *Ustaša* under Ante Pavelić. It was never clearly established which of the two allies would have supremacy in Croatia, and original joint control – the Germans in the north, the Italians in the south – quickly turned into a clear hegemony of the former.

Italian policy in the occupied territories, which were governed partly by civilian and partly by military administrations, was on the whole very harsh.[28] In the annexed territories –just as in the area of Menton in south-east France – a census and screening of the population were carried out to distinguish the politically trustworthy, and those who could be granted at least conditional Italian citizenship, from the undesirables. The latter were to be removed. Mussolini proclaimed: 'Population exchanges and forced exoduses are providential.'[29] Racial elements were present in the regulations issued, but they also left room for political and judicial considerations.

The second planned step was the Italianization of the annexed territories. However, this became impossible because of a lack of personnel, time and resources. The Italianization of place names was started, but existing educational structures were touched only slightly. More significant results were obtained in the economic field through forced expropriations and seizures. But in this area, too, Italy remained subordinate to German power. The final step foresaw the colonization of the annexed territories with Italian citizens. Civilian and military authorities were in broad agreement on this matter, but the vague plans remained unfulfilled.

By contrast, a cruel policy of forced internments and population transfers was implemented in limited areas to cut local support for the partisan movement. Just in the concentration camp that the Italian military authorities built on the Dalmatian island of Rab in the summer of 1941, 10,000 people were detained in very harsh conditions, and at least one tenth of them died from privation. A network of camps was created in which at least 30,000 people were detained for various periods, and the city of Ljubljana was closed off with a system of barbed wire.[30]

The situation was exacerbated by the rise of a communist resistance movement, deeply rooted in the population and led by Josip Broz – Tito. The Italian civilian and military authorities were aware of the difficulties they faced, with a weak military machine scattered over a large territory whose natural characteristics favoured guerrilla warfare. Attempts were made to exploit ethnic tensions by enlisting collaborationist troops, such as the *domobrani* in Slovenia. However, the annexation, denationalization and colonization plans produced by civilian and military authorities never amounted to anything because of the difficulty in maintaining public order. The Italian occupiers were always militarily and logistically inferior to the Germans. As a result, an unbridgeable gap separated 'imperial' dreams from the everyday realities of occupation. As Rodogno writes: 'The reality of occupation was very different from the regime's projects and ambitions, and almost nothing of the post-war new order was accomplished.'[31]

3.2 Hungary: Principles and Practice

In the period between the two world wars, as well as during the war itself, official Hungarian policy opposed the principle of a nation state. The ambition of creating an ethnically homogeneous state stood in sharp contrast to Hungarian historical traditions since the country had been the homeland of many ethnic groups throughout its long history. The ruling elite always considered it natural and obvious that only the Hungarian nation was historically destined to assume the leading role in the region. However, according to the concept of the Hungarian nation put forward by two dominant politicians of the period between 1920 and 1944, István Bethlen and Pál Teleki, this leading role entailed not oppression but rather enhanced responsibility to promote the material and cultural prosperity of the other nations of the region.[32] This principle was also accepted by Teleki's successors as prime minister, László Bárdossy and Miklós Kállay.

Despite the rejection of the concept of a nation state in official Hungarian policy, during the 1930s the 'racial' issue stirring Central Europe became an important point in Hungarian public discussions as well. Criticism was directed against the Jewish and German minorities (the latter being known as 'Swabians'). Although the Jewish population was very well assimilated, the Hungarian aristocracy and middle classes, and most of the political elite, traditionally regarded it as an alien body. Being anti-German was a new phenomenon in Hungarian public life, mostly characteristic of the young generation of populist writers and their followers who opposed the authoritarianism of the Horthy regime.

The 'Swabian question' and the 'Jewish question' were placed on the political and legislative agenda in the years when Hungary expanded its territory on four different occasions. Between 1938 and 1941, with the help of Germany and Italy, Hungary re-annexed the Hungarian-populated southern part of Slovakia and Transcarpathia from Czechoslovakia, northern Transylvania from Romania, and the 'southern region' (Backa) from Yugoslavia. In the same years the national assembly passed three laws restricting the rights of the Jews, who were now officially considered not to be part of the nation.

While the situation of the Jews gradually worsened, the Germans received favoured status. After the Second Vienna Award of 30 August 1940 had given northern Transylvania to Hungary, Germany made the Hungarian government accept the 'Vienna agreement'. This endowed the Volksbund – an ethnic German organization that had unfurled its flag in 1939 to promote Nazi ideology – with a monopolistic status in organizing the Germans in Hungary and provided a basis for giving autonomy to the German minority. The agreement also provided the ethnic Germans of northern Transylvania with the option of voluntary resettlement into the Reich. But the Teleki government sabotaged its execution.

During the Second World War the transfer of the ethnic German population out of Hungary was not broached by the Hungarian side. In a letter of 3 November 1939, Horthy reacted with polite moderation to Hitler's speech of 6 October that had called for 'repatriation'. During their visits to Germany, Prime Ministers Miklós Kállay (June 1942) and Horthy (April 1943) stated that, apart from certain atrocities committed by the Volksbund, members of the German minority in Hungary were good patriots. The idea of bringing the Germans out of the country was raised by Hitler. Horthy did not object to the proposal, but he would contemplate only the possibility of transferring those Germans and their families who had shown disloyalty. No such transfers were carried out during the war.[33]

In general, the government wanted to restore the pre-1918 ethnic composition of the newly acquired territories, but to go no further. Ethnic multiculturalism matched the Hungarian concept of the nation. The government therefore rejected any proposals for population exchanges, primarily because they would have changed the region's traditional ethnic composition. The Hungarian government accepted neither the Czechoslovak proposal for a population exchange brought up in the negotiations held in Komárom in October 1938, nor the population exchange proposal introduced during the talks with the Romanian delegates in Turnu Severin – preceding the Second Vienna Award – in August 1940. In 1942 the Hungarian government also turned down a Croatian initiative for a population transfer along the Hungarian–Croatian border. Population exchanges and forced assimilation were both considered at odds with Hungarian traditions and interests. In 1940 Prime Minister Pál Teleki proposed the introduction of different forms of autonomy for different ethnic groups – instead of their assimilation – based on their stage of development and settlement conditions. Although only certain elements of Teleki's ideas could actually be implemented under wartime conditions, in general the ethnic groups remained loyal to the Hungarian state and local conflicts did not reach a level that could have jeopardized the country's political stability.

The strip of southern Slovakia incorporated into Hungary by the First Vienna Award of 2 November 1938 was abandoned by most of the farmers and public servants who had been settled there after 1919. According to the data given by the Refugee Care Agency set up in the Protectorate of Bohemia and Moravia in March 1939, 11,625 persons fled from the territory annexed to Hungary,[34] most of them Czech nationals. This figure excluded those civil servants who had been evacuated by the Czechoslovak authorities before the territory was ceded. Their number probably did not exceed a few thousand, including family members.[35]

Some Czechoslovak sources, however, set the figure for those leaving the Hungarian-controlled areas at 80,000–100,000.[36] But these higher figures are not supported by either census data or the materials of the Refugee Care Agency. According to the Czechoslovak census of December 1938, 1,027,450 inhabitants lived on this strip of territory. The result of the census conducted by the Hungarian Central Statistical Office in the second half of December 1938 was 1,041,401 persons.[37] According to Hungarian historiography, the Hungarian authorities expelled about 5,000 people.[38] The number of Czech and Slovak settlers who remained in their places of residence even after the Hungarian annexation of the territory was considerably higher than that. The hands of the Hungarian government were tied. They could not conduct arbitrary, unilateral actions because matters concerning the expulsion of Czechs had to be negotiated with the German government following the dissolution of Czechoslovakia in March 1939. The agreement concluded with Germany on 16 October 1940 obliged Hungary to pay compensation for expropriated Czech property. The Hungarian authorities were also deterred from expelling Slovakian settlers by the fact that the Slovakian leadership intended to compensate such expellees at the expense of Hungarian landowners in Slovakia.[39]

The Slovakian government showed less solidarity towards the Czechs living on its territory. As a result of decrees issued by the Interior Ministry and the activities of the Hlinka guard, the Czech population in Slovakia decreased from the 120,926 persons registered in the 1930 census to 3,024 by 1940.[40]

Contrary to the intentions of the Hungarian government, large-scale migration took place between Hungary and Romania in 1940 and 1941, which almost amounted to a population exchange. The migration began after the Second Vienna Award of 30 August 1940, which allocated the northern part of Transylvania to Hungary. Two groups of people were particularly affected: those Romanians from northern Transylvania who had settled in the area after 1918 and Hungarians residing in southern Transylvania. In several cases Hungarians were forced to flee by the Romanian authorities. Following the Vienna Award, the living conditions of the Hungarians in Romania deteriorated fast. Public servants of Hungarian nationality were dismissed en masse and young men were pressed into military service at the front from 1942 on. The dismissed public servants and young men slated for service on the Eastern Front considered their future secure only in Hungary and fled in large numbers. This flood of refugees went against the nationality policy of the Hungarian government, the primary goal of which was to maintain the strength of Hungarians living in southern Transylvania in the hope of further territorial revisions. To stem the influx of refugees, in the spring of 1941 the government introduced measures to make immigration to Hungary more difficult. The border could only be crossed by those who possessed either a passport stamped by Hungarian consular authorities or a so-called 'home-return pass'. But Hungarians from southern Transylvania kept coming, either by eluding regulations by means of fake documents or by crossing the 'green border' without any documents. According to the records of the National Bureau for the Control of Foreigners, 190,132 persons arrived from Romania between September 1940 and February 1944.[41] At the same time, 221,000 Romanians fled from northern Transylvania.[42]

Most of them were settlers who had arrived in Transylvania as colonizers in the 1920s and 1930s.

As a result of the Hungarian exodus, the ethnic conditions in southern Transylvania changed significantly. Contrary to the intentions of the Hungarian government, the Hungarian population in the area decreased by nearly 40 per cent. At the same time, the proportion of Hungarian nationals in northern Transylvania increased considerably, since most of the refugees settled there. But these changes were subsequently largely undone by new waves of refugees in the autumn of 1944.

The Hungarian leadership also intended to restore the pre-1918 ethnic conditions in the 'southern region', annexed after the German attack on Yugoslavia in April 1941. The ethnic composition of the region had been changed significantly by the transfers carried out by the Yugoslav government. In the first instance, the Hungarian military administration wanted to reverse the consequences of these transfers. After completing the occupation of the Backa, Lieutenant General Elemér Gorondy Novák, commander of the 3rd Hungarian Army, ordered a cleansing action on 14 April 1941. The Hungarian military interned several thousand Serbian settlers and others considered of dubious national loyalty. Internment centres were set up near major transport routes, including along the Tisza and Danube rivers and the Subotica–Novi Sad railway line, so that the transfers could be carried out quickly. But the implementation of the transfers was hindered in the same way as it was in the southern strip of Slovakia re-annexed by Hungary in 1938. The transfer of the unwanted Serbs who had settled in the area after 1918 could be carried out only with the approval of the powers that controlled the Yugoslav territories, primarily Germany. The German–Italian agreement concluded in Vienna on 24 April 1941 that proclaimed the dissolution of Yugoslavia did not foresee an ethnic rearrangement – that is, transfers or organized population movements – in the territories occupied by Hungarian troops. After the occupation of the 'southern region', the Hungarian government repeatedly conferred with German diplomatic and military leaders about the issue of accommodating the Serbs who were to be expelled. From July 1941 onwards the German Foreign Office repeatedly expressed its willingness to take at least some of the internees, mentioning a prospective figure of 2,000–3,000, but the German military command in Belgrade thwarted such plans.[43] In 1942 János Bolla, Hungary's deputy ambassador to Belgrade, negotiated with the Serbs on the deportations. But the talks produced no results, as the accommodation of the 300,000 refugees and internees pouring in from Croatia and other areas of the former Yugoslavia posed an insoluble problem for the Serbian authorities. The main reason for the puppet regime's refusal to accommodate the expellees was the fear that the discontented and homeless crowds would strengthen armed resistance, both directly and indirectly.

Since the negotiations with the Germans held out little hope of actual results, between April and December 1941 the Hungarian authorities unilaterally expelled significant numbers of Serbs classified as 'non-original' inhabitants of the area. In 1941 the Hungarian civilian authorities registered 48,067 people who had moved to the region after 1918 and stayed even after the retreat of the Yugoslavian army.[44] The local Hungarian administration and military forces viewed these people as their primary targets for deportation. Contemporary German documents refer to about 35,000 deported Serbs, while the Committee for Refugees, an organization set up by the pro-German Serbian puppet government led by Milan Nedic, put the number at 56,000.[45] Hungarian historical literature generally sets the number of expelled Serbs at 15,000,[46] while the figures given in Serbian scholarly literature vary widely, from a low of 30,000 to a high of 150,000.[47] This latter figure must have originated from a report by the German military headquarters in Serbia released shortly after the Hungarian occupation of Backa in the spring of 1941. The document states that the Hungarian administration planned to expel 150,000 Serbian colonizers to Serbia in the near future, a plan that was never realized.[48]

The resettlement of Hungarian public servants in the re-annexed territories was aimed at bolstering the Hungarian ethnic presence there. The arrival of public servants also promoted the re-establishment of the pre-1918 conditions because after the First World War hundreds of thousands of Hungarian public servants had fled to the territories defined by the Trianon peace treaty. Their number can only be estimated indirectly on the basis of post-Second World War population records. From the 1948 census and the monthly reports of the Ministry of Welfare issued between 1945 and 1947 one can conclude that the public servants who had left and then returned at the end of the war numbered about 64,000, including their families. The distribution of these refugees according to the regions from which they came was as follows: Czechoslovakia (northern Hungary) 21,000; Soviet Union (Carpatho-Ruthenia) 5,000; Romania (northern Transylvania) 24,000; Yugoslavia (Backa) 14,000.[49] These figures refer to the total number of public servants and their relatives who had left Hungary's pre-1938 territories, as the Czechoslovak, Romanian and Yugoslavian public authorities returning in 1944/5 did not tolerate the presence of Hungarian officials, most of whom retreated with the Hungarian troops.

The ambition of the Hungarian government was to re-establish the ethnic status quo of 1918. Besides this aim it had no further aspiration for population transfers, although two minor actions to repatriate ethnic groups were nevertheless carried out. Both actions involved Hungarian ethnic groups living outside Hungary's 1918 borders, in the Carpathian Mountains. The first action was the transfer/ 'repatriation' of the Seklers from Bukovina, who had settled in the eastern part of the Carpathians in the eighteenth century. The situation of this group became critical when the Soviet army occupied the northern part of Bukovina in the summer of 1940. Romanian refugees from northern Bukovina were resettled in the houses of Germans who had left the region, in keeping with the Romanian–German agreement on the transfer of ethnic Germans, concluded on 22 October 1940, and in the confiscated properties of Seklers. Plundered Seklers began to move into

Hungarian territories to seek shelter. In order to channel this exodus, the Hungarian government decided to 'repatriate' the endangered group. On 11 May 1941 an agreement on the 'transfer' was concluded with the Romanian government, which was eager to get rid of non-Romanian ethnic groups. Since the fertility rate of the Bukovinian Seklers was high, the Budapest government wanted to settle them in a strategically important region where Hungarians constituted a minority. The chosen region was Backa, an area under threat from Serbian partisans. Within the framework of this colonization project, 17,700 Sekler-Hungarians were settled along Hungary's southern borderland.[50]

Hungarians living in Bosnia were also resettled because of the threat of the partisan war. A Croatian–Hungarian agreement signed in early April 1942 approved the removal of Hungarians from three Bosnian villages. During this operation, which dragged on until September 1942, 1,552 persons were transported to Hungary's 'southern region'.[51]

Although these organized population movements were relatively small, the composition of the Hungarian population altered dramatically during the last two years of the war because of the extermination of more than half of the country's Jews. To review the history of the Holocaust in Hungary would go beyond the scope of this study. But it must be mentioned that the expulsion of the Jews and their delivery into the hands of the Germans contradicted the traditional Hungarian concept of the nation. Legislation passed between 1938 and 1942 had introduced various discriminatory regulations, but the physical labelling and deportation of Jews from the provinces and the death marches of Jews from Budapest took place following the loss of sovereignty in the wake of the German occupation of the country on 19 March 1944. Ironically, the deportations subsequently carried out by the Hungarian police, acting under German supervision, significantly weakened the Hungarian position in those territories with mixed ethnic populations, such as Transcarpathia and northern Transylvania, where the Hungarian government had wanted to increase and strengthen the Hungarian presence.

3.3 Romanian Plans and Practices

Compared with other nations in Central Europe, Romania stepped onto the path of national development relatively late, in the middle of the nineteenth century. But the self-confidence of the young state was greatly reinforced by its subsequent successes. Romania had ended the Balkan Wars victorious and with territorial gains, but the country's lucky star reached its peak at the end of the First World War, when its territory increased about threefold. However, this success also brought a big challenge. Although Romanian historians and politicians did emphasize the centuries-long integrity of the newly gained territories and Old Romania, the 'digestion' of Bessarabia, Bukovina and Transylvania was likely to be a difficult task. The integration of the new territories constituted a fundamental strategic and state security objective for post-war Romanian governments, irrespective of their party-political affiliation. The proportion of ethnic minorities in Romania increased to 30 per cent from the pre-1918 figure of 8 per cent. Ethnic Romanians constituted a majority in Transylvania and Bessarabia, but only barely, and were outnumbered in Bukovina. However, it was not the relatively low proportion of ethnic Romanians in the new territories that posed the main perceived challenge, but rather the composition of the minorities. On average, two thirds of city dwellers were ethnic Germans, Jews or Hungarians, meaning that these three groups stood at the top of the social pyramid. The major dividing line within Romanian society was not between social classes but between Romanians and other ethnicities, especially between ethnic Romanians and Jews. Jews were deemed to be the antipole of Romanians, not only by the political elite but also by most of the rest of society.

The builders of the Romanian nation wanted to segregate the Jews and assimilate the other minorities. The major tool of 'romanization' in the 1920s and 1930s was cultural policy, although physical violence was not entirely absent. But the attempt to assimilate the minorities bore no fruit. The drive to transform society in Transylvania, Bukovina or Bessarabia failed. The ratio of minorities did not change significantly on the national level either. But the Second World War and the population transfers initiated by Germany provided new opportunities for Romania, too, to resolve its perceived ethnic-minority problems in a radical way. The strengthening of Germany, the dissolution of the post-First World War status quo, and internal tensions led to an enduring internal and foreign policy crisis in Romania. In December 1937 the League of National Christian Defence came to power. The government, led by Octavian Goga and Alexandru Cuza, was the second openly anti-Semitic regime in Europe.[52] After only forty days it was forced to resign by King Carol II, who imposed his own dictatorship instead. But the prestige of the new regime was undermined by the territorial losses suffered in 1940. Bessarabia and northern Bukovina were occupied by the Soviet Union after the ultimatum of 26 June 1940. Northern Transylvania returned to Hungary after the Second Vienna Award – as we have already seen – while southern Dobrudja passed into the possession of Bulgaria under the Treaty of Craiova, concluded on 7 September 1940. The final consequence of the political chaos – exacerbated by the territorial losses – was the replacement of the royal dictatorship by that of General Ion Antonescu, supported by the Germans, in January 1941.

Antonescu's regime gained strength when, a few weeks after entering the war against the Soviet Union, Romanian and German troops reoccupied the lands that had been lost the year before. During the military campaigns of 1941, Romania also gained control of other territories. The area between the Dnester and Bug rivers occupied in the summer of 1941 came under Romanian rule under the name Transnistria. The ethnic composition of the Romanian territories changed significantly because of the twists and turns of the country's foreign and domestic policies as well as the multiple territorial changes.

The dissolution of Greater Romania in the summer of 1940 reinforced the conviction shared by Romania's entire political elite that the minorities posed a deadly threat to the very integrity of the country. Their elimination, through expulsion, was therefore seen as a key national objective. There was a precedent for population movements organized on a supposedly voluntary basis. On 4 September 1936 the Romanian and Turkish governments had concluded an agreement concerning the emigration of the Turkish minority of Dobrudja to Turkey. By April 1941, 70,000 Muslim Turks had left.[53] In the new wartime situation the Romanian leadership found a radical solution to perceived minority problems in population exchanges. Foreign Minister Mihail Manoilescu openly noted (on 30 July 1940) that 'the government wishes to take more radical steps in order to give a definitive solution to the issue of minorities of the same blood with neighboring peoples, by new measures adopted in the spirit and based on the methods of our time. Among these, a measure which has yielded very good results in all countries is the population exchange.'[54] The Craiova Treaty, which handed Dobrudja to Bulgaria, contained a provision for a mandatory population exchange. Through the exchange of 61,000 Bulgarian nationals of northern Dobrudja for 100,000 Romanians of southern Dobrudja the new state border between the two countries became an ethnic boundary as well.

According to the German–Soviet agreement of 5 September 1940, the number of people resettled to Germany from the previously Romanian provinces of Bessarabia and Bukovina reached 136,000.[55] Among those who opted for relocation were not only Germans but also people of other nationalities. They decided to leave only after the Soviets arrived, making use of the opportunity provided by the German 'repatriation' programme. As a result of the transfer of Germans, the proportion of ethnic Romanians in the territories regained in the summer of 1941 increased significantly in comparison with the previous year, despite the deportations carried out by the Soviets.

On 22 October 1940, about one and a half months after the conclusion of the German–Soviet agreement on the transfer of Germans from Soviet-incorporated Bessarabia and northern Bukovina, a treaty was signed by representatives of the Reich and the Antonescu government on the removal of German minorities from southern Bukovina and northern Dobrudja. In southern Bukovina 52,000 people and in northern Dobrudja 14,500 people opted for transfer to Germany.[56] As a result of transfers and the annexation of northern Transylvania by Hungary, the number of Germans in Romania decreased from the 740,000 recorded in 1937 to 470,000. The number of Hungarians who remained on Romanian territory also dramatically decreased. Due to the territorial changes and to the migration between the two parts of Transylvania, the Hungarian population fell from a pre-war figure of 1.4 million to 200,000.

After the reacquisition of northern Bukovina and Bessarabia, the absolute number of Jews living in Romania increased again, but as a percentage of the total population their numbers decreased, since many moved into the interior of the Soviet Union, fleeing German–Romanian occupation. This was a typical phenomenon in the territories annexed by the Soviet Union. As the troops of Germany and its allies approached, the Jews who had heard about the atrocities committed in Poland and elsewhere ran away – if they could. From the territories annexed by the Soviet Union in 1939 and 1940, a total of about 140,000–170,000 Jews retreated into the interior of the Soviet Union, together with elements from the economic and public administration.[57]

Whereas the general trend in Romanian-controlled areas was towards greater ethnic homogenization, in Bukovina and Bessarabia the position of Romanians deteriorated during the Soviet occupation. While ethnic Germans from beyond the Reich were being transported into Germany, large-scale forced migrations also took place in the areas that had come under Soviet control. The Soviet operations were motivated by both ethnic and political considerations. The aim of the deportations, mass arrests and internment was to eliminate those 'hostile' classes that could constitute a potential leading force of national resistance.

Northern Bukovina and a part of Bessarabia annexed in June 1940 were incorporated into the Ukraine, while the greater part of Bessarabia became a new republic of the Soviet Union, the Moldavian SSR, proclaimed on 2 August 1940. On the very same day, Bogdan Kobulov – one of Lavrentij Berija's deputies – ordered the round-up of 'anti-Soviet elements' in the Moldavian region. The operation to track down these 'hostile elements' took several months. A decree issued on 14 June 1941 by Beria determined the fate of those put on the list of enemies.[58] The plan stipulated the arrest and banishment of former industrialists, land owners and other members of the bourgeoisie. The operation had actually started on 13 June 1941, the day before the decree was issued, but it never reached full speed because of the German invasion launched on 22 June. According to Pavel Poljan, this relatively short period was still long enough to arrest and deport 22,848 people, of whom 9,954 were taken to Kazakhstan and 5,787 to Omsk and Novosibirsk.[59] According to other sources, the number of those dragged away from the Moldavian Soviet Socialist Republic was 31,699, while a further group of 12,191 'anti-Soviet' persons was deported from the Romanian territories annexed to the Ukrainian Soviet Socialist Republic.[60]

The population exchange carried out in Dobrudja, the 'repatriation' of Germans and Seklers from Bessarabia and Bukovina, the flight of considerable numbers of Jews into the interior of the Soviet Union, as well as the mass migrations between areas of Transylvania controlled by Hungary and Romania, all led to a significant ethnic homogenization of the population of Romania. However, Romania was still very far from becoming a homogeneous nation state. The country's ethnic situation was further complicated by the annexation of another region, Transnistria.

Sabin Manuilă, director of the Romanian Central Institute of Statistics, proposed a way out of this ethnic diversity, which the country's leadership considered harmful. As early as 1929 he had spoken of the need to block emigration and to strengthen the ethnic Romanian population in border areas and in the major towns. The reports he compiled for the government in August and December 1940, and also in April and October 1941, reveal that population exchanges constituted the central idea of his conception. He argued that only population exchanges with neighbouring countries would 'lead to the ethnic homogenization of our population, and eliminate the frictions causing international tension at present'.[61] He also suggested that Romanians living in territories that could not become part of Romania should be transferred 'home' by the state. Manuilă exhorted the government to refrain from ad hoc solutions, citing the population exchange agreement with Bulgaria as an example, because it involved only Dobrudja rather than the whole country, leaving a significant Bulgarian minority within Romania. He stressed the importance of conducting population exchanges or transfers according to programmes elaborated in advance.

Manuilă summed up the essence of the draft proposal as follows:

> Politically, the time has come, or is very near, for an operation of considerable proportions, which would consist in removing to the other side of the border all the minorities with centrifugal tendencies from the future territory of Romania, bringing into the country all those with Romanian blood, wherever they may reside, and establishing the new borders of eternal Romania so that political borders and ethnic boundaries coincide accurately. … The minority populations with centrifugal tendencies are the following: 1) the Hungarians; 2) the Russians and Ukranians; 3) the Bulgarians; 4) the Serbs. All these minorities should disappear from the territory of Romania.[62]

In the first phase of the seven-stage project, the 42,000 members of the Serbian minority in Romania would be evacuated. In the second stage, Romania would claim back one third of the territory of southern Dobrudja, which had been given to Bulgaria a year before, while all 180,000 Bulgarians in Romania would be removed. At the same time the 85,000 Romanians still living in Bulgaria despite the earlier population exchanges would be 'brought home'. During the third stage the 468,000 Romanians from Yugoslavia would be settled in northern Transylvania, a territory to be seized from Hungary and cleansed of Hungarians. Manuilă proposed eliminating almost the entire Hungarian minority in Romania, numbering about 1.4 million people, by means of three transfer actions and some minor territorial cessions. In the fourth stage of the transfer programme, the Russian and Ukrainian populations in Romania, estimated at about 990,000, would leave in exchange for the Romanians living beyond the Dnester River, whose number Manuilă put at about 800,000. This is where the detailed part of the proposal ends.

The departure of the Germans of Transylvania and the Banat was taken for granted by the author, probably because of the ongoing transfers of the Bukovinian and Dobrudjan Germans. The exit of the Germans was meant to constitute the fifth stage of transfers. In the sixth stage the small Turkish ethnic group still in Romania should be gradually transferred, in cooperation with the Turkish government. About the prospective fate of the Jews, viewed as the antipode of Romanians, and the gypsies, also regarded as an alien element, Manuilă wrote: 'The Jewish problem and the "Gypsy problem" fall beyond the scope of the population exchange solutions, being unilateral transfers; they will be approached in a special memorandum.'[63] There is no trace of the promised memorandum in the available Romanian sources; probably it was never written. It is obvious, however, that by 'unilateral transfers' the author meant forced relocations.

According to Manuilă's proposal, 3.5 million non-Romanians would have been expelled from the territory of Greater Romania, while 1.6 million Romanians would have moved into the country. In territorial terms, the new Romanian nation state would have been slightly smaller than post-First World War Romania – because of the 5,000 square kilometres to be ceded to Hungary.

Apparently the available sources reveal nothing about how the addressee of the proposal, Marshal Antonescu, reacted to Manuilă's ideas. But the Central Institute of Statistics led by Manuilă did play an important role in governmental decision-making. Antonescu and his circle asked for Manuilă's opinion on population policy issues several times during the war. Manuilă also took part in the work of the Peace Bureau, set up in June 1942, whose task was to collect data in preparation for the peace settlement. One of the Bureau's sections dealt specifically with issues of ethnicities and borders. 'Manuilă's project did not become *stricto sensu* an official program of the Antonescu government. In fact, there existed no text which could have formally been adopted by the government as a program. However, the policy of the Romanian state between 1941 and 1944 toward ethnic minorities and toward Romanians living abroad was in large part in unison with Manuilă's ideas.'[64] Manuilă coyly devoted only a single sentence in his proposal to the Jews and gypsies. He must have known that the 'unilateral transfer' suggested by him was already in the process of actual implementation at the time the project proposal was drafted.

From September 1941 to the end of 1942 about 180,000 Jews were deported to Transnistria, which was considered as a dumping ground for 'alien' elements. The greater part of the deportees came from Bessarabia and Bukovina, while a minority originated from the territory of the Old Kingdom. As a result of the deportations Bessarabia and Bukovina became nearly free of Jews. About 40 per cent of the deportees died on their way to the assigned concentration camps. Shootings and epidemics also took a heavy toll on the Jews. According to Jewish estimates, out of about 180,000 deportees only 77,000 were alive in October 1943.[65] According to data from the Ministry of Internal Affairs and other governmental organizations, at the beginning of 1944 only 42,000 Jewish deportees in Transnistria were still alive.[66] Consequently, two thirds of the deportees died.

The native Jewish population of Transnistria (about 300,000) was also doomed. It is estimated that about 50–70 per cent of this population was evacuated or fled before the German–Romanian armies occupied the territory.[67] According to Romanian statistics, on 1 September 1943 the local Jewish population numbered 32,000,[68] which means that 60,000–120,000 local Jews became victims of the various forms of mass killing carried out by the units of Einsatzgruppe D and Romanian troops.

Sabin Manuilă's proposal to transfer the gypsies also came close to being implemented. The gypsies in Romania practically lived 'outside politics'. This out-of-society status even gave them a sort of security at the beginning of the war. From a juridical point of view they were unaffected by the racial and ethnic persecution instituted by the Antonescu government. They were treated as a social category rather than an ethnic group. On 22 May 1942 Antonescu made his decision on the transfer of the 'problematic' gypsies to Transnistria. The Central Institute for Statistics estimated the number of gypsies living in the county at 208,000.[69] Between June 1942 and December 1943 about 25,000 Sinti and Roma were deported to Transnistria, where they were settled in special colonies. Not being able to get either work or sufficient amounts of food, at least half of them died.[70] Those who survived escaped back into the inner regions of Romania without any sort of central command before the arrival of Soviet troops.

During the Antonescu era it was only the partial deportation of the Jews and Germans that was actually carried out from among the plans proposed by Sabin Manuilă in October 1941. Nevertheless, during the Council held on 16 November 1943 the Marshal declared the following: 'If the circumstances will help me win the war, then be sure that there is no other solution than to move the minority masses by a reform which we have to make and by eliminating these minority masses from among the Romanian element. But, until then what are we to do with the Ukrainian, Polish element? Until then we have to treat them absolutely equal in rights … we must be tolerant.'[71] Antonescu lost the war but the new wave of forced migrations of population launched at the end of the war, in the autumn of 1944, were not contrary to the Romanianizing intentions on the whole.

—4—

Population Movements at the End of the War and in Its Aftermath

4.1 The Victors' Plans and Their Implementation

From the end of 1944 the decisive element in forced migration in East-Central Europe was the westward flight – and subsequent expulsion – of Germans, who were replaced by Poles, Czechs, Slovakians, Hungarians, Serbians and Romanians. The collective punishment of Germans in East-Central Europe was carried out in the shadow of worldwide anger and hatred. Although the Allies condemned the principle of collective punishment, in practice they still made it possible. The war of the Allies had started as one against National Socialism, but it gradually turned into a war against Germans. The Atlantic Charter, proclaimed by Churchill and Roosevelt in August 1941, described a post-war peace 'which will afford to all nations the means of dwelling in safety within their own boundaries, and which will afford assurance that all the men in all the lands may live out their lives in freedom from fear and want'.[1] The Soviet government also committed itself to promoting the right of national self-determination.

As victory approached, however, the Allies diverged from their own proclaimed principles vis-à-vis the Germans, and the earlier differentiation between the German people and the Nazi regime gradually faded away.[2] This shift was reflected in the proclamation of the principle of unconditional surrender at the Casablanca Conference in January 1943. In a note of 11 October 1943 prepared for Eden, who was heading to the Moscow conference of foreign ministers, Churchill already expressed the principle of collective responsibility in an indirect way: 'We have no desire to keep any branch of the European family of nations in a condition of subjection or restriction, except as may be required by the general needs and safety of the world.'[3] At the Tehran Conference of November 1943, Stalin, Churchill and Roosevelt debated the national character of the Germans. Churchill contrasted Prussians with southern Germans, claiming about the latter: 'The people of those parts of Germany are not the most ferocious … South Germans are not going to start another war, and we would have to make it worth their while to forget Prussia.' But Stalin's opinion was: 'all Germans were the same … all Germans fought like fierce beasts'.[4] The collective responsibility of the German people, which had been implicit in declarations issued at the Yalta

Conference of February 1945, became explicit at Potsdam in July and August 1945: 'The purposes of the occupation of Germany ... shall be: ... To convince the German people that they have suffered a total military defeat and that they cannot escape responsibility for what they have brought upon themselves, since their own ruthless warfare and the fanatical Nazi resistance have destroyed the German economy and made chaos and suffering inevitable.'[5]

Besides Germans, Hungarians were the other nation whose collective responsibility was broached. This was implied by Vjačeslav Molotov, People's Commissar for Foreign Affairs, in a letter he sent to the British ambassador to Moscow (7 June 1943): 'The Soviet government believes that it is not only the Hungarian government that must bear responsibility for Hungary's armed support to Germany ... but to a certain degree the Hungarian people.'[6] A few months later, on 14 December 1943, Molotov reacted to Eduard Beneš's anti-Hungarian invective by again exclaiming: 'The Hungarians must be punished.'[7]

The defeat of Nazism also meant the defeat of Germany and its allies, primarily Hungary. The victorious powers and the world's public opinion regarded the retaliatory measures against Germans in East-Central Europe at the end of the war and in its aftermath as rightful revenge for Nazi crimes. That revenge was certainly fuelled by the brutality of the German occupation, but the expulsions that ensued were also driven by the desire to fulfil old dreams of creating a homogeneous nation state. For smaller countries on the winning side, the defeat of Nazism presented the opportunity to achieve the creation of such a nation state. The first versions of plans for forced population movements were already being drafted at the start of the war, and they continued to be revised throughout the conflict.

4.1.1 Czechoslovak Plans

Beneš and the group of people surrounding him were the primary authors of the transfer plans whose implementation would have made Czechoslovakia an ethnically homogeneous nation state. But the communist Czechoslovak émigrés in Moscow adopted similar ideas. We might never learn when the idea of expelling Germans and Hungarians first occurred to President Beneš. His statements were carefully adjusted to the political situation and the international balance of forces at any given moment. As the war proceeded, the publicized ideas about population transfers from Czechoslovakia became increasingly radical. This radicalization was not a function of increasing oppression by the occupying Nazi regime. As victory over Germany got closer, the elbow room of Czechoslovakian émigré politicians became wider, and they could propagate their ideas about the expulsion of Germans and Hungarians more openly.

In 1939, following the dissolution of Czechoslovakia, the primary goal of refugee politicians was to establish a government-in-exile and have it recognized.

The first step was the forming of the Czechoslovak National Committee in Paris on 17 October 1939. In response to events in the war, the government-in-exile was finally set up in London on 9 July 1940 and officially recognized by the British government.

During the period of Soviet–German cooperation, Beneš – adapting to the policy of Great Britain and her allies – held out the prospect of equal political rights for the German and Hungarian minorities. When the National Committee was formed in Paris, Beneš was still stressing that in a reconstituted Czechoslovak republic the mistakes of the previous two decades concerning minority issues would be corrected.[8] In November 1939 and February 1940, in his messages to Sudeten Germans who had fled to Great Britain, he also claimed that after the war the Czechs and the Germans would cooperate closely in their common home-land in which justice, equality and freedom would constitute the basic moral values.[9]

While Beneš kept announcing the granting of equal rights in the future, he began planning a reduction in Czechoslovakia's minority population as early as 1939. Prior to the summer of 1941, the British government did not really question the Munich Agreement, which had been partly based on ethnic criteria. Therefore Beneš's initial plans were relatively moderate. During the autumn of 1939 he was even prepared to make certain territorial concessions in order to reduce the number of Germans remaining in Czechoslovakia. By ceding to Germany a strip of land along the northern and north-western borderline, Czechoslovakia would have reduced the number of Germans under its dominion by half. In the plan drafted in the spring of 1940 there was no more mention of territorial concessions. The emphasis was now placed on creating ethnically homogeneous regions. The plan aimed to eliminate the scattered German ethnic islands in Moravia by internal relocation, moving people to the Sudetenland. The homogeneous German block in the border region would then have been given autonomy. Had this plan been imple-mented, the Germans would have been promoted to the status of a 'state-forming nation', alongside the Czechs and the Slovaks. This idea was supported by the émigré leaders of the Sudeten German Social Democratic Party. In the spring of 1940 Beneš still reckoned on ceding part of the southern Slovakian territories inhabited by Hungarians to Hungary, thus significantly reducing the number of Hungarians remaining in Czechoslovakia.

The government-in-exile's memorandum of 2 February 1941, which outlined Czechoslovakia's peace objectives, also contained plans for a correction of the post-First World War Czechoslovak–Hungarian borderline. Hungary was to keep only a small part of the territory it had received under the First Vienna Award of 1938. The Czechoslovaks intended to combine a modification of the border with an extensive population exchange so that the state border would coincide with the ethnographic one. The idea of an exchange of inhabitants between Czechoslovakia and Hungary became a constant feature of Beneš's plans, but after 1943 he did not talk about territorial cessions any more. On the contrary, Czechoslovak territorial claims against Hungary began to arise.

The position of the government-in-exile and its declared minority policies changed considerably after the German attack against the Soviet Union. The standing of the London-based government improved, as testified by the fact that in July it was recognized by the Soviet Union and by the United States. The contacts established with the two powers boosted the confidence of the government-in-exile, which now no longer needed the support of the Sudeten German émigré groups. At the same time, the Sudeten German émigrés lined themselves up behind the Czechoslovak policy of demanding a revision of the Munich Agreement. In exchange, they asked for a reorganization of the republic on a federative basis. But Beneš was more interested in creating the impression of seeking consensus; on 12 October 1940 he offered the Sudeten Germans six seats and the vice-president's post on the State Council established in July. But in September 1941 he postponed the admission of the German representatives, claiming that their direct involvement in policy-making would demoralize the resistance movement. In December 1942 the negotiations with the Sudeten German émigré leaders finally reached a dead end.

After obtaining the recognition of the Allied powers, Beneš and his companions began to proclaim their views about the ethnic reshaping of the region more vocally. The German occupation of Czechoslovakia also contributed to the radicalizing of the London émigré group's aims. After the appointment of Reinhard Heydrich as Reichsprotektor in September 1941, oppression assumed increasingly brutal forms. Moreover, Bohemian Germans, familiar with local conditions, constituted much of the backbone of the apparatus of oppression. As a result of the increasing terror, the Czech population could hardly differentiate between Nazi and anti-Nazi Germans, i.e. there was an increasing tendency to regard Germans as a homogeneous block of enemies. The terror campaign that unfolded after Heydrich's assassination in May 1942 further increased the Western powers' sympathy for the Czechs.

From the autumn of 1941, the leaders of the London exile group propagated their views in several articles and declarations, concluding that minority problems could not be settled without deportations. The most detailed public explanation of these views was Beneš's article 'The organization of post-war Europe' in the January 1942 issue of the journal *Foreign Affairs*. He placed the blame for Czechoslovakia's disintegration on Nazi Germany, fascist Italy and reactionary Hungary. He openly voiced the principle of collective responsibility and declared that the Germans – as a nation and a state – had produced the most devastating war in world history and were responsible for Hitler. He repeatedly declared that population transfers could not be avoided when solving minority problems. However, he did not advocate the deportation of the entire German and Hungarian minority populations, promising instead political and cultural rights to those who would stay in Czechoslovakia.

The ideas publicized by the Czechoslovak government-in-exile during the autumn of 1941 and the first half of 1942 were not detailed plans but theoretical statements. The promulgation of precise plans would have made no sense in any case, as the country's post-war borders were still indeterminate. From the autumn of 1941, the Czechoslovak émigrés in London therefore focused on winning the Allies' support for the re-establishment of the country's pre-Munich boundaries and for the principle of population transfers. The Soviets by and large welcomed these ideas. When Foreign Minister Molotov visited London on 9 July 1942, he had this to say to Beneš: 'The current moment is a historical opportunity to stop the German expansion now and forever. The Czechs might get rid of as many Germans as they can. Russia does not intend to interfere with Czech internal affairs, but if Czechs so require, Russia is willing to help with this case.'[10] On 4 July 1942 the Soviet Union nullified the Munich Agreement, thus recognizing Czechoslovakia's pre-1938 boundaries.[11]

British Foreign Minister Eden proclaimed on 5 August 1942 that Czechoslovakia's borders would revert to what they had been before the Munich Agreement. It is almost impossible to pinpoint when the British government accepted population transfers as a possible solution to perceived post-war minority problems. On 7 July 1942 Eden informed Beneš that 'his colleagues agree with the principle of transfer'.[12] At the beginning of August he also told Beneš that the British government regarded the Munich Agreement as null and void.[13] On 21 September 1942 the British Ambassador attached to the Czechoslovak government-in-exile assured Beneš that his government approved of the transfer of Germans.[14]

Beneš assumed that the Soviet Union would play a decisive role in shaping the fate of Eastern and Central Europe. Consequently, he placed great importance on gaining the Soviet leaders' consent to his transfer plans. The issue was given enhanced prominence during Beneš's negotiations in Moscow in December 1943. He held the minorities responsible for the dissolution of the republic and repeatedly claimed that only the removal of non-Slavic elements could prevent outside powers from using them in 'conspiracies against peace and the Slavs'.[15]

The Czechoslovak delegation also expounded its views on the relocation of minorities in a memorandum entitled 'The transfer of a part of Czechoslovakia's population'. The document makes clear that at that stage the government-in-exile did not yet intend to remove all the Germans and Hungarians from the country's territory. The first objective was rather to 'clean' the border regions; the minorities would not have been given collective rights. While most Germans faced expulsion, the number of Hungarians living in Slovakia and in Transcarpathia was to be reduced through a population exchange, to affect the Slovaks and 'Russians' living in Hungary. The Soviet leaders gave their blessing to this plan. But this time that consent had only theoretical significance, as neither Stalin nor Molotov committed themselves to any concrete steps, preferring to line themselves up with the somewhat more cautious standpoint of the British and US governments.

The Czechoslovak Communists exiled in Moscow underwent a peculiar metamorphosis in their stance on population transfers. The Communist Party originally opposed mass transfers on principle. Collective responsibility was deemed incompatible with the communist view of the nature of fascism. Moreover, the Czech Communist Party had 10,000 ethnic Germans among its members. But such principled considerations were ultimately outweighed by the political interests of the Soviet Union and the national viewpoint of non-communist Czech elites. During his December 1943 negotiations in Moscow, Beneš held talks with Czech communist leaders, including party general secretary Klement Gottwald. Initially the Communists rejected the radicalism of the London leaders, advocating a differentiated kind of transfer, which would have allowed Germans and Hungarians with 'democratic' (i.e. communist) credentials to stay in their homeland. But when Stalin accepted Beneš's plans, the exiled Czech Communists also had to fall in line. On 11 May 1944 Gottwald announced on Moscow radio that 'the moment when the cleaning of our homeland of the German and Hungarian traitorous scum starts is coming soon'.[16]

As the end of the war was approaching, the Czechoslovak leaders in London deemed it necessary to summarize their ideas about population transfers in another memorandum, sent to the Allied governments on 23 November 1944. The document proceeded from the assumption that ethnic minorities posed a serious threat to Central Europe. As territorial compensation had been removed from the agenda, minority problems could only be settled through the transfer of the German and Hungarian minorities.[17] Vis-à-vis the Hungarians in Slovakia, the memorandum stressed the following:

> The presence of the Hungarian minority in Czechoslovakia does not present as dangerous a problem as that of the German minority. However, the Czechoslovak government reserves the right to treat those members of the Hungarian minority who have trespassed against the Republic similarly, as proposed in the memorandum. We note that according to 1938 data a considerable Slovakian minority lives within the borders of Hungary, which renders it possible for us to settle this issue on the basis of a large-scale population exchange.[18]

The British and American leaders replied to the memorandum evasively, deferring the issue of transfers to the peace talks.

The Czechoslovak government's priority was to secure the Kremlin's backing. After the December 1943 negotiations, Beneš left Moscow for London with the conviction that he had managed to secure Stalin's agreement on all key issues. But this was only an illusion. Although he achieved a bilateral agreement of friendship with the Soviet Union and he was ready to pass Transcarpathia to the Soviets,

Beneš had no influence on Stalin's policy. Stalin complied with Beneš's wishes only for as long as they matched his own interests. In a memorandum of 24 August 1944, Beneš's government asked the Soviet Union to include in a future ceasefire agreement a specific provision about the mass resettlement of Hungarians from Slovakia to Hungary and Slovakians from Hungary to Slovakia.[19] The Soviets rejected the Czechoslovak initiative several times, stating that the issue of population transfers had to await the post-war peace talks. However, when negotiating the ceasefire agreement with Hungary in January 1945, Molotov finally took up the proposal. But presumably this was only an empty gesture by the Soviets – who had already annexed Transcarpathia – as they knew that, because of the opposition of the Western Allies, this condition could not be included in the ceasefire agreement with Hungary in any case.

Beneš's trip to Moscow in March 1945 was the last wartime occasion when the Czechoslovak government-in-exile elaborated on its ideas for forced population movements. At that time the plans envisaged the expulsion of two million Germans from Czechoslovakia; 800,000 were to stay. Beneš estimated the number of Hungarians in Slovakia at 600,000, two thirds of whom he wanted to transfer to Hungary. By the spring of 1945 preparations for the expulsion of Hungarians were already in full swing on the Slovak territories.

4.1.2 Yugoslavian Plans

The plans to achieve a Serbian nation state were rooted in the Greater Serbian idea and ideology. The firmest support for this nationalistic project came from the Četnik movement. After the collapse of Yugoslavia, Draža Mihailović organized the pro-British Četniks into guerrilla units. The Četnik military resistance organization was recognized by the Yugoslavian government-in-exile in London, and Mihailović himself served as minister of war between 1942 and 1944. One of the leading ideologists of the Četnik movement, Stevan Moljević, developed a plan for post-war population transfers as early as June 1941. The plan projected a Greater Serbia which was to be led by the Karageorgević family and would include part of Romania and Hungary, most of Croatia, as well as Bosnia, Montenegro and Macedonia. The plan, which was sent to the Yugoslavian government-in-exile in London, envisaged the transfer of 2.675 million non-Serbians, including half a million Germans, in order to establish the Greater Serbian nation state.[20]

Vasa Čubrilović – a nationalistic politician – drafted a more modest plan for Marshal Tito, founder of the communist partisan army, in November 1944. Tito's views about the plan are unknown. However, ideas for the establishment of a South-Slavic nation state were generally popular in Serbia regardless of party affiliations, and developments after the autumn of 1944 generally resembled Čubrilović's suggestions. He obviously managed to attract Tito's attention, as he was appointed minister in charge of population transfers and agriculture after 1945.

Čubrilović's proposals were based on the pre-war territory of Yugoslavia. He suggested only minor border corrections at Italy's expense. The German, Hungarian and Kosovo Albanian minorities had to be held responsible for the military defeat of 1941 and its consequences, as they had allegedly been preparing for the disintegration of unified Yugoslavia for a long time. He regarded ethnic Germans as Yugoslavia's greatest enemies: with them 'the bill must be settled for now and ever after. They well deserve this by not having been loyal to the state in which they lived, by having been cruel and traitorous.'[21] On the list of nations considered to be enemies, second place was occupied by the Hungarians.[22]

Albanians were blamed for collaborating with the German and Italian occupiers and for expelling Serbs from their homes. After listing the alleged crimes of ethnic Germans, Hungarians and Albanians, Čubrilović declared: 'by stepping up against our state in an openly hostile way, the three biggest minority groups in Yugoslavia forfeited their own civil rights. They have lost the right to call themselves our citizens anymore. They must be eliminated from the country.'[23]

The nationalistic and aggressive views of the Četnik Moljević and the nationalist Čubrilović were widely shared all over Serbia. The popularity of ideas of revenge and the elimination of minorities could be traced back to the suffering endured by the Serbs. According to Yugoslavian scholars, a minimum of 120,000 Serbs from Croatia, 42,065 from Bulgaria, 48,808 from Crna Gora and Kosovo – under Italian rule – and at least 30,000 from Backa – which belonged to Hungary – had been expelled during the war.[24]

The enumeration of the sins committed by Germans, Hungarians and Albanians served only as a pretext for the elaboration of Čubrilović's actual aim, which was nothing other than the expulsion of non-Slavic ethnic groups: 'the only right solution to the minority problem is population transfer, which brings up a series of tasks to be done. … In the course of removals, in my view, the following order of priority should be applied: Germans, Hungarians, Arnautes [i.e. Albanians], Italians and Romanians.'[25] According to the plan, Germans faced complete expulsion, while on the territories inhabited by Hungarians, Albanians, Italians and Romanians the goal was to establish a majority status for the Serbs. 'If we remove 200,000 Hungarians from Backa, we would solve the Hungarian majority question,' Čubrilović suggested.[26] The plan was moderate vis-à-vis the Italians because it advocated only the expulsion of those who had settled in Istria, Gorizia and Gradisca – all of which were considered Yugoslav territories – after 1918. The Romanians of the Banat were to leave Yugoslavia under the framework of a population exchange agreement. As for the Albanians of Kosovo, the population transfer would affect primarily those who lived in the border areas. To replace them, Čubrilović wanted to settle Serbians, so that the dominance of the Slavic ethnic element would be ensured.

Remarkably, Čubrilović connected the viability of his plan to the war: 'The solution of minority issues by population transfers can be carried out most easily in times of war, such as the current one … the military forces have to clean the territories that we want to settle with our population of other ethnicities in a planned and merciless way while the fighting still goes on.'[27] With this statement, he indirectly admitted that the planned population transfers contradicted international legal norms and therefore could not be implemented in times of peace. It is also remarkable that – much like the Czechoslovak advocates of the nation state idea – Čubrilović also expected Soviet help for the implementation of his project. In a passage of his plan that praised the Soviet model of ethnic cleansing, he wrote: 'we can duly hope that the brotherly Soviet Union will help us solve the minority question in the way that they have done and are doing'.[28]

4.2 The Fate of the Defeated Nations in the Carpatho-Danubian Basin

During and after the war, the Soviet Union's anti-fascist ideology successfully combined the desire for democracy with patriotic feelings and revolutionary universality. Undoubtedly, the presence of Soviet troops contributed to the fulfilment of the 'victorious' smaller states' ethnic cleansing plans, while the Soviet Union's ideology made a more indirect contribution to that outcome. In Yugoslavia, Czechoslovakia and Poland, nationalistic passions against Germans and Hungarians were fuelled by the idea of Slavic patriotism, which was also spread by Soviet propaganda. Moreover, Stalin invented the concept of 'Leninist new Slavism', which he elaborated on 28 March 1944 at the farewell party to Beneš as follows:

> I hate Germans. The bill of World War One had also been paid by the Slavs … It is the Slavs who have to pay the piper in this war, too. The French opened the doors to the Germans, who occupied most of France, as well as the Netherlands and Belgium. Britain is an island … And who is most affected by the war? The Germans attacked the Slavs, and the Czechs, Slovakians, Ukrainians, Russians and Yugoslavians all suffered from the consequences. But now we will smash the Germans so that attacks against Slavs will never ever happen again. The Soviet Union wants nothing else than to have allies who will be always willing to stand up against the German threat. The Soviet Union will not interfere with its allies' internal affairs. The is the Leninist new Slavism, followed by us, the Bolshevik-communists.[29]

In a great part of East-Central Europe the Soviet Union – although feared as a power – was welcomed as the big Slavic brother who finished off the German oppressors; the uplifting feeling of revenge among the Soviets was shared, for example, by the Bulgarians, the Czechs and the Serbs. The Czechs did not forget how the West had let them down at Munich, and in the aftermath of victory the

Czech Communist Party mostly owed its power to the fact that it managed to combine patriotism with ties to the Soviet Union. And Tito managed to unite the nations of Yugoslavia in a partisan army which, together with the Soviet army, liberated Belgrade. The small winning countries were so delighted to see the defeat of the Germans that they hardly realized that the Soviet assistance given in the name of Slavic brotherhood and anti-fascism meant only a stage on the way leading to a vassal's status.

The ethnic minorities that stood in the way of the victorious power suffered a series of disasters from the second half of 1944 onwards. The minorities regarded as enemies – primarily the Germans and the Hungarians – were initially depleted by a massive flight provoked by the advance of the dreaded Red Army. The Soviet military itself contributed to the weakening of the Romanian ethnic group in Bessarabia and Bukovina, the Hungarian ethnic group in Transcarpathia and Transylvania, and the German ethnic group throughout Eastern and South-eastern Europe by deporting part of the civilian population. The situation of the remaining Germans and Hungarians was further exacerbated by the atrocities carried out or tolerated by the new authorities under Soviet control, as well as by internment, arbitrary expulsions and the deprivation of rights. In the next and final stage of the process, 'organized' population transfers took place, as a result of which the ethnic map of Eastern Europe changed permanently.

4.2.1 Flight from the Red Army

The huge wave of westward migration triggered by the advance of the Red Army during the summer and autumn of 1944 played an important role in the realization of the nation-state ambitions in Poland, Czechoslovakia and, partly, Romania. From 1943 onwards, Soviet troops, gradually reoccupying lost territories, pushed hundreds of thousands of refugees of Caucasian, Ukrainian and Baltic ancestry in a westerly direction. But even this wave of refugees was eclipsed by the one unleashed when the Red Army approached the Soviet Union's pre-1939 western borders. As a result of the Red Army's spring offensives of 1944, columns of refugees left northern Bukovina and Bessarabia for the interior of Romania, just as in the summer of 1940, when these territories had first fallen under Soviet occupation. Organized flight began at the end of 1943, when Soviet troops reached the river Dnester. Everyone was allowed to cross the Prut River, the eastern border of Old Romania, but the Romanian authorities did not encourage the local Romanians to leave. They believed that the Soviet occupation would be only temporary and that a weakening of the Romanian ethnic group in the area would undermine Romania's ability to reclaim it in the future. The Romanians who had settled in Bessarabia and northern Bukovina after 1941 left the region almost without exception. Many of these refugees were leaving their homeland for the second time in four years. Unlike in 1940, this time many peasants also decided to flee. Another contrast with the previous situation was that not only Romanians but also Poles and Ukrainians fled from the approaching Soviet troops, albeit in smaller numbers. Although no exact statistical data were collected, in 1944 at least 300,000 refugees arrived in the interior of Romania from the eastern and north-eastern territories, three times more than in 1940.[30]

When the Soviets and their new allies the Romanians – who had switched sides in the war – reached the south-eastern rim of the Carpathian Mountains, a wave of refugees started to lumber from Transylvania towards the interior of Hungary. This process boosted Romanian national ambitions, as the people leaving this area of mixed ethnicity were overwhelmingly Hungarians and Germans. To stem the flood of refugees, the Hungarian military set up a blocking line along the Tisza River. 'As the fighting spread that far, order was upset again. Finally there was no chance to restore the order any longer,' wrote Géza Lakatos, Hungary's prime minister.[31] Conclusions about the numbers involved can be drawn from the Romanian citizenship law of 11 August 1945, which declared that former residents of Transylvania who had departed with enemy troops would lose their citizenship. The citizenship law affected at least 300,000 Hungarians in northern Transylvania who had left their places of residence during the fighting but returned later.[32] The number of refugees from Transylvania who remained in Hungary was 102,000.[33] This means that more than 400,000 people from Transylvania took to the road during the autumn of 1944. About 8,000 ethnic Germans also left.[34]

In 1940 – after the *Heim ins Reich* operation – there were still about 600,000 ethnic Germans in Romania, 90 per cent of whom lived in south Transylvania and the Banat. The Germans there found themselves in a privileged position compared with that of the other non-Romanian ethnic groups, as political and military coop-eration between Berlin and Bucharest gradually intensified. The local German organizations were increasingly brought under Nazi control. As a consequence, SS recruitment was especially successful in Romania, with about 70,000 ethnic Germans from Transylvania and the Banat enlisted to serve the Reich during the war.[35] They were the first group lost to the ethnic German minority of Romania, as many died in the war or in captivity, and the survivors were not allowed to return.

The idea of rescuing the ethnic Germans of Transylvania, Romania and the Serbian Banat as well as Backa, Baranja and Slavonia from the threat of revenge imposed by the Soviet army and the new civilian authorities was implemented only after the retreat of the Wehrmacht and SS units. At that point the trains and truck convoys from the towns and the rows of carts and carriages from the villages would start lumbering towards the north-west, harassed by air raids.

The evacuations at the end of the war were far from comprehensive, and not only because of the lack of time and equipment. In Transylvania and the Romanian Banat, the German population, especially the rural inhabitants, did not understand why they should fear the Soviet military and the irregular Romanian forces. The propaganda fliers dropped from Soviet aeroplanes also encouraged people to stay. According to a census conducted in the Federal Republic of Germany in 1950, 149,000 ethnic Germans from the territories of post-war Romania arrived in West Germany after the war, while 57,000 reached the Soviet zone. These numbers include not only the *Volksdeutsche* who fled from the Banat and Transylvania but also those who were taken captive and then brought to the Federal Republic and the GDR at the end of the 1940s.[36] Many of those who had left Romania during the autumn of 1944 tried to sneak back after the fighting had ended.

In early October 1944 the Red Army entered the territory of the Serbian Banat. The evacuation of the Hungarian public administration from the 'southern region' had started at the end of September. About 14,000 civil servants and their families fled with the rapidly retreating Hungarian military.[37] The wave of refugees swept up about 10 per cent of the original population, i.e. some 35,000 people. Many of them left the area only several months later, following the Serbian revenge campaign.[38]

According to the Yugoslav census data of 1930, about half a million ethnic Germans (*Donauschwaben*) lived in Yugoslavia. As a result of 'repatriation' to Germany and recruitment to the Waffen-SS, their number decreased by about 50,000 during the war. The evacuation of the German population from Backa started on 5 October 1944. On 13 October Himmler approved the transfer of Germans from Romania and Croatia to western Hungary. In practice, this decision affected only the Germans of Croatia, as by this stage there were hardly any Romanian territories still under German control. The evacuation of Backa, which had belonged to Hungary since 1941, took place in October 1944. About 70,000–120,000 Germans fled from this region,[39] and an additional 30,000 Germans escaped from Baranja.[40] At the beginning of November the military front stabilized along the Serbian–Croatian border and remained there until Germany's general retreat in early May 1945. At that point a new wave of refugees was set in motion. The total number of ethnic Germans who fled or were evacuated from Yugoslav territories may have reached 300,000.[41]

The final months of the war saw massive migration from Hungary. Approximately 580,000 Hungarian soldiers and other military personnel together with 300,000–400,000 civilian refugees moved to Germany.[42] As the front was approaching, the Arrow Cross government ordered some of those employed in the strategic industries as well as public servants to emigrate to Germany. At the same time, considerable numbers of people left for Germany voluntarily, with the retreating German and Hungarian armed forces, to get away from the Soviet military. During the spring of 1945 fear of the Red Army was no longer fuelled solely by anti-Soviet propaganda but also by the reports of people fleeing westward. Altogether, approximately one million Hungarian citizens left the country at this stage, some 20,000–60,000 of whom were ethnic Germans.[43] Most of the Hungarian refugees returned to their homes in 1946, but about 100,000 stayed behind, primarily in the western zones of Germany. Most of these émigrés came from the officer corps and the higher ranks of the civil service.[44]

Prior to the Second World War, the present-day territory of Slovakia had ontained some 600,000 Hungarian and 140,000 German residents. The London-based government-in-exile, the Communists in Moscow and the Slovakian partisans operating under their control all shared the expectation that Soviet troops would help them to eliminate the Hungarian ethnic group. As early as the summer of 1944, the Czechoslovak side reckoned that the advancing Soviet armies would force Hungarians to abandon their homes. One of the aims of the Soviet offensive launched in support of the Slovakian Uprising that broke out in late August 1944 was 'to clean Slovakia completely of all intruders and traitors ... the cleaning of the Republic from Germans, Hungarians, traitors is starting only now'. However, the expulsion of Hungarians was cancelled at this time because of the failure of the Red Army's offensive and the crushing of the Slovakian Uprising.[45] Because Soviet troops were approaching Slovakia and the strip of territory it had ceded to Hungary in 1938 from the south- east, the expulsion of Hungarians could not be carried out at a later stage either.

The ethnic German minority in Slovakia was concentrated in three regions: Bratislava and its vicinity, Nitra, and Sepes county. Because of the approach of the front, the leadership of the Deutsche Partei opted for an initially partial and subsequently complete evacuation. Between September 1944 and January 1945, about 100,000–120,000 people abandoned their homes in several consecutive waves, but some 10,000–20,000 returned immediately after the war.[46]

4.2.2 Deportation of Civilians by the Soviet Authorities

The second disaster that hit the defeated nations of Europe was the campaign of deportations carried out by the Soviet occupying forces. It was targeted primarily at ethnic Germans, but Hungarians and Romanians from Bessarabia and Bukovina were also hit heavily. Although the primary goal of the deportations was not to alter ethnic conditions but to collect workers, the operations did have an indirect impact on changes in the ethnic composition of certain regions. The Kremlin considered the war a good opportunity to collect as big a foreign workforce as possible for Soviet industry and agriculture.

On 19 September 1939 People's Commissar of the Interior Lavrentij Berija ordered the establishment of a new forced-labour camp system for prisoners of war and foreign internees.[47] The new camp system, called the Directorate for the Affairs of Prisoners of War and Internees of the Commissariat of the Interior, was usually referred to by its acronym UPVI (Upravlenie Voennoplennych i Internirovannych). In February 1945, when the camp system already comprised 350 large and 4,000 minor camps, the Directorate was upgraded into a Chief

Directorate (Glavnoe Upravlenie po delam Voennoplennych i Internirovannych – GUPVI).

The fact that the camp system was set up at an early phase of the war proves that the Soviet leadership did not make a distinction between civilians and soldiers and that the war was seen as useful for the purpose of supplying a labour force, along with expanding the communist system. The subsequent combination of forced labour and reparation claims also stemmed from the logic of the Soviet system. During British Foreign Secretary Anthony Eden's visit to Moscow in December 1941, Stalin already made clear that after the war the Soviet Union would claim not only financial reparations but also restitution in kind. Jenő Varga, the head of the Institute of World Politics and Economics of the Soviet Academy of Sciences, was the first to introduce the idea that the defeated enemy countries should not only pay financial reparations but also contribute to the Soviet Union's post-war reconstruction through their workforce.[48]

In August 1943 a committee led by Ivan Maisky, the former Soviet ambassador to London, was set up within the Commissariat of Foreign Affairs to prepare a detailed plan for the 'Soviet reparations programme'. On 24 November 1943, after the Western Allies had agreed that German reparations would be paid partly in the form of forced labour, the 'Governmental Reparations Committee for the Damages Caused to the Soviet Union by Hitler's Germany and Its Allies' was also established. Even the first plans elaborated by the Maisky committee included the idea that using prisoners for the reconstruction of devastated areas would constitute part of the reparations. At both Yalta and Potsdam, Stalin, too, explicitly stated that he wanted enemy POWs to work on the territory of the Soviet Union to provide partial compensation for the country's tremendous human and material losses.

Besides the acquisition of forced labourers, the deportations were also driven by considerations of collective punishment and political cleansing. According to Soviet sources, 380,000–390,000 people were deported into the interior of the Soviet Union from the Eastern European territories annexed by the USSR between 1939 and 1941.[49] However, some Polish historians contend that nearly one million people were deported from Polish areas alone.[50] The collective punishment conducted by the Soviets on an ethnic and class basis resumed in Eastern Europe in 1944–5 in a manner that closely resembled the practices of 1941. The forward march of the Red Army opened the way to the exploitation of the material and human resources of the defeated countries. The deportations from Romania were partly rooted in the armistice agreement of 23 August 1944. It obliged the Romanian government to send Soviet citizens residing in Romania back to the Soviet Union. From the time the agreement was signed until December 1945 the two signatories kept arguing over who exactly should be considered a Soviet citizen. Finally, on 7 December 1945 – with the approval of the Soviet-led Allied Control Commission – the Romanian Armistice Enforcement Commission took measures that made it possible for most of the people who had fled from

Bessarabia and northern Bukovina to decide whether they wanted to settle in the Soviet Union or in Romania. But this agreement – the result of long negotiations – had only theoretical significance, as the great waves of deportations had largely subsided by the time of its signing.

On 11 November 1944 the Allied Control Commission called on the Romanian government to begin sending refugees from Bessarabia and northern Bukovina to the Soviet Union without delay. Despite the evasive reply that the Romanian government issued three days later, the Soviet occupation authorities started to round up these people themselves. The first group of refugees was transported to the Soviet Union in December 1944, and a further wave of deportations was launched in January 1945. Under pressure from the Soviet military authorities, the Romanian police helped to track down refugees from Bessarabia and northern Bukovina. But the manhunts brought relatively poor results, as some of the targets hid during the round-ups and others used false identity papers. Some 56,450 people were forcibly 'repatriated' to the USSR between 23 August 1944 and 30 September 1946.[51]

Most of the refugees were not taken to their previous homelands but to labour camps in the interior of the Soviet Union. In reality 'repatriation' therefore meant a round-up of forced labourers. This was even admitted by the deputy chairman of the Allied Control Commission in Romania, Vladislav P. Vinogradov. When the chairman of the Romanian Armistice Enforcement Commission, Savel Rădulescu, asked him to postpone the 'repatriation' scheduled for 30 December 1944, the Soviet general replied: 'The labour force is so necessary to us that we cannot delay [the repatriation].'[52] Occasionally political motives could help to outweigh economic interests, however. Such considerations contributed to the Soviet leadership's decision to allow some 40,000 Jews to leave Bessarabia and northern Bukovina for Palestine at a time when other refugees from the same regions were being transported back into the Soviet Union.

The available sources contain no information on when Stalin ordered the deportation of ethnic Germans of working age from the territories occupied by the Soviets. In his 24 November 1944 report Berija wrote about having started the preparations for such operations. By that time, NKVD officers had already estimated how many persons could be deported from each area. Originally Berija had planned to target only men. But a later directive of the State Defence Committee, issued on 16 December 1944, also encompassed women:

All German men aged 17–44 and German women aged 18–30 who live in the territories of Romania, Hungary, Yugoslavia, Bulgaria and Czechoslovakia liberated by the Red Army must be mobilized and directed to work in the Soviet Union. The NKVD, and specifically Comrade Berija, is to be assigned the supervision of mobilization. The NKVD is to be in charge of organizing transit camps, the admission of mobilized persons, the establishment and launching of marching columns, and overseeing their guard en route.[53]

The plan divided the occupied areas into ten zones. Six were on the territory of Romania, which harboured the greatest German minority population. There were also two zones in Yugoslavia and another two in Hungary. The scheduled round-ups foresaw the collection of Germans from the Yugoslav and Hungarian territories between 28 December 1944 and 5 January 1945. In the area east of the Danube River, the Germans of working age were scheduled to be captured from 1 to 10 January 1945, while a similar round-up in Romania and Transylvania was planned to take place between 10 January and early February.

The implementation followed the plans only loosely. In Hungary, the round-up of ethnic Germans cannot be separated neatly from broader deportation campaigns that also targeted other civilians. In theory the action aimed at the Germans there started on 28 December 1944, but the capture of deportees had actually begun in September, as Soviet troops arrived in the country. It is difficult to form a clear picture of the deportations from Hungary because of numerous variations: the place where the arrests took place, the methods used, the personnel implementing the operations, as well as the composition of the groups of victims.

Both subsequent recollections and contemporary records show that the Soviets rounded up and deported some of the civilian population shortly after they occupied a given area, often within a few days. This first wave of deportations hit the population of Budapest particularly hard. The number of those deported from the capital in the aftermath of the fighting is estimated at 50,000–100,000.[54] The scattered initial deportations were followed by actions of a different nature. The goal of these subsequent operations was not only to increase the number of forced labourers in the USSR but also to 'pacify' a given region and to change its ethnic composition. Able-bodied Hungarians were systematically rounded up in each village of Transcarpathia and the adjacent regions of north-eastern Hungary.

The third type of deportation took place within the framework of the campaign to round up ethnic Germans from South-eastern Europe. The list of those targeted for deportation – or for 'communal work', to cite the contemporary euphemism – was not compiled on the basis of standardized criteria. The Hungarians tried to reduce the number of those 'in employment', but the final decision rested with the local NKVD officers, who interpreted the concept of 'ethnic German' as widely as possible and very often 'mobilized' Hungarians as well. The local public administration was in charge of rounding up the people on the lists, but chaotic conditions often meant that Soviet troops had to arrest and transport the designated persons. As a consequence, most of those deported from Hungary as 'Germans' were not even native speakers of German.

The Soviet units had to fulfil regional quotas of deportees. If the targets in a given area could not be met with captured Germans, Hungarians with German names were rounded up next, followed by Hungarians with Hungarians names. But if the quotas had been met, not even all the local Germans were targeted. In

Hungary, the number of deportees was more important than their ethnicity. The total number of deportees from Hungary's present-day territory can be put at 120,000–200,000, on the basis of various estimates. Another 50,000 were deported from Transcarpathia, Transylvania and the strip of land in the Uplands re-annexed in 1938.[55] Both Soviet and German sources agree that about 30,000–35,000 of this group were German nationals.[56]

In Yugoslavia the 'mobilization' of Germans capable of work started on 23 December 1944: 21,000–22,000 had been deported by the end of January, but the action had to be abandoned because of the worsening situation at the front.[57]

In Romania the deportations of able-bodied Germans who had not fled with the retreating Wehrmacht took place between 11 January and 2 February 1945. The arrests were ordered by Soviet General Vladislav P. Vinogradov, the representative of the Allied Control Commission in Bucharest, on 3 January 1945. The implementation was left primarily to the Romanians,[58] although NKVD squads participated in the round-up. The Romanian authorities had presumably been preparing these actions for a while, as they had conducted a registration of German nationals in the country between August and October 1944. The subsequent arrests were carried out on the basis of these registration lists. City dwellers were rounded up first, followed by rural residents. In the third and final stage, German nationals serving in the local troops of the Romanian army were picked out. According to Soviet sources, about 70,000 Germans were deported from Romania.[59]

4.2.3 Revenge Campaigns and Arbitrary Expulsions

The deportations conducted by the Soviets weakened the German ethnic group in South-eastern Europe, especially in Romania. The revenge campaigns and arbitrary expulsions that proceeded in parallel with these deportations also contributed to the destruction of the ethnic minorities unwanted by the victorious powers.

Within a few days of Romania's switch away from the Axis on 23 August 1944, decrees were issued by the Interior Ministry in Bucharest to make possible the internment of ethnic Germans and Hungarians 'posing a hazard to the order of the state' in Transylvania and in the Banat. In October 1944, after Soviet and Romanian troops had occupied northern Transylvania, which had been attached to Hungary by the Second Vienna Award of 1940, the ministry extended the internments to this region, too. Referring to point two of the cease-fire agreement, the Romanian authorities arrested droves of northern Transylvanians with Hungarian passports. The arrests were extended to men of working age, who were later declared 'prisoners of war', even if they had never fought. The captured Hungarians and Germans were transported into one of the thirty-six internment and prison camps established in the country. The number of internees can be estimated at several thousand.[60]

Although prisoners were often taken from internment camps to Soviet POW camps, the internments usually took place independently of the Soviet-run deportations described above. A memorandum by the Soviet Foreign Ministry, issued on 26 January 1945, makes it clear that the Soviet leadership did not approve of the mass internment of Hungarians in Transylvania.[61] However, most of the internment camps were still 'operating' months – or even years – after the war had ended.

The revenge campaign in Transylvania pursued by Romanian paramilitary forces set up in late August 1944 exacted a numerically lower toll than the internments but caused greater trauma. The massacres committed by these squads contributed to the fact that in the middle of November 1944 the Soviets ordered the recently returned Romanian administration out of northern Transylvania. Romanian officers were allowed to resume control of the province only in March 1945.

In Tito's Yugoslavia unwanted minorities were hit by even more severe disasters. The direct antecedent of ethnic cleansing in Voivodina was the imposition of military rule on 17 October 1944 by the People's Liberation Army. The declared reason for the introduction of a military administration was the need to exploit the almost intact economic potential of the region. But in fact ethnic and political considerations had more importance than economic ones. In a notice issued on 22 October 1944 Brigadier General Ivan Rukovina, the head of the military administration, openly announced that military rule was necessary in order 'to secure the nation's future and the southern-Slavic character of the territories'.[62]

The Yugoslav authorities regarded ethnic Germans and Hungarians as hostile nationalities. The Germans were also collectively held responsible for the German occupation. On 21 November 1944 a decree was approved by the Anti-Fascist Council of the People's Liberation of Yugoslavia (AVNOJ) which clarified the intentions of the Communists towards the German ethnic group. It declared all ethnic Germans to be enemies of the state who would be deprived of their Yugoslav citizenship, civil rights and property. In official announcements, ethnic Hungarians were labelled somewhat less harshly, but in practice the prevailing attitude was to extend the notion of collective responsibility to them, too. On 18 November 1944, when the internment of ethnic Germans started, Hungarian men between the ages of 16 and 50 were also 'mobilized'. They were forced to work, mostly in agriculture and forestry. Hungarians also became subject to internment. The populations of villages that were on the territory of the round-ups of 1942 were expelled in their entirety as a form of collective punishment. In Voivodina about forty internment camps were set up.[63] The number of Germans confined to camps can be estimated at around 140,000–150,000.[64] We have no data on the number of interned Hungarians.

Indiscriminate executions and other killings hit ethnic Germans and Hungarians even more devastatingly than forced labour or internment. Such retaliations were carried out by the Department for the Protection of the People, established in

September 1939 and known as OZNA (Odeljenje za zaštitu naroda). As John R. Schindler comments: 'OZNA was a particularly Serbian preserve, unlike the multinational Yugoslav army. Indeed, the secret police chief, Alexander Ranković ... was a top Serb in the Yugoslav communist hierarchy, and chose his countrymen for most leading positions. Together with his assistant, Svetislav Stefanović, another Serb, Ranković oversaw the destruction of the hated "svabi" acting as much in Serbia's interest as in the party's.'[65] The number of Germans killed by OZNA was probably about 10,000, but German sources claim that some 60,000–70,000 German nationals died in the internment camps.[66]

The killing of Hungarians in post-war Yugoslavia became a theme of historical research in Serbia after several decades of neglect. The number of Hungarians executed in October and November 1944, on the basis of the lists prepared by OZNA, was about 5,000. But this number does not include those executed as a result of death sentences passed by Yugoslav people's courts. In addition, the massacres went on until the spring of 1945 – although with decreasing intensity – despite the fact that military rule in the area ended in the middle of February. According to a later statement by Svetozar Kostić Čapo – OZNA's leader in Voividina – Yugoslav troops killed about 20,000 Hungarians.[67] On the basis of eyewitness testimonies and documents, most Hungarian scholars in Serbia put the number of Hungarians killed at about 15,000–20,000.[68]

Another feature of the retaliation campaign was the expulsion of Hungarians and Germans from their places of residence. The Hungarian documents include several notes about the fact that between April and November 1945 armed Serbian forces were driving ethnic Germans and Hungarians across the border to Hungary in groups of 5,000–10,000. The expulsions continued until June 1946. The fact that the Hungarian prime minister, Ferenc Nagy, publicly supported Yugoslavia's claims to the city of Trieste played a very important role in putting an end to these actions.

The only significant ethnic minority on Hungarian territory that remained largely untouched as the war neared its end, except for the loss of three villages, comprised the Germans. As mentioned in the previous chapter, Germanophobia did not have a strong basis in Hungary. The activities of the Volksbund and SS recruitment drives had caused some tension in certain provincial settlements, but open clashes between Hungarians and ethnic Germans had not occurred. The Nazi occupation that began on 19 March 1944 did not provoke strong anti-German emotions either. The majority of the population was more afraid of a Soviet occupation than a German one. With the arrival of the Red Army, discrimination against the Germans initially grew out of economic necessity rather than theoretical considerations. There was not enough land available for the rural proletariat or the hundreds of thousands of incoming refugees. The reform law of 17 March 1945 thus declared: 'All landed property must be confiscated completely, regardless of its size, from all traitors, Arrow Cross, National Socialist or other leaders, members of the Volksbund, as well as all those guilty of committing war crimes or crimes against the people.' The law did not discriminate between war criminals and rank-and-file members of an organization in which only a small minority had fully espoused National Socialist ideology.

Ethnic Germans in Hungary were threatened with the loss of not only their land but also their personal freedom. In accordance with its obligations under the armistice signed in Moscow on 20 January 1945, Hungary's provisional national government issued a decree ordering the internment of German citizens. A few months later the decree was extended to Hungarian citizens who had served in the SS. Under the terms of the decree issued by the Interior Ministry on 14 May 1945, the internment of the family members of the previously targeted groups and of the sick and elderly was also made possible. We have no data about the number of Germans interned. In a note of 1 December 1945 prepared for the representatives of the Allied powers in Budapest, Hungarian Foreign Minister János Gyöngyösi put the number of Germans affected by the confiscation of property at 103,000.[69] Internal population transfers carried out in conjunction with the property seizures affected about 40,000 Germans.[70]

In Czechoslovakia the time to pursue the implementation of Beneš's nation state concept arrived in the spring of 1945. Beneš and his circle had based their plans on a united Czechoslovakia, but in fact the situation in Bohemia-Moravia differed greatly from that in Slovakia, where before the war ethnic Germans had consti-tuted only 4.5 per cent of the total population. As a result of evacuations, even that low proportion had declined drastically, and at the end of the war only about 20,000 ethnic Germans remained in Slovakia.

Immediately after liberation, the first targets of anti-German anger in Slovakia were the abandoned houses of those who had fled. They were pillaged first by Soviet soldiers and then by local inhabitants. After the fighting subsided, some of the refugees returned to their homes, and the number of ethnic Germans in Slovakia increased to 57,000 by the spring of 1945.[71] Those who returned found their houses looted and often had to face attacks. Fearing persecution, many took refuge in the mountains, and there were numerous suicides. Despite the land and house seizures, in Slovakia there was no outbreak of such elementary Germanophobia as in Bohemia and Moravia.

The greatest obstacle to the building of a nation state in Slovakia was the Hungarian ethnic group of about 600,000. In theory, Moscow supported the depor-tation of the Hungarians, along with the Germans, but the situation of the two minorities was not the same. Although Czechoslovak politicians pressed the issue, the armistice agreement concluded with Hungary did not oblige the country to accommodate expelled Hungarians. Initially even the Slovakian leadership was uncertain about whether the same rules could be imposed on the Hungarians and the Germans. During the negotiations held in Moscow in February 1945, Gustáv Husák, a leading Slovak communist, accepted the ideas of Beneš and the

Moscow-based Czechoslovak Communists concerning a gradual 'transfer' of the ethnic Hungarians.

The anti-Hungarian atmosphere in Slovakia intensified after the war as a result of the influence of the Czechoslovak government programme, Beneš's presidential decrees, and the various rulings issued by the Slovakian National Council. Beneš and his government-in-exile, together with members of the communist emigration, arrived in the Slovakian town of Košice via Moscow on 3 April 1945. There the new Czechoslovak government was formed and its programme, approved by the Soviet leadership, announced. The plan of creating a purely Slavic state was explicated in chapter eight. Chapters ten and eleven addressed the confiscation of the property of the two minorities. Chapter fifteen exhorted the government to demolish the German and Hungarian school systems.

The primary 'legal bases' of the anti-German and anti-Hungarian measures were the 143 presidential decrees issued by President Beneš between 14 May 1945 and 27 October 1945. On 5 March 1946 they were retroactively ratified by Czechoslovakia's Provisional National Assembly, set up on 28 October 1945. Thirteen of the decrees referred directly to the German and Hungarian minorities, and others also contained regulations that were indirectly connected to the punishment of the two minorities for their perceived collective guilt. Decree 5 regulated 'the National Administration of the property assets of Germans, Hungarians, traitors and collaborators and of certain organizations and associations'.[72] Paragraph four declared: 'From the state's point of view all persons must be considered unreliable who a) are of German or Hungarian nationality, b) performed activities against the sovereignty, independence, integrity, democratic-republican regime, security or defence of the Czechoslovak Republic'.[73] The same decree also defined who should be considered a German or Hungarian national. Apart from all those who – on the basis of the ethnic data of the 1930 census – had declared themselves to belong to one of the two minorities, the decree covered all the members of any German or Hungarian political party or organization registered by the Czechoslovak authorities between the two world wars.

The other twelve relevant decrees also treated the national minority groups as collectively guilty. Decree 12, for example, addressed the confiscation of the agricultural property of the Germans and Hungarians, while decree 16 concerned the punishment of Nazis and war criminals and the establishment of extraordinary people's courts. Decree 33 (2 August 1945) was also significant as it declined to grant Czechoslovak citizenship to ethnic Germans and Hungarians despite the fact that the Munich Agreement and the First Vienna Award had been declared void. Four decrees dealt with the confiscation of the agricultural property of German and Hungarian nationals in Slovakia.[74] Decree 105 (23 August 1945) provided for the establishment of labour camps in Slovakia.

The issue of locking up Slovakia's ethnic Germans and Hungarians in internment camps had already been discussed by the Slovakian National Council in

April 1945, and the Slovakian authorities had begun to build camps even before the decree was issued. Some fifty internment and labour camps, with about 20,000–22,000 inmates, were set up. Of the internees 82–5 per cent were Germans, 9–12 per cent Hungarians, and 5–6 per cent Slovakians.[75] For the Germans, internment meant an initial step towards expulsion – a fate that the ethnic Hungarians of Slovakia experienced as the most widespread form of their persecution by the summer of 1945. Among the roughly 35,000 Hungarians forcibly deported at that time were not only those who had settled in Slovakia after 1938 but also so-called 'original inhabitants' who lived near the border with Hungary. However, even those whose homes lay further inland could not feel secure since the expulsion plans encompassed all Hungarian nationals.

4.2.4 Organized Transfers

Public opinion and scholarly research in West and East link the expulsions of Germans to the decisions made at the Potsdam conference. Indeed, the Czechoslovak and Polish governments asked the leaders of the United States, the Soviet Union and Great Britain to use the Potsdam summit to authorize the transfer of their respective German population groups to Germany. Yugoslavia did not turn to the victorious powers with such a request because most of its ethnic Germans had already left the country. However, Budapest unexpectedly joined the cause promoted by the Polish and Czechoslovakian governments. On 26 May 1945 the Hungarian government asked the Soviet Union to approve the forced transfer of 200,000–250,000 'fascist' Germans to the Soviet occupation zone of Germany. In the census of 1941, 490,000 people living on what became Hungary's post-1945 territory had declared themselves German nationals. The Hungarian political leadership therefore considered about half of its ethnic German population 'guilty' of fascism because of Volksbund membership, SS service, or for some other reason.

On 2 August 1945 the representatives of the three victorious powers, meeting at Potsdam, approved the 'transfer' of the German population out of Poland, Czechoslovakia and Hungary. But the fate of the Germans did not depend primarily on the Potsdam decisions, as their deportation from Poland, Czechoslovakia and Yugoslavia had already started in late 1944. Through their decision at Potsdam, the victorious powers attempted, in part, to replace chaotic expulsions with more orderly population transfers in areas where this was still possible. The deportation of the German population from Slovakia started in the spring of 1946. Almost the entire German population still in the country was deported by train via Košice. Slovakian statistics indicate that 24,000 Germans left the country in 1947, but, according to the census of 1950, only 5,179 German nationals remained out of a community that had once numbered 150,000.[76]

Despite the intentions of the Czechoslovak government and the support of the Soviet Union, the Postdam decision did not endorse the deportation of the Hungarian minority of Slovakia. With a 600,000-strong Hungarian minority population still in the country, the goal of creating a Slavic nation state, as outlined in the Košice government programme, could only be achieved by means of a population exchange agreement with Hungary. The Czechoslovak side projected the transfer of about 300,000–500,000 Slovakian nationals out of Hungary, although in the Hungarian census of 1930 only about 105,000 people had declared themselves to be native speakers of the Slovakian language. The Czechoslovak authorities also intended to follow up the population exchange with further measures to eliminate the Hungarian minority still in the country, including internal and unilateral transfers. Through its persecution of Hungarians, the Czechoslovak government managed to persuade Budapest to conclude a population exchange agreement, according to which the number of Hungarians transferred to Hungary from Czechoslovakia would equal the number of Slovakians who volunteered to move in the opposite direction. Contrary to expectations, the Czechoslovak side managed to transfer only 73,000 Slovak nationals from Hungary under this agreement. For the time being, the great majority of Czechoslovakia's ethnic Hungarians remained in place; about 120,000 of Slovakia's Hungarians – along with the expelled post-1938 settlers and 'war criminals' – resettled in Hungary.[77]

The implementation of the Czechoslovak–Hungarian population exchange agreement had not even started when Prague's Interior Ministry made a decision about a unilateral transfer of 200,000 Hungarians. The decision received a political boost through the communist victory in the Czechoslovak parliamentary elections of May 1946. The Communists' success greatly contributed to the intensification of Czechoslovak–Soviet contacts. Supported by the Soviet leadership, the Czechoslovak government requested a unilateral transfer of 200,000 Hungarians. But the Western Allies rejected the request; thus the incorporation of the Hungarian population of Slovakia into Hungary was not included in the peace treaty concluded with Hungary. The Czechoslovak plans having failed on the international stage, the 'solution' of the 'Hungarian question' within the country was broached. On the basis of the president's decree number 88 concerning forced labour, 44,129 Hungarians were forcibly transferred to abandoned areas of the Sudetenland – previously inhabited by Germans – between November 1946 and 1947.[78] They were allowed to return to their homes in Slovakia only years later.

The plan to create an ethnically homogeneous state, populated exclusively by Slavs, required the importation of Czechs and Slovaks from abroad along with the expulsion of internal 'aliens'. At its meeting of 25 May 1945 the Slovakian National Council accepted a resolution calling on Slovak and Czech nationals living outside the borders of Czechoslovakia to return home. The 'home transfer' of Slovakians from Hungary was carried out within the framework of the bilateral population exchange agreement. 'Repatriation' from Romania, Poland, Yugoslavia and Bulgaria proceeded through unilateral transfers; the governments of these countries allowed the propaganda activity of Czechoslovak officials and the emigration of Slovaks, but they turned down the financial claims of the migrants. The 'calling home' of ethnic Slovaks from Romania began in the spring of 1945 and gained new impetus in June 1947, when the Czechoslovak leadership started to promote the transfer of well-to-do Slovak nationals from Romania to the Hungarian-populated regions of southern Slovakia. The repatriation of Slovak nationals from Yugoslavia was put on the agenda only in the autumn of 1946. Between 32,000 and 35,000 'home settlers' were expected, but in the end the 'repatriation' was restricted to a few hundred young intellectuals.[79] In January 1947, 270 Slovakian families from Bulgaria moved to Czechoslovakia. The ethnic Slovaks from areas that had been incorporated into Poland in 1938 and again after the war constituted a separate group. In November 1945 the Polish authorities moved 1,213 Slovakian families across the border. The expelled Slovakians were accommodated in the houses of previously expelled Hungarians and Germans.

After Prague ceded Transcarpathia to the Soviet Union, the Czechs and Slovaks living there were allowed to resettle in Czechoslovakia. On 29 June 1946 the Czechoslovak government concluded a citizenship agreement with the Soviet Union, which conferred Soviet citizenship on all residents of Transcarpathia. In fact the treaty was a population exchange agreement, which made it possible for Czech and Slovak nationals who had been Czechoslovak citizens before 1938 to move to that country, while Ukrainians, Russians and Ruthenians living in Czechoslovakia were allowed to resettle in the Soviet Union. Officially, 5,078 people left Soviet Transcarpathia.[80] In late 1945 and early 1946 a further group of 20,000 people crossed the Soviet border into Czechoslovakia.[81] According to the Soviet Union, 95 per cent of those who left were neither Czechs nor Slovaks but of Jewish origin. Although this official Soviet statement is heavily exaggerated, there were undoubtedly many Jews among the migrants.[82] No official statistics are available concerning those who moved from Czechoslovakia to the Soviet Union. Ukrainian historians estimate their number at 12,000. As a result of ethnic persecution as well as organized and arbitrary population transfers, Czechoslovakia nearly became a pure Slavic state. The ethnic homogenization was not complete, however, because most of the ethnic Hungarian population remained in place. After the communist takeover in 1948, even the Soviet Union – previously a firm supporter of Czechoslovak nation-state projects – instructed Prague to restrain its ambitions.

In Hungary, the Potsdam decision concerning the expulsion of the country's German population was unexpected, although it had been requested by the country's political leadership. The earlier concord among Hungary's political elites relating to the deportation of Germans disintegrated in August 1945. The standpoint of foreign policy elites differed greatly from that of the formulators of domestic policies, and an increasingly harsh debate broke out among the political parties. At the same time the Soviet Union exerted increasingly intense pressure on the Hungarian government to extend the transfers as widely as possible and to implement them quickly. Just one week after the Potsdam Conference, Lieutenant General Vladimir P. Sviridov, the Soviet Vice-chairman of the Allied Control Commission, demanded from the Hungarian government the expulsion of 400,000–450,000 Germans. Foreign Minister János Gyöngyösi repeatedly asserted in the Hungarian Council of Ministers that the concept of collective responsibility had been Hitler's idea, and that Hungary would lose the moral basis to defend its own minorities abroad if it accepted that principle.[83] In August 1945 the government, with the full support of the National Peasant Party and the Communist Party, nonetheless pronounced itself in favour of the total expulsion of the Germans. The Social Democrats and the Smallholder Party regarded the stance adopted by the Great Powers at Potsdam as merely an option rather than a directive. Although they accepted the principle of expulsion, they wished to determine the circle of those to be expelled on the basis of individual accountability. Thus the Hungarian government rejected the principle of collective responsibility; yet the implementation order issued on 29 December 1945 made the expulsion binding on all those who in the 1941 census had declared themselves to be of German nationality or native German speakers. All members of the Volksbund, and those who had served as volunteers in the German armed forces, were also to be deported.

> The deportations were conducted differently in each village, depending on several variables, such as the relationship between the commissioner in charge of the action and the local government, the party-political divisions in the village, the current political situation in the country, and even the available means of transport. But commonalities were also evident. The poor preparation of the actions and the erratic legal regulations, together with the uncontrollable activities of the organizations charged with carrying out the deportations, caused constant problems.[84]

From 19 January to 1 July 1946 about 110,000 ethnic Germans were deported from Hungary. After that, the transports had to be suspended, at American request. The reception camps situated in the western zones of Germany had reached full capacity, and the accommodation and provision of the expellees were becoming an excessive burden for the American authorities. American diplomats called the attention of both the Soviet members of the Allied Control Commission and the Hungarian government to the fact that the deportations were being carried out in an inhumane way and that the Germans from Hungary were arriving in the reception camps without money, personal belongings or sustainable amounts of clothing, deprived of everything.

The suspension of the deportations in mid-1946 was also partly caused by political developments within Hungary. Resistance to the deportations increased during the spring. The Smallholders' Party and the Social Democratic Party initiated exemption procedures to weaken the practice of collective punishment. The first – the country's strongest party in terms of the number of its supporters – objected to the deportations of the Germans and to the parallel internal relocations within Hungary partly on humanitarian grounds and partly because these actions threatened to disrupt agricultural production. As a result of internal political pressure, a decree issued by László Rajk, the Minister of Internal Affairs, on 10 May 1946 exempted from the expulsions those native speakers of German who had declared themselves Hungarian nationals in 1941 and had not joined the Volksbund or any German military formations. After the Hungarian government allowed the deportees to take with them a small amount of money and some effects beyond their most immediate personal belongings, the expulsions resumed on 8 November 1946. Following the deportation of some 6,000 people, the American authorities stopped the process again in mid-December 1946, referring to difficulties in accommodating the expellees. During the negotiations held within the next few months, it became obvious that the decision was final; in the American view, the western zones of Germany were full.

After Prime Minister Ferenc Nagy (Smallholders' Party) had been forced out of office in a takeover that resembled a coup d'état, a communist-controlled government was set up in Budapest under the lead of Lajos Dinnyés. The new government sent an official note to the Allied Control Commission on 11 July 1947, in which it asked for permission to deport Germans from Hungary into the Soviet occupation zone of Germany. The Soviet government agreed to receive such deportees. The resulting third and final phase of the expulsions from Hungary started on 19 August 1947. The plundering character of this deportation wave is reflected in the fact that primarily well-to-do people were placed on the list of deportees. The implementation was marred by major difficulties, as many of the Germans did not want to go to the Soviet zone. To pre-empt escapes, police forces usually rounded up the families in unexpected night-time raids.

Instead of the projected total of 50,000, only about 35,000 Germans had been transported to the Soviet occupation zone by 15 June 1948, at which point the deportations ended.[85] The number of ethnic Germans in Hungary, which had been almost half a million in 1941, decreased by 200,000–220,000 as a result of flight and deportation. In the 1949 census only 22,455 people categorized themselves as native speakers of German and a mere 2,600 as German nationals.[86]

4.3 The Expulsion of Germans from Poland and Czechoslovakia

The expulsions of Germans from Poland and Czechoslovakia at the end of the Second World War unfolded in roughly parallel fashion, with many similarities between the two states. As we have seen, the plans for the forced removal of Germans had been advanced during the war in both countries as an integral part of broader blueprints for demographic engineering that targeted other ethnic minority groups as well, particularly Hungarians in Czechoslovakia, and Ukrainians, Belorussians and Lithuanians in Poland. However, the actual implementation of these plans was quite different for each ethnic group.[87] Whereas the removal of Hungarians from Slovakia, for example, was realized only partially, the expulsion of Germans became nearly total. By the end of the 1940s up to 10.5 million Germans had either fled or been expelled from the post-war territory of the two states, some 7.5 million from Poland and slightly over 3 million from Czechoslovakia.[88]

The earliest stage in the removal of Germans from what were to become post-war Poland and Czechoslovakia came with the widespread westward flight of the German civilian population as the Red Army advanced into eastern Germany in late 1944 and early 1945. Recent estimates indicate that during this period at least six million Germans either fled or were evacuated westwards from the territories that would later be incorporated into Poland.[89] The exodus was less extensive in the case of Czechoslovakia, with several tens of thousands escaping from the eastern Sudetenland in the first months of 1945 and at least 100,000 fleeing or being evacuated from Slovakia.[90]

Like earlier mass flights and evacuations of ethnic Germans from areas further east, Germans took to the wintry roads in large numbers, more often than not on their own initiative, as the implementation of the evacuation plans drawn up by Nazi authorities was frequently postponed until the front had already reached the area in question. As a result, many German refugees were caught up in the war zone. While a considerable number ultimately managed to reach relative safety further west, many others found their path blocked either by the Red Army or, in some cases, by the Wehrmacht, which occasionally simply pushed refugee treks out of its way.

A large number of Germans decided to stay in their homes rather than risk a dangerous escape into the unknown. In the future Polish territories, up to 3.6 million Germans remained after the first wave of flight and evacuation caused by the arrival of the Red Army. More than 60 per cent of them were women; just over a third were under 18 and one sixth older than 60 years of age.[91] In the Slovakian half of Czechoslovakia, the majority of the German population had left by the end of the war, with only some 30,000–40,000 of the 140,000 ethnic Germans remaining, but elsewhere in the country, particularly in the Sudetenland, the German presence was still strong.[92] According to estimates, some 3.5 million Germans, including about 400,000 refugees from areas further east, were still in Czechoslovakia in May 1945.[93] At the end of the war, these figures increased again as large numbers of Germans who had fled before the advancing Red Army either returned on their own initiative or were sent back to their homes by the newly established Allied authorities. Estimates of the number of German returnees to the post-war Polish territories go as high as 1.25 million.[94]

Many of the Germans who had been overrun by the Soviet army and its allies during the final stages of the war experienced a prolonged reign of terror, involving plunder as well as widespread sexual assault against women and girls. For those who survived this onslaught, the experience served as a transition to the state of general disenfranchisement, ostracization and arbitrary lawlessness that set in once the front had passed further west, giving way to an assertion of control by Polish and Czechoslovak authorities, backed up by Soviet occupation forces.

During this transitional stage between war and emerging peace, the power relations and dynamics on the ground in German settlement areas in both Poland and Czechoslovakia were often confused and unclear. The Soviet military ultimately sat at the top of the power hierarchy. Violent outbursts against the German population by members of the Red Army continued, caused partly by a desire for revenge and partly by the general lawlessness that accompanied the end of the war. In certain areas, particularly in Upper Silesia and East Prussia, the Soviets put together transports of ethnic Germans and sent them to the USSR for forced labour to rebuild the country left devastated by the German invasion.[95]

Occasionally Soviet officials dealt directly with what was left of previous German administrative structures or intervened to protect the local German population against Polish or Czechoslovak actions perceived to be excessive or counterproductive. Most of the time, however, the Soviets left the initiative in dealing with the Germans to Polish and Czechoslovak authorities, whose behaviour and actions were inspired and determined by a range of factors and considerations. In both Poland and Czechoslovakia, high-level politicians set the general tone with pronouncements and declarations about their intentions and expectations vis-à-vis the German populations, generally encouraging retaliatory and punitive measures that were meant to pave the way for an anticipated mass expulsion.

In Czechoslovakia, the new government established in Košice in early April 1945 under the leadership of Beneš and Zdeněk Fierlinger issued a series of public statements in favour of collective punishment of Germans, including a call by Beneš himself to 'cleanse our land culturally, economically and politically of everything German'.[96] The 143 directives issued by President Beneš between May and October 1945 authorized a wide range of measures against the German and Hungarian minorities in the country, and Interior Ministry directives provided for the deportation of almost the entire German population, with temporary exemptions only for those defined as anti-fascists or as essential skilled workers and experts.

In Poland, the provisional government, spearheaded by its communist members, adopted a very similar line, backed by the Soviet Union. The communist Interior Minister Edward Ochab, for example, advocated forced deportation for the overwhelming majority of Germans left in Poland's so-called 'recovered territories', exempting only skilled workers in particular fields and others whose labour contributions were considered essential.[97] The authorities typically made a distinction between the so-called *Reichsdeutsche* – Germans who had been citizens of the inter-war Reich – and the *Volksdeutsche* – ethnic Germans, who had been citizens of pre-1939 Poland. Whereas the former were usually encouraged to leave as quickly as possible, many of the latter were initially held back and conscripted to forced labour, in large part as punishment for their perceived – and in many cases real – disloyalty to the Polish state.[98]

However, the ability of each country's re-emerging central authorities to control events on the ground was initially quite limited, and at the local level several often competing actors typically sought to assert themselves, thereby contributing to a cumulative radicalization in the treatment of German populations under the chaotic end-of-war conditions. Indigenous civilian and military authorities frequently disagreed over questions of jurisdiction, and both also had to adjust to the demands of the Red Army. In the Czechoslovak borderlands, for example, the competing sources of authority included the National Committees (groups of citizens charged by the provisional government with the maintenance of public order in the various localities); the Revolutionary Guards (bands of partisans and hangers-on that functioned as a police force); military detachments wearing Czechoslovak, Soviet and in some areas also American uniforms; as well as self-styled security units composed of partisans and other volunteers.[99] This typically produced chaotic circumstances, with a good deal of leeway for local initiative. Actions taken against Germans were not necessarily dictated by any one authority, which often resulted in the adoption of harsh and retributive measures.

The treatment meted out to Germans in both Poland and Czechoslovakia during the transition to peacetime had many similarities. The new rulers imposed a variety of anti-German measures, which were in part retaliatory but also served longer-term purposes by disenfranchising, isolating and intimidating the Germans, thereby easing the way towards their planned forced relocation. The most obvious and predictable targets of retaliatory action in both countries were men in Nazi or Wehrmacht uniforms, many of whom were subjected to attacks as well as incarceration or forced labour. However, the measures implemented reached well beyond the most obvious agents of Nazi oppression, typically encompassing the entire ethnic German population in various ways.

Arrests, interrogations and forced labour assignments became widespread, with large numbers of people (in Poland in particular the *Volksdeutsche*) being forced to clear the streets of rubble and do other heavy manual work, frequently punctuated by violent attacks, often regardless of age or gender. Attempts followed to ostracize and isolate the Germans in a fashion that drew on Nazi precedents, including bans on using public transport or speaking German in public; confiscation of radios, telephones and other means of communication; and even the requirement to wear special armbands that identified their bearers as Germans. Pillage and plunder accompanied the process, particularly after growing numbers of Germans had been forced to leave their homes and interned in camps and other detention centres, some of them taken over from the Nazis, for purposes of control and forced labour deployment. The withdrawal of legal protections from the Germans and the seizure of their property were facilitated by policy statements and decrees, in Czechoslovakia in particular by the Beneš decrees, which underscored the presumed collective guilt of the Germans and explicitly endorsed the expropriation of their assets and possessions.[100]

The mob justice, incarceration and property loss faced by the Germans provided a transition to the actual expulsions, which began in May and June 1945 in both Poland and Czechoslovakia and unfolded in several stages during the following months and years. The first phase comprised the so-called 'wild' or 'military' expulsions that continued roughly until the beginning of the Potsdam Conference of the Big Three in July 1945. While the emerging central administrations of both countries supported the expulsions, their practical implementation lay primarily in the hands of local leaders. Military or paramilitary units played the key role in executing these operations, although in Poland civilian authorities also ran extensive parallel deportations of their own.[101] The general objective was to remove large numbers of Germans in order to create a *fait accompli* before the upcoming Potsdam Conference, at which the Big Three were scheduled to discuss Germany's eastern borders and any accompanying population transfers. By removing Germans and replacing them with Polish and Czech settlers, the governments of both countries intended to engineer a dynamic on the ground that could be presented as irreversible, particularly to the British and the Americans, who had not yet expressed official support for these demographic projects.[102]

In Poland, the pre-Potsdam 'wild expulsions' focused primarily on areas just to the east of the country's projected new frontier with Germany, along the Oder and the western Neiße rivers. The typical procedure was for groups of soldiers to surround the German communities, give the residents a few hours to pack the small amount of personal luggage allowed to them, usually no more than 20 kilos, and then march them to the borderline, with theft, assault, rape and even murder occurring frequently along the way. On the western side of the projected new frontier, in the Soviet occupation zone of Germany, the expellees were simply left to fend for themselves in chaotic conditions.

In Czechoslovakia, the expulsions originated from a wide range of locations throughout the German settlement areas, particularly the Sudetenland, and often involved train transports in goods and cattle wagons, along with forced marches. The practical implementation closely resembled that in Poland, with sudden forced departures, overseen by military or paramilitary units, brutal transit conditions, and an abrupt, unceremonious end to the journey just on the other side of the boundary of the US or Soviet occupation zones of Germany or Austria.

In both Poland and Czechoslovakia, the 'wild expulsions' reached their peak in June and early July 1945 and then tapered off by the latter half of July, partly because of the need for additional labour for the agricultural harvest and partly because of pressure from the victorious Allies, who began to object to the strains placed upon them by the arrival of large numbers of German expellees in their occupation zones. Such objections were understandable, not only because of the looming start of the crucial Potsdam Conference but also because the numbers of Germans swept westwards in the tide of 'wild expulsions' grew very high indeed; it is estimated that some 800,000 from Czechoslovakia and around 400,000 from Polish-controlled lands east of the Oder–Neiße line were affected. Initially, almost all the expellees from the Polish-controlled areas arrived in the Soviet zone of occupation. The majority of the expellees from Czechoslovakia – approximately 450,000 – were also deported to the Soviet zone, while the American zone received another 200,000 and Austria the remaining 150,000.[103]

The Potsdam Conference marked a turning point in the expulsion process. In the run-up to the meeting, the Polish and Czechoslovak governments had lobbied intensively for Great Power endorsement of their post-war plans, both the anticipated forced deportations and – especially in the case of Poland – the accompanying territorial imperative of pushing the future Polish–German boundary westward to the Oder and Neiße rivers. Similar efforts continued during the conference itself, with Polish representatives making their case in official negotiating sessions.[104]

Such endeavours paid off in the end, as the Potsdam Agreement adopted by the three Allies in early August decided in the Poles' and Czechs' favour on both key counts. The 'former German territories' east of the Oder–Neiße line desired by Poland were placed 'under the administration of the Polish state', with the de facto expectation that this status would become permanent, even though the agreement technically described the changes as provisional, pending a definitive peace settlement, which never arrived. Even more decisively, Article XIII of the Potsdam Agreement gave formal three-power approval for the 'orderly and humane' 'transfer' of the remaining German populations from Poland and Czechoslovakia – and also from Hungary.[105] However, underscoring the burdens faced by the occupation authorities in Germany in the face of the deportee influx, the article also called on Warsaw, Prague and Budapest to 'suspend the expulsions' until the Allies had been able to study the issue and 'submit an estimate of the time and rate at which further transfers could be carried out'.[106] In other words, the Allies asked the Polish, Czechoslovak and Hungarian governments to halt the expulsions until they received explicit authorization to continue. Such authorization came a few months later, in late 1945 and early 1946, through Allied Control Council directives and bilateral agreements between the expelling countries and the occupation powers in Germany.

In practice, however, large-scale expulsions from both Poland and Czechoslovakia continued without the post-Potsdam pause envisaged by the Big Three. Both governments wanted to maintain the momentum behind the deportations, expelling large numbers of Germans as quickly as possible. Secret directives issued by Czechoslovak Defence Minister General Svoboda at the end of the Potsdam Conference, for example, ordered his subordinates to continue with the mass deportations without interruption.[107] At the same time, the Polish and Czechoslovak governments were keen to avoid any appearance of open defiance of the decisions of the Big Three. Each government left much of the implementation of the expulsions in the hands of local authorities so that they could deny responsibility if necessary. Predictably, this led to important variations in the timing and the modalities of the operations from region to region. Whereas large-scale expulsions from Polish-controlled Upper Silesia, for example, resumed immediately after Potsdam, many other parts of Poland, including neighbouring Lower Silesia, did not witness deportations on a similar scale until the autumn.[108] In another attempt to avoid unwanted international attention, both governments also sought to curtail public discussion and media coverage of the details of the expulsions. The Czechoslovak Information Ministry, for example, instructed the country's press not to address the topic unnecessarily.[109]

However, the primary strategy in both Warsaw and Prague for downplaying the severity and scale of the continuing expulsions was to portray the German exodus as 'voluntary'. In both states, Germans were encouraged to flee on their own initiative, and several administrative steps were implemented to facilitate this, such as a relaxation of the bureaucratic formalities necessary for exiting the country and, in some areas, for a limited time, even the provision of discounted or free train tickets to German territory.[110] However, the supposedly voluntary nature of the mass departures was a fiction, intended to mask the underlying iron fist of coercion. Even those Germans who did ultimately leave on their own initiative did so under strong duress, in a context of violence and systematic oppression that had been building up for months, at a time when growing numbers of Polish and Czech settlers were arriving and assuming control of properties previously held by Germans, and incarceration and forced labour typically formed the alternative to 'voluntary' departure. Many others were forced out through organized mass deportations, conducted under harsh conditions, with sudden departures from homes or holding camps with a bare minimum of possessions, at most 30–50 kilos per person, much of which was typically stolen or seized along the way.[111]

The call for a voluntary exit did not encompass all Germans still left in Poland and Czechoslovakia, however. In Poland, *Volksdeutsche* tended to be kept back and, more generally, able-bodied men and women – particularly those whose special skills stood in high demand – were often not allowed to leave, even if they wanted to volunteer. Already during the earlier 'wild expulsions', those Germans regarded as economically unproductive – the old, the sick, children and women with young offspring – had been given priority for expulsion, and this policy was now enforced more consistently. In Czechoslovakia, in a change of policy, the Germans previously defined by the authorities as anti-fascists in recognition of their loyalty to the Czechoslovak state and their resistance to Nazism were now also slated for deportation, despite earlier plans to allow them to stay. The vast majority of these anti-fascists – an esti-mated total of some 96,000 – were expelled into the Soviet and American zones of occupation in several waves between October 1945 and mid-1947.[112]

The post-Potsdam 'wild expulsions' from Poland and Czechoslovakia continued until December 1945 and ended only when the Soviet Union, at this stage the occupation power most willing to admit expellees into the territory under its control, refused to accept any more Germans from either country. Deportations from Poland ceased in early December 1945 and those from Czechoslovakia shortly before Christmas. The total number of Germans deported during this four-month period is impossible to determine precisely, but recent estimates suggest just under 600,000 from Poland, overwhelmingly transported to the Soviet occu-pation zone, and some 373,000 from Czechoslovakia, approximately two thirds of whom were moved to the American zone and the others to the Soviet zone.[113]

Even as the unauthorized, post-Potsdam mass expulsions ran their course during the last months of 1945, planning and preparation for the next stage of the process, as endorsed by the victorious Allies, progressed steadily behind the scenes. On the national level, the Polish and Czechoslovak governments worked to create the infrastructure to implement the planned deportations. Attempts were made to con-centrate as many Germans as possible in labour camps or similar places of intern-ment where they could be controlled more easily, and to coordinate the tasks of different ministries, agencies and military offices.[114]

On the international stage, the key event was the release of the Allied Control Council's plan for the 'transfer of the German population' from Poland, Czechoslovakia and Hungary on 20 November 1945. As promised at Potsdam, the victorious Allies gave the green light for the resumption of deportations from these three countries into occupied Germany. The plan foresaw the 'transfer' of 3.5 million Germans from Poland and 2.5 million from Czechoslovakia, to be carried out according to a strict and ambitious schedule between December 1945 and mid-1946. The expellees from Poland were to be divided up between the Soviet and British occupation zones, with 2 million destined for the former and the remaining 1.5 million for the latter, whereas 1.75 million of the expelled Sudeten Germans were earmarked for the American zone and 750,000 for the Soviet zone.[115] The plan was complemented by subsequent bilateral agreements between the Polish and Czechoslovak governments and the affected occupation powers, which regu-lated some of the practical modalities of the 'transfers', such as the transport routes, timetables and transit conditions. The first of these was reached between American and Czechoslovak representatives in early January 1946.[116] A similar agreement between Britain and Poland was concluded in February 1946, soon to be followed by others between the Soviet Union and Poland in May 1946 and the Soviet Union and Czechoslovakia in early June 1946.[117]

The internationally sanctioned post-Potsdam expulsions began in late January 1946 when trains carrying Sudeten Germans out of Czechoslovakia started to roll in the direction of the American occupation zone.[118] At the end of February 1946 similar train transports of expellees began from Poland, as the British launched 'Operation Swallow', aimed at fulfilling their obligations under the guidelines adopted by the Allied Control Council. The volume of the railway transports grew quickly. During the early stages of 'Operation Swallow', some 6,500 Germans were shipped towards the British zone from Poland each day, while the daily total from Czechoslovakia in the direction of the American zone was at least four trains with 1,200 deportees each. The launch of a British-run sea link from Danzig to Lübeck, which operated from late March until June 1946, increased these numbers by an additional 43,000 during these three months.[119]

Just like the earlier 'wild expulsions', these more organized expulsions were implemented in a very similar fashion in both countries. Military and police units rounded up the targeted Germans from their homes, work camps or other detention sites at very short notice and marched or drove them to specially prepared collection points, at which the deportees and particularly their possessions were subjected to various inspections, and, after a very variable period of waiting, loaded onto trains or ships. Almost all the Germans still remaining in Poland and Czechoslovakia were now targeted for deportation; only small groups of workers with specialized skills were deliberately held back, often against their will. In the early months of 1946 the transport conditions were very severe. Cold weather compounded the hardships imposed on people locked in crowded cattle cars, often for days, with a bare minimum of possessions and supplies. Most expellees arrived at their destinations – typically makeshift reception centres operated by Germans under Allied supervision – exhausted and ill. Deaths, especially of the elderly, were a frequent occurrence during these early transports. Plunder and theft along the way also remained common, even if the most brutal violence characteristic of the 'wild expulsions' increasingly became a thing of the past.[120]

The conditions began to improve somewhat from the spring and summer of 1946 as the procedures became increasingly established and interventions by British and American authorities brought about small ameliorations, such as an increase in the baggage allowance of Sudeten German deportees to approximately 70 kilos per person.[121] By mid-1946 the expulsions reached their numerical peak, when the Soviet Union re-joined the effort. During the first months of the year the only transports allowed into the Soviet occupation zone had been small contingents of the so-called German anti-fascists from Czechoslovakia, and it was only in June 1946 that the Soviets again began to accept large-scale expellee transports from both Poland and Czechoslovakia. This first wave of organized post-Potsdam deportations into the Soviet zone from Poland continued until October 1946 and from Czechoslovakia until November 1946, and it affected some 750,000 and 790,000 Germans, respectively.[122] The conditions of these transports were roughly comparable to those of the transports bound for the British and American zones. The expulsions from Poland into the British zone began to taper off after July 1946 and finished completely in early January 1947. By that time, some 1.2 million Germans had arrived.[123] The Americans, in turn, stopped accepting transports from Czechoslovakia in November 1946, by which time their occupation zone had absorbed some 1.4 million Sudeten German expellees.[124]

By the beginning of 1947, the main phase of the expulsion of Germans had passed. Despite pressure from Poland and Czechoslovakia, neither the British nor the Americans were willing to receive further large-scale transports after that date, although relatively small numbers – a total reaching just under 100,000 people – still arrived from these two countries during the rest of the decade.[125] For the Soviet zone, too, 1947 was the last year of a numerically significant expellee influx. Nearly 600,000 Germans arrived there from Poland between April 1947 – when forced transports were resumed after a halt imposed the previous November – and the end of the year.[126] After that, the westward flow of Germans slowed to a trickle. Between 1948 and 1949 the total number of Germans who left Poland was no higher than 77,000, and although the total from Czechoslovakia is difficult to determine with any precision, it was considerably lower, perhaps no higher than 17,000.[127]

By the end of the 1940s the expulsion of Germans from Poland and Czechoslovakia was for all practical purposes complete. The newly founded Federal Republic of Germany had absorbed approximately 8 million Germans who had either fled or been expelled from Central or Eastern Europe beyond Germany's post-war borders. The expellees made up 16 per cent of West Germany's population and included some 4.5 million people from the territories that had come under Polish rule and nearly 2 million from Czechoslovakia.[128] The proportion of expellees in the German Democratic Republic (the earlier Soviet zone of occupation) was even higher. According to the last reliable statistics from 1947, the Soviet zone had taken in 4.3 million people defined as expellees – 24 per cent of the population – of whom 3.1 million had come from Poland and 900,000 from Czechoslovakia.[129] By 1949 the German Democratic Republic no longer compiled official statistics of its expellees – or 'resettlers' (*Umsiedler*), as this population group was formally called – largely for fear of upsetting the Soviet authorities. Around half a million German expellees settled outside Germany, mostly in Austria.

The Germans still left in Czechoslovakia and Poland at the end of the 1940s – many of them against their will and under oppressive conditions – were few in number, probably some 200,000 in the former and, depending on the definition of 'Germanness', between 125,000 and 431,000 in the latter, with the higher figure probably closer to the truth.[130] During the 1950s these numbers declined further, largely due to efforts to reunite families separated by the expulsions. The first major initiative of this kind was 'Operation Link', a programme run partly under the auspices of the International Red Cross, through which nearly 60,000 Germans from Poland and perhaps some 10,000–20,000 from Czechoslovakia were resettled into the Federal Republic and the GDR in 1950 and 1951.[131] A modest level of westward migration by Germans continued during the rest of the 1950s, particularly from Poland, where by the end of the decade only several thousand or, at the very most, some ten thousand Germans remained. The issue of the German minorities was to remain on the international agenda in the following decades but was not regarded with a great sense of urgency.[132]

4.4 Towards a Nationally Homogeneous State: Poland 1944–6

The ethnic cleansing that took place in Poland's eastern provinces during the German occupation between 1941 and 1944 had a substantial influence on Stalin's thinking about the fate of these captured lands. The recent events seemed to demonstrate that the peaceful coexistence of different nationalities was impossible and that the only answer to this perceived problem was ethnic homogenization. For both quantitative and political reasons, such a policy had become much simpler to pursue by the end of the war than it would have been a few years earlier. When the Red Army entered the region in 1944, only half of its original four million Polish inhabitants were still there; of the more than one million Jews probably not more than tens of thousands remained. On the other hand, the presence of the USSR in the anti-German coalition, and the fact that until mid-1944 it had borne the main burden of the war in Europe, prompted the Western democracies to adopt a less principled attitude towards Soviet political and territorial claims. The respite guaranteed by the Red Army was worth a high price: handing to Stalin half of Europe, including Poland's eastern provinces. Polish resistance was not considered a factor in the game. The protests of the Polish government-in-exile, with which Moscow had refused to deal since April 1943, were effectively neutralized by the Western Allies.[133] The Polish Communists, who in their exile in the USSR were preparing for the takeover of Poland, accepted Moscow's territorial demands – most notably in the treaty concerning Poland's post-war borders signed on 27 July 1944 – while striving for an ethnic homogenization of post-war Poland.

Undeniably, the Polish Communists, many of whom had gone through tragic experiences in the USSR, wanted to save as much as possible of the 'human substance' expelled from Poland's pre-war eastern provinces and from central Poland. Even the first major proclamation of the new authorities – the so-called 'Manifesto of the Polish Committee of National Liberation' issued on 22 July 1944 – strongly advocated the return of emigrants. That term, of course, referred not so much to the Poles in Great Britain as to those dispersed in Kazakhstan or Siberia. They were supposed to populate the German territories that Poland was to be given in compensation for the eastern provinces incorporated into the USSR. It is difficult to say how much weight that argument carried in the summer of 1944. But it certainly became more important by the spring of 1945, once the

Polish administration of the so-called western territories became a fact. It seems that in 1944 it was more important to argue in this way for a 'mutual exchange of people', which meant the removal of the Ukrainian, Belorussian and Lithuanian minorities from Poland.

The Soviet republics bordering Poland, to which Moscow shifted the organization of the projected relocations, were also interested in a population exchange. There is little doubt however, that the general regulations governing the migrations were worked out in the Soviet capital. This is indicated, for instance, by the fact that the three treaties signed by Poland with the respective Soviet republics were practically identical.[134] The agreements concerning the mutual 'evacuation of people'[135] signed by representatives of the Polish Committee of National Liberation with the Soviet republics of Ukraine and Belarus (on 9 September 1944) and Lithuania (on 22 September 1944)[136] foresaw the 'voluntary transfer' of the Polish and Jewish populations from the Soviet Union and of the Ukrainians, Belorussians and Lithuanians from the so-called 'Lublin Poland'. The criteria for determining who was to be transferred were not precise; it was not clear whether the transfer should apply only to pre-war Polish citizens or to all those who declared themselves Polish. Given the complicated ethnic situation in Poland's pre-war eastern provinces, this was bound to provide cause for serious conflicts. The agreements paid a good deal of attention to organizational problems. Each family could take up to two tons of movables, such as clothing, shoes, food, furniture and farm animals. The self-employed, such as physicians and artists, were also allowed to take along the tools necessary for their jobs. All resettlers were exempted from taxation, levies, and the like.

The agreements between Poland and the Soviet republics were overly optimistic in terms of timing: the registration of the candidates for relocation was to be completed between 1 October 1944 and 1 April 1945. These deadlines proved unrealistic, and the treaties required repeated amendments involving extensions of the closing dates. The relocation of Poles was finally stopped in June 1946. The agreements signed in September 1944 applied only to the Poles located in the Soviet Union's western republics at the time, leaving out those deeper in the interior of Russia, including Siberia or Kazakhstan. The treaty concerning the repatriation of this latter group was signed on 6 July 1945 and applied only to pre-war Polish citizens, excluding all those who had lived in the USSR before the war.

While the plans for relocating people from both sides of the new Polish–Soviet boundary emerged coevally with the final drawing of that border line, schemes for the removal of the Germans from Poland matured much earlier. Initially, these plans focused mainly on the Germans who had lived in pre-war Poland and signed the *Deutsche Volksliste* during the war. Various forms of punishments were foreseen, including imprisonment and the loss of property and civil rights. But from 1943 onwards, the idea of removing the Germans from the country began to gain acceptance. The first acts of the Home Cabinet during the Warsaw Uprising included decisions to withdraw Polish citizenship from Germans and to expel them from the country. An exception was made for those whose conduct had been 'loyal' to the Polish state.[137] Post-war Polish legislation concerning the so-called *Volksdeutsche* relied extensively on the acts prepared by the wartime underground authorities. However, whereas the laws promulgated in the years 1944–5 concentrated on punishing or rehabilitating the ethnic Germans, the legislation published in 1946 focused on depriving them of their Polish citizenship and relocating them to Germany.[138]

The fate of the Germans who lived on territories to be adjoined to Poland after the war was of less concern to the resistance planners.[139] Generally, the idea of deporting the Germans to Germany proper prevailed, avenging the expulsions conducted by the Germans in the regions incorporated into the Reich in 1939. However, although the fate of the Germans inhabiting the Opole province or East Prussia may have been an issue of little significance in occupied Poland, the London-based government-in-exile paid as much attention to the promise of territorial acquisitions in the West as to the prospect of losses in the East. All this was part of the 'Polish problem', one of the most contested issues within the anti-Axis coalition. On the question of the country's post-war borders, the Polish government in London was constrained by the decisions of the Big Three. Concentrating their efforts on the eastern borders and fearing that exaggerated claims in the West – such as Lower Silesia or Western Pomerania – could facilitate an Anglo-American capitulation vis-à-vis Russian demands, the 'London Poles' decided to lay claim to Danzig, East Prussia and the Opole province. One of the arguments used was the impossibility of relocating several million Germans from the other western regions, although the government-in-exile did advocate deportations from the provinces that it demanded.

Such a 'minimalist' attitude was possible only if one assumed very limited territorial losses in the East. But ever since the Tehran summit of late 1943, it had been clear that Poland would forfeit all its eastern territories. Hence, the compensation at the cost of Germany had to increase, as did the number of people slated for potential relocation. It was becoming obvious to the émigré politicians that post-war Poland should be an ethnically homogeneous state. However, as the end of the war drew closer, the opinions of the government-in-exile were losing significance. Stalin had decided not to talk to the Polish émigrés in London, although – to keep up appearances of legality – he acquiesced in the possibility of a coalition cabinet encompassing both émigré politicians from London and Communists. Ultimately, it was the latter group that took control of Poland in the summer of 1944, with Stalin's blessing. The Polish Communists residing in the USSR during the war had no 'German plans' of their own. They were completely dependent on their Soviet patrons and also lacked the intellectual wherewithal to master the challenges before them. However, the Poles also exercised their own initiative, sometimes in a very far-reaching way, particularly at the organizational level.

After the German attack on the Soviet Union in June 1941, all of Poland's eastern territories found themselves under German occupation. A small part of these new conquests – the Galicia district – was incorporated into the General Government; the Białystok region was added to East Prussia; and the remainder was divided into two units: the Reichskommissariat Ostland and the Reichskommissariat Ukraine. German rule, which lasted three years, resulted – as we have seen – in far-reaching demographic changes in the region. The Jewish community was annihilated almost totally. A considerable percentage of the several hundred thousand people – probably some 500,000 – moved from these lands to Germany as forced labourers were Poles.[140] The ethnic cleansing conducted by Ukrainian nationalists, discussed in chapter 2, killed about 100,000 Poles and made refugees out of another 300,000. To this number must be added the victims of German terror as well as the casualties of resistance campaigns.

When the Red Army finally conquered these territories in July 1944, only half of the pre-war Polish population was still there, totalling about two million. Crossing the former Polish–Soviet border on the night of 3/4 January 1944, the Red Army treated these territories as Russian soil. The Polish government in London protested, but Moscow left no room for illusions. In their reply to the Polish government-in-exile on 11 January 1944, the Russians stated that Poland should be a strong and independent state but that it could not be reborn 'by annexing Ukrainian and Belorussian territories'; the country's eastern border should be drawn along the Curzon line. Stalin was determined to settle the Polish question without the émigré government. But he delayed setting up his own 'Polish government', composed of exiled Polish Communists, until the Red Army had crossed the 'border' river Bug and seized some bigger towns. The Polish Committee for National Liberation – Stalin would not use the term 'government' yet – was finally constituted in Moscow on 21 July 1944. The existence of this body and its 'manifesto' were made public in Chełm Lubelski, a town on the 'Polish side' of the projected border. Although a statement about the Curzon line was removed from the text at the last minute, it was obvious that this divider would form Poland's new eastern border, with minor modifications. This was officially confirmed in the agreement between the Polish Committee of National Liberation and the Council of People's Commissars signed in Moscow on 27 July 1944. The manifesto said nothing about population displacements, but at least one clause stressed the homogeneity of the new Poland: 'The Polish lands for Poland; Ukrainian, Belorussian and Lithuanian lands for the Soviet Ukraine, Belarus and Lithuania.'

As previously stated, little is known about the negotiations between the Polish Committee of National Liberation and the governments of the Soviet republics bordering Poland conducted in September 1944. But it would be an oversimplification to place all of the responsibility for the subsequent population movements on the Kremlin. While Soviet authorities were keen to remove Poles from what had previously been Poland's Eastern Borderlands, Warsaw was also eager to rid itself of ethnic minorities and looked forward to the prospect of an ethnically homogeneous state. According to the estimates of the Polish State Office for Repatriation, in the autumn of 1944 over 546,000 people fulfilled the criteria for evacuation to the East.[141] Ukrainians were the largest affected group, and the Polish authorities were very keen to deport them, to the point of being willing to use brutal force.[142] The Polish–Ukrainian agreement on the 'mutual exchange of population' was signed on 9 September 1944, and already on 20 September a group of Soviet apparatchiks appeared in Lublin. The Soviet delegation joined the propaganda drive aimed at persuading Poland's Ukrainians to move voluntarily to the Ukraine. The methods used included special meetings at which the availability of state assistance for those prepared to go was emphasized. The propaganda, combined with the attacks of the Polish underground against Ukrainian villages, did bring some results. By the end of 1944, 10,449 families (39,864 people) had chosen to relocate.

Soon the Ukrainians left in Poland began to receive information about the actual conditions that the migrants were encountering on the other side of the border. As a result, the number of volunteers dropped dramatically. The Polish authorities responded by imposing additional taxes, duties and labour obligations on the Ukrainian villages.[143] These measures did not change much in Ukrainian attitudes towards the relocations. In August 1945 the Polish army was involved in the relocation process. Ukrainians living near the border were ordered to move within fourteen days – or to face expulsion by force. This was no mere threat; forced expulsions did take place in many cases, frequently accompanied by arrests.[144] Finally, 122,622 Ukrainian families (482,880 persons) out of the 125,949 families (497,682 persons) registered for relocation did leave Poland. Only 4.8 per cent of the Ukrainian migrants declared that they had moved voluntarily. According to the Polish State Office for Repatriation, a total of 518,718 Ukrainians, Belorussians and Lithuanians had been transferred out of Poland by August 1946.[145]

Although the Lithuanian and Belorussian minorities caused relatively little concern in Warsaw – the former because of their low numbers and the latter because of their comparatively low national consciousness and organizational activity – the Polish leadership was intent on solving the perceived problem posed by the 150,000 Ukrainians left in the country after the agreed populations 'transfers' with the USSR had been completed. Because the Soviet side refused to accept more deportees, the only available option was to move these people within Poland. Military authorities argued that such measures were necessary in view of 'possible disloyalty' in the future. The Ukrainians were portrayed as the natural support base for the Ukrainian Insurgent Army (UPA), although by 1946/7 this force posed no threat to the Polish state. The preparations for the internal deportations began in the autumn of 1946, with Moscow's consent, and the plans were ready by March 1947. The launch of the operation was facilitated by the probably incidental death of Deputy Defence Minister General Karol Świerczewski on 28 March 1947. On the following day the Politburo of the Polish Workers' Party decided to start the expulsions of the Ukrainians and to disperse them across the western territories acquired from Germany, primarily East Prussia and Western Pomerania. The so-called Operation 'Wisła' was conducted by the army. By 17 July 1947 the Polish forces had deported approximately 140,000 people, at times with the utmost brutality.[146]

The significance the Polish authorities attached to the expulsion of the Ukrainians at the turn of 1944/5 is attributable not only to the desire to attain a homogeneous nation state, but also to the pressing need to find homesteads for the Poles 'repatriated' from the Ukrainian Soviet Republic. Whereas the 'transfers' from the Belorussian and Lithuanian Soviet republics did not start until 1945, the operations from the Ukraine, where the situation was more complicated, began in 1944. Official statistics claim that around 117,000 people were 'evacuated' from the Ukraine into Poland in 1944. One can assume that about 100,000 of these evac-uees were refugees escaping Ukrainian terror. Such people usually found their way to the 'new' Poland without the knowledge of the institutions which were supposed to oversee the relocations on both sides. The coordination of the operations in Poland was assigned to the State Office for Repatriation, established on 7 October 1944.[147]

The influx of 'repatriates' from the Eastern Borderlands gained momentum in the summer and autumn of 1945, when the climatic conditions were favourable and the western territories became open for the incoming migrants. Whereas in 1944 the 'official' relocation had encompassed only Poles from the Ukraine (the 117,212 persons mentioned above), in 1945 the transfers affected 511,877 people from the Ukraine, 135,654 from Belarus, 73,042 from Lithuania, and 221,717 from other parts of the USSR. Relocations from Lithuania, Belarus and the Ukraine were largely over by mid-1946. In total, during the years 1944–8, 1,517,983 Poles were swept up in the 'official' transfers.[148]

This figure must be augmented by an unspecified number of 'irregular' settlers. Contrary to the pre-Potsdam expulsions of Germans – conducted by the Polish army in June and July 1945 – the 'irregular' migrations in the East were under-taken chiefly on the initiative of the local inhabitants. Many of the migrants were people who had been politically compromised in the eyes of the communist authorities, such as soldiers of the underground Home Army. In the Vilna district, considerable numbers of Poles illegally crossed into Poland's Białystok region, fearful that the Lithuanian administration might force them to stay.[149] Another group of 'unauthorized migrants' consisted of Poles escaping from Ukrainian nationalist terror into the Lublin and Rzeszów regions.[150] The statistical yearbook for 1949 includes the category of 'irregular' immigrants, whose number was esti-mated at 22,815. But the calculations produced by Polish historians point to a figure of 200,000, which seems closer to the truth.[151]

As far as the repatriates from the interior of the USSR were concerned, the exchange agreement covered only those who could claim pre-war Polish citizenship. The vastness of the Soviet Union's territories and the underdevelopment of its transport and communication links frequently presented insurmountable obstacles. The Soviet administration often displayed a reluctance to repatriate Poles. Moreover, many Poles were deprived of their Polish citizenship and coerced into obtaining Soviet passports. Theoretically, this did not prevent repatriation, but in practice it often proved too high a hurdle. These problems applied chiefly to the Poles located deep within the USSR. The implementation of the agreements of September 1944, particularly from the perspective of individual and group experiences, will be discussed in detail in the next chapter. Here, we must limit ourselves to more general observations.

The act of leaving was typically the result of various factors. National consciousness was one of these, but frequently not the decisive one. The administrations of the individual Soviet republics approached the problem of nationality in various pragmatic ways. In the Ukraine, for instance, the authorities pressured the Poles to leave, particularly from the cities. In rural areas the terror of the Ukrainian nationalist underground persuaded many others to go. The Lithuanian authorities, by contrast, put up numerous obstacles to deter the Poles – most of them rural folk – from leaving.

Differences in the treatment of urban and rural residents were common. Soviet authorities were typically interested in removing the more nationally conscious minority population of the cities – particularly in Vilna and Lwów, which were steeped in Polish history and tradition[152] – whereas the relocations of peasants were frequently postponed, or even sabotaged, especially in Lithuania and Belarus. Revealingly, the registration of migrants in Vilna began on 28 December 1944 and ended in March 1945, while in smaller Lithuanian communities the process started only in January–February 1945 – or not at all.[153] This reluctance to relocate the rural population was often caused by concerns over a possible decrease in agricultural production. The following excerpt from a report (written in November 1945) by an apparatchik involved in organizing relocations from the Belorussian Soviet republic illustrates the point: 'The peasant was not allowed to register [for relocation] until he had finished sowing. After the sowing was finished, after 1 May the registration was closed, and there were no railway cars for those already registered, so the people had to wait again. The townsfolk and all those who have higher easy earnings had more opportunities for getting transport and leaving.'[154] As a result, in the Vilna region, where about 380,000 people registered for relocation, only about half actually left, but with a wide discrepancy between town and country: 80 per cent of those registered within the city migrated, whereas outside the urban area the percentage was only 31.3.[155] In general, the proportion of registered Poles who actually left was 90 per cent in the Ukraine, 50 per cent in Lithuania, and about 55 per cent in Belarus.[156] For various reasons, ranging from delayed registration to imprisonment in a gulag, both in the Eastern Borderlands and in the interior provinces of the Soviet Union, from 600,000 to 1.6 million Poles stayed behind. Some of them managed to make their way to Poland during the so-called second wave of repatriation in 1955–9.[157]

The agreements did not specify where in Poland the repatriates were to be settled. Many of the resettlers wanted to be placed in 'historical Poland', i.e. within the boundaries of 1939. There they would be much nearer to their former home-lands; they often had families in the region, and the milieu was more familiar than cities like Szczecin or Wrocław. Unfortunately, such wishes clashed with the plans of the Polish authorities, on both the national and local levels. The government wanted the newly acquired western territories to be populated as quickly as pos-sible for political and economic reasons.[158] The authorities were also reluctant to burden 'historical Poland', especially regions adjacent to the new eastern border, with elements hostile to the Soviet neighbour. The central government's policies were largely in accord with those of local elites, particularly the Communists, for whom the migrants were a political nuisance. The resettlers also exacerbated the ongoing competition for the farms and houses left by the expelled Germans and Ukrainians, which were much coveted by the 'locals'. Hence, the authorities tried to restrict – or even prohibit – the settlement of the newcomers in central Poland.[159]

Ultimately, the majority of the migrants from the Eastern Borderlands – 121,846 from Lithuania, 247,936 from Belarus and 612,405 from the Ukraine – and from the distant provinces of the USSR – some one million in total – settled in the ter-ritories taken over from Germany. The trail went westwards; the migrants from Lithuania and Belarus typically settled in East Prussia and Pomerania, while those from the Ukraine ended up in Silesia. Of the Poles from the Vilna region, 25.1 per cent settled in the Gdańsk administrative unit, 25.9 per cent in the Olsztyn region, but only 14.8 per cent in the vicinity of Wrocław. On the other hand, 37.9 per cent of the people transferred from the western Ukraine went to Silesia and 35.4 per cent to the Wrocław district.

4.5 The Exodus of Italians from Istria and Dalmatia

Between 1945 and the mid-1950s, along the eastern border of Italy, about 250,000 people of Italian nationality were forced to leave the towns and villages in which most of them had been living for many generations; these towns and villages were situated along the eastern coast of the Adriatic Sea, from the Gulf of Trieste to Istria, and reaching as far south as Dalmatia.

At least two points should be borne in mind to place the exodus of the Istrians and the Dalmatians in its proper historical context: the policies of the Italian fascist government vis-à-vis population groups defined as 'alien' between the two world wars, and the political and military events in the Balkans during the Second World War. With regard to the former, the fascist regime implemented or planned a series of measures, ranging from the closure of Slovenian and Croatian schools to the forced Italianization of the names of places and people and the adoption of oppressive policies towards Slovenian clergy.[160] However, the fascist regime's denationalization drive was not particularly successful;[161] as Raoul Pupo has written, 'the efforts to wipe out Slovenian and Croatian national identity did not even come close to succeeding'.[162] Of course the denationalization policy did have some effects. On the one hand, it speeded up the emigration of Slovenians and Croats, between 50,000 and 100,000 of whom left Italy. On the other hand, it provided an incentive for the formation of underground groups of anti-fascists.

After the invasion of Yugoslavia by German and Italian troops in April 1941, the occupiers subjected the region to a radical 'Balkanization', with the aim of stirring up national tensions and thereby reducing the risk that the area would produce a united resistance movement. Ex-Yugoslavia was divided among the countries of the Axis, thereby satisfying their respective expansionist or nationalist desires. Mussolini got control of the so-called province of Ljubljana in central and southern Slovenia, the Dalmatian coast and Montenegro, areas that were placed under military administration. As we have seen in the third chapter, Italian measures in the occupied territories were, on the whole, very repressive.[163] A case in point was the policy of internments and forced population movements, aimed at weakening the support base of the partisan movement.[164] These harsh policies were fuelled by the emergence of a fierce resistance movement that enjoyed broad popular backing. The Italian civilian and military authorities were aware of the difficulties they faced, given the weakness of their military machine, which was scattered over a vast territory, and the widespread support that the guerrillas enjoyed among the population. They attempted to exploit ethnic tensions by enlisting collaborationist forces, such as the so-called *domobrani* in Slovenia. However, the annexation, denationalization and colonization plans, drawn up by civilian and military authorities, remained just pieces of paper.

After the collapse of fascism in July 1943, Tito's partisan movement in Istria and Dalmatia gained strength and began to develop long-term political plans. The Communists found common ground with nationalist groups. In fact, one reason for the success of Tito's movement in building a strong base of popular support was its emphasis on the national question, with marked anti-Italian overtones. The political programmes of the partisan movement envisaged the annexation of the whole of Dalmatia and Istria. The post-war objectives of the partisans also included the acquisition of Trieste, Gorizia and, further north, Maribor.[165] Italian anti-fascists would be allowed to take part in the democratic liberation of post-war Yugoslavia, but in a subordinate position.

With the Italian armistice of 8 September 1943, a power vacuum was created in the occupied territories, a vacuum that was soon filled by a period of brutal violence associated with the term *foibe*.[166] The *foibe* are subterranean cavities typical of the karst regions of Istria, which had often been used as pits and dumps. Groups of partisan and – in some cases – ordinary citizens conducted a series of brutal attacks, which killed between 500 and 700 people, mostly Italians; their bodies were dumped in the *foibe*. According to the most recent scholarship, there was no genocidal intent behind this first phase of killings. Italians were targeted because they represented the denationalizing power. Fascists, carabinieri and other public officials were prominent among the victims, but teachers, pharmacists and other members of the middle classes also lost their lives.

In the following months, the Germans set up a zone of operations in Italy's eastern border areas, named the Adriatic Littoral Operation Zone (*Operationszone Adriatisches Küstenland*). This action served primarily strategic purposes, and, to keep the territory under control, the Germans made use of Slavic and Italian collaborationist forces.[167] Confronted with German military occupation, Yugoslavia's communist resistance movement outlined its political programme in summer 1944.[168] Its aims were twofold: maximizing its military successes in order to facilitate the establishment of a communist regime at the end of the war and making Yugoslavia's national and ethnic borders coincide, as we have already seen in regard to Hungarians and Germans. Yugoslav resistance organizations set up contacts with Italian partisan formations operating in the country's eastern border area. The links to their closest ideological ally, the Italian Communist Party (PCI), were particularly important. The PCI, led by Palmiro Togliatti, reacted with caution to its Yugoslav comrades' requests for a recognition of their territorial claims, which were very clear: the Isonzo river was to become Italy's eastern border. This implied that both Trieste and Gorizia, as well as the important industrial centre of Monfalcone, should belong to the Yugoslav state after the war. Only in May 1945 did Togliatti condemn the Yugoslav occupation of Trieste, 'an indisputably Italian city'.[169] The local Communists had a different attitude and ended up agreeing fully with the Yugoslav position.

Once the Yugoslav partisans reached Trieste on 30 April 1945, they tried to establish their sovereignty over the region. Even Italian anti-fascist groups came under attack. From that moment, Trieste and Italy's eastern border region became an important source of tension in the rising Cold War. In the middle of May, firmer pressure from the United States to drive the Yugoslavs from Trieste produced a compromise with the Soviet Union. In accordance with the agreement signed in Belgrade on 9 June 1945, Venezia Giulia was divided into two zones: Zone A – including Trieste and its immediate hinterland – under Allied administration and zone B – which included northern Istria – under Yugoslav administration.[170]

The Yugoslav occupation authorities set out to sweep away all obstacles, in particular all political enemies. A second and more radical wave of violence took place. The operations continued for several months and assumed a variety of forms: summary court cases, spontaneous executions, planned deportations to camps from which the majority never returned. 'Actions from below' were mixed with policies implemented by communist political authorities. The victims of this second phase of the *foibe* were primarily Italians. The new rulers acted in a similar way in other parts of Yugoslavia as well, with preventive purges of entire categories of people regarded as politically, culturally and socially dangerous. In Venezia Giulia these categories happened to consist primarily of ethnic Italians. It is very difficult to quantify the number of victims of this second wave of the *foibe*. The figures of 15,000–20,000 given in nationalistic Italian historiography are exaggerated, but the total probably did reach several thousand. Subsequent interpretations have also overemphasized the presumed causal link between the *foibe* and the ensuing exodus of Italians. It is likely (and deducible from available documents) that the Yugoslav violence left lasting scars of anguish and uncertainty in the Italian communities, but it is also a fact that 'the turbulent transition of power, from Nazi-fascism to Yugoslav communism, took place without per se causing large-scale population transfers'.[171]

It does not appear that an official decision for the general expulsion of the Italians from Yugoslavia was ever taken. According to Edvard Kardelj, one of the leaders of Tito's regime, a series of 'national rights' was to be granted to the Italian population. However, there was a crucial precondition: the Italians would have to accept the new regime. A clear distinction was made between 'honest, anti-fascist' Italians, who could become part of the new regime, and 'reactionary' Italians and 'enemies of the people', who could not. For long and short-term historical reasons, the great majority of the Italians were placed in the second category. They came primarily from the middle class and lower middle classes, lived in the towns and cities, and had been steeped in the myth of Italian nationalism for decades. As property owners, many had much to lose from the policies of nationalization and social re-equilibration advocated by Tito.

The exodus of Italians, which is often described as an essentially unitary process, should, in reality, be broken up into specific territorial cases that, apart from some general similarities, had their particular characteristics. The first wave came from the city of Zadar. The city had endured terrible air raids throughout 1944, which caused more than half of its inhabitants to seek refuge in Italy. In May 1945, as communist partisans entered the city, there were just a few thousand people left, very few of them Italians.[172]

Let us consider a case closer in time to the end of the conflict, i.e. that of Rijeka. In that city, inhabited by an Italian majority, the arrival of the Yugoslav liberators brought a series of repressive actions, aimed at disrupting the local autonomist movement, whose anti-fascist credentials were no longer important. The Yugoslav partisans perceived the autonomists as dangerous because they could advocate Italian interests during peace negotiations. The liberators carried out a series of public murders and instituted an intense policy of Croatization in the city, ousting the Italian ruling class for good. The inadequate preparation of the improvised new ruling class exacerbated the difficult material conditions, creating a particular crisis for the Italian population, which suffered from an extensive policy of confiscations in 1946/7. The Italian inhabitants, accused of being 'enemies of the people', found themselves in an unbearable situation. Consequently, a stream of emigration began in early 1946, initially involving about 20,000 people. Yugoslav communist authorities reacted to the exodus with violent criticism of the emigrants and attacks against the ecclesiastical hierarchy, which was accused of instigating the mass flight.[173] The exodus continued in the two subsequent years, in the form of an option made possible by the peace treaty. In this first phase of the migration, hundreds of workers, especially from Monfalcone, convinced that the building of socialism was now possible only in Yugoslavia, moved to Rijeka, taking the place of the departed. They viewed Tito's Yugoslavia as a utopia. However, they were soon to be bitterly disappointed; Tito's split from Moscow in 1948 disoriented them. They had to endure accusations of 'deviationism', and some were deported to concentration camps.[174]

The exodus from Rijeka took place quietly, whereas that from Pula unfolded in the international limelight. The agreement of June 1945 between the victorious powers had made the city an enclave to zone A, under Allied military administration. In the early post-war period, Italians were very active in an inter-party group.[175] In early spring 1946 the possibility of the city passing under Yugoslav occupation arose. This prospect threw the Italian-speaking inhabitants into a panic. There were attempts at a collective response, such as the great popular demonstration organized on 22 March 1946 during the visit of an Allied delegation. However, the city was isolated, and the economic conditions of the Italian population were growing worse. In the summer of 1946 the news from Paris caused a dramatic change in the Italian community's attitude, and all hopes crumbled. In the end, more than 28,000 of Pula's approximately 32,000 Italian inhabitants chose the exit option. The exodus began at the end of the year.

In the interior of Istria the immediate aftermath of the war exposed Italians to terrible violence (the *foibe*) as well as property confiscations and forced labour. These developments worsened the living conditions of the Italian population and undermined any residual sympathies for the new communist regime. The more the Italian population displayed its discontent, the more the Yugoslav authorities hardened their stance. But it was the news from Paris, establishing the definitive borders between Italy and Yugoslavia, that sparked off a rush for the emigration options at the beginning of 1948. Interestingly, those taking advantage of the exit option included not only a high percentage of the inhabitants of the coastal towns, as could be expected in light of their deep-rooted connections with Italian culture, but also many residents of the interior. Yugoslav authorities tried to curb the flow of emigrants, putting up a series of bureaucratic hurdles. The emigration of Italians reached its initial peak in the years 1947 to 1949. Thanks to Italy's diplomatic intervention, the terms for the options were reopened in 1950. The behaviour of

Yugoslav authorities in the face of large-scale Italian emigration was contradictory. On the one hand, there were attempts to stem the exodus by threatening its
'instigators', while, on the other hand, Italians were pressured to leave quickly and
en masse. Our knowledge of Yugoslav decision-making processes is insufficient to
explain the reasons behind such contradictions. But the number of Istrian Italians
involved in this phase of the exodus was more than 50,000.

In the northern part of Istria, assigned by the victors to zone B, the exodus took
place later, at the beginning of the 1950s. The measures implemented were similar
to those in the other territories: summary killings, confiscations, pressure from the
governmental authorities and the press. Here, too, a part of the Italian population
– primarily members of the working class close to, or active in, the Communist
Party – tried to protest, highlighting the gap between Yugoslav policies and public
opinion among the Italians. The workers' protest in Koper in October 1945 –
directed against the Yugoslav authorities' economic policy – was symptomatic of
this dynamic. The Yugoslav administration reacted by moving people from the
countryside into the town, thereby applying a characteristic strategy of Yugoslav
nationalism, i.e. pitting the Slavic countryside against the Italian city.

The main reason why the exodus from the Koper area began so late was the
region's proximity to Trieste and the hope that the territory would be returned to
Italian sovereignty. Initially the British and the Americans entertained the idea of
setting up a buffer state that would include the A and B zones and the so-called
Free Territory of Trieste established in and around the city. However, they abandoned this idea because they realized that Yugoslav pressure would make the existence of this little state impossible. These decisions were not announced to the
Italian government, let alone to the Italians of Koper, who continued to hope for
an internationalization of their region's status and a concomitant Yugoslav withdrawal. In reality, however, the Yugoslav authorities stayed, and, with the situation
between the two zones becoming increasingly rigid, they were able to implement
their policies more and more effectively. They put the Italian population under
increasing pressure, branding them fascists, while the Italian Communists were
disparagingly labelled 'extremists'. The Italian schools were closed and the
teachers forced to leave. Heavy pressure was also brought to bear on the Italian-
speaking clergy. In April 1950, as a reaction to the local elections in Trieste in
which moderate Italian parties had triumphed, the Yugoslav authorities organized
administrative elections in zone B.[176] The Communist Party scored a clear success
in an atmosphere of intimidation which convinced many Italians not to vote.

The October 1953 note of the two Western powers that put an end to the existence of zone A, ceding it to Italy, sparked off the final Italian exodus from zone
B. Confronted by Yugoslavia's harsh reaction, Italians realized that the region was
now lost to Italy. Amidst apparently spontaneous outbursts of violence, thousands
of people were forced to abandon their homes. A few months later they were followed by the great majority of the Italians of northern Istria, when it became clear

that zone B would officially become Yugoslav territory. Between October 1953 and August 1956 about 25,000 people fled the zone.[177]

The exodus came to an end in the summer of 1956. It is difficult to give an accurate number of the Italians who fled. The total given by the associations of the refugees is 350,000, but this figure includes many non-Italians. A real census was never carried out. In 1956 the Italian government estimated that the exiles numbered 270,000; other estimates are slightly lower, mostly around 250,000.[178] In light of pre-war Italian censuses, this latter figure seems to be a 'realistic estimate of the migratory flow'.[179] Slovenian and Croatian researchers have suggested a much lower number of 190,000. This estimate fits with the tendency to downplay the phenomenon, placing it within the parameters of normal, voluntary migration, driven primarily by economic motives.[180] However, regardless of the quantitative issue, the fact that a whole community was undermined and forced to abandon its areas of settlement remains important.

What were the motives propelling the exodus of Italians? In the first instance, there was the fear fuelled by the initial waves of violence, which struck many as inexplicable. The repressive, inquisitional atmosphere established by the communist regime also contributed to the sense of dread. But there were other reasons as well, such as the subversion of traditional social and cultural hierarchies, and the crumbling of a tight network of habits and customs, especially religious ones. This factor was probably underestimated in the older, predominantly nationalistic historiography, which emphasized the link between Yugoslavia's 'ethnic cleansing' project and the Italian reaction. Social and economic factors were given only secondary importance in this scholarship, whereas the most recent historiography has tended to place them in the forefront.[181] The Italians of Istria and Dalmatia experienced a dramatic change in their lives during the transition from war to peace, which increased their feelings of unease. They underwent what could be described as a serious identity crisis, linked to the modernization process that the new communist regime was promoting. A sense of being 'out of place' in what should have been one's own country often became the main reason for the agonizing decision to leave. These arguments, however, do not mean that the exodus should be interpreted as a purely voluntary option.

–5–

The Experience of Forced Migration

Although the many millions of Europeans affected by forced migration during and after the Second World War were a diverse group, underneath the multiplicity of personal destinies lay certain patterns and commonalities. This chapter seeks to illuminate some of these patterns and commonalities, as well as differences and contrasts, by drawing on the experiences of two of the largest groups of forced migrants, Poles and Germans, in several wartime and early post-war contexts. The first section focuses on the millions of individuals caught up in Nazi Germany's 'Heim ins Reich' programme from the autumn of 1939 onwards: ethnic Germans transported into the Reich, with the expectation of swift resettlement, as well as Poles and others singled out for brutal relocation in order to make room for newcomers. The second section examines the experiences of Poles and Germans transported eastwards to the USSR by Soviet authorities during the war, usually for forced labour service. The concluding section addresses the massive forced migrations that accompanied the war's final stages and aftermath: the westward flight and expulsion of Poles and Germans that went hand in hand with far-reaching changes in the political geography of the region.

5.1 The 'Heim ins Reich' Programme and Its Impact

The more than half a million ethnic Germans transported into Nazi Germany as part of the 'Heim ins Reich' programme, primarily between late 1939 and late 1941, had widely divergent regional, social and cultural backgrounds. Few bonds beyond a language recognizable as a German dialect and a vaguely shared Germanic cultural background united wealthy nobles from the Baltic states and simple peasants from rural Romania, for example. But the Nazi resettlement programme ultimately imposed broadly similar experiences on the bulk of the ethnic German deportees, regardless of their backgrounds.

The first widely shared experience was surprise, even shock, at the news that a mass relocation would have to take place. The various ethnic German communities lacked the power to participate in the high-level decision-making that led to their resettlement or to shape the practical procedures implemented on the ground. They were simply expected to respond to the call to evacuate to the Reich – a land that most had never even seen – typically at very short notice, abandoning homes and communities that they and their ancestors had in many cases inhabited for generations.[1]

Such an abrupt displacement was obviously a difficult step, but the vast majority of the affected ethnic Germans ultimately agreed to take it. Several different motives contributed to this outcome. The most elemental – and arguably strongest – motive was fear, particularly in areas where the *horror sovieticus* loomed large, such as the three Baltic states of Estonia, Latvia and Lithuania and the formerly Polish and Romanian territories incorporated into the Soviet Union in 1939–40. The desire to escape from 'the powers of darkness' embodied in 'the immense danger of Bolshevism' predominates in the subsequent reminiscences of evacuees from these regions.[2]

Several other motives also played a role, both in these areas and in those that lacked an equally imminent communist threat but nevertheless witnessed large-scale evacuations, such as the southern Bukovina and Dobrudja districts of Romania or the South Tyrol province of Italy. Social pressure was an important factor in the typically close-knit ethnic German communities. The evacuations assumed an air of inevitability as the majority of the ethnic group, typically urged on by its community leaders, accepted their necessity. As one evacuee subsequently put it, many concluded that 'because everyone else is going, I am too'.[3] Considerable importance also accrued to a nationalistic fervour for Germany and Germanness, fuelled by the Third Reich's seeming strength. According to one ethnic German, his community in Romania was swept by 'a great enthusiasm for the German cause. ... Germany was like the sun in the sky. Nothing could cast shadows in its path.'[4] Such sentiments were further reinforced by Nazi propaganda, which underscored the ethnic Germans' duty to respond to the 'call of the Führer' and promised them a bright future in the Reich, with full compensation for any material losses and many subsequent improvements in their lives. Under the combined weight of these and other influences, the vast majority of the ethnic Germans targeted for resettlement heeded the call. There were variations, of course; South Tyroleans proved considerably less willing to move than did ethnic Germans of Eastern Europe, for example, and in most communities older and wealthier individuals were predictably less eager to jump into the unknown than the young and less affluent. But even the more cautious ones usually managed to lighten their 'heavy hearts' with hopes for a better future in the Third Reich.[5]

The resettlement itself began with registration procedures conducted by Nazi officials in cooperation with local authorities in areas of German settlement. Once the German ethnicity of the relocation candidates had been verified and their property recorded, evacuation typically followed promptly, often within weeks or even days. Varying means of transport were used, depending on conditions. The Baltic Germans undertook the voyage by sea, aboard large German liners, while in other regions mixtures of river boats, trains, buses, and even horse-drawn wagons were employed. Sometimes a separation by age and sex was involved. In the evacuation of ethnic Germans from Soviet-occupied eastern Poland in late 1939 and early 1940, for example, most women and children and the elderly took motorized transport, primarily trains, while many younger and middle-aged men lumbered westwards in horse-drawn wagons and carts.[6] In other areas women and children travelled in the relative comfort of passenger trains and buses, while men and older boys rode in unheated trucks or freight trains.[7] The property that the evacuees were allowed to bring with them was strictly limited, often to no more than 50 kilograms of goods and small amounts of money and other valuables per person, although those transported by horse-drawn wagons could usually manage to take more, not least the horse itself. Despite the obvious hardship and stress involved, the transports to the Reich typically ran smoothly, and many evacuees subsequently commented on their general efficiency. One ethnic German from the Dobrudja region of Romania even praised the operation as 'a masterpiece of organization'.[8]

Nazi propaganda had led most evacuated *Volksdeutsche* to expect, upon arrival in the Reich, swift resettlement into homes and jobs at least equal and probably superior to those they had previously possessed. But only a small minority, composed in the first instance of the first 20,000 or so Baltic Germans evacuated in the late autumn of 1939, experienced anything resembling a smooth and speedy transition to a new, settled existence.[9] Within weeks of their arrival, this group had received farms or urban dwellings recently expropriated from Jews and Poles in the districts of Danzig-West Prussia and the Warthegau. The economic opportunities available to these Baltic Germans, in town and country, were generally superior to those they had left behind, and many were initially happy with their new conditions, in material terms at least, even if some wondered about the origins of their new possessions and suffered from mental and psychological strains caused by the sudden transformations in their lives.[10]

For most others, arrival in the Reich inaugurated a lengthy period of uncertainty and waiting, typically in holding camps and other similar institutions, as will be discussed below. As the Nazis' over-ambitious ethnic re-engineering projects were increasingly foiled by practical realities, most of the uprooted ethnic Germans never got to try their hand at colonizing the newly conquered east. But even for those ethnic Germans who ultimately did get resettled in the Reich's eastern territories, primarily in the districts of Danzig-West Prussia and the Warthegau, reality ultimately did not live up to the promises of milk and honey originally made by the Nazi propaganda machine, particularly over the longer term.

To be sure, in material terms many did benefit. In most cases they received sizeable, functioning farms, complete with houses, cattle and farm equipment, vacated by forcibly dispossessed Poles and other local residents, some of whom stayed behind as poorly paid and ill-treated agricultural labourers, enhancing the wealth and power of their German overlords. But some of the ethnic Germans found that their new material situation compared unfavourably with what they had left behind, and most had considerable difficulty adjusting to the conditions in the new settlement areas. Some of the problems were of a technical and professional nature. A Bessarabian German resettled in the Warthegau, for example, subsequently complained that the 'very strange' local 'methods of farming' had caused him 'a good deal of trouble and worry'.[11] A more general sense of unease and uprootedness was promoted by the Nazi policy of disrupting existing village and other communities by scattering *Volksdeutsche* from a particular locality to different parts of the eastern territories in order to homogenize the German community and to pre-empt potential opposition. Some also struggled with their consciences; in the words of one resettler, 'it was always an unpleasant feeling for me and my family to be sleeping in a house that had been seized from its previous owners'.[12] As the fortunes of war gradually turned against the Third Reich, armed resistance and sabotage became yet another increasingly serious problem for the German resettlers, especially in the conquered Polish territories.[13] Under such conditions, few of the newcomers could feel particularly settled or comfortable, and one of them later described the post-resettlement conditions in the East as 'the greatest disappointment' in the entire 'Heim ins Reich' enterprise.[14]

However grave the disappointments faced by the German settlers may have been, they paled in comparison with the intense and extremely widespread hardship endured by the residents of the conquered Polish lands who were deported to make room for the newcomers. These brutal relocations, launched by the Nazi authorities in the autumn of 1939, aimed to deprive Polish society of its leading elements and economic basis and to remove Jews and gypsies from the region. The first targets included the intelligentsia and the clergy, landowners, politicians, members of veterans', economic and social organizations, Poles who had settled in the region after the First World War, and persons classified as 'asocials', including the mentally handicapped and physically disabled, alcoholics, prostitutes and criminals.[15] Factory workers and petty office employees were generally left alone, to avoid disrupting economic production. Individuals with any connection to 'Germanness', such as those with German spouses or close relatives in Germany, were also spared. The same applied to other privileged ethnic groups, such as the Kaszubi, Mazurzy, Silesians and Ukrainians. Many decisions depended on the backgrounds of the incoming German resettlers: migrants from Volhynia, Galicia or Romania typically needed farms, whereas those from the Baltic states mainly required urban housing and employment. Deportations were conducted accordingly.

Regardless of their backgrounds, the German resettlers were supposed to find everything they needed in their new apartment or house, workshop or business. Therefore, the owners of the most desirable residences were typically the first to go. The decision to put someone on the deportation list was made by township mayors and district superintendents on the basis of intelligence materials, seized Polish documents and the advice of local Germans, who were often very well

informed. Personal animosities, prejudice or pure greed also frequently contributed to the decisions.

On the day before the expulsion, the institutions overseeing the enterprise delivered to the police and the gendarmerie secret lists of the persons to be removed.
The operations were always conducted with strong assistance from the SA, the SS,
the police and – particularly in the first months of the occupation – the
Selbstschutz, the paramilitary organization of local Germans. In order to surprise
the targets and to find them at home, the expulsions were usually carried out late
in the evening, with whole villages or town quarters sealed off by armed forces.
The officials then entered the chosen houses and apartments and delivered the
relocation orders, in most cases in writing. The documents listed the names of the
people to be resettled and enumerated their many obligations and few rights. The
latter included an entitlement to take with them a small amount of personal
belongings, initially 12 kg and from spring 1940 25–30 kg per adult. Children
were allowed half this amount. The permitted items included personal effects and
documents, bedding, eating utensils, a small supply of food, a modest sum of
money, and a wedding ring. Sometimes the time allowed for packing did not
exceed fifteen minutes. The rest of the deportees' possessions, including savings,
jewellery, bonds and works of art, were confiscated – or simply looted.
Occasionally Poles were ordered to cover their beds with clean sheets before
vacating their homes because 'those who will take the place over tomorrow must
find everything clean'.[16] Such behaviour reflected not only care for the incoming
inhabitants but also the Germans' conviction that the changes would be permanent
and irreversible.

Even the most difficult situations produce coping strategies. In the case of the
expulsions, these included escapes, temporary absences, the hiding of valuables,
and so on. In an attempt to stop escapes and the uncontrolled removal of possessions, on 13 November 1939 the German administration of the Warthegau technically prohibited Poles and Jews from moving residences and from 'emigrating'. In
practice, however, permissions to leave for the General Government were issued
without particular formalities, albeit on the condition that the 'émigrés' abandoned
all their possessions.[17] Sometimes people nevertheless managed to take along
valuables, but only in rare cases were they able to bring these into the General
Government, where such items could prove vital for survival. Jewellery and valuables were confiscated in the course of frequent searches in the interim camps and
transports. Wealthy Jews were searched with special brutality, and in response they
often attempted to salvage their remaining possessions by depositing them with
Christian house servants, who were controlled less diligently.[18]

To confuse the Poles and to pre-empt any opposition, the Germans deliberately
conducted the expulsions in unpredictable patterns. Evading expulsions was somewhat easier in rural than in urban areas, partly because the marking of farms
assigned for resettlement was a clear indication of impending danger. In addition,

the relations between German and Polish communities were less strained in the countryside than in the cities. Germans sometimes warned their Polish neighbours or purchased their belongings. Hiding was also easier in the countryside.

By the spring of 1940 it became clear that Poles living in villages had managed to develop efficient defence mechanisms. If the expulsions had uprooted some 75 per cent of their intended targets in the early days, once Polish society had recovered from the initial shock, the figure soon fell to around 25 per cent. Even when the Germans started searches, sweeping forests and rigorously observing the rules for personal registration, the figure still remained as low as 40 per cent in some regions.[19] Overall, however, the majority of those on the relocation lists, seeing little possibility of resisting, did accept their fate and only tried to minimize their material losses. People strove to prepare themselves as effectively as possible, packing the most necessary items in advance and often storing bundles of essential foodstuffs in corridors or entrance halls.

Along with the sudden departure from home, the interim camps and the transportation to the General Government proved particularly traumatic for the expellees. Chaos and poor organization characterized the relocations, particularly in their earliest phase at the turn of 1939/40. The first collection points were market halls, factories and other incidental sites. Because the infrastructure and resources did not match the number of the migrants, the expellees often found themselves locked up for days – sometimes even weeks – in interim camps, subject to racial and economic screening. The first interim camp, chiefly for landowners and the intelligentsia, was set up in Cerekwica on 26 October 1939, and others soon followed. The largest, through which 31,400 persons were transported to the General Government, was located in Poznań. These camps were closed in spring 1940 with the introduction of a new organizational scheme, according to which all migrants from the Warthegau had to pass through Łódź. The Łódź camp remained operational until the end of the occupation.[20] Other interim camps included Potulice, Toruń and Tczew in the Danzig-West Prussia region, Działdowo in the Ciechanów district, and similar sites in Silesia.[21] Many of them, including Potulice, Toruń-Rudak and Działdowo, were again used as collection points after 1945, this time for Germans awaiting expulsion from post-war Poland.

The conditions in the interim camps were appalling, particularly during the first phase of the relocations. In the small Kalisz camp, for instance, the inmates had to sleep on bare cement floors. The big camps were not much better. In Poznań, the Germans used former storage buildings of the Polish army. The premises held 4,000–4,500 people. Only some of the internees were provided with wooden beds; others slept on straw spread over concrete floors. Sanitary conditions and food were very poor. These problems forced both the prisoners and the guards to look for ways to reduce the hazards and to improve the living conditions. The fact that approximately one fifth of the internees were children aggravated the situation. Self-organization of the internees helped a good deal. The so-called Polish

Committee, which was active in the camp, managed to obtain assistance from the outside, including packages from relatives and friends, establish workshops, improve the sanitary conditions and the supplies, and provide medical aid. The Committee strove to offer cultural and sporting activities and religious assistance. From the beginning of 1940 living conditions in this camp improved. But the low number of fatalities – a minimum of twenty-six, chiefly among the elderly and infants – was primarily an achievement of the internees.

Prolonged camp life – albeit under conditions far less stringent than those faced by the interned Poles – was an experience shared by most of the ethnic Germans transported into the Reich. Only a small minority of the relocated *Volksdeutsche* underwent prompt resettlement in the East. For the others, arrival in Germany heralded a lengthy period of uncertainty and institutionalization, as they found themselves trapped within an interlocking system of camps run by the Liaison Office for Ethnic Germans (Volksdeutsche Mittelstelle, VoMi), the Nazi organ primarily responsible for their welfare. The VoMi operated no fewer than 1,500 camps throughout the Reich specifically for the ethnic German resettlers. As in the case of the Polish internees, most were not purpose-built camps as such, but sites originally designed for other activities, such as schools, cloisters and monasteries, even hospitals and mental institutions, some of which had just been cleared of their previous occupants by the killing squads of the Nazi 'euthanasia' programme.[22]

Three different kinds of camp existed within the VoMi system. The first – the transit camps (*Durchgangslager*) – were temporary, makeshift structures, often located outside the Reich proper, through which the resettlers passed towards the end of their journey. During their stay, which usually lasted no more than two or three days, they had the chance to rest, fortify themselves with warm meals, and receive appropriate medical care. Next, they were taken to larger assembly camps (*Sammellager*) within Germany, in which they typically remained for up to a week while being examined and processed by Nazi authorities. Once these procedures had been completed, the inmates were transferred to one of the observation camps (*Beobachtungslager/Umsiedlerlager*) scattered around the Reich. In theory, they were supposed to stay for only a few weeks for a period of quarantine, additional testing and observation, after which they were to be taken to their new homes, ideally in the Reich's new eastern territories. But in practice many of the ethnic Germans languished in the observation camps for months or even years as the Nazi project of ethnic re-engineering and forced Germanization in the East gradually ground to a halt. Even in January 1942, well over two years after the launching of the 'Heim ins Reich' programme, more than 125,000 resettlers were still stuck in camps, and for tens of thousands this routine continued throughout the war.[23]

For most of the evacuated ethnic Germans, camp life was a confusing and increasingly alienating experience. To be sure, things often started on a relatively high note in the initial transit camps, which many perceived as a welcome refuge from the emotional and physical strains of their journey into the unknown. One resettler from North Bukovina, for example, was deeply impressed: 'There was a clean station, new uniforms and German Red Cross nurses busily hurrying to and fro, attending to the women and children and especially to the weak and the invalids. Coffee was poured out for us and we began to have medical attention. It was as though it were the middle of a long period of peace.'[24] But this positive perception soon began to change, in part because of the complex and mystifying series of tests and examinations to which the newcomers were subjected in the assembly and observation camps. Some of the procedures were straightforward enough, including assessments of the resettlers' property compensation claims and occupational capabilities. But there were also political evaluations and – most significantly – racial screenings, conducted by the SS under the guise of routine medical examinations.

The results of the racial classifications were of fundamental importance for the unwitting *Volksdeutsche*, most of whom had no idea that they were undergoing anything other than somewhat odd 'heart and kidney tests' and an unrelated 'selection' of who was to be settled where.[25] In reality, the ethnic Germans were divided into three categories, primarily on racial grounds: the 'O-cases' (*Ost*), the cream of the crop, valuable enough for colonization duties in the newly conquered eastern territories; the 'A-cases' (*Altreich*), those of slightly inferior Germanic stock, to be resettled within the old Reich; and the 'S-cases' (*Sonderfälle*), a smaller group deemed to be racially dubious and usually slated for additional camp life, followed by deportation back to their areas of origin or to the General Government in occupied Poland.[26]

Although some of the O-cases did receive expedited opportunities for resettlement in the East, the majority of the ethnic Germans, particularly those in the other two racial categories, spent many months in various observation camps, typically growing increasingly discontented. The very conditions of their confinement irritated many. As one camp veteran bitterly recounted, 'they were keeping us there like prisoners; we were not being treated like resettlers but rather like convicts'.[27] The perceived arrogance and condescension of the camp authorities often exacerbated such resentment. In one camp, for example, adult resettlers from Dobrudja were being retaught how to read and write German, while also being subjected to an array of arbitrary rules, such as a ban on 'l[ying] down during the day'.[28] Corruption and other abuses by camp leaders occurred frequently. Sheer boredom was another problem for many, despite the sporting and cultural activities and other diversions available at most camps. To be sure, boredom became less of an issue from the spring of 1940, as all able-bodied resettlers were ordered to work at local farms or businesses and growing numbers of young men were drafted into the military or the labour service. But these measures also stoked additional discontent among the ethnic Germans as extended families were broken up and the reality of local employment made permanent resettlement in the East seem an ever more remote possibility.[29] In addition, a wide range of practical, everyday problems continued to antagonize the newcomers: overcrowding, insufficient or qualitatively poor food provision, and a variety of cultural tensions, often epitomized by religious clashes between pious ethnic Germans and their anti-Christian Nazi hosts. As the disappointments piled up, growing numbers of resettlers apparently muttered things like: 'If we had known what expected us, we would not have come.'[30] Many also expressed a desire to go back to their former homelands, but in most cases the Nazi authorities banned such moves. Usually only the old, weak or racially and politically unreliable were given permission to return, at their own risk and expense.[31]

Again, however, the hardships faced by the ethnic German internees did not match the cruelties endured by the 'non-Germanic' population of occupied Poland, which found itself at the mercy of the Nazi authorities. Forced transports from German-annexed areas into the General Government began in late 1939. These deportations took many more Polish lives than had the holding camps, particularly during the autumn and winter of 1939–40, when harsh weather and poor organizational conditions exacted a deadly toll. An average transport included twenty to thirty railway cars, or some 1,000 persons, assembled at interim camps, collection points or railway stations, usually with little care for heating and provisions. The first transport, launched on the night of 30 November 1939, lumbered around the General Government for several days before finally reaching its destination in Ostrowiec Świętokrzyski. Subsequent shipments, dispatched in equally difficult conditions, moved somewhat faster. Transportation facilities were scarce because trains sent to the General Government were often utilized by the German authorities for other purposes. Although the Germans reorganized the deportations in February 1940, the losses of life remained high, up to several dozen per transport. Finally, from May 1940, all deportees were routed through interim camps in Łódź because the city had good railway connections with the entire General Government. Between 6 May 1940 and 20 January 1941 ninety-two shipments involving 91,956 people were dispatched from Łódź.[32]

Theoretically, the commanding officer of each transport was expected to hand the deportees to Polish officials, who in turn were to place them with local families. But in most cases the relocated were left to their own devices. Those who had relatives or friends in larger cities, particularly in Warsaw, often tried to make their way there. The remainder were dependent on Polish or Jewish charity organizations, at least in the first weeks after the relocation.[33] Their situation was difficult, especially in small towns that had no facilities to accommodate them, but charity organizations managed to help many of the deportees, thanks in large part to generous individual donations.[34]

Substantial assistance was also provided by the Delegacy of the government-in-exile, whose first Delegate, Cyryl Ratajski, was a member of the Labour Party and himself expelled from Poznań. The Delegacy quickly established its Western Bureau, a special branch to assist the deportees, particularly artists, teachers and scientists. The last two groups immediately began illegal teaching, creating educational structures for all levels from primary to higher education. In 1943/4 more than 2,000 students attended secondary school, and 777 received their underground secondary school certificate. In November 1940 the University of the Western Territories, which continued the traditions of the University of Poznań, was established in Warsaw. Secret university courses were also run at other locations with large concentrations of deportees, including Kielce, Częstochowa, Ostrowiec and Świętokrzyski. In 1945 no fewer than 754 university diplomas were issued on the basis of these courses, and another 725 followed a year later. Research was also conducted, primarily in history and German studies. 1941 saw the opening of the Western Seminar, which in 1944 expanded into the Western Institute in Poznań that still continues to function.[35]

The deportees were settled in the parts of the General Government that had the most developed resistance structures, i.e. Warsaw, Cracow, Kielce, Lublin, Częstochowa and Radom. This circumstance, together with the fact that a large percentage were young or veteran soldiers or both, resulted in many wholeheartedly joining the resistance movement. The underground organization 'Fatherland', founded in Poznań in September 1939, established its Warsaw unit three months later to maintain contact with the political underground and to assist the deportees. In the spring of 1941, as a result of its activity, the 'Western Corps', a special military unit consisting of soldiers from the Wielkopolska region, was established. Numbering between 240 and 300 officers and soldiers, this organization was incorporated into the Home Army in 1944. Deportees from the territories annexed by the Reich also fought in other military organizations, including the right-wing National Military Forces and the Peasant Battalions.[36]

Research on the forced migrants in the General Government between 1940 and 1944 remains insufficient. Information on the deportees quickly disappears from the reports of the charity and underground organizations, which partly reflects successful adaptation. The conditions in the General Government were not as difficult as those faced by the people transported from Poland's Eastern Borderlands to Siberia or Kazakhstan, to be discussed in the next section; there was no language, cultural or religious barrier. In addition, many of the deportees in the General Government were educated, which facilitated their adaptation. Particularly for the younger people who had no property ties to the Poznań or Łódź regions, integration proved rapid. Little is known of returns after the war, which began on an individual basis, without institutional assistance, as soon as the front had passed westwards in January–February 1945.[37] Frequently, the returnees found their homes plundered or destroyed.

To close this section, another large-scale deportation programme aimed at clearing Poles, Jews and others from the path of planned German settlement deserves brief discussion, both for its brutal impact on the deportees and its subsequent significance for the post-war memory of forced migrations in Poland. This was the failed Nazi drive to create an area of German settlement in eastern Poland, in the Zamość region, which precipitated extensive expulsions of the local population between November 1942 and August 1943.

Unlike the earlier expulsions from areas incorporated into the Reich, these deportations targeted entire villages rather than individuals selected according to specific criteria. The classification of the deportees was usually done after the expulsions, at collection points. In December 1942 the Government Delegacy reported:

> The division [of the deportees] into classes is done after a personal interview of the *Prüfer* individually with each inhabitant. The result of that examination is recorded on a red card, and the entry under the rubric *Urteil* – where the appointed 'class' is inscribed – determines the fate of the Pole. ... Those assigned to the first group – 'Deutschstämmige' – remain in place. Group two – young persons of both sexes, able to work – are sent to Germany as labourers. The third group – the better farmers and particularly healthy elements capable of work – remain in place, but will be relocated to villages for the Poles. Group four – racially unwanted elements – are sent to labour camps, where, according to Globocnik's own words, they will soon die.

> The *Prüfer* are SS-men with special training. Their evaluations are based on local documents and interviews with the given individual but in practice depend on the person's appearance. Amongst the deciding factors are such physical features as an inclined forehead, slanting eyes, protruding cheekbones, Semitic looks, etc.[38]

The most traumatic and deadly fates awaited those who ended up in the Auschwitz-Birkenau or Majdanek extermination camps, including nearly the entire Jewish population. But the situation in the smaller camps in Zamość, Zwierzyniec and Budzyń was also appalling. Terrible sanitary conditions, no medical assistance and poor provisions resulted in many deaths: of the 36,389 people arrested in the summer of 1943, for example, as many as 514 died before the classification described above had even begun.[39] Mortality rates were particularly high among the roughly 3,200 elderly persons and the 2,150 children under twelve shipped to villages in the Warsaw district, particularly among the children whose parents had been sent to concentration camps or to forced labour. The fate of the children, both those who arrived in the villages near Warsaw and those who were sent to the Reich for 'Germanization', caused great agitation in the General Government – and provoked widespread acts of charity. In late 1942 and early 1943, for instance, as the transports stopped in Warsaw, volunteers bribed German guards to try to release the children.[40] When circumstances allowed, the deportees also received assistance in their new places of settlement.[41]

The people expelled from the Zamość region – like those deported from Poznań or Łódź – lost their possessions. They were allowed to take only a small piece of luggage and had to leave everything else behind. It was therefore only natural that villagers threatened with deportation attempted to flee with their most valuable movables. Entire localities were suddenly deserted.[42] While women and children sought shelter with relatives or hid in the forests, occasionally visiting their homesteads, most men joined the guerrilla fighters.

Whereas in the territories incorporated into the Reich deportations hindered resistance, in the Zamość region and, to a degree, in the rest of the General Government they fuelled it. In December 1942 guerrilla units started a campaign of burning villages taken over by Germans, which led to skirmishes with the German police. On 1 January 1943 the Polish Home Army carried out operation Wreath II, stopping railway traffic on the lines used for the deportations.[43] The Germans reacted with further brutalization of the relocations, whose last phase – from late June to early August 1943 – was characterized by the 'pacification' of numerous villages, featuring the burning of farm buildings and the execution of the inhabitants.

The return of the deportees started during the German occupation; peasants reclaimed their land as soon as German settlers ran away or were evacuated. Once the front had passed the area in July 1944, the returns became more frequent. The last to come back were the approximately 33,000 forced labourers shipped to Germany. Very few of the roughly 2,000 individuals sent to Auschwitz survived, and the search for the children taken from their families continued for years. After the war, the deportations from the Zamość region became one of the foremost components of Poland's 'politics of history' – the struggle to shape the public memory of the Second World War and the German occupation.

5.2 Deportations into the USSR

Although Nazi Germany and its policies of conquest and demographic re-engineering were the direct or indirect cause of most forced migrations in wartime and early post-war Europe, the Soviet Union also had a major role in carrying out forced population movements in the region. The best-known Soviet contributions came with the various expulsions and 'population transfers' at the end of the war. But the Soviets also engaged in a related practice: the forced shipment of hundreds of thousands of captured civilians and military personnel into the interior of the USSR, generally for forced labour.

Although the Soviets targeted a number of Eastern and East-Central European nationalities for these shipments, Germans probably constituted the largest ethnic contingent, with an estimated total of some 380,000. The deportations began from the ethnic German communities of Romania, Hungary and Yugoslavia in December 1944 and January 1945, as the Red Army pressed westwards, and continued from some of Germany's eastern provinces, particularly Upper Silesia and East Prussia, until April 1945. The usual procedure was for men and women of a suitable age – normally between their late teens and mid-forties to early fifties – to be arrested by the Soviet military, interrogated and examined, and, if found acceptable, detained for a time in an internment camp and then shipped eastwards in tightly packed cattle trains. The transport conditions were typically very harsh, with overcrowding, poor food provision and insufficient heating, and reports indicate that significant numbers of the deportees perished in transit. At the end of the train journey, which could last up to several weeks, the survivors were put to work in Soviet labour camps, carrying out predictably demanding physical duties. For many the sojourn in the Soviet Union proved long and arduous. Although some of the German labourers were released as early as late 1945, the final wave of discharges did not occur until 1949, and up to 100,000 may have died as a result of the deportations.[44]

The treatment given to these German deportees was in large part an extension of practices introduced and honed by the Soviets during earlier waves of similar transports. Highly important and formative were the four waves of eastward deportations conducted between February 1940 and June 1941 from the parts of interwar Poland occupied and annexed by the USSR in 1939, known in Polish parlance as the Eastern Borderlands.

The first two deportation waves of February and April 1940, which targeted soldiers, foresters, local government officials, landowners, policemen and family members of these groups, highlighted the strained ethnic situation of eastern Poland. The relocations provided an opportunity to settle personal and inter-ethnic scores, particularly in rural communities, where ethnic divisions were deepest and from where most of the deportees came. In the memoir literature one finds a recurring element: a local Jew, Ukrainian or Belorussian accused of denouncing Poles to the authorities and assisting in their deportation. It seems that this alleged mass collaboration of Belorussian or Ukrainian peasants with the occupiers can be explained on not only ethnic but also pragmatic grounds. Unlike the German-run relocations from the Warthegau, which consisted of numerous dispersed actions, the Soviet relocations from the Eastern Borderlands were massive, meticulously prepared operations, executed in a very short period, usually just one day. Such operations necessitated the mobilization of extensive resources, including local collaborators. The satisfaction allegedly voiced by many of the locals was painful to the victims, although instances of sympathy and help were also numerous.

An element of surprise was crucial for the smooth functioning of the forced relocations. Particularly in the first round of deportations, the Soviets were remarkably successful at keeping their victims in the dark, despite the extensive preparations. So total was the surprise that although the operations began on the night of 9/10 February, Polish resistance leaders in Lwów did not learn of them until 12 February.[45] To retain a similar advantage, subsequent deportation waves followed set procedures, too. Like German officials in the Warthegau, NKVD functionaries in the Eastern Borderlands commenced the operations in the evening or at night.

The instructions issued by the Deputy Commissar for Internal Affairs on 17 January 1940 ordered that the deportations be conducted in a 'humane' manner, allowing 500 kg of luggage per family – including clothing, personal items, utensils, money, valuables and food for a month – and two hours for packing. But what really mattered was the attitude of the NKVD functionary on the ground. In many instances the deportees were given just a quarter of an hour for packing and allowed no more than 15 kg of luggage per person. This was chiefly dictated by what the NKVD intended to do with the possessions left by the migrants. Only a portion was transferred to collective farms or other state-owned economic institutions. Some went to the families of local Soviet administrators, some to persons relocated from territories along the Soviet–German border, and some to the poorest local inhabitants. Predictably, then, many people wanted the deportees to leave with as little as possible, and many of the abandoned possessions were looted immediately.

Although the deportations from the Eastern Borderlands resembled those from the areas incorporated into the Reich or from the Zamość region at this initial stage, subsequent events were very different. There were no interim camps in the Eastern Borderlands. The deportees were brought to the nearest railway station, from which they departed after a short wait, usually no more than two or three days. The Soviet-run relocations, unlike the German ones, were police-administrative operations, planned and conducted by a specialized bureaucratic apparatus. In the first deportation of 9/10 February 1940, 100 trains carried off 139,000–141,000 migrants; in the second deportation of 13 April 1940, 61,000 people were dispatched in approximately 50 transports.

According to official regulations, each train transport was supposed to consist of a specific number of appropriately equipped carriages.[46] The regulations also specified the maximum number of persons per carriage, the level of food rations and medical assistance, and the number of guards. But often these rules were disregarded, which greatly affected the deportees' experiences. The fact that the journey usually lasted two to three weeks aggravated the situation. Hot meals were issued rarely, and the deportees were largely left to their own resources. Most of the memoirs emphasize the appalling sanitary conditions: no possibility of washing, and an uncovered opening in the floor of the carriage as a lavatory. During the winter, when the temperature often fell below –40°C, a lack of heaters and fuel was a common problem. Whereas cold was the chief killer in the winter, in the summer the heat took its deadly toll, as the appalling sanitary situation spread diseases very rapidly. Most memoirs portray the transport conditions as the most traumatic – and deadly – element of the whole deportation. One must note, however, that deaths during the transports were generally fewer than the plentiful memoir literature suggests. According to relatively trustworthy official Soviet data, the average death rate did not exceed 1 per cent. The transports to Siberia in February 1940 reported a mortality rate of 0.7 per cent. Most of the fatalities occurred among small children and the elderly.

The social make-up of each deportation wave affected the mortality levels. The first wave of February 1940 was composed primarily of 'full' families. They were chiefly inhabitants of rural areas, accustomed to difficult living conditions and often well provided with food. For these reasons the losses were comparable to those of the transports of April and June 1940. The victims of the 'second deportation' were primarily family members of previously arrested men: women, children and the elderly. There were relatively few children among those deported in June 1940; the majority were adults, originating from the cities and representing 'white collar' professions.[47]

The decisive influence on the experiences of the relocated was their final destination, which varied greatly, given the deliberate dispersal of the deportees to twenty-one different Soviet republics, territories and regions. The victims of the forced migrations of February 1940 were slated chiefly for forestry and mining in the far north, western Siberia and the Krasnoyarsk and Altai territories.[48] The deportees of April 1940 were sent primarily to northern Kazakhstan, where the majority were employed in agriculture and others in industry and construction. Most of the forced migrants of June 1940 went to western Siberia and the north. The last wave of May–June 1941 was directed to Siberia and Kazakhstan.

After the trains had reached their destinations, the deportees were divided into groups and sent to their places of settlement, sometimes still many days' travel away. This last segment of the journey was usually undertaken in lorries, horse-drawn carts or sometimes ships. At the place of settlement, the convoy guards handed the deportees to local NKVD units, who, together with functionaries of the local administration, allocated living quarters. Theoretically, each family was entitled to an individual room, with no fewer than three square metres per person, but in most cases this regulation was ignored. Shortages of housing, construction materials, foodstuffs, clothing and medical assistance were universal. This did not necessarily result from negligence but from the chronic scarcity that haunted the USSR and from strict centralization, which prevented unorthodox decision-making. However, the deprived situation of the Polish migrants also reflected their low status.

Those designated for work in the forests were usually placed in so-called 'special settlements', rigorously overseen by the NKVD. These deportees dwelled in primitive barracks, with more than ten families in each. The victims of the 'second deportation' of April 1940 had better living conditions. At least theoretically, they enjoyed many of the rights of normal citizens of the USSR. Unlike the earlier deportees, they were not isolated in separate, guarded settlements but were allowed to mix with the local population. However, they were primarily women, children, elderly people and – to a great extent – members of the former Polish elite, not accustomed to manual labour and difficult living conditions.

The first months were the worst for the deportees, but in time they began to adapt. Survival necessitated coping strategies, particularly in the hardest jobs, such as mining or forestry, and in areas with the worst living conditions. To a large extent, these strategies were borrowed from local society. Deportees learned how to avoid and simulate work, and how to bend the rules to their advantage. They developed local connections and learned how to acquire better work and housing and higher rations. They built personal contacts and liaisons with the locals. The most significant obstacles to adaptation in the Asian republics were cultural differences and the language barrier. Interestingly, the cultural gap was less stark in Siberia, where dietary customs and sanitary habits were similar to those in Poland.[49]

Another strategy for survival was the attempt to maintain old customs and standards of behaviour, including religious practices, although such conduct often provoked misunderstandings. Keeping to one's own ethnic circle and limiting outside contacts was another common behaviour pattern. Frequently, old prejudices and conflicts, such as Polish–Ukrainian or Ukrainian–Polish–Jewish animosities, were also transferred with the people.

Hunger was a shared experience for all the deportees. The tiny food rations were normally issued only to those who worked, and not all the deportees found work. Even those who were employed could not afford to buy expensive food on the black market with their low wages. The deportees were also burdened with numerous taxes, partly to cover the NKVD's expenses. Those who had managed to bring some belongings were in a better situation because they could barter various items for food. The army settlers proved industrious in acquiring foodstuffs; sometimes they also tried to acquire plots of land to produce their own food. Members of the former privileged classes generally abstained from such initiatives, not only because they lacked farming skills but also because they counted on rapid liberation. However, the members of the intelligentsia also enjoyed some advantages; they understood the circumstances better, were psychologically more flexible and resilient in extreme situations, had in many cases some knowledge of the Russian language, and coped with the Soviet system more effectively. Artisans, relatively rare among the deportees, were also 'privileged'; they could find jobs without major difficulty.

Hunger and general hardship caused many losses during the first months of the deportations, particularly among children and the elderly. Vitamin deficiency and dystrophy were the most frequent causes of death. The precise number of fatalities among the deportees is still unknown, but it was considerably lower than the estimates of 300,000 to 900,000 that still circulate in Poland. According to official data, the deportees of February 1940 suffered 10,864 fatalities, i.e. 7.7 per cent. Of those deported in June, some 1,900 died, i.e. 2.4 per cent. In the deportations of April 1940 the death rate was probably no higher than 2.5 per cent. Hence, one can assume that up to mid-1941 the number of the deceased was approximately 15,000. Somewhat paradoxically, the death rate rose sharply after August 1941, when the deportees were released because of the so-called 'amnesty' (discussed below). This was caused by a general deterioration of living conditions in the USSR following the German invasion.[50]

The outbreak of the German–Soviet war and the establishment of diplomatic relations between Moscow and the exiled Polish government in London changed the status of the Polish deportees in the USSR. The supplementary protocol of the so-called Sikorski–Maisky agreement of 30 July 1941 provided for an 'amnesty for all Polish citizens who are currently deprived of their freedom in the USSR, as prisoners-of-war or for other reasons'. They received the right to choose their place of residence, albeit only within appointed regions, and to possess a document confirming their identity. By September 1941, 265,000 people had been released from areas of forced settlement, although local administrators, desperate for labour, often resisted their liberation.[51]

An exodus of Poles to the south of the USSR ensued immediately after the proclamation of the 'amnesty'. Survival in the south was supposed to be easier, and a Polish army was being formed there. This mass migration, which probably encompassed over 100,000 people and was undertaken primarily by the young and fit, was so spontaneous that the Soviet authorities were alarmed by their inability to control it. But the journeys, which frequently took weeks, caused further fatalities and weakened the migrants, making them vulnerable to maladies common in the southern USSR, such as malaria. As a result, by 1943 approximately 11,500 Poles had died in Uzbekistan, Kirgizia and Kazakhstan alone.[52]

The hope of finding better living conditions in the south proved illusory. Neither the Polish army nor the Soviet administration could provide effective aid, and the charitable institutions organized by the Polish Embassy in Kuibyšev became operational only in late 1941. Conditions improved by early 1942, but the capabilities of the Polish government remained very limited, despite aid received from organizations such as the American Red Cross and the purchase of provisions from outside the USSR. The civilian population had to rely on its own industry or on the Red Army's aid. Poor conditions also prevailed in the soldiers' camp in Buzuluk. Inadequate provisioning was one of the reasons why the Polish army was transferred to Iran. By the end of August 1942 as many as 78,600 soldiers and 38,000 civilians had been evacuated there.

The Polish army's withdrawal to the Near East contributed to the deteriorating relations between the Polish government-in-exile and Moscow. The growing conflict immediately affected the treatment of Poles in the USSR. To survive, they still had to perform hard labour. Because of the war, conditions went from bad to worse, as work quotas were drastically raised and food rations systematically reduced. Despite the 'amnesty', many former deportees and GULAG prisoners were denied the right to Polish citizenship. They were issued Soviet documents instead, sometimes by force. This 'passportization', as the undertaking was called, affected nearly 191,000 Poles. Some 165,000 were granted Soviet citizenship; over 24,000 refused it or had their Polish citizenship acknowledged; some 1,500 were imprisoned. Interventions of the Polish authorities made little impact. The Embassy's delegacies were closed or their activity hampered, and in April 1943, when diplomatic relations were severed, the delegacies stopped functioning altogether.

The Polish population in the USSR was not left entirely without protection, however. As Stalin severed relations with the Polish government-in-exile, he recognized the rival structures established by Polish communists. In the spring of 1943 the Union of Polish Patriots emerged and took over most of the charitable functions of the Embassy's delegates. First, the Union's functionaries tried to determine the number of Poles in the USSR. This proved no easy task, partly for technical reasons, including the somewhat cavalier attitude to problems of ethnicity and citizenship evident in Soviet statistics. For instance, the official statistics acknowledged as Polish only ethnic Poles and Jews, treating the Ukrainians and Belorussians who had been Polish citizens prior to 1939 as Soviet citizens. In June 1944 the number of Polish citizens in the USSR was estimated at over 329,000, in September 1944 at approximately 260,000 and in December 1944 at circa 229,000, half of whom were ethnic Poles and the other half Jews.[53]

By spring 1944 the military units formed by the Union of Polish Patriots had managed to recruit some 40,000 soldiers, mostly former deportees. Extensive attention was paid to appearances and symbols of national identity; the uniforms reflected pre-1939 Polish models, and Polish national and religious traditions were observed. Army service freed tens of thousands of men and women from hard labour and improved morale among the Poles in the USSR. The humanitarian work of the Union of Polish Patriots was of enormous importance: Polish canteens, kitchens, nursing homes, orphanages, libraries and schools were established, and vigorous publishing activity began.[54] Because the situation of the Poles was still very difficult, particularly in the far north, efforts were made to move them to the milder climate of the south. Thanks to these efforts, over 70,000 people were resettled in 1944.

These were only provisional measures, however, as the principal aim of the Polish institutions in the USSR was to help with survival and future repatriation. The September 1944 agreements between the Polish Committee for National Liberation and the authorities of the neighbouring Soviet republics provided only for the resettlement of the Poles resident in those republics. The return of ethnic Poles and Polish Jews from deep within the USSR became possible only with the Polish–Soviet agreement of 6 July 1945. People who had been Polish citizens prior to 17 September 1939 received the right to renounce their imposed Soviet citizenship and migrate to Poland.

Repatriation proved a difficult task, hampered by problems with verifying Polish citizenship, by the bureaucracy, by the dispersal of Poles around Soviet territories, and by transportation difficulties. The first official transport left Kiev on 29 January 1946. Many repatriates were in very poor health and deprived of all belongings. After their return, they required much more medical and material assistance than the people from the Eastern Borderlands, to be discussed below.

The necessity of providing them with furnished flats, houses or farms frequently led to conflicts with local administrators and with other deportees.[55]

The transfer of people from the interior of the USSR took longer than similar operations from the Eastern Borderlands. The Soviets stopped the repatriations at the end of 1947, but, thanks to the interventions of Polish authorities, small groups were still able to return in 1948.[56] The 'evacuation' was finally closed by an agreement of 30 April 1949. Altogether some 268,000 ethnic Poles and Jews left the USSR.[57] It is difficult to establish how many people managed to cross the river Bug on their own initiative, outside official channels. It is equally difficult to tell how many Poles remained in the USSR, for whatever reason. Some failed to register for repatriation in time or could not prove their citizenship; others were imprisoned. Even after the war, the NKVD arrested and deported to the USSR tens of thousands of resistance activists, Upper Silesian miners and others, both from the Eastern Borderlands and from within Poland's post-war boundaries.[58] Some were released relatively quickly, but a large proportion, if they survived, had to await the so-called 'second repatriation' of 1955–9.[59]

5.3 Flight and Expulsions of Poles and Germans at the War's End

The deportations of Poles, Germans and others into the interior of the USSR were ultimately overshadowed by the massive westward flight and expulsion that affected both Poles and Germans during the war's final stages and aftermath. These latter population movements were far bigger in numerical terms, and their political and psychological significance also loomed large, in good part because of the complicated links between the forced migrations, the accompanying territorial and political changes, and the resulting international, societal and individual problems. The legacies of the expulsions therefore became key challenges of the post-war era for Poles and Germans alike.

5.3.1 Relocations from Poland's Eastern Borderlands, 1944–6

With memories of the Soviet occupation of 1939–41 still fresh in most people's minds, the Poles of the Eastern Borderlands had few illusions about what awaited them when pressures for a departure began to grow by 1944. But decisions to stay were not rare, at least in the early phase of the relocations. Such decisions were motivated by hopes for positive results at the peace conference and by a will to resist 'Russification' and to uphold the Polish character of the region. The latter motives were most common among the intelligentsia. In the end, the decision to go usually prevailed, frequently aided by propaganda from Warsaw. In rural areas of Belarus and Lithuania, where local authorities sought to persuade and sometimes to coerce Poles to stay, the support provided by delegates from Warsaw often proved decisive. Lithuanian and Ukrainian officials complained that Polish delegates exceeded their authority. Stanisław Ochocki, the Delegate-in-Chief of the Polish Government in the Lithuanian Soviet Socialist Republic, was arrested and sentenced to fifteen years in the GULAG.[60]

The role of Polish institutions in inducing Poles to migrate westwards was only secondary, however. The major factors tipping the balance, apart from the desire to live within Poland, were fear and coercion. The coercion assumed various forms, ranging from outright terror, such as the anti-Polish activities of the Ukrainian nationalist underground, to arrests, forced 'Ukrainization or 'Lithuanization', and professional and educational discrimination. The reasoning that it was much better to go west, where the future was uncertain, than to stay and eventually go east, where the future was more certain, also influenced decisions. This reasoning was strengthened by the ongoing forced deportations to the Donbas coalmines and other regions of the USSR. There was widespread fear that the registration for relocation to Poland would be suddenly cancelled or not continued beyond the initial deadline of 1 April 1945. It also seems that Poles from the Eastern Borderlands acknowledged as early as 1945 that the changes in the region's political geography were final and irreversible.

As previously stated, the experiences of urban and rural inhabitants differed extensively, particularly in Belarus and Lithuania. Whereas the authorities were keen on getting rid of the more nationally conscious townsfolk, they tended to obstruct emigration from the villages, fearing a decline in agricultural production.[61] Registration and emigration were also impeded in areas where ethnicity had been a problem before 1939, such as Belarus.[62] But the priorities of the Soviet authorities were not the only factor privileging urban emigration. Urban inhabitants were also nearer information sources, registration points, Polish relocation institutions and transport facilities. As a social group, they were far more mobile than peasants, who had to worry about their farm animals and machines. Characteristically, there were far fewer negative reports about transport problems from Lithuania than from the Ukraine or Belarus. To a large extent, this was due to the fact that urban residents constituted 44 per cent of the migrants from Lithuania but only 26 per cent of those from Belarus.

The main factors preventing people from registering for relocation were 'uncertainty about the future of the repatriates in Poland and terrifying transport conditions'.[63] The experiences of Poles relocated 'voluntarily' were in fact remarkably similar to those of Germans expelled from Poland and Czechoslovakia. Although the Eastern Borderlands had no interim camps like those through which many Germans had to pass, the same basic rule applied: people had to assemble before the trains arrived. The migrants typically had to spend 10 to 15 days at railway stations, waiting, 'without the possibility to cook a hot meal, with nowhere to hide from the rain and wind, and constantly exposed to robbery during the night'.[64] The relocation procedure provided numerous opportunities for corruption. Bribes had to be given to board a train, to facilitate its departure from each station, and particularly to speed its release from the halt at the border, which could otherwise take days.

Much more traumatic than the bribery, however, were the inhuman conditions that typically prevailed during the transports, which were conducted in open coal carriages and sometimes lasted for weeks. Inefficient organization, carelessness, corruption, violence and looting all contributed to the misery. Because of the unrealistic deadlines set in the relocation agreements and the mounting pressure of the Ukrainian nationalists in Volhynia, the transports were not disrupted even in severe frost during the winter of 1945/6. In the coldest months between October 1945 and March 1946, 346,033 people were relocated.[65] The difficulties were exacerbated by the poor condition of the trains and the tracks and by war priorities. In May 1945, for instance, on the orders of Marshall Žukov, all the carriages had to be sent further west immediately. The migrants were simply thrown out of the trains that were supposed to take them to Poland.[66]

The combination of harsh weather and organizational inefficiency led to a relatively high loss of life, although we still have no reliable data on mortality rates. However, transports such as the one that left Buczacz in East Galicia on 19 November 1945 with 961 people on board – including 143 children – in fifty-five carriages, only fourteen of them roofed, and took twenty-one days to cover the 250 km to Rzeszów were nothing out of the ordinary. Four people on this train froze to death just during the stop at the border.[67]

The situation on Polish territory was little better. It took from 28 November to 8 December 1945 to transport a group of highly qualified workers, originally from Lwów, between Katowice and Wrocław, for example – a distance of some 200 km. Upon arrival in Wrocław, 'the carriages contained three corpses that had been travelling with the living for several days, numerous children with frostbite, bad colds, and everybody in a state of extreme exhaustion'.[68]

Reaching one's destination did not necessarily improve things. Sometimes the migrants were taken off the trains at remote locations, where they again had to wait for weeks before being assigned living quarters or farms. Makeshift huts composed of planks, bags, cardboard and other similar materials immediately arose along the railway tracks. The poor sanitary conditions promoted the rapid spread of disease, particularly dermatological and digestive illnesses. A report by an official who visited Popielowo and Siołkowice in Lower Silesia in July 1945 makes distressing reading: 'The repatriates' encampments are a scene of dire poverty and misery. Apart from an acute lack of food, diseases decimate the repatriates. The same applies to the livestock. Myriad flies fodder on the leftovers, the nearby dung heaps, and the animals, providing a macabre picture. The repatriated families that managed to find lodging in nearby villages are frequently removed by the Russians to make room for Germans.'[69] The reports emphasized problems and abuses, but there were many staging points which, despite the difficulties, operated without reproach, such as Brynów, in Silesia, or Cracow.

According to the 'evacuation' agreements made with Soviet representatives, the Polish migrants were allowed to take along two tons of possessions, but governmental decrees often failed to translate into reality. Much depended on local conditions and officials. The Lithuanians, for example, treated all home utensils as furniture and disallowed their removal. Attempts to take away items of furniture led to their confiscation.

The possessions left by the 'evacuated' population in the Eastern Borderlands were supposed to be evaluated by bilateral Polish–Soviet commissions and compensated in the places of resettlement. However, only possessions whose ownership could be proved with official documentation were to be considered, which caused problems. In many cases people had to depart in a hurry or under pressure, frequently leaving behind even the evacuation cards that certified them as migrants. Hence they lacked all documentation of their lost possessions. It also happened that the Lithuanian, Belorussian or Ukrainian authorities deliberately declined to issue such certificates to the Poles in order to destroy all traces of a Polish presence in these lands and to pre-empt any future claims.[70]

Having arrived in Poland, the migrants without documentation had difficulty obtaining compensation for their lost possessions. Although the authorities tried to adopt a 'flexible' attitude, those who lacked proof of their former possessions were in a weak position.[71] Nor was documentation the only problem. According to the Polish Workers' Party, farms given to the resettlers were to range between 7 and 15 hectares in size, regardless of how much land they had left behind.[72] With town properties, the rules were even stricter – the housing provided in western Poland was not to exceed 220 square metres per family, which was particularly unfair to those who had possessed large homes. Through 1947 the State Bureau for Repatriations (PUR) made 153,473 decisions regarding compensation, including 123,187 agricultural and 30,286 urban objects.[73] Certain legal matters concerning the resettlers' possessions remain unresolved even today.[74]

The 'repatriates' from the Eastern Borderlands were not unaware that they might be viewed as a competing, alien element by the local population. Letters sent by refugees attest to feelings of alienation and estrangement.[75] But resettlement in Poland proper was still the lesser evil for them. There they were relatively close to their native territories, in some cases had family nearby, and faced less unfamiliar surroundings than in the areas further west that had been taken over from Germany. However, settling the 'repatriates' in central Poland was contrary to the plans of both the central government and the local authorities of western Poland. For political and economic reasons, Warsaw was eager to repopulate the so-called Regained Territories taken from Germany as swiftly as possible, even at the cost of chaos. The authorities were also unwilling to leave in central Poland, in the vicinity of the new border with the USSR, elements that for obvious reasons were negatively inclined towards the Soviets. The local elites of these regions, in particular the Communists, who were still in the process of establishing their control, wanted to avoid political disturbances. Moreover, the 'repatriates' partly upset the clientele system under construction at the time because, at least theoretically, they were the first in line for the farms and houses seized from Germans and Ukrainians, which the local population also coveted. In practice, the locals usually prevailed. 'The settling of a repatriate – as was reported from a town 130 km north-west of Warsaw – is very difficult ... The Polish Worker's Party prohibits settling these people in the district, threatening them with removal. All formerly German farms are in the hands of trustees, allegedly all very meritorious to the State. The removal of such a trustee is impossible. The Secretary of the Polish Worker's Party said that he would obey only orders coming from the political parties, and none other.'[76]

Similar attitudes towards the relocated also prevailed in other parts of 'Old Poland', where slogans such as 'Wielkopolska for the Wielkopolanians' or 'Pomorze for the Pomeranians' were becoming increasingly popular. The situation was strained to the point of homicides being committed against the newcomers from the East. Directives from Warsaw failed to change the picture, and the 'repatriates' from the Eastern Borderlands and far-away regions of the USSR managed to take over only 21.4 per cent of the farms in central Poland previously possessed by Germans. As late as the spring of 1956, a journalist from the weekly *Po prostu* published a story about a farm assigned to a woman 'repatriated' from the Lwów region that was still being held by a local peasant who refused to hand it over to its legal owner.[77]

Theoretically, the situation should have been different in the western regions, where land and housing were plentiful, even if the weakness of the administrative, economic and social systems, combined with a lack of security, caused problems. But even there the local administration was bent on having its own policy vis-à-vis the settlers. The district of Wałbrzych is a case in point. At the end of 1945, local decision-makers wanted to stop the influx of migrants from the USSR into the area, claiming that most of the 'repatriates' were farmers whereas the region needed urban professionals.[78] There were also attempts to settle the relocated population in areas where all the individual farms had already been distributed so that the newcomers had to be placed on former landed estates, which were being turned into collective farms, or added to farms already assigned to other settlers.[79] Such actions caused understandable opposition. As a result, entire transports were sent back to central Poland.

It must be stressed, however, that the resettlers from the East formed a minority in the former German lands. The dominant majority, both numerically and politically, came from central Poland. Conflicts between these groups were also fuelled by the fact that, following 'repatriation', the majority of the Polish Jews who had survived the war in the USSR settled in the west, chiefly in Wrocław and Szczecin, which often exacerbated anti-Semitic attitudes.[80] A May 1946 report from Szczecin, for example, states: 'the ethnically Polish repatriates are greatly embittered by the problem of the influx of the Jews. ... Their big influx to Szczecin causes a ferment that is not yet visible on the outside but has the potential to decrease greatly the attractiveness of Pomerania, which is low anyway.'[81]

The conflict between resettlers from the East and people originating from 'Old Poland' was sufficiently serious to be reflected in the press and to cause the central authorities to intervene. As the future was to reveal, integration progressed faster in those territories of 'Old Poland' where the migrants from the East were dispersed. In areas where they lived in more concentrated groups, such as Wrocław or Gliwice, they were better able to retain their separate identity, and the memory of the lost Eastern Borderlands endured much longer.

5.3.2 The Expulsion of Germans

The flight and expulsion of Germans from Eastern and East-Central Europe unfolded in several successive but partly overlapping phases, stretching from the final stages of the Second World War well into the post-war years. The process began with the large-scale evacuation and flight provoked by the steady westward march of the Red Army. The first organized evacuations occurred in the autumn of 1943, as the withdrawing Wehrmacht transported ethnic German communities out of the southern Soviet Union, particularly from the Crimean peninsula and its vicinity. By the following autumn the ranks of westward-bound German civilians had swelled by further hundreds of thousands as additional major evacuations took place from Romania, Hungary, Yugoslavia and Slovakia, and many other ethnic Germans fled on their own initiative. This growing mass of refugees was composed overwhelmingly of women, children and the elderly, as most younger men had by then been drawn into the Third Reich's war machinery in one way or another. Their evacuation and flight was typically a wrenching experience, involving sudden departures from familiar environments, long and arduous treks towards undefined destinations, often in horse-drawn carts or even on foot amidst the chaos and destruction of total war, with enduring danger to life and limb.[82]

The situation grew even more chaotic and difficult once the Red Army began to press into the eastern parts of Germany proper in late 1944 and early 1945. Plans for the evacuation of the civilian population – which here too consisted primarily of women, children and the elderly – had been drawn up for most of the Reich's eastern districts, and in some areas these blueprints were implemented effectively. In the town of Insterburg in eastern East Prussia, for example, the local authorities managed to move the vast majority of the population to relative safety further west through decisive evacuation measures.[83] But such forceful action formed an exception; more typically, planned evacuations of civilians were delayed until the last minute because of the unwillingness of Nazi leaders to admit military defeat and the ongoing bureaucratic battles among different party, governmental and military authorities. All too often the result was utter chaos that left large numbers of German civilians stuck and exposed as the military front line swept through their domiciles. A German doctor caught up in the Red Army's big offensive of January 1945 described the reality faced by many of his compatriots laconically but aptly:

> No evacuation order. In the afternoon German soldiers alone and in groups: tired, nervous, wounded, some without weapons, fleeing westwards. Air-raid alarm again. Bombs. Panic amongst the thousands at the train station. No shelter ... The first Russian tanks drive into town. Utter despair.[84]

Despair and terror at the thought of the Red Army's arrival were widespread sentiments among the residents of eastern Germany during the war's final stages. Building in part on pre-existing anti-Slavic prejudices, Nazi propaganda had played up the supposed dangers of Soviet *Untermenschen* for years; the resulting negative stereotypes were then reinforced by actual events, themselves amplified and distorted by additional Nazi propaganda, so that the stage was set for full-scale panic. The small East Prussian village of Nemmersdorf, which the Soviets had briefly captured, only to massacre its entire population of at least seventy civilians in late October 1944, became a byword for Russian bestiality, loudly proclaimed by Goebbels' propaganda machinery.[85] Petrified by the prospect of other atrocities, large numbers of Germans made desperate efforts to flee the Reich's easternmost provinces on their own in late 1944 and early 1945, as organized evacuations floundered.

Many got away successfully, often under extremely difficult conditions. In an arguably representative effort, a pregnant 22-year-old woman residing in the western Warthegau tried to flee on foot through the ice and snow of a mid-January 1945 night, got caught in the firing line just outside her home town, turned round, milled around the local railway station along with thousands of others, boarded an overcrowded westbound train and, after a long and hazardous journey by train, car, foot and horse carriage, ultimately reached relatives in Pomerania. Like the vast majority of German refugees at the time, she regarded her flight as a temporary measure and fully expected to return home once the fighting had ceased. But, like millions of others, she soon discovered that her escape had been only the first stage in a longer process that would culminate in renewed flight or expulsion once more systematic efforts at the permanent removal of Germans from areas slated for incorporation into post-war Poland, Czechoslovakia or the Soviet Union got under way.[86] According to recent estimates, some six million Germans resident within the Reich managed to escape from the Red Army's path, either by fleeing on their own or by being evacuated by the authorities.[87]

For hundreds of thousands of Germans, however, attempted flight ended prematurely in the face of more powerful forces. In most cases it was the advancing Red Army that stopped them, but occasionally rapidly retreating Wehrmacht units also blocked their path. Under such circumstances, many sought to return to their homes, thereby joining the minority – particularly older, well-settled residents of the countryside – who had all along preferred the relative stability of their familiar surroundings to the uncertainty and danger of an escape through the middle of a war zone.

The Germans who, willingly or not, remained in the parts of the Reich overrun by the Soviets in late 1944 and early 1945 were promptly exposed to the full fury of the Red Army. Brutalized by the bitterness of warfare on the Eastern Front and egged on by anti-German propaganda, Soviet soldiers paid back to the German population some of the cruelty that had earlier been inflicted upon them and their compatriots.[88] Although subsequent eyewitness testimonies suggest that many front-line troops 'behaved decently' towards German civilians, often simply stealing valuables such as 'watches and rings' before rushing on to the next military engagement, the reserve units that followed usually left a very different impression.[89] These troops, which sometimes stayed as an occupation force in conquered German territories, promptly unleashed a comprehensive reign of terror, whose main features included rampant plunder and theft, severe and often indiscriminate violence, including frequent murder and – probably most strikingly – endemic, at times even systematic, rape of German women. In one Danzig neighbourhood, for example, Russian soldiers reportedly raped every woman they could find, 'without exception', from 'very young girls to old women of over 60', often very brutally, and similar scenes took place at many other locations.[90] The violence was at its worst in the easternmost parts of the Reich, particularly in East Prussia and Silesia, during the first days following the Red Army's arrival. Further west and later on the brutality tended to taper off, but even then an atmosphere of lawlessness and menace remained, particularly for women, who continued to be frequent victims of rape and other forms of sexual assault well after the fighting had ceased.[91]

The Red Army's initial bursts of violence gave the German civilians a foretaste of the arbitrary lawlessness that ensued during the subsequent transitional period of rule by Soviet occupiers and re-emerging national authorities, particularly in Poland and Czechoslovakia, which in turn paved the way for the large-scale expulsions that would shortly follow. Violent retaliatory outbursts against Germans by Poles and Czechs became commonplace once the heavy yoke of Nazi rule had been lifted. One of the most extreme examples was the anti-German uprising that engulfed Prague in early May 1945. The roughly 200,000 Germans left in the city found themselves at the mercy of revolutionary guards and other elements bent on exacting revenge for the suffering imposed on them by the Nazi regime. Predictably, men in Wehrmacht or SS uniforms were prime targets, many of them summarily shot, but the civilian population was also subject to a wide array of abuse. Most were chased out of their homes; incarcerated in makeshift detention centres, such as schools, sports stadiums or cinemas; beaten or otherwise abused and humiliated; and put to work in menial, physically demanding tasks, such as clearing rubble from the streets. Sexual assault, rape and murder were also widespread.[92]

The picture was similar, albeit somewhat less extreme, in many other areas of German settlement that came under Polish or Czech control at the war's end. An initial wave of violent harassment, assault, rape and at least occasional killings was typically followed by arrests and interrogations aimed, at least in part, at identifying people implicated in the Nazi regime. As the next step, Germans were typically forced to perform heavy labour. Rubble clearance was one common task, but duties more laden with symbolic significance were also frequent. One resident of West Prussia, for example, subsequently recalled being forced to use his bare hands to exhume the badly decomposed bodies of Poles executed during the Third Reich, and similar assignments were handed out at many other locations as well.[93]

Measures to exclude Germans from normal interaction in civil society followed. In imitation of some of the exclusionary policies adopted by the Nazis against perceived racial and other enemies, Polish and Czech authorities imposed a series of restrictions on the Germans under their control. Germans were forbidden from using public transport or going to bars and restaurants; their bicycles, radios and telephones were confiscated; they were sometimes required to wear special armbands identifying them as Germans and banned from publicly speaking their native language; their food rations and personal freedoms were severely curtailed. Large numbers were also locked up in concentration camps of various sorts, some of which had been used by the Nazi authorities only a few months before. Several, such as Lamsdorf in Upper Silesia, gained rapid notoriety for the vindictive brutality routinely inflicted on their inmates, and many exhibited high mortality rates, caused primarily by poor sanitary and dietary conditions and by the resulting communicable diseases, although deliberate physical abuse and murder also played a contributory role. The primary purpose of the camps, however, was to isolate Germans and to channel them into forced labour, often outside the camps themselves, in agriculture, mining and various types of post-war reconstruction.

The cumulative impact of these and other measures was to turn the Germans into social pariahs, beyond the rule of law and marginalized in an increasingly desperate existence of hardship and deprivation, as reflected, among other things, in heightened suicide rates. To make matters worse still, these exclusionary measures were accompanied by an even more discouraging development: the arrival of growing numbers of Polish and Czech resettlers, who began to take over businesses, residences and farms previously owned by the Germans. Under these conditions, the various German communities were rapidly losing their bases of existence, and thoughts of escape began to preoccupy many of their increasingly desperate members.[94]

Even as the ground was being prepared for their massive westward expulsion, during the winter and spring of 1945 large numbers of Germans still continued to move in the opposite direction, both voluntarily and involuntarily. The involuntary migration consisted of the forced transports of labourers to the Soviet Union discussed above. The voluntary migrants were hundreds of thousands of returnees heading back to the Reich's eastern provinces from which they had recently fled. Unaware of ongoing Allied deliberations that were paving the way for their former domiciles' separation from post-war Germany and eager to reclaim their old homes, the returnees endured long and hazardous journeys that typically ended in disappointment. Many were forced to turn back along the way, and those who did reach their destinations were often shocked by the sheer devastation they found. 'Desolate, empty, abandoned, covered in rubble and dirt', was how one returnee summarized his impression of his old home town in East Prussia, while another found that 'there was practically nothing left of my old apartment, not even in the thoroughly plundered basement'.[95] Additional disappointment and shock then promptly followed, as the returnees became subject to the ostracism and terror that had already been imposed on the rest of the German population.

Despite the forced labour transports and the continuing efforts of displaced Germans to return to their former homes, by the late spring and early summer of 1945 massive numbers of Germans again began to stream westwards as systematic expulsions from areas under Polish and Czechoslovak control began. Eager to create a *fait accompli* before the victorious Allies met to discuss Germany's eastern borders and accompanying population transfers at Potsdam from mid-July, military and civilian authorities in both countries rushed to rid themselves of unwanted Germans. These early, pre-Potsdam expulsions were characterized by loose central direction, with extensive local and regional initiative, and by particular harshness and brutality in the treatment of the targeted Germans. The operations – labelled the 'wild expulsions' in subsequent German parlance, in contrast to the more coordinated and somewhat more orderly post-Potsdam actions – commenced by May and reached a crescendo in June and July. They occurred primarily in border regions – areas east of Poland's projected western frontier along the Oder and Neiße rivers and various parts of the Sudetenland – and generally followed a roughly similar pattern.

Military contingents or other armed units burst into villages and settlements inhabited by Germans and ordered the residents to vacate their homes at very short notice, often half an hour or even less, and to take along property that they could carry, up to a maximum of some 20 kilos. Once the Germans had complied, their dwellings were typically plundered and many of the goods they had brought with them seized by militants or local residents. Physical abuse occurred frequently. The Germans were then herded towards the borderline, often in long columns on a forced march, although lorries and trains were sometimes used over longer distances. The marches, which could drag on for days, were punctuated by additional plunder, beatings, sexual assault, even deliberate killings. The bulk of the Germans were taken to the western side of the Oder–Neiße line or of Czechoslovakia's boundary with Germany and Austria and then left to their own devices in difficult, overcrowded conditions, although some were interned in camps, pending later deportation. A number of particularly violent incidents accompanied the expulsions. Anti-German riots in the Bohemian town of Aussig (Ústî nad Labem) on 31 July 1945, for example, resulted in at least one hundred and possibly more than a thousand German deaths.[96] The forced march of Germans out of the Czech city of Brünn (Brno) at the end of May culminated in a comparable tragedy as the Germans, refused both entry into Austria and return to Czechoslovakia, languished in no-man's land, plagued by hunger and epidemic disease; some 1,700 of them lost their lives.[97] Although no precise figures exist for the Germans expelled prior to the Potsdam conference, recent estimates suggest a total of over one million, with some 800,000 from Czechoslovakia and roughly 400,000 from areas that were being incorporated into post-war Poland.[98]

Once the Potsdam conference had given formal Allied approval to the 'orderly and humane' 'transfer' of the remaining German populations out of Poland, Czechoslovakia and Hungary, the stage was set for the second, better organized stage of the expulsions.[99] In theory, the forced migrations were supposed to be suspended after Potsdam, pending official authorization for their continuation from the Allies, so that the occupation authorities in Germany could prepare for a renewed refugee influx. But although such authorization was not issued until late 1945 and early 1946 through Allied Control Council directives and various bilateral agreements, expulsions in fact continued in the meantime from both Poland and Czechoslovakia. In both countries, the process grew more coordinated and organized, as exemplified by the selection of the deportees. Even in the pre-Potsdam period the Germans had not been targeted completely at random; the authorities in both countries had made some effort to retain workers with badly needed specialized skills, and in Poland ethnic Germans who had been citizens of pre-1939 Poland were more likely to be held back than their compatriots who had lived in the inter-war Reich. Both selection principles now came to be applied more consistently. In particular, the least economically productive sectors of the German population – the old, the sick, children and women with young offspring – were typically targeted first, whereas able-bodied men and women – especially workers with specialized skills – were often kept behind, to be exploited as cheap labour. This led to many families being torn apart, sometimes for years.

Another contrast with the pre-Potsdam period was that although organized expulsions continued, often in as brutal and abrupt a fashion as before, Germans were increasingly encouraged to flee on their own initiative. In Polish-controlled East Prussia, for example, the authorities exhorted Germans to 'leave their areas of residence voluntarily', while in Danzig Germans willing to depart for the Soviet occupation zone were even able to obtain free train tickets during the autumn of 1945.[100] The de facto coercion behind the supposedly voluntary departures was never in doubt, however; the living conditions of the German population remained extremely harsh, and in East Prussia, for example, the call for voluntary departure was explicitly coupled with a threat: 'those who refuse to depart voluntarily will be brought into a camp'.[101] Such coercion worked to the degree that nearly a million additional Germans were resettled from Poland and Czechoslovakia to Germany between August and December 1945.[102]

The final, organized stage of the expulsions, as sanctioned by the Big Three at Potsdam, finally began in early 1946. Significant forced transports took place from Hungary, with some 170,000 ethnic Germans shipped to the US zone of occupation in 1946 and another 50,000 or so to the Soviet zone during the following two years.[103] The bulk of the expulsions still originated from Poland and Czechoslovakia, however, and the numbers grew very large, particularly during 1946, the peak year of the operations, when nearly 4.2 million Germans were expelled from the two countries. Detailed numerical data on this phase of the expulsions can be found in section 4.3 above and will not be repeated here, except to restate that by the time the operations finished at the end of the 1940s, they had brought a total of some 12 million refugees to the two German states, approximately eight million to the Federal Republic and another four million to the GDR.[104] According to the most reliable estimates to date, some 600,000 Germans lost their lives in the course of their flight and expulsion, mostly in war-related incidents during the early stages of the process.[105]

The organized, post-Potsdam expulsions that began in 1946 followed a very similar pattern across different locations, particularly in the main staging grounds of Poland and Czechoslovakia.[106] In this phase, nearly all Germans, with the primary exception of small groups of specialized skilled workers essential for the local economy, were targeted for deportation. As before, the Germans were rounded up very abruptly, with no more than about twenty-four hours' notice, and allowed to take along only a limited amount of baggage, usually no more than 40 kilos, and small amounts of money. They were then marched or driven to special collection points or, alternatively, simply transferred to such points from the camps or other sites in which they had already been incarcerated. After some arbitrary inspections of their possessions – in the course of which items tended to disappear – and a variable period of waiting, ranging from hours to days or even weeks, they were shipped westwards, in the vast majority of cases by train, although a sea link between Poland and western Germany also existed for a time in 1946. The train journeys still typically took at least a few days, and often longer, in overcrowded, poorly provisioned and often unheated cattle cars. To be sure, outright plunder, rape and other forms of extreme violence were much rarer than they had been in earlier stages of the expulsion process, and, after a grim start, the transport conditions generally improved from the spring and summer of 1946.[107] But even in late 1946, at the end of the peak period of expulsions, frightening scenes persisted. According to a Polish report about a train carrying deported Germans from Breslau to Lower Saxony in December 1946, for example, during this particular six-day journey in tightly packed, unheated cattle cars, the 1,543 deportees – composed mostly of children, the elderly and the sick – received only one cold meal and four cups of warm coffee and arrived in western Germany with no fewer than 58 fatalities.[108] Even in their most organized phase, the expulsions were thus neither very orderly nor particularly humane, Potsdam provisions notwithstanding.

For those who survived the flight and expulsion, arrival in what was left of Germany was a confusing experience. Particularly during the early stages of the forced migration process – amidst wartime flight and evacuations and the immediate post-war expulsions – reaching the German border brought only limited relief, as the tired and traumatized refugees were left to fend for themselves in chaotic conditions of destruction and deprivation, with no organized support networks. The experiences of a 75-year-old woman expelled from East Brandenburg to Frankfurt an der Oder in June 1945 were illustrative – and arguably in some ways representative. As she subsequently recounted, she and her companions were 'left to [their] fate' once they had crossed the river Oder. The city of Frankfurt had been flooded by 'hundreds of thousands of refugees,' with new ones arriving steadily. There was 'nowhere to stay and no bread'. Her first four nights were spent 'in the tunnels of the main railway station', waiting for an opportunity to board one of the westbound freight trains. Once that had proved impossible, because of the 'thousands' of others who tried to storm every outgoing train, she and several others set out on foot, covering '15 to 20 kilometres each day, in constant fear of being attacked by the Russians', sleeping 'in the forests or in abandoned barns' and eating 'carrots and potatoes from the fields', until she managed to reach relatives living further west.[109]

Later on, after Potsdam, the situation improved, as special reception camps, supervised by the Allies but operated by German authorities, were established for the incoming refugees in all the affected occupation zones. These camps, too, were insufficient in various ways, particularly at first. An inspection of the Ragelswick camp in the Soviet occupation zone in the autumn of 1945, for example, revealed poor sanitary conditions and severe overcrowding, with fifty-four people crammed into a room measuring only seven metres by three.[110] But at least an infrastructure was being created to provide the refugees – particularly those who arrived during the more organized, post-Potsdam expulsions – with a place where they could find rest, sustenance, medial care and other kinds of initial assistance after the tribulations they had endured. The resulting sense of relief was clear in the testimony of an East Prussian woman who reached the Soviet occupation zone in early 1946 after a long and traumatic journey: 'Although the conditions and the treatment at the Blankenburg refugee camp were not exactly ideal, our first reaction was that this felt like heaven. It was an indescribable relief for us to be able to sleep at night in peace and without being disturbed and to get food … every day.'[111]

The initial stay at a reception camp represented merely the tentative first stage in the expellees' long and difficult readjustment and integration into life in post-war Germany. For a significant minority the next step was a residential refugee camp, where some ended up living for years. But the majority were eventually distributed to ordinary communities, particularly rural villages and small towns, which had typically suffered much less war damage than the heavily bombarded bigger cities and were therefore deemed more capable of accommodating the newcomers. The predictable result of a major influx of impoverished strangers into small, conservative communities was conflict, acted out on a number of levels. There was a clash of cultures as different accents, dialects, customs and confessions collided in previously homogeneous and inward-looking areas. However, ultimately most of the almost universal hostility and discrimination faced by the newcomers was rooted in economic realities: at a time of severe scarcity an influx of strangers in search of food, housing, jobs and other valuable commodities was hardly going to be a welcome phenomenon to the locals. Predictably, the expellees, lacking in resources and useful social networks, typically drew the short straw and endured lasting privation, particularly in comparison with the local population, long into the post-war years.[112]

Integration from such beginnings was never going to be plain sailing for the expellees. A sense of deprivation in everyday life, a feeling of rejection and conflict in the new communities, a persistent desire to return to the lost *Heimat*, whose image often grew ever more idealized with growing temporal and geographical distance – all these factors and others militated against quick, enduring adjustments. Some, particularly many members of the older generation, never did adapt very successfully, and even among the younger expellees feelings of cultural exclusion and unresolved identity problems persisted long into the coming decades.[113] But, at least on the social and economic levels, increasing integration did gradually take place, aided by economic growth, internal migration, urbanization and other broad societal and trans-national trends.[114] However, these were all long-term developments, and in 1949 – when Europe's decade of mass expulsions drew to a close just as the two new German states were established – their main impact still lay well in the future. The present remained one of relative hardship and difficulty for most victims of forced population movements, wherever they happened to reside.

–6–

Forced Migrations and Mass Movements in the Memorialization Processes since the Second World War

6.1 Introduction

In the last two decades, memory has become a theme of central importance for historians and social scientists. A quick glance at the tables of contents of history journals and the catalogues of the major publishing houses confirms this, as does the rediscovery of the fundamental work of the French sociologist Maurice Halbwachs, who coined the terms 'social memory' and 'collective memory'.[1] As the French historian Henry Rousso writes: 'Our relationship with the past is subject to evolution and therefore possesses a historicity, which should be brought to light.'[2]

The study of the so-called 'sites of memory' has become particularly popular. After the pioneering collection for France, edited by Pierre Nora,[3] similar collections have been published for Italy and Germany.[4] Related fields that have flourished in recent years include the study of monuments[5] as well as research that draws on contemporary testimonies, based mostly on the methods of oral history.[6] The study of memory and forgetting[7] is an interdisciplinary area par excellence, and it has involved historians, anthropologists,[8] sociologists, people of letters and artists, as well as politicians. It is also of high political significance, because it connects the present with the past, whereby the past 'is called upon' to legitimize or undermine the present. This is especially true of the memory of the Second World War because of its peculiar ideological character.[9] Moreover, there is the sheer extent of the tragedy that the war itself represented. It caused tens of millions of deaths, many of them civilians, partly because of the harsh occupation policies implemented by Germany and its allies, including Japan. It also had severe demographic, social and political effects. These included the extensive border changes and population movements involving Germany, Poland and the Soviet Union, with the forced transfer of millions of civilians. The war's most significant legacy was arguably the division of the continent into two politically and ideologically opposed blocs, which also affected the character of public memory. Particularly in the communist bloc, collective memory was strictly imposed by the respective regimes, although in post-war Western democracies, too, collective memory was shaped by the specific interventions of the state or the ruling classes.

Analysing the linkage between history and memory offers striking possibilities, but it also presents difficulties. There is a risk of being overwhelmed by the sheer volume of sources. Personal testimonies have increasingly assumed not only scholarly but also ethical-public significance. This is perhaps best shown in recent publications on the Holocaust, which express fear of a 'dictatorship of the witness'.[10] This is a reversal of the situation that prevailed in the first two post-war decades, when the victims' viewpoints were largely ignored.

The fundamental risk implicit in the 'over'-evaluation of personal testimonies, which are limited and distorted by the passage of time, is that they prevail over other sources, thereby unduly influencing our perception of past events and our memory. What weight should the historian give to the perception of the individual? And, vice versa, how close is the relationship between the construction of public memory – by ceremonies, monuments, etc. – and private memory? It is not easy to link the public production of memory or specific events – such as the success of a book or historical exhibition – with the perception of those processes and events by individuals. These are some of the significant methodological problems that the field of the 'social history' of memory faces.[11]

Forced migrations have been, and continue to be, at the centre of highly politicized processes of memorialization. These processes are very complex because they have evolved over time and because they have involved, in different ways, those directly affected by the population movements, and their descendants, as well as the rest of society. The forced migrants were uprooted from their social and territorial context, and they typically became victims of not only the war but also often discrimination in their 'new' homelands or, in the case of Soviet prisoners of war and forced labourers, in their original homelands when they returned after the war.[12]

In all the countries of the communist bloc, public memory of the population transfers imposed by the USSR in their sphere of influence remained suppressed for a long time. Persistent private memories, although fading with time, could counterbalance the silence of official memory only to a small extent. Since 1990 we have witnessed an extraordinary revival of acts of commemoration, ranging from the erection of monuments to the re-evaluation of previously neglected sources.

The collapse of official memory after 1989/90 gave way to a complex, though fruitful, period of rereading national memories in the Soviet Union/Russia. In the other former communist countries, it reopened old wounds that had previously been covered by the predominant official memory.[13] However, in the West, too, the public narratives of apparent post-war success that had allowed the dramatic memories of expulsion and uprooting to be cast aside had to be revisited. Political shifts, such as Italy's transition to a government dominated by a party of the political right in 1994 and again in 2001, sometimes brought dramatic conflicts over memory to the surface. In Italy this entailed giving fresh attention to the Italians who were expelled from Istria and Dalmatia in the years 1945–53 and whose experiences had been largely confined to private memory or the representations of refugee organizations. For some years now they have been the subject of public controversies and of new official memorialization.[14]

After 1945, questions of memory were particularly crucial for Germany and Japan, the main aggressors – and losers – of the war.[15] In the German case, public and private reflection on the war was complicated by the fact that the country was divided and found itself at the centre of the Cold War.[16] During most of the 1950s and well into the 1960s, the view of Germans as victims prevailed in West German public and private memory.[17] In contrast, the GDR suppressed the memory of the expulsions of Germans, confining it to the private sphere.[18] The unification of the two German states does not yet seem to have produced a genuinely shared collective memory of the Second World War in Germany.[19]

Memories of forced migrations caused international tensions after the Second World War – and in some cases continue to do so even today. The potential claims of German expellees against Eastern European states for compensation, for example, led to political friction in the context of German unification and have periodically made waves since. Internationally, collaborative attempts to define areas of shared memory have started only slowly in the last few years and encountered many problems. The eastward expansion of the European Union might contribute to the shaping of common memories; however, the question again arises as to how much of this is imposed from above, and how much is actually shared by the populations.[20] As the memory of the various forced population movements during and after the Second World War was, and still is, particularly contentious in Germany and Poland, these two cases will be discussed in greater detail in the following. They are both crucial and in many ways illustrative of the general processes that have shaped collective memories since the end of the Second World War.

6.2 Memory and Commemoration of Flight and Expulsion in Germany

6.2.1 The Divided Germany

For more than forty years the forced migration, or forced resettlement, of millions of Germans from Central, Eastern and South-eastern Europe after the end of the Second World War did not feature very prominently, if at all, in German collective memory.[21] The individuals themselves who experienced this uprooting and permanent displacement remembered their personal histories and articulated their memories in individual narratives. Shared, or common, memories of the refugees and expellees developed as well – in West Germany more openly than in the German Democratic Republic. However, for a long time these individual and group memories were not incorporated into the dominant national narrative, nor did they become part of the national patterns of official remembrance and commemoration – or, to be more precise, only those elements of the individual and group memories of the refugees and expellees found their way into the national memory which were seen as politically acceptable or expedient.

A personal testimony – one of many – illustrates how the German collective memory of flight and expulsion was shaped in the post-war period. Annerose Rosan was born in 1928 in the small village of Gilgenau (today Elgnówko) in East Prussia. In January 1945 she fled westward with her parents to escape from the advancing Red Army, and the family initially settled in the village of Morsum near Bremen in north-west Germany. She recalls that the local schoolteacher tried to bring native and refugee children together by staging plays in the local pub, many of which he wrote himself:

> They all followed – with little variation – the same plot: a refugee girl – hard-working, very neat, very pretty – works for a peasant on his farm. The son of the peasant falls in love with her. Against the wishes of his mother, and with the support of the grandfather, they actually get married. In her anger, the mother trips up and sprains her ankle. The young daughter-in-law nurses her in a self-sacrificing way, runs the whole household at the same time, and thus wins the heart of her mother-in-law. All are happy.[22]

The German refugees and expellees not only lost their homes and most if not all of their belongings, but many also lost relatives and friends in the course of their forced resettlement, and their social networks and communities were destroyed. The native schoolteacher in the little village of Morsum most definitely meant well and intended to give the refugees and expellees hope for the future by showing in his plays that they could be integrated into the host society soon – as indeed they would be. However, at the same time his plays denied the newcomers their own personal histories and specific memories because they assumed and almost expected that in the course of successfully settling into post-war Germany the refugees and expellees would lose, or 'shed', their old collective identities and mentalities, and also the specific experiences and individual memories which they had brought with them from the East, and would thus become like the natives.

In the former German Democratic Republic this was much more obvious than in West Germany. Here, the refugees and expellees were officially referred to first as *Umsiedler* (resettlers) and then as *Neubürger* (new citizens), and from 1950 the category disappeared altogether from all official statistics. The East German government pursued a policy which made it clear that their loss of home was permanent. The state doctrine of anti-fascism which was imposed from above to define the 'new' society of the 'socialist nation' after 1945 and the notion of a specific

GDR citizenship left no room for the memories and experiences of the refugees and expellees from the East. The experience of flight and expulsion and everything related to it were excluded from the official discourse and remained so until the last days of the East German state.[23]

The case was nothing like as clear-cut in West Germany, but ultimately the refugees and expellees did not fare much better, even though themes of flight and expulsion were taken up both in the political discourse and in popular culture in the 1950s and well into the 1960s. Refugees and expellees were officially referred to as *Heimatvertriebene* (expellees from their homes), and maps, including those used in schools, continued to show Germany with the borders of 31 December 1937, labelling the territories east of the Oder–Neiße line as 'temporarily under Polish administration' (or Soviet administration, in the case of the northern part of East Prussia). From 1947/8 onwards, the displaced were allowed to form their own cultural and political organizations, which became powerful interest groups in the first decade of the Federal Republic; their meetings and rallies were attended by leading politicians. In their manifestos and official speeches, these organizations propagated the right of the refugees and expellees to return to their homes in the East (*Recht auf Heimat*), and, with the exception of the Communists, all the main political parties and pressure groups officially supported this position.[24] In addition to the major parties, the newly formed Bund der Heimatvertriebenen und Entrechteten (BHE) was particularly dedicated to representing refugees' demands; it entered a number of coalition governments both at the state (*Länder*) and the federal level.[25]

Numerous special museums and institutes for the history of the German populations in Central, Eastern and South-eastern Europe, as well as annual conventions (*Heimattreffen*) and a wide range of cultural activities of the refugees and expellees, were generously funded by the West German state.[26] Schools were requested to teach about the 'German East' (*der Deutsche Osten*) and its contribution to German culture and Western civilization in general.[27] The introduction of an annual 'East German Week' (*Ostdeutsche Woche*) was encouraged,[28] and a new school discipline, Eastern Studies (*Ostkunde*), was developed, even though this had only a very limited impact.[29]

In 1951 the Federal Ministry for Expellees commissioned the collection of testimonies from individual refugees and expellees for a documentation of their mass flight and expulsion during and after the Second World War. However, the thousands of testimonies gathered in what became a huge research project do not document anything of the life of the refugees and expellees in their old homelands before their displacement. They start with the Red Army approaching the villages and towns, and they focus exclusively on the traumatic events of flight and expulsion – the violence, the hunger, the lootings, the rapes, the countless deaths, the deportations to Poland and the Soviet Union for forced labour and, above all, the continuous and ever-present fear.[30]

Popular culture in the 1950s and 1960s also took up the topic of flight and expulsion. Like the *Dokumentation der Vertreibung*, the novels of this period focused mainly on the outrages which the refugees and expellees suffered before their arrival in the West.[31] In contrast, most West German cinema films showed refugees and expellees as innocent victims of the war who lost everything but did not allow this to get them down for long, and who successfully established new lives for themselves in the West – which made them like the natives there, especially if they were hard-working, tidy, undemanding and, in the case of women, young and pretty. Flight and expulsion were thus trivialized into a soap opera with a happy ending.[32]

However, all these manifestations of flight and expulsion in the public and the popular discourse of West Germany in the 1950s and 1960s (and beyond) did not amount to a true acknowledgement and remembering of the pasts of the refugees and expellees by the West German polity and society. Instead, they represented a highly selective acknowledgement and thus a highly selective remembering: only those aspects of the individual pasts of the newcomers which served a broader function in post-war West Germany were incorporated into the political and popular discourse. The desire was to stabilize a society which had unravelled in the course of war and defeat and to give the new West German state some form of legitimacy and an acceptable form of dealing with the past.

In the political context of the Cold War, the refugees and expellees were useful pawns. Their memories and experiences were instrumentalized, or functionalized, and their sufferings exploited in the propaganda battle with the Soviet Union and communism in general.[33] Both the Western powers and the West German government found it opportune to keep alive the hopes of many refugees and expellees for a return to their former homes by emphasizing that the definite settlement of Germany's post-war borders required an official peace treaty and that until such a peace treaty was concluded, the future of the territories east of the Oder–Neiße line had to be regarded as open under international law. Flight and expulsion were equally useful, to establish that Germans, too, were victims of the Second World War and had suffered injustice and hardship, and to suggest that the crimes committed against Germans were perhaps comparable to the crimes committed by Nazi Germany against the Jews, by implicitly or even explicitly equating both as 'victims driven from their historic homelands because of their "ethnicity" (*Volkszugehörigkeit*)'.[34]

Thus, the life histories of the refugees and expellees were basically reduced to two aspects in the post-war West German collective memory: victims of tragedy and crime in the course of German defeat, on the one hand, and resilient individuals who bounced back against all the odds through their successful integration into the post-war economy and society, on the other. All regional characteristics that were more than picturesque folklore, as well as their personal and group histories before their displacement, were widely disregarded.

The collective memory in both German states was the collective memory as defined by the 'natives'. In the GDR, refugees and expellees were not permitted to develop a publicly visible collective identity based on their common experience of forced displacement from their homelands, and their specific experiences and memories were suppressed. In West Germany, the creation of such a collective identity was encouraged and at times even actively supported, but the refugees and expellees were individualized and socially marginalized, shunted off into a special niche, and became museum pieces. The commitment of the West German state to the cause of the refugees and expellees remained superficial and formal. At best, it helped the refugees and expellees to keep their specific group identity, while at the same time it gave the native society the comforting feeling that it was fulfilling its obligations in acknowledging the past of the refugees and expellees. No shared past of native and refugee populations and no shared collective memory emerged. The overall result, therefore, was ultimately similar in both West and East Germany. The refugees and expellees had to integrate into the post-war polity, economy and society without their memories and experiences getting a proper place in a common narrative of the areas which received them.

The 1960s saw a change in the public discourse in West Germany towards a more (self-)critical assessment of the Nazi period.[35] Willy Brandt, the new Chancellor, a Social Democrat who had fled Nazi Germany, embarked on a foreign policy of rapprochement with Eastern Europe (*Ostpolitik*) and declared that the treaties that his government was concluding with the Soviet Union and Poland gave nothing away that had not been lost long ago. Brand dated the origin of this loss not to 1945 but all the way back to 1933 or even before.

The refugee organizations continued to hold their annual meetings, and testimonies of flight and expulsion were still available, but it was now mostly only the refugees and expellees themselves who took notice of this. The wider population regarded them more and more as relics of the past, whose continued insistence that their loss and pain had to be acknowledged seemed to threaten the newly established dialogue with the Eastern European countries. Politicians, the media and historians alike emphasized the successful integration of the refugees and expellees into post-war Germany and moved on to more 'exciting' topics.[36] The wave of *Alltagsgeschichte* (history of everyday life) which had begun in the 1970s passed over and omitted their historical experience – in contrast to the historical experiences of other social groups such as women or workers, which were given a proper place in public discourse. As a result, the memories of the refugees and expellees were all but obliterated from public consciousness and denied a place in a comprehensive and shared collective memory. This meant that the concerns of this social group became an increasingly easy prey for the political far right.

After the Christian Democrats returned to power in West Germany under Chancellor Helmut Kohl in the early 1980s, it seemed for a moment that the refugees and expellees would again become more connected to the main political discourse. However, the fortieth anniversary of the end of the Second World made clear that West German society as a whole had come to see 8 May primarily as a day of liberation,[37] whereas for most refugees and expellees it still represented unacknowledged loss and suffering: the beginning of their displacement. Almost as if protesting against the prevailing mood, the Schlesische Landsmannschaft, the interest group of those Germans whose homeland had been Silesia, planned to hold their annual meeting in 1985 in Hanover under the slogan: '40 Years of Expulsion – Silesia Remains Ours' (*Schlesien bleibt unser*).[38] It was easy to dismiss this as nationalist rhetoric and just another sign of the continued existence of revisionism and revanchism among the refugees and expellees, but it could also be argued that for the large majority of the members it was an almost desperate appeal to society at large to acknowledge their life histories and group memories in a way that did not simply exploit them for political and other purposes.

During all this time, even those refugees and expellees who were, from today's standpoint, reasonably successful in their 'new' lives in the West kept a lingering feeling that they retained some of the qualities of a stranger, of an outsider, in the regions where they now lived, and that they did not totally 'belong' there.[39] In both German states, the memories of displacement by flight or expulsion and of the new beginning in the West were only handed down within the affected families, and often not even there.[40] Most refugees and expellees tried to tell their stories after arriving in their new homes in the West, but especially in the rural regions most got the feeling that the natives were not interested and did not want to know. Throughout the period from the end of the Second World War until the collapse of communism in Eastern Europe (and perhaps until today), the refugees and expellees had to come to terms with the trauma and the grief over the loss of their former homes and with their memories on their own, outside the public domain, since post-war German society did not offer any collective patterns for dealing with them.[41]

Very few histories of individual German communities and districts, including those which were written recently, make more than passing references to the thousands of refugees and expellees from the East who were taken in after the Second World War. If they feature at all, it is basically as a sudden influx of people which caused tremendous problems for the receiving regions: problems of housing, of feeding, of employment.[42] There are hardly any places of public commemoration of the particular experiences of the refugees and expellees and their contributions to the areas where they settled; where they do exist, they are more often than not in obscure places.[43]

Most refugees and expellees, especially those who had settled in rural areas, saw with feelings of sadness and helplessness that their specific past and the stories they had to tell were more and more regarded as irrelevant by society at large, whilst for them their past and their stories had remained burning issues, becoming for many even more so as they got older. The instrumentalization of their experiences was followed by collective forgetting and suppression. As a result, the refugees and expellees have continued to feel, until today, to a greater or lesser degree emotionally somewhere in-between their 'old' homes, which now only exist in memory, perhaps in some family traditions and in a distant country, and their 'new' homes, which even after fifty years still show a trace of strangeness and of unfamiliarity for them. This marks the complex duality of past and present which is so typical for many refugees and expellees and which they sum up by referring to the place where they were born and grew up as their *Heimat*, and to their home in the West where they have lived for more than fifty years as their *Zuhause*.

6.2.2 Re-sitings of Memory since 1989–90

With the unification of the two German states in 1989–90, a chance opened up for a re-siting of memory and the development of a new cohesive and inclusive narrative. Cautious moves to reappraise flight and expulsion had, in fact, already got under way just before unification. One of the first manifestations was a conference in Göttingen in 1986.[44] A similar reassessment had begun, even more cautiously, in the German Democratic Republic.[45] In both German states the emphasis was still predominantly on the growing-together of native and refugee populations in the receiving areas in the post-war period, but increasingly the individual refugee, the individual expellee and his or her life history were taken into consideration as well. Lutz Niethammer reminded the Göttingen conference that historians needed to accept the challenge of writing a history where the specific experiences of all people could be linked in a meaningful way to a larger context.[46]

At the time of unification, after forty years of separation, West Germans and East Germans had few common experiences and memories left apart from National Socialism, the Second World War and the uprooting many suffered as a consequence of these. This meant that the flight and expulsion of large numbers of Germans from the East became a focus of public attention and discussion again.[47] In the western part of Germany this new interest was also encouraged by the fact that, after the collapse of communism, it became much easier to travel to the former homelands of the German refugees and expellees. Such visits had already taken place earlier, from West Germany since the 1970s in the wake of the *Ostpolitik*, but it had been almost exclusively refugees and expellees that had made these journeys. They had often been ridiculed as 'homesickness tourism' (*Heimwehtourismus*) or 'pilgrimages to the old homelands' (*Pilgerfahrten in die alte Heimat*),[48] but they had the important function of helping the refugees and expellees to come to terms with the dramatic turn which their lives had taken after the Second World War. From 1989–90 increasing numbers of people who had no family connections with these regions travelled there as well, and they discovered similarities between the expelled Germans and the people who live in these areas today, many of them refugees and expellees themselves with similar experiences of displacement.

Writers, novelists, professional historians, the media and even politicians rediscovered the theme of flight and expulsion, raising public consciousness and instigating a public debate on a level not seen since the end of the Second World War. The disturbing pictures from former Yugoslavia contributed further to the sense of the relevance of this discussion. Books about areas formerly inhabited by Germans and the accompanying television programmes on flight and expulsion found an audience far beyond the refugees and expellees.[49] In particular at the local level, new projects were started which explored the composition and identity of communities.[50] Flight and expulsion from the East and arrival and settling in the West were no longer seen as isolated incidents but rather as integral elements of biographies. The impact which these often traumatic events had on the lives of the individuals affected by them moved to centre stage.[51]

A powerful expression of this new approach to the past was Günter Grass's novella *Im Krebsgang*, published in February 2002 (English translation: *Crabwalk*, 2003) and regarded as the first attempt by a major German author to deal in a work of literature with the mass flight and expulsion of German populations from Central and Eastern Europe. The novella tapped into the already simmering debate about what constitutes German historical consciousness and collective memory. It moved beyond the selective remembrance of flight and expulsion and linked the events at the end of the Second World with their origins in 1933 and earlier, on the one hand, and their legacy for the present time, on the other. Grass himself, in the guise of 'Der Alte' (the old man), pointedly acknowledged in the novella that it should have been the responsibility of his generation to put into words the horrors experienced by the German refugees and expellees, but that they had spectacularly failed to do so:

> [His generation] should have found words for the hardships endured by the Germans fleeing East Prussia ... Never ... should his generation have kept silent about such misery, merely because its own sense of guilt was so overwhelming, merely because for years the need to accept responsibility and show remorse took precedence, with the result that they abandoned the topic to the right wing.[52]

Grass was repeating what some politicians and historians had noted earlier: that because of a perhaps well-meant but ultimately false understanding of political correctness, particularly those who thought of themselves as being on the left or the centre-left had avoided acknowledging the specific memories and experiences of the refugees and expellees. The result of this neglect was – and this is the main theme of Grass's novella – that flight and expulsion became an issue of nationalist-conservative propaganda.[53] As early as 1955 the German-Jewish historian Hans Rothfels had pointed out that the past had to be remembered 'in its horrifying totality'.[54] This does not just mean remembering Germans as both perpetrators and victims: it means remembering more than just the year 1945; it means remembering what happened before and what came after and why. Hartmut Boockmann had already emphasized the linkage between these issues some ten years before Grass, pointing out: 'If we Germans do not know what happened to us in 1945, we will also not remember what we had done since 1933.'[55] The moral obligation to remember the victims of National Socialism does not mean that it is not possible to remember the victims of the consequences of National Socialism; indeed, one might argue that one necessitates the other. Recognizing the pain experienced by individuals does not mean negating collective responsibility or guilt.

Grass's novella *Im Krebsgang* intensified the national (and international) debate about how to remember flight and expulsion, and even journals such as the centre-left weekly news magazine *Der Spiegel*, which had shunned this topic in the past, now put it on the front cover.[56] As what can almost be seen as an attempt at a final, or authoritative, statement, the Haus der Geschichte der Bundesrepublik Deutschland (Museum of the History of the Federal Republic) in Bonn opened a national exhibition in December 2005 with the title 'Flucht – Vertreibung – Integration' ('Flight – Expulsion – Integration') in the presence of the Federal President, Horst Köhler, who also acted as the exhibition's patron.[57] The flight and expulsion of Germans was shown in the wider context of twentieth-century forced population resettlements and Nazi Germany's rule over much of Europe. Most critics agreed that the exhibition set a new standard because of 'the sober way' it told 'of grief, loss, farewell, and arrival'.[58] The general public seemed to agree; the exhibition was seen by a record number of visitors.

Historical consciousness, public memory, collective identity, and politics are closely linked. In the case of flight or expulsion, the situation is further complicated by the fact that it affected not only Germany and ethnic Germans, but also Poland, the Czech Republic and the other countries from which German populations were forcibly removed after the Second World War. In all these countries, a reassessment of national narratives is currently taking place.[59] The gradual appreciation of a common European experience of displacement and forced migration, promoted by political and intellectual elites and shared by many of those actually affected, could potentially lead to the formation of a common supranational collective memory of the immediate post-war period. However, in the short run it has instead given rise to new national divisions and even confrontation based on deep-seated fears and traumas, in particular between Germany and Poland and Germany and the Czech Republic.[60]

Political clashes and nationalist rhetoric have focused in particular on the plans of the Bund der Vertriebenen (BdV), the federation of German refugees and expellees, to set up a documentation and information centre dealing with flight and expulsion in the twentieth century (Zentrum gegen Vertreibungen).[61] Critics of this proposal have expressed their fear that it would lead to 'the emergence of an officially sanctioned re-interpretation of the past – indeed a historical revisionism

– which would endanger the social and political discussions which aim at a common European dialogue'.[62] All Polish governments, no matter what their political make-up, and most of the Polish intellectual elite have vehemently opposed such a centre for the same reason.[63] The Red/Green coalition, which governed Germany from 1998 to 2005, kept a careful distance from the project, whereas it was enthusiastically supported by the then conservative opposition. In July 2002 the German parliament passed a resolution in favour of 'establishing a European centre against displacement' as 'a European task' and 'with European partners'.[64] Three years later, in 2005, Germany, Poland, Slovakia and Hungary established the 'European Network Remembrance and Solidarity', with a coordinating office in Warsaw, in order to reappraise their common history in the twentieth century, including population displacements.

The biggest dispute about the Zentrum gegen Vertreibungen is raging around its location: the BdV and conservative groups insist on the German capital Berlin, whereas the Red/Green coalition suggested Wrocław, formerly Breslau, in Silesia, if such a centre was to be set up at all.[65] No compromise seems to be possible at the moment that would not be perceived as a defeat by one side or the other. The Grand Coalition government in Germany, formed in November 2005 under the CDU Chancellor Angela Merkel, has not taken any clear stand yet, despite Merkel's support during the election campaign for the establishment of the centre in Berlin.[66]

There are indications that the exhibition in Bonn was meant to make the establishment of the Zentrum gegen Vertreibungen unnecessary,[67] but this idea was rejected by the BdV.[68] They are pressing ahead with their plans, and a preliminary exhibition under the title 'Erzwungene Wege' (Forced Paths) was opened at Berlin's Kronprinzenpalais in August 2006 in the presence of the President of the German Bundestag. It, too, presents German flight and expulsion in the wider context of the twentieth century.[69] Some commentators were surprised at how similar this exhibition was to the one shown in Bonn, wondering how far it really foreshadowed the intentions for the Zentrum.[70] Others, however, felt that the exhibition amounted to an attempt to rewrite history, thus putting German–Polish relations under great strain – a view shared by most Polish politicians and much of the Polish media.[71]

For the time being, Germany is left with two competing narratives of flight and expulsion.[72] They differ from each other at the moment perhaps less in the overall narrative but definitely in the style and outlook of their presentation. This demonstrates yet again how politicized the memorialization of the flight and expulsion of German populations from Central, Eastern and South-eastern Europe remains even today. The Polish writer Stefan Chwin suggested in 1999 that 'the chance of a normal life and normal feelings' would only come when the generation of victims and witnesses had died, or had at least grown old.[73] In Olaf Müller's novel *Schlesisches Wetter*, the narrator meets an old Polish woman who has lived in

Wrocław, the former German Breslau, since the end of the war and is now witnessing more and more Germans visiting the town. She voices the opinion 'that the Germans could at least wait until we are dead, if they need to come back at all'.[74] All the indications are that there is still quite some way to go before a comprehensive narrative emerges which allows all groups of society to link their individual experiences and memories without attempting to balance the pain suffered by one side against that endured by others. At the moment it seems that the best chance of achieving this goal is within a wider European setting.

6.3 Memory and Commemoration of Flight and Expulsion in Poland

Outlining the actual deportations and expulsions seems a relatively easy task compared to analysing the Polish 'relocation memories' of the forced migrations during and immediately after the Second World War, as they are diverse and complex. Collective memories of forced migrations are formed on several levels; moreover, individual perspectives are dependent on numerous factors.

Predictably, the injustice and trauma experienced by Poles are remembered vividly in Poland, whilst the wrongs committed against others, such as the Germans or the Ukrainians, were widely omitted from the collective memory or even became taboos. The post-war division of the world also influenced remembrance in general and the memories of forced relocations in particular, as they were so closely linked with wartime and post-war changes to the Polish borders. Under communist rule, memories of certain events were either suppressed or thoroughly censored. As a consequence, the memory of the relocations was, to a large extent, reduced to the level of personal experiences and family history. This produced selective memories, strengthened stereotypes, produced popular myths, and created painful voids in the Polish historical consciousness. The memories of those Poles who remained in the West after 1945 and were not subjected to ideological restrictions were distorted as well. They filtered out the multi-ethnic character of the Borderlands to produce a scenario in which the minorities were relegated to the role of stagehands in a purely Polish drama. The fact that for a long time it was impossible to obtain accurate information about the forced migrations in the East gave rise to myths about their magnitude, and when the information became available, hardly anybody attempted to correct the firmly established stereotypes.[75]

Time also shaped the memory of the relocations. In post-war Poland, time was measured by a series of political disruptions – 1956, 1970, 1980, 1989 – which either weakened or strengthened censorship, thereby expanding or narrowing the boundaries of the 'official history'. The changes of 1989 were particularly significant for collective memory. However, the sudden disappearance of ideological restrictions did not mean that politics pulled out of history altogether. It was only the dominant perspective that changed, as the focal point of collective memory shifted eastwards. The sudden interest in formerly forbidden subjects such as the Soviet occupation and the loss of the Eastern Borderlands, the deportations to the USSR and Stalinist crimes, which overwhelmed the media, politicians, scholars as well as the wider public, marginalized the memory of the German occupation and the accompanying mass relocations from the Warthegau, Pomerania or the Zamość region for the entire 1990s.

This phenomenon was all the more important because the forced migrations under German occupation had never been the focal point of historical interest in post-war Poland. Although a number of accounts of these relocations had appeared immediately after the war, when the memories were still very vivid,[76] from the 1950s onwards the topic was taken over predominantly by professional historians.[77] Their publications found a very limited readership, and thus their impact on shaping collective memory was minimal. In the official version of history – transmitted through schools, literature, movies, museums and memorial sites – the forced migrations were placed within the framework of German extermination policies, together with economic exploitation, forced labour, concentration camps and terror.[78] One could even argue that the relocations were portrayed as a less serious measure of repression: insufficiently 'martyrological' on the one hand and inadequately heroic on the other. In the commemoration of the Second World War prior to 1989 – in museum exhibitions, memorials, commemorative mural plaques, and similar – the expulsions were a marginal theme, overshadowed by more spectacular events such as mass executions or the extermination of the Jews.

It is also difficult to say to what degree, and in what way, comparisons between the experiences of those who were forced to relocate and those who stayed impacted on the memory of the relocations. For those who had to leave their homes, the relocations were traumatic experiences, comprising sudden uprooting and subsequent brutalities endured in interim camps, on transports and during resettlement in the General Government. Nevertheless, it must be stressed that on the whole their wartime existence in Warsaw, Lublin, Radom or Częstochowa was much less inhumane than the fate of their countrymen who remained in their own homes in the territories incorporated into the German Reich. The expellees in the General Government were still able to speak Polish without fear of being punished, to attend Polish churches, to read Polish newspapers, to drink coffee in Polish cafes, and to send their children to Polish primary schools. It seems that the assumption of an 'easier' life in the General Government did much to make the forced migrations appear less painful in the collective memory.[79]

Similar processes can be observed with regard to the expellees from the Eastern Borderlands. The Polish writer Stefan Chwin recalls in his memoirs:

> I knew … inhabitants of Gdansk [deported] from the former eastern parts of Poland, who harboured in their hearts an authentic exile complex …, whose hatred would

sometimes surface with loud exclamations like 'Lwów and Vilnius should be ours again', while at the same time ... they felt actual relief that they no longer had to live in the Borderlands, the boiling pot of nations constantly dealing blows one to another, ... and that they could lead a quiet life in a Polish Gdansk.[80]

Indeed, looking back at the loss of the Eastern Borderlands from the perspective of the twenty-first century, it seems that the memory of those territories changed even faster than the borders. However, while the memories of a Pole deported from the 'Kresy' in 1940 or 1941 tended to be one-sided and permeated by a yearning for the lost ancestral lands, the recollections of a Jew relocated from the same territories would be dramatically different. For Jews, the eastward migration into Soviet territory ultimately turned out to be the escape from extermination. Although life in a kolkhoz, or a 'special settlement', or even a gulag in Siberia or Kazakhstan, was extremely difficult, it nevertheless gave the Jews much more of a chance to survive than did the German occupation.

The memories of expulsions which were particularly painful, such as those from the Zamość region, have been preserved in a more distinct manner than those of the somewhat less harsh deportations from the Poznań or Łódź regions. In many of the villages whose populations were expelled – or subjected to 'pacification actions', as the operations were labelled by the Germans – there are monuments and commemorative plaques. The Zamość Museum of Martyrology devotes a major part of its space to the expulsions. In Zwierzyniec, where a temporary holding camp was located, there is a monument and a church with an altar recalling the fate of the Zamość children. The expression 'Children of the Zamość region' became a prominent reminder of the suffering caused by the German occupation. However, measured not by chapters in history textbooks but by the streets, squares and schools named after the events, public commemoration of the Zamość expulsions is mainly confined to the eastern regions of Poland. Street names reminiscent of the expulsions, for example, can be found only in Zamość, Lublin and Siedlce.

The territorial aspect of upholding the memory of a particular deportation is not restricted to Wielkopolska, Pomerania or the Zamość region, but applies to Warsaw as well. Much has been written about the importance of the memory of the Warsaw Uprising for the maintenance of the traditions of Polish independence. However, on the national level it is the 'heroic' part of the Uprising – the armed resistance between 1 August and 2 October 1944 – which is commemorated publicly, much less so the subsequent 'Exodus' of the city's inhabitants. The wall encircling the Pruszków railway depot, where the biggest collection centre was located, bears the inscription: 'Through this place passed Warsaw: 6 August – 10 October 1944'. However, despite the relatively large number of books devoted to the 'Exodus',[81] until recently the tragedy was known only to a declining number of the original inhabitants of Warsaw. The opening of the Warsaw Uprising

Museum in 2004, which dedicated space to the 'Exodus', marked a turning point in this respect.[82]

It seems that the gaps in Polish collective memory can be explained by both 'regionalism' and the insufficiently 'heroic' appearance of the deportations in question. The expulsions from Wielkopolska or Pomerania in 1939–40 or from Warsaw in 1944 were traumatic experiences. The cost in lives went into the hundreds of thousands, while additional hundreds of thousands survived but literally lost everything they possessed. However, the majority of those who survived the expulsions from Poznań, Leszno, Gdynia, Zamość, Skierbieszów or Warsaw returned to their homes after the war. Although their houses, flats and farms were destroyed or ransacked, their personal links with the local area were not severed.[83] For all – those who were able to return as well as those who lost their homelands forever and could visit them only in their recollections – post-war reconstruction became an important element of their identities.

After the change in the political system in 1989, the interest of historians and of society at large focused on previously forbidden subjects: the Eastern Borderlands or the fate of the Germans after the war, including their expulsion. The public debate centred on a new, internationally burning question: Polish responsibility for crimes committed against others, especially Germans and Ukrainians.[84] The Polish–German attempts at reconciliation soon brought results. The Polish side voiced regret for the expulsion of Germans after 1945, most notably in the speech of the Minister of Foreign Affairs, Władysław Bartoszewski, at a special joint session of the German Bundestag and Bundesrat on 28 April 1995.[85] The German parliament, in turn, tried to address in 2001 the problem of material compensation for wartime forced labourers.[86]

Initially, these discussions were limited to a relatively small group of intellectuals, but by the turn of the century the subject of the deportations was attracting mass interest. As a result, politicians, particularly from the political right, became involved, aiming to enhance their popularity. This proved an easy task because the intensifying debate in Germany about the establishment of a 'Centre against Expulsions' led to a deterioration in Polish–German relations. In retaliation against potential material and memorial claims from Germany, the Polish side began to talk about compensation for the destruction wreaked by the German occupation. Although the German president and the German chancellor both distanced themselves from any demands by Germans for compensation for their losses, the Polish Parliament passed a resolution in September 2004 'on Poland's right to war reparations from Germany and on the unlawful claims against Poland and Polish citizens forwarded in Germany'.[87] The cover of the weekly news magazine *Wprost* of 21 September 2003, depicting the 'German Trojan Horse',[88] gained worldwide notoriety. The televised debate organized by the journal *Rzeczpospolita* on 16 September 2003, with Erika Steinbach and leading Polish intellectuals, was watched by a large Polish audience.

The public discussion in Poland also generated renewed interest in the wartime deportations carried out by the Germans.[89] The former Polish expellees, who had started to form associations by the early 1990s,[90] began to document their experiences and to claim their rights,[91] and the Institute of National Remembrance, established in 2000, also paid attention to forced migrations in its publications and exhibitions.[92] However, the commemoration of forced migrations was not always a spontaneous activity from below but often an aspect of a wider 'political project'. The sixtieth anniversary of the expulsions from the Zamość region is a good example. In November 2002 the Middle School in Skierbieszów, the first village to be relocated in 1942, was given the name 'Children of the Zamość Region', and a commemorative plaque was unveiled. It appears that the interest stirred up by politicians will lead to permanent changes in the perception of the relocations during the Second World War: new monuments are being set up and others planned; publications are being written and exhibitions prepared.[93]

However, it is important to note that the renewed emphasis on Polish losses during the Second World War and the deterioration in Polish–German relations did not affect one of the most important achievements of Polish historiography of the 1990s: the realization that Poles, too, had inflicted harm upon others. The most fundamental post-1989 changes in this area have taken place with regard to the Germans. The expulsion of the German population was meant to contribute to the stabilization of the post-war Polish state, and the eradication of the memory of their existence, as well as of the material remains of their presence, was an element of the 'Polonization' project in the newly acquired territories in the west and the north.[94] However, the broader international significance of the expulsion of the Germans – particularly in view of the new Oder-Neiße border between Germany and Poland – and the illegality, plunder and brutality that accompanied the deportations, led to the formation of a specific Polish 'expulsion complex', which turned the whole issue into a taboo. This explains, for example, the extremely sharp reaction of the Polish authorities to a letter of the Polish bishops of autumn 1965, which addressed the German Catholic hierarchy with the words: 'we forgive, and ask for exculpation'.[95]

Under communist rule, official propaganda placed the organizations of West German expellees among the main 'enemies of Poland'.[96] Historians or journalists never used the term 'expulsion'. More neutral and euphemistic substitutes were applied instead: 'repatriation', 'migration', 'relocation', 'exit' or 'exodus'.[97] However, it was impossible to delete the memory of the presence and removal of the Germans from the so-called 'regained territories' altogether, although when the Germans appeared in literature or in films, it was usually in the roles assigned to them by official propaganda: as saboteurs, or murderers from the Werewolf organization. Violence against Germans was portrayed either as a series of sporadic incidents provoked by the victims themselves or as acts committed by criminals.[98] Historians were also not above reproach: in a 718-page book on the history of

Western Pomerania, for example, there was just one page on the removal of the German population.[99]

In the late 1960s the first monographs on the relocation of the Germans from Poland were published, focusing on demographic problems and on the transfer process itself.[100] Questions such as the origins of the deportations, the attitudes of Poles towards the Germans, the everyday life of the German population under Polish rule, the camps or German forced labour were either ignored or vaguely addressed as 'problems', 'deficiencies' or 'certain faults'. The best book of the time, a monograph by Stefan Banasiak, had a print run of only 60 copies, and the official letter that accompanied copies sent to public libraries advised that 'this work is not intended for wide circulation and should not be copied'.[101]

The official limitations imposed on scholars were crossed only once in the pre-1989 period, and not by a historian but by Jan Józef Lipski (1926–91), a journalist, Second World War Home Army veteran and renowned opposition activist. In 1981 he published a booklet with the title 'Two Mother Countries – Two Patriotisms: Remarks on the National Megalomania and Xenophobia of the Poles', which initially came out as an underground (*samizdat*) publication and has been reprinted many times since. By describing forced population movements as always harmful – although justified in some instances – and admitting that the Poles had actively participated in them, Lipski broke a taboo. It is impossible to overestimate the influence of this text on the younger generation of Polish historians who began researching the deportations of the Germans after 1989.

The list of relevant monographs, primary source editions, and scholarly and journalistic articles published in the 1990s is long. All the previously forbidden themes are represented: the 'unauthorized relocations' of June–July 1945, the working and living conditions of the Germans, the camps, the mortality rates, the illegal repression (by the authorities and individual Poles alike), as well as the participation of the Red Army and the Soviet authorities in the removal of the Germans.[102] However, an opinion poll of May 1996 showed that the Polish view of the expulsion of the German population was only changing very slowly.[103]

The lost Eastern Borderlands were remembered differently inside Poland than among the Polish émigré communities in the West,[104] in part because a large percentage of the émigrés, perhaps even the majority, came from those territories.[105] For them emigration became 'not only a form of protest against the territorial changes, but also a place of double expulsion, from their ancestral regions and from their mother country'.[106] The Eastern Borderlands were recalled in sentimental and nostalgic ways typical of exiles as an idealized, happy 'Arcadia' with a purely Polish character. The list of books, brochures, memoirs, novels and poems published by the emigrants about the Borderlands is enormous,[107] as is the number of cultural events, anniversaries and ceremonial religious services organized primarily by the émigrés from Lwów. In London, Toronto and New York the former inhabitants of the 'Kresy' attempted to revive the life of Vilnius or Lwów. The

Polish émigré organizations remained loyal to the principle of the territorial 'integrity of the Republic' and demanded the re-establishment of the Polish borders laid out in the Riga Peace Treaty of 1921. At the same time, these organizations regarded Poland's post-1945 western boundary along the rivers Oder and Neiße as the 'only proper' and 'just' demarcation line, flatly rejecting any revision.[108] The memory of the Eastern Borderlands was a delicate barometer of émigré life. Whereas in communist Poland censors meticulously erased each and every 'improper' statement about the territories east of the River Bug almost until the end of the regime, in London any suggestion of acquiescence in the post-war reality immediately met with reproach.

However, over time some of the émigrés did integrate into their new milieus. For a growing percentage, particularly of the younger people, the demands for a return of these lands to Poland became increasingly anachronistic. It was recognized that people of other nationalities were living in that area now and that for the Ukrainians, Belorussians or Lithuanians the Borderlands were not 'territories lost' but 'territories regained'. The literary and political milieu gathered around the Parisian periodical *Kultura* and its editor Jerzy Giedroyć was the first to voice such opinions.[109] From the mid-1960s onwards new ideas also started to circulate in the milieu of the Polish emigrants in London. There was a growing acceptance that the future configuration of Poland's eastern borders depended not so much on the decisions of the Great Powers as on agreements between Poland and its neighbours, and that a return to the Eastern Borderlands would become possible only through European integration.[110] At the General Convention of the Poles in Great Britain on 25–28 February 1978, for example, the old demand for a return to the borders of the Riga Peace Treaty was replaced by a statement proposing talks with neighbouring countries about the future of the borders.[111]

It appears that people in Poland were quicker to adopt a realistic stance towards the 'Kresy' than were Poles in exile. However, this did not mean forgetting what had happened in Poland's eastern territories. Immediately after the war, when the relocations were still in progress, the terms 'Kresy', 'Wilno' and 'Lwów' were present in everyday media and political discussions and carried no additional connotation. However, from 1946/7 onwards, communist censorship suppressed these terms with a determination that sometimes bordered on the ridiculous, for example when the setting of the novel *Szkoła orląt* by Janusz Meissner unexpectedly shifted from Vilnius to the vicinity of Białystok. As in the case of the German expulsions, historians rarely turned their attention to the relocations from the East. Until the 1980s these topics remained practically taboo. When authors did wish to get something through the tight net of censorship, they usually focused on the 'repatriations' of 1944–6 and avoided descriptions of the political context, the numerous illegal actions or the catastrophic conditions of the deportations.[112] The authorities attempted to erase all traces of the Borderlands not only from literature and historiography but also from personal biographies. From 1951 onwards, the identity cards of all Poles who were born in the Eastern Borderlands showed 'USSR' as the place of birth.

Complete amnesia proved impossible to achieve, however. Some 140 'holy' Madonnas were smuggled into Poland from the East, sometimes under the most dramatic circumstances. Placed in shrines in Warsaw, Cracow, Wrocław and Legnica, these icons constituted – and indeed still do – an important integrating factor for the former inhabitants of the 'Kresy'. On particular religious holidays, the former inhabitants of a given area would congregate at the new location of the devotional objects from their former parish.[113] In everyday life, small artefacts, family photographs and other similar items created an illusion of living in the old world.[114]

The Stalinist regime was thus unable to remove all traces of the Eastern Borderlands from Polish life. It is difficult to determine whether the task proved too formidable or whether the regime deliberately abstained from overly harsh measures. In Warsaw, for example, none of the street names referring to the 'Kresy' were changed. Within six months of Stalin's death, information about the territories east of the Bug appeared in the Polish press. The taboo was soon broken by Polish Radio as well, when a September 1953 programme about the achievements of Soviet Belarus mentioned not only Witebsk and Minsk but also the former Polish town of Grodno.[115] A year later the Polish media noted that the Borderlands had been previously inhabited by Poles. A newspaper published a short notice about a former inhabitant of the town of Kołomyja in search of people who might know the fate of his family.[116]

After the beginning of the so-called second repatriation of Poles from the Soviet Union in 1955, the 'Kresy' featured still more prominently in the Polish press. A year later, when political changes brought less strict censorship and more freedom of speech, even the official press organ of the Communist Party printed stories about the 'Kresy'.[117] At the meetings organized throughout Poland in the autumn of 1956, in addition to political freedom, economic reform and the removal of 'Soviet advisers', popular demands included the return of the Eastern Borderlands. There were even proposals for a referendum on this question, and for bringing the matter before the United Nations.[118] In the following years, although the political thaw ended, radio and press reports from the territories east of the Bug continued to be broadcast and printed in relatively large numbers.

However, in Poland, as among the Polish émigrés, the 1960s witnessed a distinct generation change. The young generation had a more distanced attitude towards the 'Kresy', which for them were only a created myth. Recovery from what was sometimes called 'memory schizophrenia' was noticeable in journalism as well as in the film industry. In 1967 the film *Sami swoi* (Among Themselves), directed by Sylwester Chęciński, appeared. This comedy, one of the biggest successes in the history of the Polish cinema, tells the story of two families relocated from the 'Kresy' to Lower Silesia. The Borderlands references in the film – the language, the mentality, the behaviour – were reconstructed by Chęciński with close attention to detail. However, although the characters miss their lost homeland, they are perfectly aware of the fact that their life in the 'Kresy' belongs to the past, and they act accordingly.

The Eastern Borderlands were slower to emerge as a major theme in the work of Polish poets and novelists, a considerable number of whom originated from the 'Kresy'. After 1956 the Borderlands appeared, or reappeared, in their writings but, in contrast to the émigré publications, the 'happy Arcadia' yielded to reality and to rational, if not cold, observation of the 'Kresy',[119] and it seems that censorship was not the only reason for this. Interestingly, many writers who originated from the Borderlands joined the political opposition to the Communists. Roman Graczyk was obviously right in his comment that:

> in the Communist days, to come from the 'Kresy' was nearly equivalent to opposing the system. Anyone who exclaimed with pride 'I am from Lwów' was in a way challenging the Communist authorities. … The 'Kresy' functioned in collective consciousness nearly as a cradle of true 'Polishness', free of Communist depravation. … The Borderlanders, just like the soldiers of the Home Army, were an important social evaluation point. The fact that Jacek Kuroń originated from Lwów, and that Jan Józef Lipski was a Home Army veteran, was very important for forming opinions about the KOR.[120]

Somewhat paradoxically, this circle of democratic 'Borderlands' activists was the first group of the Polish opposition to accept the territorial decisions reached at the Tehran and Yalta conferences. As early as the summer of 1966 the publicist Stanisław Stomma, born in the 'Kresy' in 1908 and raised there, argued that Poland would have lost the Borderlands regardless of the Second World War; the Poles would have had to evacuate it, just as the French had been forced to pull out of Algeria.[121] Stomma's text foreshadowed an attitude change towards the 'Kresy' on the part of the entire Polish opposition, which gave up all claims to these territories during the next decades, except for some marginal groups of die-hard revisionists. This was the result of two considerations: that a return of the Poles to the eastern territories would be a political and social anachronism and that the end of the Yalta system had to bring independence not only to the Poles but to the other peoples of the region too. Hence, when émigré Poles used the fortieth anniversary of the Yalta conference to confirm their insistence on the Polish boundaries as defined by the Riga and Potsdam treaties, the opposition in Poland subscribed to the so-called 'Yalta Appeal', issued on 4 February 1985, which protested against the European order established forty years before but did not question the contemporary national borders.[122]

It must also be noted that for the majority of the opposition within Poland the Borderlands were a marginal issue. This was reflected in the modest presence of

'Kresy' themes in the underground (*samizdat*) publications. Of the circa 4,700 underground books and brochures printed in the years 1976–90,[123] only just over twenty dealt with the 'Kresy', and even they focused primarily on the Second World War. This phenomenon is partly explained by the fact that most of these publications appeared in the late 1980s, when growing numbers of books on the Borderlands were starting to emerge.

The period of the 'First Solidarity' from August 1980 to December 1981 – a time of unrestrained cultural activity in Poland – turned out to be decisive for the presence of the 'Kresy' in the nation's collective memory. In 1980 Czesław Miłosz, a writer and poet born in the Polish East who had dedicated much of his work to the 'Kresy', won the Nobel Prize for Literature, and this helped to break taboos surrounding the Borderlands. Unlike in 1956, when the territories east of the Bug became the subject of revisionist demands, in 1980–1 the 'Borderlands renaissance' was largely confined to the cultural sphere. However, for the first time in many years a discussion about compensation for the properties lost in the East began again in the Polish press.[124]

The martial law imposed on Poland on 13 December 1981 failed to suppress interest in the 'Kresy' for long. In fact, it appears that a kind of tacit agreement was reached between the authorities and society. The continued, even if controlled, public discussion of 'Kresy' themes was a way of letting off steam. The first scholarly works in Polish on the Borderlands and on the activities of the Home Army in the East were written in this period. From the mid-1980s the 'Kresy' started to attain a wide presence in journals of all types, from the religious to the orthodox communist. The appearance of a book on the Łyczakowski Cemetery in Lwów in 1988 was the final proof that the former taboo had ceased to exist, and a steady flow of all kinds of publications on the Borderlands followed.[125]

The political changes of the late 1980s included the agreement of the authorities to the establishment of 'Eastern Borderlands' societies, i.e. organizations of former residents of the 'Kresy'. In September 1988 the 'Lwów Society' was registered in Wrocław, and its Warsaw section was officially established at a meeting in December of the same year, which attracted more than 3,000 people.[126] Three months later the communist authorities began the Round Table talks with the political opposition, which opened a new phase not only in the political history of Poland but also in the history of the Polish memory of the 'Kresy'.

From 1989 even the most 'reactionary' or 'revisionist' publications on the Borderlands were free to appear. New Borderlands societies were established; travel agencies organized 'sentimental' tours of the 'Kresy'; and an annual Borderland Festival of 'Kresy' culture was held in the Masurian town of Mrągowo from 1995 onwards. At the same time, the public fascination with the Borderlands waned. For the average Pole of the early twenty-first century, the 'Kresy' no longer symbolizes resistance, defiance and the old, free Poland, as a free Poland is now a reality. The Borderlands publications have lost their popularity, and the 'Kresy' societies usually only feature in the context of claims for compensation. Symptomatically, research on the relocations from the Borderlands in 1944–6 has made little progress since 1989, apart from a few specialized monographs.[127]

The young generation is interested in the Eastern Borderlands, but this interest resembles the attitude of many young Germans towards areas such as Lower Silesia or the Masurian region. The reason is simple and easily understandable: emotional memory cannot be transferred; passing on true nostalgia is impossible. It remains the exclusive preserve of those who have really lost their ancestral homes – the generation of the parents and the grandparents. Ryszard Terlecki wrote in 2000:

> Lwów, as remembered by the victims of the deportation, who leaned out of the windows of the departing trains to look at their city for the last time, is no more. Lwów of those years is gone, although the walls and the houses are still standing and the cobblestones are the same. Memory is the shelter of the exiles. The history of Lwów will remain a part of our collective memory.[128]

The majority of contemporary Poles consider the Eastern Borderlands a closed chapter, a sentimental and touching myth, but one that belongs to memory only.

–7–

Forced Labourers in the Third Reich

Forced labour is not a phenomenon unique to the Nazi state. The exploitation of labourers in the colonies of the nineteenth century or the deployment of forced labourers in the Soviet GULAG ('Main Administration of the Camps') or in Mao Zedong's China come to mind as other prominent examples of the practice. Forced labour was, and still is, used in dictatorial states as a method of political repression and economic exploitation. In the Third Reich, however, forced labour and the associated transfers of people reached enormous dimensions. Millions of people were carried off into Reich territory specifically to perform forced labour and were held there against their will. Many found themselves thousands of kilometres away from their homes in what was for them an utterly strange and largely hostile environment. Their work became a fixed and, with the progression of the war, indispensable component of the German war economy.

The forced labourers in the Third Reich constituted a heterogeneous group: they differed in terms of gender, age, origin, race and class. Different groups of civilians were among them, as were concentration camp inmates and prisoners of war who – according to the Geneva Convention – should not have been forced to work. The term 'forced labourer' applied to more than nine million people in the German Reich.[1]

The treatment of foreign prisoners of war and civilian labourers in the Third Reich was dependent on racial-ideological criteria and political calculations. From the very beginning, a conflict existed between racial and xenophobic Nazi ideology on the one hand and pragmatic economic policy on the other.

At the end of the war, a huge flow of people began to move again, but this time in the opposite direction. With their liberation from camps, forced labourers obtained the status of 'displaced persons' (DPs). The majority attempted to return to their homes by the quickest route possible. But there were also former forced labourers who wanted to remain abroad or emigrate to a third country. Former Soviet prisoners of war and civilian labourers were accorded a special role, as they were regarded as traitors in their homeland and in many cases faced reprisals as a result.

This chapter provides a brief overview of several central aspects of the deployment of forced labourers in the Third Reich. The primary focus is on three issues.

The first is the area of conflict between racial ideology and economic policy in which the forced labourers were placed. The second concerns the impact of this dilemma on the experience of forced labour, including several areas of daily life. The third addresses the consequences of their deployment as forced labourers for former Soviet civilian workers and prisoners of war, who were subjected to decades-long discrimination in the Soviet Union.

The majority of these areas have already been explored extensively; a wealth of literature has appeared on the subject, especially in the last few years, in connection with German and Austrian compensation payments and the related public debates. The following comments therefore draw in large part on existing research results.

7.1 Conflict between Racial Ideology and Economic Policy

With the passage of time, the German war economy became increasingly dependent on the deployment of foreign labourers, who came predominantly from France, Poland and the occupied areas of the Soviet Union. As early as the end of 1940, agriculture – from which many men were initially drafted into the Wehrmacht and which was also affected by strong migration into the armaments industry – would have been unable to provide for the provisioning of the population without the approximately two million foreign forced labourers deployed in it. By autumn 1941 at the latest, foreign labour had become indispensable for the entire Nazi war economy.[2] In July 1944 – the point when armaments production reached its peak – over 5.7 million foreign civilian labourers, more than 1.9 million prisoners of war and around 400,000 concentration camp inmates made up just under 26 per cent of all labourers and employees in the German Reich.[3]

However, the massive deployment of foreign forced labourers in Reich territory was by no means planned from the outset. Within the decidedly xenophobic regime, political-ideological and racial considerations militated against it. Above all in the Party leadership and in the security apparatus led by Heinrich Himmler, it was feared that the deployment of foreign labourers would lead to a 'mingling of blood', sabotage and communist subversion.[4] On the other hand, economic pragmatists emphasized the importance of the deployment of foreigners for the war economy. In this way, calculations about the effective utilization of available manpower collided with concerns about exposure to 'racially inferior' peoples and deleterious ideological influences.

The conflict between the regime's ideological and economic aims was closely linked to the progression of the Second World War. Here one can follow the classic division of the war into the 'Blitzkrieg phase' that lasted until summer/autumn 1941, the phase of reorientation from 'Blitzkrieg' to a war of attrition that ran up to the beginning of 1943, and the phase of 'total war' that finished in May 1945. Parallel to the deterioration of the military situation and the intensification of labour shortages, economic problems grew increasingly urgent. The worse the war situation became, the more the pragmatists asserted themselves. German industry had access to a group of labourers that was available in sufficient numbers and promised an optimal relationship between investment and return. Initially this applied to skilled workers from Western Europe, but when they were no longer available in adequate numbers, Poles began to be deployed from 1941, followed by Soviet forced labourers, growing numbers of concentration camp inmates and, finally, in the last year of the war, Jews.

The pragmatists could claim a comprehensive victory only on the question of whether foreign forced labourers should be deployed in the Reich. The determination of what concrete form this deployment should take had to be left to the racial ideologues within the framework of a 'power trade-off' (Ulrich Herbert). All areas of Nazi forced labour deployment were defined by racial-ideological considerations. This fact cost the lives of tens of thousands of foreign prisoners of war and civilian workers as well as hundreds of thousands of concentration camp inmates, so-called 'work Jews' and Soviet prisoners of war.[5]

The conflict between economic interests and ideological principles is demonstrated with particular clarity by the example of the Soviet prisoners of war in the Third Reich. Prior to the German invasion of the Soviet Union, a labour deployment of 'Soviet Russians' was not foreseen because of racial-ideological reasons. Indeed, such a deployment had been explicitly forbidden by Hitler himself. The introduction of Slavic 'sub-humans' into the Reich did not appear to be conducive to German aims. Accordingly, no provisions were made for maintaining the working capacity of Soviet prisoners. In fact, the economic burden imposed by these 'useless eaters' was underscored, thereby justifying the regime's annihilatory intentions. As a result, 60 per cent of the approximately 3.5 million Soviet prisoners captured in 1941 died, 1.4 million of them already by the beginning of December 1941.[6]

Only Germany's deteriorating military situation on the Eastern Front from autumn 1941 and the continuously increasing demand for labour within the Reich brought about a decision in favour of 'Russian deployment', and an initial improvement in the catastrophic living conditions of the Soviet prisoners of war.[7] But it took some time for these measures to take effect: on 28 February 1942 Reich Minister Rosenberg informed Chief of the Supreme Command of the Wehrmacht Field Marshal Keitel that of the 3.6 million Soviet prisoners of war only about a hundred thousand were fully fit for work.[8] At the beginning of 1942 a mere 11.2 per cent of them could be recruited for labour deployment, whereas 70 per cent of all French prisoners of war were fit for work. The treatment of Soviet prisoners of war improved in parallel with the deterioration of the military situation, so that by August 1944 32.7 per cent of them were fit for work. In their case, economic 'utilization' had led to an improvement in the catastrophic living conditions in German captivity.[9]

7.2 Definition and Categories

The term 'forced labour' contains the most important and most obvious component of its meaning: the enforcement of labour. According to the definition of the International Labour Organization (IAO) from 1930, the term 'forced labour' is to be understood as 'any form of work or service which is demanded from a person under the threat of some sort of penalty and for which they have not volunteered'. Military service, standard civic duties, community service on the basis of criminal conviction or duties in a state of emergency were exempted from the definition.[10] The term was defined more precisely during the course of the discussion regarding the indemnification of 'forced labourers in the Third Reich'. According to this definition, forced labourers for the Nazis were classified as 'persons who were deployed for work by the National Socialist regime using force or under false pretences ..., or who were prevented from returning home after a voluntary stay ..., forced to work here, subject to particularly harsh living conditions'.[11]

The intake of workers could to all intents and purposes take place on a voluntary basis. Decisive for the forced nature were two characteristics: firstly, the legally institutionalized indissolubility of the employment contract for the foreseeable future and, secondly, the meagre opportunities of the workers to exert an influence on the conditions of their labour deployment.

No two forced labourers were in exactly the same position, however. Their divergent living and working conditions and legal status in the Third Reich, combined with the partly conflicting aims of the diverse power groups within the regime, ensured this. The categorization that follows is based on legal status on the one hand and racial-ideological criteria on the other. A further differentiation within the three large groups of civilians, prisoners of war and concentration camp inmates is also required, as each was to be treated in a distinct fashion.

The system was based on the National Socialist racial scale, at the summit of which stood the German 'master race', followed by Germanic, Anglo-Saxon, Romance and Slavic peoples. Beneath them were Jews, 'gypsies' and non-whites. A decree of the Reich Security Main Office (RSHA) of mid-January 1941 established this racial hierarchy as the official guideline for the treatment of foreign forced labourers in the Reich. Accordingly, the RSHA differentiated between 'workers of Germanic descent' (the Norwegians, Danes, Dutch and Flemish) and 'foreign national workers' (all others). Admittedly, the decree completely ignored political realities. Italians, Slovaks and Hungarians, for example, enjoyed certain privileges as citizens of allied states. In February 1943, therefore, the RSHA devised the following, more differentiated categorization:

(1) Germanic peoples, (2) non-Germanic allied peoples, (3) non-Germanic peoples under German sovereignty and (4) civilian workers from the occupied areas of the Soviet Union.[12]

Of the estimated nine million forced labourers in the German war economy, the overwhelming majority – approximately 7.6 million – were civilians. Around 1.4 million were prisoners of war. In addition, 400,000 concentration camp inmates carried out forced labour, above all in the final phase of the war. Civilians were transported from all parts of Europe occupied by the German Wehrmacht for forced labour in the Reich. In September 1944 there were 5.7 million civilian workers in the German Reich. Only a small proportion of them had arrived voluntarily or partly voluntarily, enticed by various promises, and many of those who had done so were subsequently forced to remain in the Reich. The largest group were the 2.8 million so-called 'eastern workers' (*Ostarbeiter*) deported from the Soviet Union. The living and working conditions of the civilian forced labourers varied greatly, but one can differentiate in principle between two large, yet in themselves heterogeneous, groups.

One group consisted of civilian workers from Poland and the Soviet Union. They had a mortality rate distinctly higher than average and no noteworthy influence on their conditions of existence.[13] The Nazi regime divided the forced labourers from the Soviet Union into *Ostarbeiter* and 'Ukrainians', whereby geographical origin was the decisive factor in the categorization.[14]

According to the 'Ordinance regarding Deployment Conditions for Eastern Workers' of 30 June 1942, 'eastern workers' were understood to be 'those workers of non-German nationality who are to be acquired in the Reich Commissariat Ukraine, in the General Commissariat Belarus or in those territories that lie to the east of these territories and in the former independent states Latvia and Estonia, and those that, following the occupation by the German Wehrmacht, were brought into the German Reich, including from the Protectorate of Bohemia and Moravia, and deployed here'.[15] Ultimately, the category 'eastern workers' embraced civilian workers from all Soviet territories within the USSR's borders of 1939. Poles from 'former Soviet' territories (particularly from the Reich Commissariat Belarus) were also defined as 'eastern workers'.

The status 'Ukrainian' referred only to those labourers from the Ukraine who originated from the General Government. Ukrainians from the territory of Lwów were subjected neither to the decrees pertaining to 'eastern workers' nor to those relevant to Poles and were placed on a par with other foreign workers.[16] The treatment of Poles, whose forced labour deployment in the German Reich began in 1939, was governed by the Nazis' 'Pole decrees'.[17]

The second group of forced labourers comprised workers from Western and Northern Europe, but also Estonians and people of Southern and South-eastern Europe, including Croats, who were declared to be 'Germanic peoples' because of foreign policy considerations.[18] The largest group among the forced labourers of

'Germanic origin' was composed of the 300,000 workers from occupied Western Europe – including French, Dutch and Belgian citizens – with an additional 270,000 Italians, 80,000 Slovaks and 35,000 Hungarians.[19]

Prisoners of war in the Third Reich can be divided into two categories, based on their judicial position: those who were treated in accordance with the legal provisions of the Geneva Convention of 1929 and those who were not. Under the terms of the convention, prisoners of war could be made to perform work of which they were physically capable, according to their abilities and rank, except for officers and non-commissioned officers, who were to be exempted. However, activities directly connected with acts of war were explicitly forbidden, in particular the manufacture and transport of weapons or ammunition of any kind.[20] Those prisoners of war who were made to perform work which contravened the provisions of the Geneva Convention are to be regarded as forced labourers.

The category of prisoners of war that, according to the Nazi view, fell under the protection of the Geneva Convention included prisoners from the USA, Belgium, France, the United Kingdom, Yugoslavia, Norway, Poland and the Netherlands. Officers and non-commissioned officers were to some extent urged to register for work 'voluntarily'. From May 1940 onwards 90 per cent of Polish prisoners of war were given the status of civilian workers.

The POWs without the protection of the Geneva Convention included Polish-Jewish and Soviet prisoners of war as well as Italian 'military internees', taken into captivity after Italy switched sides in the war in 1943. According to the Nazi judicial view, Soviet prisoners of war were not entitled to the protection of international law because the USSR had not signed the Geneva Convention, and the Hague Convention on Land Warfare of 1907 had been signed only by Tsarist Russia, not the Soviet Union. For racial-ideological reasons, Soviet prisoners of war stood de facto at the very bottom of the Nazi POW hierarchy, a fact that manifested itself in their poor living conditions and extremely high mortality rates.[21]

Jewish prisoners of war from Western states were generally treated the same as their non-Jewish compatriots. This did not apply, however, to Jews who had served in the Polish or Soviet armies and had been taken into captivity. They were treated with particular brutality and had an extremely high rate of mortality.[22]

International protection provisions also did not apply to the Italian military personnel taken prisoner from 1943 onwards. Because no state of war existed between the former allies at the time of their capture, they were allocated the status of Italian military internees (IMI). This affected more than 600,000 Italians on Reich territory who ended up in German captivity after the Italian surrender of 8 September 1943. The living conditions of the military internees, most of whom were housed in POW camps, sank to the level of Soviet POWs within a few weeks of Italy's 'betrayal'.[23]

At the very bottom of the Nazi forced labour hierarchy stood Jewish workers, who were entirely without rights or protection, in particular the Hungarian Jews who were transferred to 'deployment in the Reich' after 1944 and concentration camp inmates. Inmates of concentration and labour camps exerted no influence at all over their conditions and suffered extremely high mortality rates. This very heterogeneous group included prisoners of war, civilians of various nationalities, political prisoners, homosexuals, Roma and Sinti and 'those engaged in oppositional activity', who had been committed to a concentration camp for various reasons. Many Jewish prisoners in particular were exposed to 'annihilation through labour'. At the beginning of the war the number of camp inmates totalled approximately 25,000; by the end of the war it had risen to about 700,000. While the political functions of camp detention (the annihilation of political-ideological opponents, the persecution of minorities) prevailed until 1942, from 1942 onwards the exploitation of camp inmates for the war economy took priority. The prisoners of concentration camps were at the disposal of the Reichsführer SS and subject in particular to the following SS organs: the Inspector of the Concentration Camps, the Economic and Administrative Main Office (Wirtschafts- und Verwaltungshauptamt, WVHA), and the Reich Security Main Office (Reichssicherheitshauptamt, RSHA).[24]

7.3 Abduction to the Reich

The experience of forced labour deployment, the living and working conditions, depended largely on two key factors: the legal framework that specified the treatment to be given to each of the various groups of forced labourers, and the practical implementation of these specifications. The stages of forced labour that will be discussed below – from the deportation to the camps to the labour deployment – therefore varied between different groups of forced labourers.

The category of civilian workers included foreigners who had 'voluntarily' registered for 'deployment in the Reich' on the basis of various inducements or under 'the decisive influence of external conditions', those who had gone to Germany as a result of age-group conscription, and those who had been forcibly deported to the Reich.

Among the largest group of civilian forced labourers – the 'eastern workers' – voluntary registration for deployment in Germany was short-lived. Germany's brutal occupation policies and reports of bad treatment by those already enlisted quickly acted as a deterrent. What followed was a ruthless abduction of mainly very young women and men, in part also of children, which constituted a traumatic experience. The victims were generally caught flat-footed and torn from their family circle by the German occupation forces without prior notification. Many were denied the possibility of taking their leave from parents, siblings and other loved ones and carried off to an uncertain fate in a strange, largely hostile environment. Irrespective of how the abductees were ultimately treated in the Reich, the inhuman methods applied by the German occupation forces and their local collaborators left a lasting impression.

In the second year of the war with the Soviet Union, the abductions assumed enormous proportions. With the appointment of Fritz Sauckel as Plenipotentiary for Labour Deployment in March 1942, the round-ups became increasingly organized. In Poland and in the western Ukraine, countless quarantine camps were set up for the purpose of disinfecting the 'eastern workers'. After journeys lasting days or even weeks, the men and women, boys and girls were given the opportunity to leave the train for the first time. They received a meal, were deloused and were subjected to a medical examination. 'And without sentimentalities …' is how Sauckel characterized his approach to the 'eastern workers' brought into Reich territory. He understood his duty as follows: 'I have been commissioned by Adolf Hitler, and I will bring the millions of eastern workers to Germany without any consideration of whether they want that or not.'[25]

Anastasia V., eighteen years old at the time, still remembered her abduction very clearly more than half a century later. Together with her sister, three years her junior, she was transported to the railway station of Saki in the Crimea in September 1942.

> We were assembled, not like passengers, but like one would transport cows. Forty people at one go, forty from our village, men and women. One bucket was provided for us. … We were let out in Poland. Men and women were separated. These moments are so particularly difficult. We were stripped completely naked, then lined up in rows of two. Large barrels with some sort of liquid were set up. A long stick lay there. Cloths hung on the stick. … Alongside stood soldiers, the Germans. They looked at us and laughed. We were led to these barrels, these cloths were immersed – and on the head. Tears were in our eyes.[26]

After the 'disinfection', the abductees received new uniforms made of a thin, cheap material. Instead of their own shoes, they were given clogs. Underwear was not distributed as, according to German documents, it 'would be barely known to the Russians and unfamiliar'. Afterwards the young people were driven into carriages, the doors were bolted, and the carriages were sent further westwards.

The former 'eastern worker' Antonina Kopylova, née Michailova, from Novočerkassk in southern Russia, also recalls this first stage of her forced labour deployment only reluctantly. Her abduction in autumn 1942 came as a surprise. She had only a few minutes to pack the most necessary items and to take leave of her parents. In Rostov on the Don, Kopylova and her companions were loaded onto a train: 'We were transported in an awful, dirty freight car; only – excuse the expression – *pigs*[27] should be transported in this way. … This is how we were taken to Poland. … We were loaded on quickly, *quick, quick, quick*, and the dogs, Alsatians and the Germans.'[28]

In Poland the customary 'disinfection' was carried out without consideration for the sense of shame among the mainly very young girls:

> There we were washed, and our belongings were taken into a room, and that was it. We screamed; it was unpleasant for us; the Poles were walking about. Men were walking about, and we were naked; you know what I mean, that was simply not nice. … It was degrading; we were just girls, young; I was seventeen years old. … And they walk about and laugh, with our belongings in the room and us naked. … Simply everything was taken from us. It was enough to make you cry.[29]

Scenes that passed during the journey through Poland allowed the deportees to guess what awaited them. During stops, Soviet prisoners of war working on the railway laid siege to the transport. 'When we arrived in Poland, my God, what we saw there! Our poor prisoners screamed: "Brother, sister! Throw us a piece of bread!" … Such terrible figures. They had such an appearance, so emaciated. They did some kind of work there, on the railway, … at least a piece of bread!'[30] But the men and women on the transports had barely anything to eat themselves.

Maria Viets, née Kuznecova, now living in Florida, recalls the journey into the Third Reich in a similar way. The then eighteen-year-old, together with her cousin and some school friends from Krasnyj Sulin, a village in the district of Rostov, was carried off to 'Ostmark' (Austria): 'They closed the door and we slept on the floor. Once a day we stopped and they cooked a type of soup for us. … There were lots of military men, German soldiers with dogs and everything; we had to go into the bushes in order to … So, when we had finished, we came back. … Sometimes we were brought to a station and we didn't know where we were, where we were going; we had no idea. We stayed there three, four days. … And then we continued.'[31]

7.3.1 Accommodation, Food and Medical Care

At the places of labour deployment, the most basic requirements of the forced labourers – accommodation, food, clothing, medical care and, increasingly, air-raid protection – were meticulously regulated. The individual provisions were determined according to National Socialist racial doctrines. Thus, the two groups of foreign civilian workers most discriminated against had to wear their own emblems ('P' for Poles and 'Ost' [East] for 'eastern workers'), which stigmatized them publicly and prevented them from entering shops and other public places or using public transport.

As early as 8 March 1940 Poles were required to affix to the right breast of every item of clothing a five-by-five centimetre piece of material imprinted with the letter 'P'. They were thus the first group of people to be subjected to discriminatory external marking in the Third Reich. The 'P' emblem provided the model for the subsequent adoption of the Jewish Star as an external marker of Jews.[32] The 'eastern workers' who went to the Third Reich after 22 June 1941 had to wear a 7 × 7.7 centimetre piece of material with the word '*Ost*' (East) on it. In mid-1944 it was replaced by 'nation-specific' emblems for Ukrainian, Russian and Belorussian 'eastern workers'. Fixed penalty regulations for the non-wearing of the obligatory emblems remained in force throughout.[33]

The accommodation of foreign civilian workers also corresponded to their respective ranks within the Nazi racial hierarchy, although a caesura can be established for 1942. At the beginning of 1942, more than 2.1 million foreign civilian workers were employed in the Reich. The Poles among them numbered about a million and were primarily forced labourers, approximately three-quarters of whom were lodged with farmers. Of the remaining foreign civilian workers, almost 90 per cent laboured outside agriculture, mostly in urban areas. The provision of their accommodation was still a manageable task at this point, above all because the proportion of volunteers among them remained fairly high.[34]

The number of foreign civilian workers in the Reich almost doubled during 1942, primarily because of the large-scale transports of 'eastern workers'. The high number of newcomers overstretched the resources available to the authorities. At the same time, the accommodation standards for the 'eastern workers', who – according to Nazi propaganda – resided in shacks and holes in the ground in their homelands in any case, were lowered. The huts provided for them were frequently overcrowded and allowed no privacy.

Polish forced labourers and 'eastern workers' were to be kept in strict separation from the German population. Their barrack camps were to be encircled by barbed wire and guarded. They were supposed to remain in their lodgings whenever they were not at work. In practice, however, these guidelines were frequently disregarded. The 'eastern workers' deployed in agriculture were the only Soviet forced labourers not supervised by guards.

In accordance with an April 1942 decree, each room of the standardized barracks of the Reich Labour Service (RAD) was supposed to have enough space for eighteen civilian workers (or non-Soviet prisoners of war) or thirty-six Soviet prisoners of war. The sleeping area consisted of nine double beds for the former group and of plank bunk beds for the Soviet prisoners of war. Mattresses and cushions were filled with straw. Even eating utensils were meticulously regulated: whereas the Soviet prisoners of war were entitled to one bowl, one beaker and one spoon, the other prisoners of war and civilian workers received an additional plate, knife and fork each.[35]

The qualitatively and quantitatively inadequate food supply had a particularly strong impact on the lives of forced labourers in the German Reich. 'We were hungry, … without sugar, without fat',[36] recalls one former 'eastern worker', who laboured in an armaments concern near Graz. Her breakfast typically consisted of a quarter of a loaf of bread, two pieces of sugar and a cup of coffee. For the midday and evening meals there was watery soup with potatoes or cabbage. Only on holidays were the meals somewhat better, featuring primarily potatoes.[37]

No other group of foreigners was subjected to such measly rations as the Soviet forced labourers. Until 1944 foreigners, including most Poles, received – at least on paper – the same rations as Germans, although prisoners of war and 'eastern workers' got noticeably less. Soviet prisoners of war received the same rations as the 'eastern workers'. In addition, distinctions were made between normal workers, heavy labourers and those who worked below ground. In practice, all this meant years of starvation for the Soviet forced labourers.[38]

It was usually advantageous to be employed in agriculture, despite the strict regulations of the Nazi authorities. Although living conditions varied greatly, depending on the circumstances of individual farms and the attitudes of the employers, both forced labourers and prisoners of war were much better provisioned in agriculture than in industry.[39]

As in the case of food, the regulations regarding the provision of clothing and shoes had a major impact on foreign civilian workers and prisoners of war. Once again, Poles and Soviet citizens were treated particularly harshly. To be sure, the other groups of civilian workers rarely received replacements for their threadbare clothing, but they could make purchases on the black market, thanks to their higher wages. Prisoners of war were strictly forbidden to wear civilian clothing because of fears that this would facilitate escape attempts. However, their provisioning with uniforms proved difficult even as early as 1940 because of a lack of 'booty uniforms'. The Supreme Command of the Wehrmacht therefore decided to ease the shortage by dyeing signed-out Wehrmacht uniforms for their use.[40]

The 'eastern workers' initially only possessed the clothing they had worn during their abduction or brought with them, provided that these items had been returned to them following their 'disinfection' in Poland. The shortage of clothing proved so serious that the production of simple and robust garments specifically for 'eastern workers', and subsequently also for all other workers from Eastern and South-eastern Europe, was begun in late 1942. The clothing was supposed to be wearable on and off duty. Shoes and clothing had to be ordered by the firm employing the workers, which received them from the Economics Office and then sold them to the 'eastern workers'. Subsequent statements by 'eastern workers' suggest that the local population sometimes provided them with additional materials from which they could make further items of clothing.[41]

The footwear manufactured specially for the 'eastern workers' contained no rubber or leather. The shoes were made entirely of wood or at least had wooden soles, which made them exceptionally uncomfortable.[42] A former 'eastern worker' recalls that the clogs were bad for the health as well, particularly in winter: 'It is cold in winter, always wet with the clogs. The feet got wet. That was all awful!'[43]

The existence of two classes of civilian workers was also apparent in medical care, although all foreign civilian workers – apart from the 'eastern workers' prior to April 1944 – were entitled to some social security. Initially, the 'eastern workers' only possessed medical insurance cover. In principle, the instructions stated that the medical treatment of foreigners – once again with the exception of Poles and 'eastern workers' – was to be no worse than that of German patients. However, hospitals were obliged to admit foreign workers only when there was a threat of communicable disease. The foreign civilian worker was a de facto hostage of the medical insurance agencies.[44]

The shortage of clean clothing, bed linen, towels and articles of personal hygiene was also problematic. Poles and 'eastern workers' were, again, entitled to fewer of these than were other civilian workers. Furthermore, sanitary facilities were frequently inadequate and disinfecting agents lacking. A plague of vermin in the huts was often the consequence. After only a few weeks in the Reich, many of the Soviet forced labourers, especially the prisoners of war, therefore appeared to correspond to the image of the 'Slavic sub-human' propagated by Nazi propaganda.[45]

7.3.2 Labour Deployment, Discipline and 'Spare Time'

The German Reich became a state of slaveholders during the Second World War.[46] Not a single concern of appreciable size failed to utilize forced labourers, although not all firms employed concentration camp inmates. In 1940 around 60 per cent of all foreign workers were engaged in agriculture; in the final years of the war this figure dropped to one third.[47]

In keeping with all areas of forced labour deployment in the German Reich, the principle of discrimination was also consistently applied to wages. The principle of 'same wages for the same work' was valid only for foreign workers from states allied with Germany, and only initially. The wage levels of foreign workers were fixed at between 50 and 80 per cent of those of German workers in the 'Reich Tariff System for Polish Agricultural Workers' of January 1940. Polish agricultural workers were thus about 50 per cent cheaper than Germans, which is why many farmers went so far as to dismiss expensive German workers and replace them with cheaper Poles during the opening phases of the war. But the employment of prisoners of war was even more cost-effective. In order to combat the undesirable effects of the wages gap, a special tax of 15 per cent was introduced for Poles in 1940 under the designation 'Social Equalization Contribution'. This meant that part of the foreign workers' wages was siphoned off without any advantage to the employer. The contribution was soon extended to Jews and 'gypsies' and later to the 'eastern workers' in general.[48]

In the case of the deployment of 'eastern workers', employers were required to make an 'Eastern Worker Contribution', as a result of which the workers' actual earnings shrank to the level of mere pocket money. In addition, the employers were entitled to subtract a contribution for board and lodging from the wages, which meant that many 'eastern workers' received no payment whatsoever. Thus, from the beginning of December 1941 to mid-June 1942, 'eastern workers' were simply slaves. They could barely afford to improve their limited food rations, especially since until the end of 1942 they were not allowed to leave their camps during non-working hours.

From mid-June 1942 onwards the proportion of the 'Eastern Worker Contribution' was reduced, thus increasing the net pay. But the decisive factor was that henceforth the 'eastern workers' were paid extra for greater work performance. With these additional earnings, they could purchase goods for their daily use, particularly as the rules for going out during non-working hours were also gradually relaxed. In May 1943 a further increase in net pay levels took place as part of the propagandistic drive to improve the position of the 'eastern workers', who were supposedly fighting 'against Bolshevism' side-by-side with the Germans. In April 1944 there followed an extensive realignment of the wages of the 'eastern workers' with those of the Poles. The 'Eastern Worker Contribution' was replaced by an income tax and a 15 per cent Social Equalization Contribution. As a result, the 'eastern workers' were now entitled to social security, just like all other foreign civilian workers.

Following further reforms, by the end of the war the wages of 'eastern workers' were set at the same level as those of German workers. This had been done for other non-Polish workers from Eastern Europe as early as 1943. But because of their meagre food provisions, the 'eastern workers' had to spend a higher-than-average proportion of their wages on increasingly expensive foodstuffs, especially on the black market.[49] However, one former 'eastern worker' subsequently recalled that she was nevertheless refused entry to most shops: 'At the beginning we didn't receive anything, but then they began to pay six roubles [meaning Reich marks]. But what should we do with them, either in a shop or anywhere else? We weren't allowed in, only for photos.'[50] Many therefore found that the successive wage increases in no way constituted an appreciable improvement of their situation.

Depending on their nationality, status and gender, the foreign labourers were subject to punitive measures that far exceeded the punishments meted out to Germans. For ideological hardliners, the foreigners posed primarily political and 'blood-related' threats. Hence, an RSHA decree of June 1943 stated 'that the Pole and Soviet Russian constitutes a danger for the German national order by virtue of his presence on German territory alone, and for this reason it is not so much a question of finding an appropriate punishment for his crime as of preventing a further endangerment of the German national order'.[51]

Two offences were considered particularly serious and always fell under the jurisdiction of the Gestapo: 'forbidden contact' with Germans and 'breach of employment contract'. They posed a threat to the economic-pragmatic and

political-ideological interests of the Nazi regime, namely the economic exploitation of foreign forced labourers on the one hand and the 'racial separation of
Germans' and foreigners on the other.[52]

The penalties were draconian. In March 1940 the RSHA regulated the punishment of Poles in the following way: in the case of 'habitually casual work, cessa-
tion of work, incitement of workers, leaving of the workplace of one's own accord,
sabotage activities etc.',[53] transferral to a 'work education camp'
(*Arbeitserziehungslager*) was to be the initial response. In the event of 'stubborn
reluctance to work', transfer to a concentration camp was prescribed. For particularly serious infractions, the death penalty could be imposed. The authority of the
Gestapo was extended to include the right to decide whether to initiate proceed-
ings or to resort to state-political measures in cases of serious violations. In this
way, the judiciary was de facto excluded from the punishment of foreign
workers.[54]

In addition, individual companies enjoyed considerable leeway in administering
disciplinary measures against foreign civilian workers. But recorded punishments
comprised only one aspect of the disciplinary regime imposed on forced labourers.
Daily beatings were commonplace, particularly for Polish and Soviet forced
labourers and Italian military internees. To be sure, corporal punishment of prisoners of war was expressly forbidden, and in August 1942 the ban was extended
to cover the 'eastern workers' as well. But employers often disregarded these rules.
Penalties against Soviet prisoners of war were particularly brutal, whereas Western
workers or prisoners of war rarely suffered physical punishment.[55]

The Nazi authorities paid particular attention to contacts between the resident
German population and the forced labourers. Sexual contact was considered a
capital crime for Poles, Soviets and – from 1943 – Italian prisoners of war. The
'German woman', whose sexual transgression was regarded as an 'offence against
the nation' and 'race defilement', was also liable to be prosecuted.[56]

Although the purpose of their residence in the Reich was work, forced labourers
also had some 'spare time'. In this area, it is necessary to differentiate between
three groups, each of which faced different regulations: 1) civilian workers who
were not stigmatized by the wearing of racial emblems; 2) the marked Poles and
'eastern workers', and 3) the forced labourers who lived under prison conditions,
namely prisoners of war and detainees.

The first group was entitled to take advantage of the normal cultural offerings
of cinemas, theatres, concerts and operas. They were able to pay the resultant costs
as they received wages which usually equalled those paid to Germans.[57]

Poles and 'eastern workers' were excluded from many free-time activities. It was
not for nothing that the Reich Security Main Office had marked them with the
obligatory emblems on their clothing. In March 1940 a package of prohibitions
was imposed on the Poles which forbade the use of public transport, attendance at
German functions of a cultural and festive nature, the frequenting of public

houses, and intimate relations with German men and particularly women. Admittedly, local police authorities could make guesthouses available to Polish workers at certain times, although they could only be served alcoholic drinks on Sundays and public holidays between 2 p.m. and 6 p.m. The 'occurrence of intoxication' was to be avoided at all times.[58]

'Eastern workers', insofar as they were not engaged in agricultural work for small enterprises, were initially allowed to leave their accommodation only for work. In April 1942 the ban on leaving the camps was relaxed, and in December 1942 it was lifted altogether. Thereafter, 'proven workers' could be granted permission to go out in closed groups under German supervision. Later on, they were given more freedoms. In winter, for example, they were generally granted permission to go out on Sundays between 2 p.m. and 6 p.m. From mid-June 1944 they – as well as Polish forced labourers in general – were given permission to go to the cinema, although they were only allowed to occupy seats in the first three rows.[59] A former 'eastern worker' subsequently recalled that she managed – obviously before June 1944 – to buy a cinema ticket and make her way into the auditorium. When the film began, however, the auditorium was inspected and all 'Russians' were forced to leave the cinema.[60]

Many used their 'spare time' to augment their scarce food rations. When the season allowed, they collected berries and mushrooms from nearby woods, for example.[61] On Sundays, with the agreement of the camp leadership, farmers hired 'eastern workers' who, in return for their labour, were allowed to take food or eat their fill. These sorts of survival strategies were also common among prisoners of war. 'Spare time' thus offered the chance primarily to maintain one's existence rather than to indulge in distraction or pleasure.

For closely guarded prisoners of war – above all those from the Soviet Union and Italy – and for detainees, 'spare time' meant primarily time off work, which they used to wash themselves and to rest. But prisoners of war also managed to organize an at times brisk cultural, educational and sports programme in their camps. The higher the prisoners stood in the Nazi camp hierarchy, the more intensely they could devote themselves to these activities. The theatre performances, educational sessions, sporting competitions and similar activities were also supposed to help to prevent feared camp 'fever'.[62]

7.4 The Fate of Forced Labourers at the War's End

On their liberation by Allied troops at the end of the war, the forced labourers became displaced persons. Most of them initially remained in their camps, although they no longer had to work. Many wandered about and 'arranged' provisions, clothing, furniture or other objects for themselves. Among the local population, fears of rape, plunder and murder by 'marauding' former forced labourers spread. Conversely, liberated female 'eastern workers' became the victims of rape by Red Army soldiers.[63]

Despite the destruction of the German infrastructure, however, the repatriation of the DPs proceeded astoundingly quickly. The Allies estimated that around 11.1 million DPs were dispersed throughout Europe at the end of the war, of whom 10.3 million were in the former 'Greater German Reich' (Germany, Austria, parts of Czechoslovakia and Poland), 215,000 in France and 110,000 in Norway. By the end of September 1945, over 10 million people had been repatriated. The high point in the process was reached in June, with a daily return rate of almost 100,000 persons.[64]

Not all DPs longed for a speedy return to their homelands, however. Soviet prisoners of war and 'eastern workers' stood under the general suspicion of having collaborated with the enemy and become traitors to their country. As early as 1941 Stalin had threatened them with the corresponding penalty. In spite of these reproaches, for at least three reasons Moscow sought to persuade 'every Soviet citizen down to the last one'[65] to return home, in many cases under de facto coercion. The first reason was economic: as a result of the extensive war damage, the USSR faced a shortage of workers, which was to be addressed, in part, by the Soviet DPs 'to be repatriated'. Only with the mobilization of the available workforce could the country be rebuilt. Particularly in the farthest reaches of the Soviet Union, where an enormous industrial base was being established, there was a dearth of workers. Thus, a proportion of those returning home were sent to work battalions or work camps, often in inhospitable regions.[66]

The second reason was ideological: the Soviet government feared that the Soviet citizens remaining abroad would allow themselves be turned into 'enemies of the USSR' and Western spies under the influence of damaging 'capitalist' ideas and anti-Soviet propaganda. With the escalation of the Cold War, this latent fear of a Western conspiracy increased steadily. The screening ('filtration') of the returnees by Soviet security organs is also to be seen in this context. As prisoners of war or forced labourers, they had been in direct contact with the West and had seen that the people there led lives that were in no way worse than under communism. In the eyes of the Soviet government, this experience had destructive potential for their state structure, which is why they viewed those returning home as potential opponents. Partial isolation in work battalions or camps was the logical conclusion, in the view of the Soviet leaders. It was supposed to prevent any 'undermining' of Soviet society by the repatriates.

The third reason reflected the aim of tracking down those former forced labourers and prisoners of war who had turned against the Soviet Union and therefore deserved 'just' punishment. However, the charge of treason applied to practically everyone returning home: from the start, the Soviet leadership had judged the forced labour carried out in the Third Reich to have been 'work for the enemy'. In his order no. 270 of 17 August 1941,[67] Stalin had labelled all Red Army soldiers taken prisoner as traitors to their country who, together with their relatives, would be punished at home. They stood under the collective suspicion of collaboration. Until autumn 1945 there were no major differences between the interests of the Western Allies and those of the Soviet Union with regard to repatriation. Out of military, administrative and supply-technical considerations, the American and British army leaderships even supported the policy of relocating displaced Soviet citizens to the territory of the USSR. The basis for this was the Yalta agreement of 11 February 1945, in which the Western Allies consented to the desire of the Soviet Union to repatriate Soviet DPs regardless of their individual wishes.

In practice, however, massive coercion proved necessary in order to fulfil this agreement. Many DPs physically resisted the handover or chose suicide over repatriation. Nevertheless, the American and British forces delivered Soviet DPs to the Soviet Union until the first cracks started to show in the alliance of convenience.[68] Prominent victims of this policy included the Cossacks, who were handed over by the British to Soviet units in the Austrian towns of Lienz and Judenburg, among other places. Many chose to commit suicide rather than return to the Soviet Union.[69]

Stalin's manic desire to lead all Soviet citizens back into the homeland, paired with the latent fear of a Western conspiracy, would form the basis of Soviet foreign policy in the years after the war and fundamentally influence the fate of hundreds of thousands of former forced labourers and prisoners of war.

7.4.1 'Without Any Exceptions': Repatriation and 'Filtration' of Soviet DPs

For the implementation of the most complete possible repatriation to the USSR, the 'Administration of the Plenipotentiary for Matters Concerning the Repatriation Attached to the Council of the People's Commissars (SNK) of the USSR' emerged in October 1944. The return was to be effected 'without any exceptions', regardless of the individual wishes of the DPs, and, if required, even with violence.[70] The Administration was subordinated to the former leader of the Main Administration for Intelligence in the General Staff of the Red Army, Colonel General Filipp I. Golikov. Together with his two deputies, Colonel General I.V. Smorodinov and Lieutenant General Konstantin D. Golubev, Golikov presided over a staff of 200 employees in Moscow as well as 210 military personnel abroad.[71]

Not only the return but also the screening of each and every individual by officers of the Soviet secret services was obligatory. The backdrop to this was an institutionalized mistrust of those who had spent time abroad and been exposed to foreign influences. As early as 1941 the idea of a complete screening of all Soviet citizens who had been in 'enemy territory' was born. At first, this primarily affected soldiers and officers of the Red Army who had fallen into captivity.[72]

The Soviet government decided to construct a new kind of camp system for the screening of the millions of people returning home, intended to cover all of Eastern Europe and the Soviet occupation zone in Germany and Austria. In the summer of 1945 the system on German territory and in other European countries comprised twenty-two collection and transit sites and seventy-four 'Screening-filtration Camps' (PFL), which were under the jurisdiction of the GULAG. On Soviet territory there were an additional eighteen 'Screening-filtration Points' (PFP), forty-three special camps of the GULAG, and twenty-six 'Screening-filtration Camps'.

The screening was conducted by a 'troika', composed of one representative each of the NKVD (People's Commissariat for Internal Affairs), the NKGB (People's Commissariat for State Security) and SMERSH (Smert' Shpionam [literally, 'death to the spies'], Soviet Counterintelligence), under the chairmanship of the NKVD representative.[73] The 'exposure of traitors to one's country, spies, traitors and other questionable persons' had always been a matter for the security services of the USSR. The interrogation sought to establish the identity of each repatriate, determine particulars about his or her place of residence, status and activity abroad, and conduct a thorough investigation of his or her social and family background. It was also of interest how the person in question had ended up abroad, under what circumstances the return to the USSR had taken place, and whether he or she could identify 'traitors' by name. Decisive for the future of the repatriates was whether the screening and filtration file contained compromising material or whether the interviewee appeared to be 'unsuspicious'.[74]

The organization of the registration, 'filtration' and special screening of former forced labourers was regulated by Ordinance of the Council of the People's Commissars of the USSR No. 30-12s of 6 January 1945. As a rule, only those who were liberated from a concentration camp or had been under fifteen years of age at the time of their abduction to the Reich were regarded as not incriminated. The former 'eastern workers' got off relatively lightly. Most of them were deployed in reconstruction and dismantlement works for another few months and then allowed to return home. However, return to the cities of Moscow, Leningrad and Kiev was prohibited in principle. The Red Army took back into its ranks soldiers of call-up age who did not arouse any suspicions and sent officers, stripped of their rank, to a punishment battalion. Invalids returned to their home towns, where they underwent further screening by local organs of the NKVD. The secret services sent a proportion of those who were seriously incriminated to forced labour camps or even shot them.[75]

There were exact guidelines on different degrees of 'suspiciousness'. Those who had served in German military formations, police units or in the the collaborationist Vlasov Army were transferred to the Screening-filtration camps of the NKVD for 'further screening'. Individuals who 'appeared suspicious' were brought to their places of residence and subjected to an interrogation by the local

NKVD. Persons about whom there existed particulars regarding 'enemy activity' were detained and transferred to the NKVD or SMERSH, which would initiate an inquiry.[76]

The goal-orientated activity of the Repatriation Administration yielded results, particularly in the second half of 1945.[77] As Colonel General Golikov disclosed, more than 5.2 million people, of whom 3.1 million were men, 1.5 million women and 600,000 children under sixteen years of age, had returned to the USSR by the beginning of October 1945.[78] According to Soviet statistics, 5.3 million DPs had returned to the Soviet Union by March 1946, of whom three million had been liberated by the Red Army and 2.4 million by the Western Allies.[79]

The extent of Stalinist terror against former prisoners of war and civilian workers can now be quantified. According to Viktor Zemskov, around 4.2 million Soviet repatriates had passed through the camps of the NKVD by 1 March 1946. Up to that point in time, of these 'screened' repatriates 58 per cent (2.4 million) were allowed to return home, 19 per cent (801,000) were called up by the army, 14 per cent (608,000) were assigned to work battalions and finally 7 per cent (272,000) were transferred to the secret service, NKVD. The last group was composed primarily of people whom the secret service regarded as collaborators, including captured Soviet officers and members of pro-German military formations. A further 2 per cent (89,000) were still at the collection sites or had been enlisted for dismantlement works in Germany or Austria, for instance.[80]

7.4.2 Remaining in the West

Some 100,000 to 200,000 former forced labourers and prisoners of war remained in the western occupation zones of Germany and Austria, and a proportion of them emigrated to the Western hemisphere. They originated for the most part from the Baltic states, Belarus and the western Ukraine. Washington and London did not define them as Soviet citizens under constitutional law and therefore did not hand them over to the Soviets. Soviet citizens were defined as those who had resided in the Soviet Union on 1 September 1939, thus excluding Balts, Ukrainians or Belorussians of former Polish nationality. Many former 'eastern workers' who did not want to return therefore declared their places of residence as having been in pre-war Poland in order to avoid repatriation. Nevertheless, Moscow made every effort to bring these people back as well.[81]

In most cases, those who wanted to avoid repatriation to the USSR were motivated by one or more of the following five considerations:

1. The fear of punishment: particularly among the Balts and the Ukrainians there were many who had collaborated with the Germans in one way or another. Many Soviet prisoners of war – left in the lurch by their homeland and facing

certain death in a German camp – had switched sides. However, charges of desertion and treason against one's own country were generally levelled against all those who had fallen into German hands, worked for them and survived. In this way, the suspicion of collaboration was attached to all 'eastern workers', although most of them had been abducted or recruited under false pretences. In any case, Nazi propaganda had stoked up fears of possible reprisals. After 1945 the British and Americans would also use this method in order to persuade Soviet DPs not to return to the USSR.

2. Economic considerations: the Soviet economy had been devastated by the Second World War. At the same time, exposure to the West had demonstrated that lives under capitalism were in no way worse than those in the Soviet Union. By remaining in Western Europe or emigrating overseas, many hoped for a better life in economic terms.

3. Ideological-political motives: here resistance against the communist system manifested itself. Many refused repatriation because of the incorporation of the Baltic states, western Ukraine and Belarus into the Soviet Union.

4. Private reasons: these were first and foremost a matter of relationships with non-Soviet citizens. Even after a marriage ceremony, the partner would not have been allowed to live in the Soviet Union without reprisals. The loss of family members in the war made an impact, as some no longer felt emotionally attached to their homeland. This bolstered their decision to begin a new life in the West.

5. Finally, religious motives: the desire for freedom of religious expression could sometimes play a role.

The flow of repatriates into the USSR dwindled with each passing year. In 1947, 30,346 people were repatriated. In the ensuing years, the following totals applied: 1948 – 14,272, 1949 – 6,542, 1950 – 4,527, 1951 – 2,297. In the period from January to July 1952 just 732 people returned, only 131 of whom came from 'capitalist' states. Accordingly, a total of 5,458,588 persons were brought back to the USSR after the war.

In view of these circumstances, on 20 August 1952 the Ministerial Council of the USSR issued an instruction for the repatriation apparatus to be dissolved. The corresponding decree was passed on 29 December 1952. However, this in no way meant the end of the repatriation campaign, which was merely decentralized. Almost nothing changed in the nature of the repatriation process itself. The screening of those returning to the USSR continued to be a matter for the local branches of the MGB.[82]

7.4.3 Stalin's Third Betrayal: Propaganda Aimed at Soviet DPs

The Repatriation Administration built up a formidable propaganda machinery. Its primary task was to try to eradicate rising fears among former forced labourers and prisoners of war, and thereby persuade unwilling Soviet citizens to return to the USSR.[83]

The liberated Soviet forced labourers and prisoners of war were told that they could return home without fear of reprisals. 'The homeland has forgiven! The homeland summons you!', clucked the newspaper *Rodina zovet!* ('The Homeland Calls!'), which was published for Soviet DPs in Germany. With all available means, a specially established propaganda department attempted to persuade 'every single Soviet citizen' to return to the USSR. Many must have learned a bitter lesson after their return in how the actual 'call and care of the homeland' differed from what they had been promised. Aleksandr Solženicyn calls this deception the third betrayal of the soldiers of the Red Army.[84]

The political work of enlightenment among the Soviet DPs was based on Ordinance of the Council of the People's Commissars of the USSR No. 1344-402s of 6 October 1944 as well as on Ordinance of the Organization Office of the Central Committee of the VKP(b) No. 225 of 4 August 1945: 'On the Organization of the Political Work of Enlightenment among the Soviet Citizens who are to be Repatriated'.[85] Its admonition 'to show the repatriates that during the Great Fatherland War the Soviet state was tirelessly concerned for the Soviet citizens in German custody and now assures their return to the homeland as well as their professional and financial care' appeared cynical.[86]

The Political Enlightenment Administration of the Plenipotentiary for the Repatriation of Citizens of the USSR, attached to the Council of the People's Commissars of the USSR, functioned as a coordinating point. At the beginning of January 1945, its head, Colonel Georgij S. Logunov, submitted to Georgij F. Aleksandrov, chief of the Department for Propaganda and Agitation of the Central Committee of the VKP(b) and one of Stalin's leading ideologues, his plan for permanent political-enlightenment work among the Soviet repatriates. Logunov stressed his aim of teaching the returnees about the 'great victories of the Red Army, the position of the Soviet Union, the re-establishment of the people's economy destroyed by the Germans, and the fact that the homeland has not forgotten its sons and daughters and will receive them with consideration and care'. In this way, all citizens of the USSR who had been taken to Germany and the German-occupied territories during the Second World War would be persuaded to return to their homeland.[87]

In a plan composed in 1944, Logunov divided the work between the 'territory of Germany', the transport trains to the USSR, and the reception points for repatriates located in cities such as Kiev, Leningrad, Odessa or Kaliningrad. For the 'territory of Germany', he envisaged the establishment of a total of twelve agitation points ('agitpunkty') in Berlin, Vienna, Munich, Prague, Leipzig, Warsaw, as well as Oslo and Copenhagen, among other locations. Each of these facilities was to receive radio equipment, a travelling cinema, a library with 20,000 brochures, newspaper cabinets, portraits of Stalin and of 'Heroes of the Soviet Union', maps of the USSR and Western Europe, and board games. The tasks of the agitation points included the promulgation of information about reception points and registration and evacuation procedures through radio transmissions and specially prepared pamphlets.

If the citizens of the Soviet Union were already on the transport trains, the ongoing political work of enlightenment was to be pursued through presentations and discussions in the carriages and during longer stops at stations. Reading matter in the form of newspapers and brochures was also to be made available.

For the third stage of repatriation, the reception points in the USSR, Colonel Logunov envisaged evening meetings with 'Heroes of the Fatherland War', collective artistic activity, presentations and film screenings.[88] The goal of the political work of enlightenment was thus not only to persuade the DPs to return home but also to cleanse them of 'Western' influence.

From autumn 1944, a formidable propaganda machinery that drew on all the means and methods for political manipulation available at the time was unleashed on the Soviet DPs. The means and methods included: the publication and distribution of appeals from the Soviet government for its citizens to return to the homeland as quickly as possible; the publication of printed agitation materials, such as wall newspapers, newspapers with titles like *The Homeland Calls!* or *News from the Homeland*; a total of six posters from leading Soviet poster artists; several brochures; articles in Soviet daily newspapers on questions of repatriation and reintegration; special radio programmes on the Berlin radio station 'Volga' and stations in Vienna and the Soviet Union on questions of repatriation and life in the homeland; films and photo reports on the life and work of those who had already returned home; the dispatch to Soviet citizens abroad of letters from repatriated relatives and friends that called for a return to the USSR; the showing of Soviet films in cinemas and the transmission of radio programmes from the USSR; the distribution of Soviet newspapers, journals, brochures and literature to the DPs; the implementation of so-called mass cultural work in various artistic, musical, literary or informative forms, such as puppet theatre performances for Soviet children in DP camps and individual and group discussions with Soviet DPs about their return.[89]

The basic tenor for the propaganda campaign was set in an interview with the head of the Repatriation Administration, Colonel General Filipp I. Golikov, published in *Pravda* on 11 November 1944.[90] All the propaganda work among the Soviet DPs was to orientate itself according to his theories.[91] Golikov sketched out the attitude of his government in the following way:

The Soviet land remembers its citizens who fell into German slavery and worries about them. At home they will receive a reception as sons of the homeland. In Soviet circles, one is of the opinion that even those Soviet citizens who, under German pressure and terror, committed acts which ran contrary to the interests of the USSR will not be called to account if they honestly fulfil their duties upon returning to the homeland. ... All returning Soviet citizens will comprehensively be offered the possibility to partake immediately and actively in the annihilation of the enemy and in the gaining of victory; first with a weapon in hand, second at the workbench, and third in the cultural sphere.[92]

The interview with Colonel General Golikov was soon published as an individual pamphlet as well, initially in late November 1944, with a circulation of 500,000 copies, and again in January 1945, with a circulation of one million. A second pamphlet with the title 'Hitler Germany is clamped in a vice between two fronts', with a print run of 500,000 copies, was also published at the same time.[93] Together with the leaflets 'Soviet citizens! The motherland receives you with love and care!' (a letter from a Soviet citizen liberated from German hands) and 'Soviet citizens abducted to foreign parts', these pamphlets, which were thrown from aeroplanes and distributed in the liberated camps, had a total circulation of 3.1 million copies between October 1944 and March 1945 alone.[94]

Among the printed propaganda materials were also several posters and newspapers designed to give the Soviet DPs a feel for life in the USSR and to make a return seem appealing.[95] This is reflected in the title of the first issue of the repatriation newspaper *For the Honour of the Homeland* (*Za čest' rodiny*) which followed Golikov's interview, stating: 'The homeland awaits you, her sons and daughters, she receives you with love and care.'[96]

The names of the other newspapers also referred to the 'call of the homeland' aimed at the DPs; transmitted 'news from the homeland'; or blazed a trail back 'into the homeland' and wished 'bon voyage'. Nineteen issues of the weekly newspaper *The Homeland Calls* (*Rodina zovet*)[97] appeared in Bielefeld between 22 June 1945 and 17 October 1945, intended for all the Soviet collection points in North-Rhine/Westphalia. The political department of the collection point for former Soviet prisoners of war in Fallinbostel also published a newspaper under the same title.[98] The weekly newspaper with the largest circulation, *Bon Voyage* (*Sčastlivyj put*),[99] was published in Hemer. In Switzerland the newspaper *In the Homeland* (*Na rodinu*)[100] appeared, and for the former prisoners of war in the area of a Scottish division there was *News from the Native Soil* (*Vesti s rodnoj zemli*).[101]

In addition, the newspaper *News from the Homeland* (*Vesti s rodiny*),[102] issued by the Soviet embassy in France on 22 February 1945, reached a circulation of up to 100,000. In accordance with the plans of the Repatriation Administration, this pamphlet was for a long time the only Soviet newspaper available to the millions of Soviet citizens in France, Belgium, the Netherlands and western Germany.[103]

In October 1944 preparations began for a series of small-format brochures for Soviet DPs. The first two brochures – I. Fomičenko's 'The Truth about the Victories of the Red Army' and N. Bryčev's 'Back Home, to the Homeland!' – appeared in December 1944, each with a circulation of 50,000. 'Back Home, to the Homeland!' was particularly popular, which is why a second issue with a print run of 75,000 appeared in July 1945.[104] The Repatriation Administration explained its success as follows: 'the author of the brochures recounts simply and in an accessible fashion how the liberated Soviet citizens have been received in the homeland and how the homeland takes care of them'.[105]

By 1946 a total of nineteen brochures had appeared in the Russian language, with a total circulation of 1.1 million copies. By order of the Repatriation Administration, the brochures also appeared partly in Belorussian, Ukrainian and the Baltic languages.[106] Among the authors were the later Party Secretary Nikita S. Chruščëv and the Polish author Vanda Vasilevskaya, who was also popular in the Soviet Union.[107]

The work of the Political Enlightenment Administration was aimed in particular at Baltic, Belorussian and Ukrainian DPs. Specially produced films and radio programmes were therefore transmitted not only in Russian but also in these other languages. They documented the individual stages of repatriation, the 'loving reception in the homeland', and the successful integration into work and society.[108] For example, in 1945 the East Berlin radio station 'Volga 2' broadcast biweekly, one-hour reports on returning Belorussians. The reports were meant to allay fears of possible reprisals in the Soviet Union on the part of those DPs who had not yet returned.[109]

From 1946 onwards, the effects of the developing Cold War became increasingly apparent. The members of the former anti-Hitler coalition increasingly mistrusted each other rather than the one-time mutual enemy, Nazi Germany.[110] Soviet DPs in the western occupation zones of Germany or in Austria were now confronted with accusations of cooperation with the American or British secret services and of carrying out 'anti-Soviet agitation'. Special radio stations called for the 'exposure of nationalists – agents of the English and Americans, who practice defamatory propaganda in the displaced persons' camps abroad against their return to the homeland'.[111]

At the same time, the British and Americans were blamed for actively carrying out 'anti-Soviet activity' in the western occupation zones of Germany and Austria that dissuaded DPs from wanting to return to the Soviet Union. Furthermore, repeated assaults on Soviet repatriation officers were said to have occurred.[112] As a counterbalance to this 'defamatory propaganda', Soviet propaganda and agitation were intensified.[113]

Towards the end of the 1940s, the Political Enlightenment Administration increasingly used the medium of film; the two documentaries *In the Homeland* (*Na Rodinu*) and *They Returned to the Homeland* (*Oni vernulis' na Rodinu*) emerged, as did the feature film *You Have a Homeland (U nich est' Rodina)*. These audio-visual productions were supposed to help to persuade Soviet citizens who still remained abroad to return to the USSR.[114] Around the beginning of 1949, Golikov submitted his plans for the further strengthening of propaganda among Soviet DPs in Western Europe to the head of the Department for Propaganda and Political Agitation, Dmitrij Šepilov, and the Secretary of the Central Committee of the VKP(b), Michail Suslov.[115] The propaganda departments of the Central Committee of the VKP(b) from the Ukraine, Belarus and the Baltic states were to receive additional support.[116]

Even after Stalin's death in 1953, the new Soviet leadership continued to pursue former Soviet citizens who remained abroad. The simple fact that the number of these people remained high was enough to trouble the Kremlin. In the view of Stalin's successors, potential danger and harm emanated from them. According to Interior Minister Sergej Kruglov, more than 400,000 former Soviet citizens remained in the western occupation zones of Germany and Austria, as well as in the USA, Great Britain, Argentina and other 'capitalist' states. Kruglov feared that they would be used as 'agents in the forthcoming war against the USSR'. According to him, 'indoctrination in the anti-Soviet spirit' was taking place among them. Kruglov proposed the installation of a 'propaganda organ' in the Soviet sector of Berlin, which should bear the name 'Union for the Return to the Homeland' and be staffed with 'trustworthy agents of the MVD [i.e. the Ministry of Internal Affairs], who are themselves repatriates or returning emigrants'. The aim of this Union would be the prevention of emigration and the furthering of the struggle against anti-Soviet propaganda.[117]

Following their arrival in the Soviet Union, many returnees realized that the 'call of the homeland' was very different from what they had been led to expect. The promising slogans and pledges of the Repatriation Administration were ultimately exposed as the 'language of betrayal', the consequences of which were expressed in decades of repression. The former 'eastern workers' and Soviet prisoners of war became victims of a totalitarian regime once again.

7.5 Forced Labour in the Memorialization Process

7.5.1 Memory and Commemoration of Forced Labour in Germany and Austria

During the Second World War, millions of foreign forced labourers became a fixed component of everyday life in wartime in the German Reich. Their manpower constituted the most important 'war booty' of the Nazi regime. Without their deployment, the Nazi war economy, both industry and agriculture, would have collapsed in autumn 1941.[118] Although the foreign women and men were always present in Nazi everyday life, they were in many cases perceived by the native population as an anonymous mass. Individual contact was possible predominantly in agricultural enterprises and in German families, although officially undesirable. Depending on nationality, status and gender, their working and living conditions were shaped by a complex system of discrimination and repression.

Retrospectively, despite their deployment in their millions in the Third Reich, forced labourers were generally regarded as a 'matter of course brought about by the war'. To this day, the dominant view is that it was 'just war' and they 'just came to the farm'. In agriculture, every larger farmer 'had a Frenchman' or a 'Russian'; such is the recollection of many 'eyewitnesses'. Any differentiation between prisoners of war and civilian forced labourers is generally overlooked, as is the 'forced nature' of their stay. To the fore are memories of how the 'foreign workers' integrated themselves into the farming family and even befriended the locals in spite of tough conditions and threats of punishment.[119] 'If we work together, we should also eat together'; thus a woman from Lower Austria recalls the forbidden shared mealtimes with 'her' Soviet prisoner of war.[120]

After the end of the war, contact was in most cases severed, as the forced labourers of the Third Reich sank into oblivion. Those who remained at the scene of their forced labour deployment attempted to integrate themselves as far as possible into the local community and to conceal the 'blemish' in their biography. Only with the fall of the 'Iron Curtain' and the increasingly public discussion of compensation for forced labourers did more and more eyewitnesses set out to search for those people whom they had met as forced labourers during the war and then lost track of. And vice versa, former forced labourers sought contact anew and a reunion after five or six decades.

Alongside this marginalization in the collective memory of the Germans and the Austrians, in particular civilian forced labourers for the Nazis left barely any traces in the so-called 'stony consciousness'.[121] This is particularly indicative, as memorials are enduring testaments to public recollection. In the case of all forms of memorial – commemorative plaques, stone memorials, crosses, inscriptions and the like – the remembrance of positive but also tragic events in the history of a societal fragment is 'cast' in a fixed form and is thus an enduring component part of public life. While the landscape is littered with war memorials to the indigenous victims of the Second World War – primarily soldiers killed in action – and memorial events take place annually at these sites, memorials to civilian forced labourers are rarely to be found. Little in public reminds us of their work, of the crimes that were perpetrated against them, or even of their simple existence.[122]

By contrast, many memorials commemorate the fate of prisoners of war in the Third Reich. They were usually established either on the site of the former camps or on the prisoners' cemeteries.[123] While a few prisoner-of-war museums and memorials even came into existence in Germany and Poland, there is so far nothing comparable in Austria. However, some of these initiatives in Germany have been met with considerable local resistance, such as the exhibition which opened at Sandbostel near Bremen in 1994. The actual camp site at Sandbostel was used commercially up to 2004, with the buildings left to go to ruin.[124] It is only very recently that this seems to have changed, at least at Sandbostel, with the state government of Lower Saxony coming out in strong support of the establishment of a permanent memorial at this site.

In Austria, mainly the former prisoners of war themselves or, following the end of the war, the occupation forces mounted commemorative plaques, although the latter are to be maintained by the Republic of Austria in accordance with the Austrian State Treaty of 1955. From 1945 onwards, the Soviets carried out count-less reburials of their prisoners of war and normally furnished the burial grounds with obelisks from which the red Soviet star hangs.[125] The local population, however, pays little attention to these memorials. They are, therefore, only to a limited extent part of the collective memory.[126]

Only in exceptional cases did the official Austrian authorities or the local popu-lation seize the initiative to commemorate the fate of foreign prisoners of war. Even at the sites of the large former Stalags (*Stammlager*, or 'regular camps'), such as Wolfsberg, Krems-Gneixendorf and Kaisersteinbruch, few traces of the camps remain today, not to mention memorials. In Wolfsberg, for example, the sur-viving original camp barracks were torn down in the 1990s. Apart from the street name Lagerstraße, only an inconspicuous commemorative plaque for former French prisoners of war makes reference to Stalag XVIII A.[127]

Memorial sites for concentration camp inmates and Hungarian Jews murdered in the course of the death marches in 1944/5 are to be encountered comparatively often. The large former concentration camps at Auschwitz, Bergen-Belsen, Mauthausen and Dachau have been converted into memorial sites. On the respec-tive liberation day, survivors, family members and government representatives congregate each year at official memorial events. Furthermore, at many satellite camps, which were scattered across the entire Reich territory, commemorative plaques or memorials are to be found. The memorial landscape for murdered Hungarian Jews along the routes of their death marches is also fairly dense. This is a sign that the sense of public injustice is stronger when it comes to concentra-tion camp inmates and the murdered Hungarian Jews than it is for prisoners of war and civilian forced labourers. The extreme brutality of the crimes and the pictures of emaciated concentration camp inmates have penetrated the consciousness of the population to a much greater extent.[128]

Apart from the deployment of concentration camp prisoners for forced labour, the topic of forced labour in the Nazi economy in general has only recently become the subject of public and scholarly discussion in Germany and Austria. In addition to those forms of commemoration which were set up at particular localities (usually the sites of former camps), more and more local archives and museums have put on travelling exhibitions. One good example is an exhibition organized in 2002 by the Historische Centrum Hagen together with a number of towns and districts in Northrhine-Westphalia. Similar projects exist in Saxony. It is hoped that they will contribute to the topic becoming part of the regional historical consciousness. In addition, comprehensive websites have been created with visualized topographies of slave labour in specific regions. They allow schools and youth groups to search for historical evidence of such events in their own vicinity. One example is the website developed by the Documentation Centre 'Köln im Nationalsozialismus' (Cologne during the National Socialist Period – the centre is housed in the former Gestapo prison of Cologne) in conjunction with a special exhibition on Nazi slave labour in 2003.

The trigger for this process was first and foremost the public debate over the material compensation of former forced labourers in the Third Reich, in which Germany led the way. Ulrich Herbert refers to the question of compensation for former forced labourers after 1945–9, a – politically and historiographically – particularly difficult problem. This question was not posed for the GDR inasmuch as it in general did not pay out any compensation to non-German victims of National Socialism. For the FRG, on the other hand, this issue constituted one of the most long-winded and difficult developments in the already far-from-straightforward field of legislation for granting compensation. The Federal Republic did indeed declare itself prepared financially to compensate those persecuted by the Nazi regime, but this rule contained far-reaching exceptions. Thus, forced labourers did not qualify for the category of 'persecution', as they had not been deployed for political, religious, racial or ideological reasons, but rather for war-economic reasons. Consequently, they – initially – remained exempt from compensation.[129]

A decisive change came when, with the end of the division of Germany, the prerequisites for the London Agreement on German External Debts of 1953 fell away, according to which German reparation payments were to be agreed on only after a peace treaty. In order to contain the considerable demands which resulted from this, the Federal Republic arranged with the CIS and Poland the payment of a one-off sum of 1.5 billion marks (767 million euros), of which 500 million (226 million euros) flowed to Poland and a billion marks (511 million euros) to the CIS. These countries set up their own foundations, which paid out the financial assistance to the former forced labourers. The Federal Government insisted, however, that forced labour for the Nazis was not a typically Nazi injustice that brought a right to compensation with it. Further demands from former forced labourers from other countries were to be put paid to this argument.[130]

In the course of the 1980s and especially the 1990s, private companies were increasingly confronted with demands for compensation from former forced labourers. Initially, they were able to reject these demands by referring to the legal situation. This began to change as a result of initiatives from the Volkswagen and Daimler-Benz firms; the well-founded, scholarly study of the deployment of forced labourers in these concerns from the mid-1990s was followed by a willingness to pay financial compensation in different ways to former forced labourers.[131] Since then, a wealth of studies have appeared examining the history of companies, as well as local and regional histories, with forced labour as their main focus. Alongside this scholarly reappraisal, former employees or their successor concerns and local authorities also set out in search of former forced labourers and invited them to Germany. These visits were in some cases accompanied by the carrying out of oral history studies.

In Austria the 'compensation debate' began in the late autumn of 1998. The fate of former forced labourers who had suffered injustices during the Nazi regime on the territory of present-day Austria was now 'suddenly' regarded as an Austrian problem as well. First of all, however, a political consensus had to be established that Austria's moral responsibility also extended to this group of victims. This discourse was accompanied by scholarly projects in the framework of the Austrian Historians' Commission,[132] and by a wide reappraisal in the media, where public discussion in letters to newspapers and newspaper commentaries was dominated by negative opinions and feelings of resentment.[133] As in Germany, countless studies examining the history of companies and local histories have also appeared in Austria in recent years.[134]

The Republic of Austria committed itself to 'voluntary payments to former slave and forced labourers of the National Socialist regime' through the 'Law on Conciliation Funds', which was enacted unanimously by the National Council in July 2000 and came into force on 27 November 2000.[135] Initially, six billion shillings (436 million euros) were raised from taxpayers' money and financial contributions from the Austrian economy, which the Austrian Funds for Conciliation, Peace and Cooperation (or 'Conciliation Funds') administered following its establishment on 20 December 2000.[136] Forced labourers deployed in agriculture and minors who had been brought into the territory of present-day Austria together with a parent, or had been born in Austria during the forced labour deployment of the mother, also qualified for payments from the Conciliation Funds. Former prisoners of war, however, were expressly excluded.[137]

Payments to former forced labourers only began, however, after the establishment of legal security had been officially confirmed following the abolition of the final legal hurdles at the end of July 2001 (collective lawsuits in the USA). In contrast to Germany, the Austrian side had negotiated the compensation for forced labourers separately from other ongoing issues of restitution. From 2001 to 2005, symbolical financial payments were made to over 130,000 former forced labourers to a total value of around 352 million euros.[138] Especially for many of the former forced labourers living in Eastern Europe, the financial compensation ensured a considerable improvement in their quality of life, for example making it possible for them to obtain medicines. At least as important, however, was the fact that they were officially recognized for the first time as victims of the Nazi regime.[139] 'Thank you for not forgetting me,' said one former 'eastern worker'.[140]

After the enacting of the law and the payment of the compensation, the public perception of the issue stagnated again. In order to work against this neglect, the 'Future Funds of the Republic of Austria' was brought into being in 2005 as a successor organization to the Austrian Conciliation Funds. Using those resources that were left over after the completion of the activities of the Conciliation Funds, the Future Funds promotes humanitarian and academic projects that 'serve the interests and the remembrance of the victims of the National Socialist regime and the commemoration of the threat from totalitarian systems and tyranny as well as international cooperation, and contribute to an advancement of respect for human rights and mutual tolerance in these areas'.[141]

7.5.2 Memory and Commemoration of Forced Labour in the (Former) Soviet Union

Forced labour deployment in the Third Reich ended with the Allied liberation at the end of the war. The vast majority of the DPs returned to their homes during 1945. For former Soviet forced labourers, however, the newly won freedom brought a new ordeal. The Soviet government placed prisoners of war and 'eastern workers' under the collective suspicion of collaboration, which was accompanied by screening by the secret services and by various forms of repression.

A first rethinking of this occurred at the 20th Party Conference of the CPSU in February 1956, when the new General Secretary in his secret address declared Stalin's rule to have been a period of terror and criticized the Stalinist 'personality cult'. In the process, Nikita Chruščëv disclosed serious mistakes in Stalin's leadership of the state and army in the Second World War. In the course of the de-Stalinization and liberalization process instigated by this new approach, which was to end with the march of Warsaw Pact troops into Prague in August 1968, the initial rehabilitation of former Soviet prisoners of war took place.

In spring 1957 condemned former prisoners of war were amnestied and released from imprisonment. The Ministerial Council of the USSR also passed a resolution to put those returning home on a par with soldiers who had fought on the front. Repatriates could also be readmitted to the Party and reclaim decorations and military ranks.[142]

In this phase, the first literary and autobiographical, as well as filmed, treatments of war captivity in the Third Reich appeared. Among the most popular works were the novella *Sud'ba čeloveka*[143] (The Fate of a Man), published in 1956/7, by the famous Soviet author Michail Šolochov, and the partially autobiographical novel *Propavšče bez vesti*[144] (The Missing) by Stepan Zlobin, in which the winner of the Stalin Prize recounted his personal experiences as a prisoner of war in Zeithain near Riesa. On the one hand, Zlobin emphasized the courage of Soviet soldiers in German camps, thus contributing significantly to the restoration of their honour in

Soviet society, and, on the other hand, he criticized the injustice with which those returning home were persecuted and imprisoned anew by the Soviet authorities.[145] Film adaptations of Šolochov's novella[146] and *Čistoe nebo*[147] (Clear Skies) represent two typical films of the 'Chruščëv Thaw'. Both addressed the issue of Soviet prisoners of war in the Third Reich and their discrimination in the Soviet Union after the end of the war, which had until then been a taboo subject. Both were extremely successful feature films and reflected political and social forms of dealing with these issues in the Soviet Union at the end of the 1950s and the beginning of the 1960s.[148]

The amnesty of February 1957, however, in no way meant the complete rehabilitation of the former prisoners of war, particularly as the 'Khrushchev Thaw' was soon followed by a 'new ice age'. The 'mark of Cain', as one of those returning home termed the stigma in his biography,[149] turned them into second-class citizens in their homeland and made them stay silent about their time in the Third Reich. Close relatives and friends often learned nothing about the years spent in German hands. On applications for a university place or a job, they had to give periods of residence abroad, which constituted a clear stain on their CVs. To acquire an identity card they had to state whether they or a relative had spent time in Germany during the Second World War. For former prisoners of war, there was a gaping decades-long hole in their military passbook or 'employment booklet', which had arisen as a result of their loss of status as a member of the military. This led to the classification of the former prisoners of war in lower wage and pension categories. A dispute as to whether prisoners of war were traitors to their country or not, conducted in 1987 and 1988 by means of heated letters to the editor in the daily newspaper *Izvestia* and the army newspaper *Krasnaja Zvezda*, demonstrates how long this social ostracism continued.[150]

The Society for Historical Enlightenment, Human Rights and Social Welfare ('Memorial') in Moscow, which had been founded in 1988 on the initiative of the civil rights activist Andrej Sacharov, was unexpectedly overrun from March 1990 onwards by a flood of hundreds of thousands of letters from former 'eastern workers'. This flood was triggered by a request of the German Green Party to 'Memorial' to support the investigation into the approximate number of living Soviets who had formerly been forced labourers for the Nazis. The demand for compensation for former forced labourers under the Nazis was to be brought before the German Bundestag for the umpteenth time. Within the framework of a press conference at the end of 1989, those individuals concerned were invited to approach 'Memorial' or the Heinrich Böll Foundation in Cologne in order to provide some input into the drafting of a law, which was expected to be of marginal significance. The widely read weekly newspaper *Nedelja* then published an article at the end of February 1990 which was to emerge as a classic newspaper hoax. Under the title 'A Pension from Abroad', the journalist Andrei Ždankin reported on the search for former 'eastern workers'; the Green Party was said to have suggested paying compensation to all those persons concerned who were still living. The article concluded with the promising and misleading sentence: 'The suggestion of the Greens has been accepted.' Neither the subsequent flood of letters nor the storm of telephone enquiries to 'Memorial' could be stopped, in spite of the fact that newspapers, radio and television were quick to proclaim that the report was false. 'Memorial', it was stated, was in no way responsible for the payment of – and moreover in no way determined – compensation.

The former 'eastern workers' had, however, broken their forty-five-year silence. They not only wanted to bear witness to their hitherto taboo past, but also to receive financial and moral compensation. A total of more than 400,000 former Soviet forced labourers contacted 'Memorial'. These semi-official declarations allow for a brief retrospective glance at the enormous number of abductions to the Third Reich, at the work, remuneration and treatment of the individuals concerned, and at their fate following their liberation. One former 'eastern worker' called Evdokija, for example, reported that – for the sake of convenience – she had received the name 'Maria' in an Austrian household. This can be seen as symptomatic of the replaceability of the individual forced labourers and the loss of their identity. In addition to their function as autobiographical sources, these letters represent an important tool in the search for former 'eastern workers'.[151]

Another five years were to pass before the final official rehabilitation of former Soviet prisoners of war and 'eastern workers' on 24 January 1995 in Decree of the President of the Russian Federation No. 63 'On the Restoration of the Legal Rights of Russian Citizens – Former Prisoners of War and Civilians Who Were Repatriated during the Great Patriotic War and in the Post-war Period'. Fifty years after the end of the war, the decree restored 'historical justice' and characterized the approach of the Soviet Party and state leadership towards the repatriates as political repression. They were thereby granted the status of victims and the corresponding privileges, for instance with regard to rent and the use of public transport. Former Soviet prisoners of war are now officially regarded as participants in the 'Great Patriotic War'. For legal reasons, however, they remain exempted from the compensation payments made by Germany and Austria to former forced labourers.[152]

Appendix: Maps

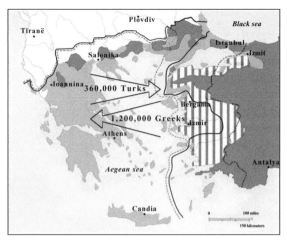

--- Greek-Turkish border proposed at the Peace conference 1919
— Greek-Turkish border 1919-1923
---- Greek-Turkish border after 1923
▓ Major concentrations of Turks/Muslims
║║║ Mixed Greek-Turkish population
▒ Major concentrations of Greeks/Orthodoxes

Map 1 Greek–Turkish population exchange, 1922/23.

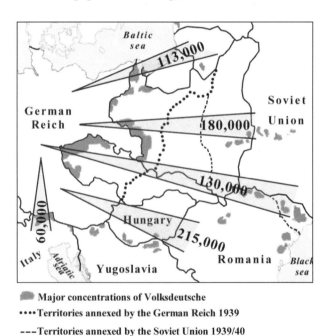

▓ Major concentrations of Volksdeutsche
•••• Territories annexed by the German Reich 1939
--- Territories annexed by the Soviet Union 1939/40

Map 2 The repatriation of Volksdeutsche, 1939/41.

Map 3 German plans for colonization (Generalplan Ost), 1940.

Map 4 Third Generalplan Ost, May 1942.

Map 5 Major forced population movements, 1944/45–50.

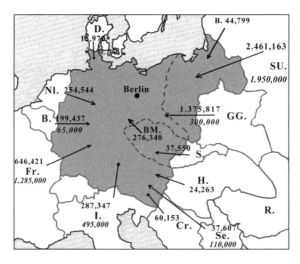

Map 6 Foreign forced workers in the Great Reich.

Notes

Foreword

1. The results of these workshops were published in *Annali dell'Istituto storico italo-germanico in Trento*, vol. 27 (2001), pp. 419–632, vol. 28 (2002), pp. 367–618 and vol. 29 (2003), pp. 517–689.

1 Introduction

1. See Hans Lemberg, 'Kulturautonomie, Minderheitenrechte, Assimilation', in Matthias Beer (ed.), *Auf dem Weg zum ethnisch reinen Nationalstaat?* (Attempto Verlag, 2004), pp. 91f.
2. See Michael Mann, *The Dark Side of Democracy: Explaining Ethnic Cleansing* (Cambridge University Press, 2005).
3. Tomáš G. Masaryk, *The New Europe (the Slav Standpoint)* (Bucknell University Press, 1972, original edition 1918), p. 69. The reference to socialism was dropped in the 1972 English translation.
4. Gusztáv Gratz, 'A Jelenkor politikai fejlődése', in Gyula Kornis, Gusztáv Gratz, Lóránt Hegedűs and Emil Schimanek (eds), *A mai világ képe*, vol. 2 (Királyi Magyar Egyetemi Nyomda, *s.a.*), p. 290.
5. Erik Goldstein, *The First World War Peace Settlements 1919–1925* (Longman, 2002).
6. It is estimated that there were about one million refugees in the first case, whereas in 1921 the Magyar government claimed it had accommodated 234,000 refugees (from Romania, Yugoslavia and Czechoslovakia); Michael R. Marrus, *The Unwanted: European Refugees in the Twentieth Century* (Oxford University Press, 1985), pp. 65f.
7. Goldstein, *First World War*, p. 105.
8. Allen C. Lynch, 'Woodrow Wilson and the Principle of "National Self-determination" as Applied to Habsburg Europe', in Henry Huttenbach and Francesco Privitera (eds), *Self-determination: From Versailles to Dayton. Its Historical Legacy* (Longo, 1999), p. 17.
9. Margaret MacMillan, *The Peacemakers: The Paris Conference of 1919 and Its Attempt to End War* (Murray, 2001), p. 21.
10. Lynch, 'Woodrow Wilson', p. 29.
11. See Carlile A. Macartney, *National States and National Minorities* (Oxford University Press, 1934).
12. Carole Fink, 'The Minorities Question at the Paris Peace Conference: The Polish

204 · *Notes*

Minority Treaty, June 28, 1919', in Manfred Boemeke, Gerald D. Feldman and Elisabeth Glaser (eds), *The Treaty of Versailles: A Reassessment after 75 Years* (Cambridge University Press, 1998) and Jost Dülffer, 'Selbstbestimmung, Wirtschaftsinteressen und Großmachtpolitik', in Matthias Beer (ed.), *Auf dem Weg zum ethnisch reinen Nationalstaat?* (Attempto, 2004), pp. 41–67.

13. See the case study by Christian Raitz von Frentz, *A Lesson Forgotten: Minority Protection under the League of Nations. The Case of the German Minority in Poland 1920–1934* (St Martin's Press, 1999). In 1934 Poland unilaterally denounced the convention on the protection of the minorities, and so even this thin protective veil failed. See Martin Scheuermann, *Minderheitenschutz contra Konfliktverhütung? Die Minderheitenpolitik des Völkerbundes in den zwanziger Jahren* (Herder Institut, 2000).

14. Marek Waldenberg, *Le questioni nazionali nell'Europa centro-orientale* (Bruno Mondadori, 1994). Polish original edition: *Kwestie narodowe w Europie środkowo-Wschodniej: dzieje, idee* (Wydawn. Naukowe PWN, 1992).

15. Ezra Mendelsohn, *The Jews of East Central Europe between the World Wars* (Indiana University Press, 1983).

16. On Poland, which had the largest Jewish community in Europe, i.e. more than three million, see Gustavo Corni, 'Motivi dell'antisemitismo in Polonia fra le due guerre mondiali', in Catherine Brice and Giovanni Miccoli (eds), *Les racines chrétiennes de l'antisémitisme politique* (École Française, 2003), pp. 231–58.

17. The most important scholar of the plebiscites in the 1800s and 1900s is without doubt Sarah Wambaugh; see in particular her monograph *Plebiscites since the World War* (Carnegie Endowment for International Peace, 1933).

18. For a brief overview, see Marrus, *Unwanted*, pp. 40–50.

19. There is a heated debate about whether what happened to the Armenians should be called genocide. The official Turkish view rejects this assessment vehemently, yet prevents any research into the events by rejecting access to Turkish archives. For some recent studies, see Donald Bloxham, *The Great Game of Genocide: Imperialism, Nationalism and the Destruction of the Ottoman Armenians* (Oxford University Press, 2005); Vahakn N. Dadrian, *The History of the Armenian Genocide: Ethnic Conflict from the Balkans to Anatolia to the Caucasus*, 6th rev. edn (Berghahn Books, 2004); Taner Akçam, *From Empire to Republic: Turkish Nationalism and the Armenian Genocide* (Zed Books, 2004); Günter Lewy, *The Armenian Massacres in Ottoman Turkey: A Disputed Genocide* (University of Utah Press, 2005). See also Wolfgang Gust (ed.), *Der Völkermord an den Armeniern 1915/16: Dokumente aus dem politischen Archiv des deutschen Auswärtigen Amts* (zu Klampen, 2005).

20. See Michael Llewellyn Smith, *Ionian Vision: Greece in Asia Minor, 1919–1922* (Allen Lane, 1973), pp. 1–20.

21. Dimitri Pentzopoulos, *The Balkan Exchange of Minorities and Its Impact on Greece*, 2nd edn (Hurst & Company, 2002), p. 38.

22. Llewellyn Smith, *Ionian Vision*, pp. 284–313. See also Henry Morgenthau, *I Was Sent to Athens* (Doubleday, 1929). Morgenthau was US ambassador in Constantinople 1913–16 and in 1923 became the first chairman of the Greek Resettlement Commission (see below).

23. Stephen P. Ladas, *The Exchange of Minorities: Bulgaria, Greece and Turkey* (Macmillan, 1932), pp. 18–23.

24. From a statement by Fridtjof Nansen, the League of Nation's High Commissioner for Refugees, at the Territorial and Military Commission of the Lausanne Conference, 1 December 1922, cited in Ladas, *The Exchange of Minorities*, p. 338.
25. Cited in Renée Hirschon (ed.), *Crossing the Aegean: An Appraisal of the 1923 Compulsory Population Exchange between Greece and Turkey* (Berghahn Books, 2003), Appendix I, pp. 281–7, here p. 282.
26. Ibid.
27. The Treaty of Lausanne of 23 July 1923, the peace treaty between Greece and Turkey, also exempted the Greek population of Imbros and Tenedos, two islands in the Dardanelles, from the forced transfer; see Ladas, *The Exchange of Minorities*, pp. 418–19.
28. Ibid., pp. 437–9.
29. Ibid., pp. 567–83 (text of the convention: Appendix VIII, pp. 817–30).
30. Ibid., pp. 27–331 (text of the agreement: Appendix I, pp. 739–43); for a brief overview, see Marrus, *Unwanted*, pp. 106–9.
31. Ladas, *The Exchange of Minorities*, pp. 618–704.
32. Pentzopoulos, *The Balkan Exchange of Minorities*, p. 225.
33. See, for example, Renée Hirschon, *Heirs of the Greek Catastrophe: The Social Life of Asia Minor Refugees in Piraeus* (Berghahn Books, 1998), which is a wide-ranging case study of Kokkina, an urban district and one of the largest refugee quarters established in 1923 near the harbour of Piraeus. The fieldwork was done in the early 1970s, and the study shows the long-term impact of the uprooting.
34. See, for example, John A. Petropulos, 'The Compulsory Exchange of Populations: Greek–Turkish Peacemaking, 1922–1930', *Byzantine and Modern Greek Studies*, vol. 2 (1976), pp. 135–60.
35. See, for example, Alfred-Maurice de Zayas, 'A Historical Survey of Twentieth Century Expulsions', in Anna C. Bramwell, *Refugees in the Age of Total War* (Unwin Hyman, 1988), esp. pp. 15–37; Christa Meindersma, 'Population Exchanges: International Law and State Practice', *International Journal of Refugee Law*, vol. 9 (1997), Part 1, pp. 335–64 , Part 2, pp. 613–53.
36. For a recent assessment of the Lausanne Convention, see the contributions in Hirschon (ed.), *Crossing the Aegean*; see also the essays published in Marina Cattaruzza, Marco Dogo and Raoul Pupo (eds), *Esodi: Trasferimenti forzati di popolazione nel Novecento europeo* (Edizioni Scientifiche Italiane, 2000), Part 1, pp. 13–101.

2 Forced Migration Plans and Policies of Nazi Germany

1. Still relevant is Eberhard Jäckel, *Hitlers Weltanschauung: Entwurf einer Herrschaft* (R. Wunderlich, 1969).
2. Adolf Hitler, *Mein Kampf* (London, 1969), p. 124.
3. Henry Picker (ed.), *Hitlers Tischgespräche im Führerhauptquartier 1941–1942* (Seewald, 1965), p. 320.
4. See Woodruff D. Smith, *The Ideological Origins of Nazi Imperialism* (Oxford University Press, 1986) and Michel Korinman, *Quand l'Allemagne pensait le monde: Grandeur et décadence d'une géopolitique* (Presses Universitaires de France, 1990).

5. Hitler, *Mein Kampf*, p. 126.

6. See Roger Chickering, *We Men Who Feel Most German: A Cultural Study of the Pan-German League 1886–1914* (Allen & Unwin, 1984).

7. Hitler, *Mein Kampf*, cited in J. Noakes and G. Pridham (eds), *Nazism 1919–1945: 3. Foreign Policy, War and Racial Extermination* (Exeter University Publications, 1988), pp. 741f.

8. Hugh R. Trevor-Roper (ed.), *Hitler's Table Talk 1941–44: His Private Conversations* (Weidenfeld and Nicolson, 1953), p. 24, conversation held during the night of 8 and 9 August 1941.

9. Gerhard L. Weinberg (ed.), *Hitlers Zweites Buch: Ein Dokument aus dem Jahre 1928* (DVA, 1961).

10. Ian Kershaw, *Hitler 1889–1936: Hubris* (Penguin, 1998), p. 292.

11. Michael Burleigh, *Germany Turns Eastward: A Study of Ostforschung in the Third Reich* (Cambridge University Press, 1988), p. 154.

12. See Michael Fahlbusch, *Wissenschaft im Dienst der nationalsozialistischen Politik: Die 'Volksdeutschen Forschungsgemeinschaften' von 1939–1945* (Nomos, 1999).

13. See Ingo Haar and Michael Fahlbusch (eds), *German Scholars and Ethnic Cleansing 1920–1945* (Berghahn Books, 2005).

14. Those who took the direct and causal connection between social sciences and extermination to its extreme are analysed in Götz Aly and Susanne Heim, *Vordenker der Vernichtung: Auschwitz und die deutschen Pläne für eine neue europäische Ordnung* (Hoffmann und Campe, 1991).

15. See Wolfgang Wippermann, *Der Ordensstaat als Ideologie: Das Bild des Deutschen Ordens in der deutschen Geschichtsschreibung und Publizistik* (Athäeneum, 1979).

16. See the second part of the documented monograph by Raitz von Frentz, *A Lesson Forgotten*.

17. Otto Dann, *Nation und Nationalismus in Deutschland 1770–1990* (Beck, 1993), p. 266.

18. See, for example, Michael H. Kater, 'Die Artamanen: Völkische Jugend in der Weimarer Republik', *Historische Zeitschrift*, vol. 213 (1971), pp. 577–638.

19. Data taken from the respective national statistics of the 1930s, except for France, which did not count the inhabitants of Alsace and Lorraine as national minorities; Dann, *Nation und Nationalismus*, p. 336.

20. Doris L. Bergen, 'The Nazi Concept of "Volksdeutsche" and the Exacerbation of Anti-Semitism in Eastern Europe, 1939–1945', *Journal of Contemporary History*, vol. 29, no. 4 (1994), p. 569.

21. Ibid., p. 571.

22. Karl-Dietrich Bracher, *La dittatura tedesca* (Il Mulino, 1973), p. 435 (original edition: Kiepenhauer & Witsch, 1969). A similar policy was pursued by Italian fascism, which tried to strengthen contacts with Italian emigrant communities on the one hand and to set up a sort of 'international fascism' on the other. But Italian fascism had primarily political and ideological aims, while the aims of Hitler's regime were of an ethnic nature. Cf. Marco Cuzzi, *L'Internazionale delle camicie nere: I CAUR 1933–1939* (Mursia, 2005).

23. Mann, *The Dark Side of Democracy*, p. 338.

24. Czesław Łuczak, *Polityka ludnościowa i ekonomiczna hitlerowskich Niemiec w okupowanej Polsce* (Wydawn. Poznańskie, 1979), p. 22.

25. Cited in Noakes and Pridham, *Nazism 1919–1945: 3*, p. 737.
26. Aristotle A. Kallis, *Nazi Propaganda and the Second World War* (Routledge, 2005), p. 96f.
27. See Renzo De Felice, *Il problema dell'Alto Adige nei rapporti italo-tedeschi* (Il Mulino, 1973).
28. Still irreplaceable is Robert L. Koehl's monograph *RKFDV: German Resettlement and Population Policy 1939–1945. A History of the Reich Commission for the Strengthening of Germandom* (Harvard University Press, 1957).
29. Cited in Noakes and Pridham, *Nazism 1919–1945: 3*, pp. 931f.
30. These points are considered by Dietrich A. Loeber, *Diktierte Option: Die Umsiedlung der Deutsch-Balten aus Estland und Lettland* (Karl Wachholtz Verlag, 1972), pp. 17f. The most relevant parts of Hitler's speech are reported there, pp. 79f.
31. Ibid., pp. 164f.
32. This promise was not always kept; ibid., pp. 44f.
33. The best examples of propaganda are the reports published by one of the most important journalists of the time: Felix Lützkendorf, *Völkerwanderung 1940: Ein Bericht aus dem Osten* (Fischer, 1941).
34. Loeber, *Diktierte Option*, p. 52.
35. Joseph B. Schechtman, *European Population Transfers, 1939–1945* (Oxford University Press, 1946), p. 24.
36. See the relevant documents in Noakes and Pridham, *Nazism 1919–1945: 3*, pp. 942f.
37. Isabel Heinemann, *'Rasse, Siedlung, deutsches Blut': Das Rasse- und Siedlungshauptamt der SS und die rassenpolitische Neuordnung Europas* (Wallstein, 2002), pp. 236f.
38. Valdis O. Lumans, *Himmler's Auxiliaries: The Volksdeutsche Mittelstelle and the German National Minorities of Europe 1933–1945* (North Carolina University Press, 1993).
39. Christoph von Hartungen, Fabrizio Miori and Tiziano Rosani (eds), *Le lettere aperte: 1939–1943 l'Alto Adige delle opzioni*, 2 vols (La Fabbrica del tempo, 2006).
40. Despite the complex bureaucratic machinery set up, Italian and German authorities managed to complete only 6,300 cases of estimates and compensation out of more than 63,000 submitted; ibid., p. 217. The main reason was that many people who had the right to claim compensation tried to slow down the process of expropriation and compensation in order to see how the situation would evolve.
41. For an in-depth historical picture, see Karl Stuhlpfarrer, *Umsiedlung Südtirol 1939–1940*, 2 vols (Oldenbourg, 1985), as well as the catalogue of the documentary exhibition: Benedikt Erhard (ed.), *Option – Heimat – Opzioni: Eine Geschichte Südtirols. Vom Gehen und vom Bleiben* (Österr. Bundesverlag, 1989). Italian edition: *Option – Heimat – Opzioni. Una storia dell'Alto Adige* (Rauchdruck, 1989).
42. Janina Kiełboń, *Migracje ludności w dystrykcie lubelskim w latach 1939–1944* (Państwowe Muzeum na Majdanku, 1995), pp. 37–8; Stanisław Ciesielski, Grzegorz Hryciuk, Aleksander Srebrakowski, *Masowe deportacje radzieckie w okresie II wojny światowej* (Instytut Historyczny, 1994), pp. 51–3; Mieczysław Wieliczko, 'Migracje przez "linię demarkacyjną" w latach 1939–1940', in Adam Marszałek (ed.), *Położenie ludności polskiej na terytorium ZSRR i wschodnich ziemiach II Rzeczypospolitej w czasie II wojny światowej* (Uniwersytet Mikołaja Kopernika, 1990), pp. 125–39.

43. Christopher Browning, *Die Entfesselung der 'Endlösung': Nationalsozialistische Judenpolitik 1939–1942* (Beck, 2003), p. 52.
44. By 1944 as many as 631,485 German settlers had been brought in: 85 per cent into the Warthegau; 7.9 per cent into Danzig-West Prussia; 5.8 per cent into Silesia and 1.2 per cent into the territories incorporated into East Prussia. Maria Rutowska, *Wysiedlenia ludności polskiej z Kraju Warty do Generalnego Gubernatorstwa 1939–1941* (Instytut Zachodni, 2003), p. 23.
45. Christopher R. Browning, *Die Entfesselung*, pp. 65–74.
46. See. Jan T. Gross, *Revolution from Abroad: The Soviet Conquest of Poland's Western Ukraine and Western Belorussia* (Princeton University Press, 1988) and Ben-Cion Pinchuk, *Shtetl Jews under Soviet Rule: Eastern Poland on the Eve of the Holocaust* (Blackwell, 1990).
47. Ewa Kowalska, *Przeżyć, aby wrócić! Polscy zesłańcy lat 1940–1941 w ZSRR i ich losy do roku 1946* (Neriton, 1998); Pavel Poljan, *Ne po svojej vole … Istorija i geografija prinuditelnych migracij v SSSR* (OGI-Memorial, 2001).
48. Lynn Viola, *Peasant Rebels under Stalin* (Oxford University Press, 1996).
49. Dominick Lieven, *Empire: The Russian Empire and Its Rivals* (Yale University Press, 2000). A good reconstruction of the ethnic-cleansing policies carried out by Stalin is J. Otto Pohl, *Ethnic Cleansing in the USSR, 1937–1949* (Greenwood Press, 1999). The best work on the argument is Terry Martin, *The Affirmative Action Empire: Nations and Nationalism in the Soviet Union, 1923–1939* (Cornell University Press, 2001).
50. Not without reason, the Russian historian Nikołaj Iwanow entitled his book on the fate of the Poles in the USSR prior to 1939 'The First Nation to Be Punished': *Pierwszy naród ukarany: Polacy w Związku Radzieckim 1921–1939* (Warsaw/Wrocław, 1991).
51. Iwanow, op. cit.; Stanisław Ciesielski, Wojciech Materski and Andrzej Paczkowski, *Represje sowieckie wobec Polaków i obywateli polskich* (Karta, 2002), online at http://www.indeks.karta.org.pl/raport.pdf, pp. 4–5.
52. Cf. Gross, *Revolution from Abroad*.
53. The so-called 'army settlers' were considered exceptionally dangerous by the Soviet authorities. Because the settlers numbered only some 6,000–8,000, the Soviets soon started to broaden the definition of the term to encompass all the Poles who had acquired farms in the region during the interwar period. On 5 December 1939 the Council of the People's Commissars took the decision to deport the army settlers and their families, and the NKVD issued appropriate directives on 19 December 1939. Viktor Komogorov et al. (eds) *Deportacje obywateli polskich z Zachodniej Ukrainy i Zachodniej Białorusi w 1940 roku* (Instytut Pamięci Narodowej, Ministerstwo Spraw Wewnętrznych i Administracji Rzeczypospolitej Polskiej with Federal'naja Służba Besopanosti RF, 2003), pp. 48–55, 712–16. On the military settlement in the Eastern Borderlands, see Janina Stobniak-Smogorzewska, *Kresowe osadnictwo wojskowe 1920–1945* (Rytm, 2003).
54. Kowalska, *Przeżyć, aby wrócić!*, pp. 78–9; Ciesielski et al., *Masowe deportacje*, pp. 36–7.
55. Ciesielski et al., *Masowe deportacje*, p. 38.
56. Kowalska, *Przeżyć, aby wrócić!*, p. 53.
57. Ibid., pp. 54–5; Ciesielski et al., *Represje sowieckie*, pp. 16–17.

58. Kowalska, *Przeżyć, aby wrócić!*, p. 56.
59. Ciesielski et al., *Represje sowieckie*, pp. 18–19.
60. Ibid., pp. 16–17.
61. Ibid., pp. 12–15; Sławomir Kalbarczyk, 'Obywatele polscy w sowieckich obozach pracy poprawczej w latach 1939–1945: Próba oceny dorobku historiografii minionego dziesięciolecia, problemy i postulaty badawcze', *Wrocławskie Studia Wschodnie*, vol. 6 (2002), pp. 195–7.
62. In 1939 the Red Army captured some 240,000 Polish officers and troops, 125,000 of whom were handed over to the NKVD. This number was reduced by the release of approximately 42,000 non-commissioned officers and soldiers who stemmed from the eastern territories of Poland and by the handing over to the Germans of about 42,500 prisoners of war, who were inhabitants of the regions incorporated into the Reich. The ranks of the remaining POWs were strengthened by about 45,400 internees. In spring 1940, 14,600 of them were executed in Katyń, Kharkov and Tver. Ciesielski et al., *Represje sowieckie*, p. 8.
63. Stanisław Ciesielski (ed.), *Przesiedlenie ludności polskiej z Kresów Wschodnich do Polski 1944–1947* (Neriton, 1999), p. 11.
64. After June 1940, for instance, the Soviet authorities relocated 13,000–16,000 Polish citizens from Volhynia and Eastern Galicia to Bessarabia and northern Bukovina. Ciesielski et al., *Represje sowieckie*, p. 18.
65. Cf. Lumans, *Himmler's Auxiliaries*.
66. From the minutes taken by Martin Bormann, dated 2 October 1940. See Werner Röhr (ed.), *Die faschistische Okkupationspolitik in Polen (1939–1945)* (Deutscher Verlag der Wissenschaften, 1989), p. 191.
67. Heydrich, giving instructions to eliminate the Polish ruling class, stated on 27 September 1939 that 'the aim for the primitive Poles is to remain permanently seasonal and migrant workers' (cited in Noakes and Pridham, *Nazism 1919–1945: 3*, p. 930).
68. From the instructions that Hitler gave to General Keitel on 17 October regarding the main lines for occupation policy, in Röhr, *Die faschistische Okkupationspolitik*, p.133.
69. Hans Umbreit, *Deutsche Militärverwaltungen 1938/39: Die militärische Besetzung der Tschekoslowakei und Polens* (DVA, 1977), pp. 91f.
70. Noakes and Pridham, *Nazism 1919–1945: 3*, p. 928.
71. Richard C. Lukas, *Forgotten Holocaust: The Poles under German Occupation 1939–1944* (University of Kentucky Press, 1986), p. 9.
72. Christof Klessmann, *Die Selbstbehauptung einer Nation: NS-Kulturpolitik und polnische Widerstandsbewegung im Generalgouvernement 1939–1945* (Droste, 1971), pp. 44f.
73. Order dated 2 October 1943, in Röhr, *Die faschistische Okkupationspolitik*, p. 281.
74. See the proposals by SD-Litzmannstadt on 25 August 1941, which suggested the mass sterilization of what were vaguely called the 'primitive classes of the Polish population': Röhr, *Die faschistische Okkupationspolitik*, p. 204.
75. Röhr, *Die faschistische Okkupationspolitik*, pp. 218f.
76. Jan T. Gross, *Polish Society under German Occupation: The Generalgouvernement 1939–1944* (Princeton University Press, 1979).
77. Order by Himmler on 30 October 1939, in Röhr, *Die faschistische Okkupationspolitik*, pp. 135f.

78. In the GG the relocations were the responsibility of the SS delegate – Oberguppenführer F.W. Krüger. This led to a conflict with Governor Frank, who was convinced that the migrations should be the responsibility of the civilian adminis- tration. Frank also suggested the suspension of relocations to the GG until the end of the war. On 16 December 1941 Bühler, chief of the cabinet of the GG, issued a cir- cular forbidding large-scale relocations without the consent of the administration. Finally Himmler had his way, and in May 1942 a Secretariat of State for Security was established under Krüger, which oversaw all police activity and the work of the RKFDV, including relocations.

79. For the relocations in the territories incorporated into the Reich, see among others: Włodzimierz Jastrzębski, *Hitlerowskie wysiedlenia z ziem polskich wcielonych do Rzeszy 1939–1945* (Instytut Zachodni, 1968); Czesław Łuczak, *Polityka ludnościowa i ekonomiczna hitlerowskich Niemiec w okupowanej Polsce* (Wydawn. Poznańskie, 1979); Janusz Wróbel, *Przemiany ludnościowe spowodowane polityka okupanta hitlerowskiego w tzw. rejencji łódzkiej w latach 1939–1945* (GKBZHwP, 1987).

80. Browning, *Entfesselung*, pp. 130–41. For the 'Madagaskar-Plan' see Hans Jansen, *Der Madagaskar-Plan: Die beabsichtigte Deportation der europäischen Juden nach Madagaskar* (Herbig, 1997); Magnus Brechtken, *'Madagaskar für die Juden': Antisemitische Idee und politische Praxis 1885–1945* (Oldenbourg, 1998).

81. See, among others, a letter addressed to Himmler on 3 July in Röhr, *Die faschistische Okkupationspolitik*, pp. 275f.

82. Heinemann, *'Rasse, Siedlung, deutsches Blut'*, p. 216.

83. Kiełboń, *Migracje ludności*, p. 133. This Jewish population originated primarily from the western parts of the Warthegau, where Jews were relatively few. The Jews from the eastern parts of the Warthegau (the Polish provinces of Łódź and, in part, Warsaw), who were far more numerous, were relocated less comprehensively. The remainder were packed into ghettos (the first one was created in October 1939 in Piotrków Trybunalski), which were then liquidated in the years 1942–4.

84. Götz Aly, *Endlösung: Völkerverschiebung und der Mord an den europäischen Juden* (Fischer, 1995), stresses this point.

85. On the policy of confinement to ghettos, see Gustavo Corni, *Hitler's Ghettos: Voices from a Beleaguered Society 1939–1944* (Arnold, 2002).

86. However, major racial theoreticians, such as Hans F.K. Günther, had determined that the oldest Slavic remains were 'mostly Nordic'; John Connelly and Michael Grüttner (eds), *Universities under Dictatorship* (Pennsylvania State University Press, 2005), p. 13.

87. While talking about the colonization of Russia, the dictator himself had portrayed an insurmountable division into two parts of the occupied territories. Germanic colonists were to reside and rule in the better lands. 'What exists beyond that will be another world, in which we mean to let the Russians live as they like'; Trevor Roper, *Hitler's Table Talks*, 8–9 August 1941, p. 24.

88. In a memorandum of 15 May 1940 he wrote: 'I want to say that our main interest is not to have the population in the East united but, on the contrary, to have it divided into the greatest possible number of bits and pieces' (Röhr, *Die faschistische Okkupationspolitik*, p. 171). The result of this segregation principle (not easily applied in everyday practice) was that the annexed territories were inundated with categorical orders that forbade and severely punished any relations between the

Polish population and the German colonists; sexual relations were the most severely punished.

89. In a report presented to Hitler on 30 June 1940, the RF-SS estimated that seven eighths of the existing population in the annexed territories would have to be expelled to the East. See Richard Breitman, *Heinrich Himmler: Der Architekt der 'Endlösung'* (Pendo, 2000), p. 127.
90. The two quotations are from Picker, *Hitlers Tischgespräche*, pp. 174 and 253.
91. Trevor Roper, *Hitler's Table Talks*, dated 12 May 1942, p. 473.
92. Mechtild Rössler and Sabine Schleiermacher (eds), *Der 'Generalplan Ost': Hauptlinien der nationalsozialistischen Planungs- und Vernichtungspolitik* (Akademie, 1993), pp. 49f.
93. See an order by O. Globocnik, dated 11 May 1943, entitled 'Hunt for German blood', in Röhr, *Die faschistische Okkupationspolitik*, p. 265.
94. Cited in Noakes and Pridham, *Nazism 1919–1945*, p. 946.
95. See the order issued by Globocnik on 11 May 1941; Röhr, *Die faschistische Okkupationspolitik*, p. 265.
96. The guidelines for this initiative had already been formulated in a memorandum by the party's Rassenpolitisches Amt of 25 November 1939; ibid., p. 144. See also the order of 19 February 1942, ibid., pp. 215f. The time that elapsed between the writing of the documents shows that the operation was carried out only partially.
97. The guidelines had already been drawn up in the RKFDV's order of 12 September 1940, ibid., pp. 186f.
98. See Himmler's detailed instructions of 9 February 1942, which reflect considerable distrust (reported ibid., pp. 213–14).
99. Michael G. Esch, *'Gesunde Verhältnisse': Die deutsche und polnische Bevölkerungspolitik in Ostmitteleuropa* (Herder, 1998), pp. 230f. Relevant sources are reproduced in Röhr, *Die faschistische Okkupationspolitik*, pp. 186ff., 213ff., 265.
100. Cited in Noakes and Pridham, *Nazism 1919–1945*, p. 949.
101. Herbert S. Levine, 'Local Authority and the SS State: The Conflict over Population Policy in Danzig-West Prussia 1939–1945', *Central European History*, vol. 2 (1969), p. 343.
102. See Bruno Wasser, *Himmlers Raumplanung im Osten: Der Generalplan Ost in Polen 1940–1944* (Birkhäuser, 1993), pp. 110f. People enrolled in class 3 of the DVL were particularly numerous in Danzig-West Prussia (725,000), Forster's declared aim being to 'Germanize' them in an easy way; Levine, 'Local Authority', pp. 345f.
103. Statistics in Elizabeth Harvey, *Women and the Nazi East: Agents and Witnesses of Germanization* (Yale University Press, 2003), p. 79.
104. Ibid., p. 296.
105. Heinemann, *'Rasse, Siedlung, deutsches Blut'*, pp. 127f. Documents in Helma Kaden and Wolfgang Schumann (eds), *Die faschistische Okkupationspolitik in Österreich und in der Tschekoslowakei (1938–1945)* (Pahl-Rugenstein, 1988), pp. 177f., 189f. See also Miroslav Kárný, Jaroslava Milotova and Margita Karna (eds), *Deutsche Politik im Reichsprotektorat Böhmen und Mähren unter Reinhard Heydrich* (Metropol, 1997), pp. 111f.
106. This was explicitly written in the order of the RKFDV, dated 12 September 1940, in Röhr, *Die faschistische Okkupationspolitik*, p. 186.
107. Hitler said: 'But they were Sorb-Wends, members of basic European stock, with

nothing in common with the Slavs'; Trevor Roper, *Hitler's Table Talks*, 6 August 1942, p. 617. Studies of Polish ethnologists and anthropologists were used to support this thesis; Connelly and Grüttner, *Universities under Dictatorship*, p. 18f.

108. Burleigh, *Germany Turns Eastward*, pp. 207f.
109. Levine, 'Local Authority', p. 347.
110. Czesław Madajczik (ed.), *Vom Generalplan Ost zum Generalsiedlungsplan* (Saur, 1994), and Rössler and Schleiermacher, *Der 'Generalplan Ost'*.
111. Michael A. Hartenstein, *Neue Dorflandschaften: Nationalsozialistische Siedlungsplanung in den 'eingegliederten' Ostgebieten 1939–1944* (Dr. Köster Verlag, 1998), pp. 85f.
112. Their sons or grandsons who had demonstrated full racial trustworthiness could possibly be allowed to reach in the future the status of independent peasants; note of 25 November 1939, in Röhr, *Die faschistische Okkupationspolitik*, p. 144.
113. Konrad Meyer, 'Neues Landvolk: Verwirklichung im Osten', *Neues Bauerntum*, no. 33 (1941), p. 99.
114. In Rössler and Schleiermacher, *Der 'Generalplan Ost'*, p. 23.
115. Cf. Gustavo Corni, *Hitler and the Peasants: Nazi Agrarian Policy 1933–1939* (Berghahn, 1990).
116. See especially the detailed plan on the *Gestaltung der Landschaft* worked out in December 1942 by the offices of the RKFDV, reproduced in Rössler and Schleiermacher, *Der 'Generalplan Ost'*, pp. 136f.
117. Connelly and Grüttner, *Universities under Dictatorship*, p. 29.
118. Wendy Lower, 'Hitler's "Garden of Eden" in Ukraine: Nazi Colonialism, *Volksdeutsche*, and the Holocaust, 1941–1944', in Jonathan Petropoulos and John K. Roth (eds), *Gray Zones: Ambiguity and Compromise in the Holocaust and Its Aftermath* (Berghahn Books, 2005), pp. 185–204.
119. Rolf-Dieter Müller, *Hitlers Ostkrieg und die deutsche Siedlungspolitik* (Fischer, 1991).
120. Cf. Aly, *Endlösung*.
121. The guidelines of the Generalsiedlungsplan are reproduced in Rössler and Schleiermacher, *Der 'Generalplan Ost'*, pp. 96f.
122. Dietrich Eichholtz, *Geschichte der deutschen Kriegswirtschaft*, 3 vols in 5 tomes (Saur, 1999), vol. II/2, p. 439.
123. Heinemann, *'Rasse, Siedlung, deutsches Blut'*.
124. See the complaints in the daily report, dated 25 July 1940, of the Łódź/Litzmannstadt police, in Röhr, *Die faschistische Okkupationspolitik*, p. 182.
125. This was clearly documented in a report, dated 26 June 1940, concerning the experience of the first phase of the expulsions, the so-called *Erster Nahplan* (First Short-term Plan) ibid., pp. 154f.
126. See the RKFDV internal report dated 26 March 1941, ibid., p. 196.
127. Harvey, *Women and the Nazi East*, p. 295.
128. See the order issued on 11 March 1943 by Globocnik, in Röhr, *Die faschistische Okkupationspolitik*, p. 265.
129. On the situation of German agriculture during the war, see Gustavo Corni and Horst Gies, *Brot, Butter, Kanonen: Die Ernährungswirtschaft in Deutschland unter der Diktatur Hitlers* (Akademie, 1997), pp. 423f.
130. See the empirical research by Peter R. Hartmann, 'Die annexionistische

Agrarsiedlungspolitik des deutschen Faschismus in den sogenannten "eingegliederten Ostgebieten"', doctoral dissertation, Rostock, 1969.

131. From a report of the RSHA, 15 October 1941, in Noakes and Pridham, *Nazism 1919–1945*, p. 979.

132. Initially, he was not aware of this operation and protested strongly. See the minutes of the meeting between Frank and Krüger, 4 August 1942, in Röhr, *Die faschistische Okkupationspolitik*, pp. 229f.

133. See the report of the Umwandererzentrale Litzmannstadt, dated 31 December 1942, ibid., pp. 238f.

134. Noakes and Pridham, *Nazism 1919–1945*, p. 980.

135. On this event see, among others, Wasser, *Himmlers Raumplanung*, pp. 62ff and 132f. Important documents are found in Röhr, *Die faschistische Okkupationspolitik*, pp. 229ff, 236, 250f.

136. See the detailed, strongly critical memo sent by Frank to Hitler on 25 May 1943; ibid., pp. 267f.

137. Letter from Himmler to Frank, dated 3 July 1943, ibid., pp. 275f.

138. The actions against the partisans during the summer did not yield the expected results, as revealed in a report of the gendarmerie, dated 8 December 1943, ibid., pp. 188f.

139. At the end of a critical report, dated 24 February 1943, Zörner asked to put an immediate end to the operation; ibid., pp. 250f.

140. Wendy Lower, '"Anticipatory Obedience" and the Nazi Implementation of the Holocaust in the Ukraine', *Holocaust and Genocide Studies*, vol. 16, no. 1 (2002), pp. 1–22.

141. Karel C. Berkhoff, *Harvest of Despair: Life and Death in Ukraine under Nazi Rule* (Belknap Press, 2004), p. 36.

142. From a report by the SS Standartenführer Hans Ehlich, dated 10 December 1942, cited in Connelly and Grüttner, *Universities under Dictatorship*, p. 31.

143. Berkhoff, *Harvest of Despair*, p. 253.

144. Bernhard Chiari, *Alltag hinter der Front: Besatzung, Kollaboration und Widerstand in Weissrussland 1941–1944* (Droste, 1998).

145. Breitman, *Heinrich Himmler*, p. 186.

146. Heinemann, *'Rasse, Siedlung, deutsches Blut'*, pp. 457f.

147. Lower, 'Hitler's "Garden of Eden"', p. 196.

148. Ibid., p. 194.

149. On the Belorussian case, see Martin Dean, *Collaboration in the Holocaust: Crimes of the Local Police in Belorussia and Ukraine 1941–1944* (Macmillan, 2000).

150. Doris L. Bergen, 'The Volksdeutsche of Eastern Europe and the Collapse of the Nazi Empire 1944–1945', in Alan E. Steinweis and Daniel E. Rogers (eds), *The Impact of Nazism: New Perspectives on the Third Reich and Its Legacy* (University of Nebraska Press, 2003), p. 115.

151. Breitman, *Heinrich Himmler*, p. 132.

152. Paul Dostert, *Luxemburg zwischen Selbstbehauptung und nationaler Selbstaufgabe: Die deutsche Besatzungspolitik und die volksdeutsche Bewegung 1940–1945* (Imprimerie Saint-Paul, 1985), pp. 205f.

153. Heinemann, *'Rasse, Siedlung, deutsches Blut'*, pp. 307f.

154. Cited in Rössler and Schleiermacher, *Der 'Generalplan Ost'*, p. 285.

3 The Population Policies of the 'Axis' Allies

1. Franco Gaeta, *Il nazionalismo italiano* (Laterza, 1981).
2. Emilio Gentile, *La Grande Italia: Ascesa e declino del mito della nazione nel ventesimo secolo* (Mondadori, 1997), p. 113.
3. For an analysis of the war culture, see the recent book by Angelo Ventrone, *La seduzione totalitaria: Guerra, modernità, violenza politica 1914–1918* (Donzelli, 2003).
4. Gentile, *La Grande Italia*, p. 155.
5. Costamagna, entry 'Nazione', in *Dizionario di politica* (Istituto dell'Enciclopedia Italiana, 1940), vol. III (1940), p. 263.
6. Cuzzi, *L'Internazionale delle camicie nere*, p. 31. See also Michael A. Ledeen, *Universal Fascism: The Theory and Practice of the Fascist International 1928–1936* (Howard Fertig, 1972).
7. Gentile, *La Grande Italia*, p. 199.
8. Pellizzi at a conference in Vienna (November 1941); cited in ibid., p. 194.
9. Michele Sarfatti, *Gli ebrei nell'Italia fascista: Vicende, identità, persecuzione* (Einaudi, 2000), pp. 103f. See also Aaron Gillette, *Racial Theories in Fascist Italy* (Routledge, 2002).
10. Entry in *Dizionario di politica*, p. 250.
11. Gentile, *La Grande Italia*, p. 211. See Nicole D'Elie, *Delio Cantimori e la cultura tedesca 1927–1940* (Vielle, 2007).
12. See the extensive anthology edited by Luisa Mangoni, *'Primato' 1940–1943: Antologia* (De Donato, 1977).
13. Ibid., p. 58.
14. Ibid., p. 107.
15. Ibid., p. 281.
16. Ibid., p. 251.
17. Ibid., p. 126. On the complex and in some respects ambiguous intellectual and political path of Pintor (shared by other leading figures of post-war culture, such as Cesare Pavese and Elio Vittorini), see the recent study by Mirella Serri, *Il breve viaggio: Giaime Pintor nella Weimar nazista* (Marsilio, 2002).
18. Renzo De Felice, *Mussolini il Duce: Gli anni del consenso 1929–1936* (Einaudi, 1996), p. 310.
19. Davide Rodogno's recent book *Il nuovo ordine mediterraneo: Le politiche d'occupazione dell'Italia in Europa 1940–1943* (Bollati Boringhieri, 2001; English: *Fascism's European Empire: Italian Occupation during the Second World War*, Cambridge University Press, 2006), in particular, has revived the study of fascist projects concerning vital space.
20. The efforts to form a widespread colonial conscience and their disappointing outcome have been analysed recently by Nicola Labanca, *Oltremare: Storia dell'espansione coloniale italiana* (Il Mulino, 2002).
21. Spampanato, in his writing *Perchè questa guerra* (Roma, 1942), quoted in Rodogno, *Fascism's European Empire*, p. 49.
22. Ruth Ben-Ghiat, *La cultura fascista* (Il Mulino, 2000), pp. 245f. English edition: *Fascist Modernities: Italy 1922–1945* (University of California Press, 2001).

23. Rodogno, *Fascism's European Empire*, p. 97.
24. Cited in Richard J.B. Bosworth, *Mussolini's Italy: Life under a Dictatorship 1915–1945* (Allen Lane, 2005), p. 404.
25. See MacGregor Knox, *Mussolini Unleashed, 1939–1941: Politics and Strategy in Fascist Italy's Last War* (Cambridge University Press, 1982) and, more recently, Giorgio Rochat, *Le guerre fasciste* (Einaudi, 2005).
26. Elio Apih, *Italia, fascismo e antifascismo nella Venezia Giulia (1918–1943)* (Laterza, 1966).
27. Pasquale Iuso, *Il fascismo e gli Ustaša: Storia del separatismo croato in Italia* (Gangemi, 1999).
28. Marco Cuzzi, *L'occupazione italiana della Slovenia (1941–1943)* (Ufficio Storico Stato Maggiore Esercito, 1998). Of fundamental importance is the collection of documents edited by Ferenc Tone, *La provincia 'italiana' di Lubiana: Documenti 1941–1943* (Istituto Friulano per la storia del movimento di liberazione, 1994). The most recent and penetrating contribution is H. James Burgwyn, *Empire on the Adriatic: Mussolini's Conquest of Yugoslavia 1941–1943* (Enigma Books, 2005).
29. Mussolini's speech of 1 August 1941, quoted in Rodogno, *Fascism's European Empire*, p. 265.
30. See Carlo S. Capogreco, *I campi del duce: L'internamento civile nell'Italia fascista (1940–1943)* (Einaudi, 2004).
31. Rodogno, *Fascism's European Empire*, p. 412.
32. István Bethlen was prime minister between 1921 and 1930, then governor Horthy's confidant and advisor until 1944. Pál Teleki was prime minister in 1920, and also from 1939 until his death in April 1941.
33. Miklos Szinai and Lajos Szücs (eds), *Horthy Miklós titkos iratai* (Kossuth Könyvkiadó, 1965), p. 307.
34. Jan Gebhardt, 'Migrationsbewegungen der tschechischen Bevölkerung in den Jahren 1938–1939: Forschungsstand und offene Fragen', in Detlef Brandes, Edita Ivaničkova and Jiří Pešek (eds), *Erzwungene Trennung, Vertreibungen und Aussiedlungen in und aus der Tschechoslowakei 1938–1947 im Vergleich mit Polen, Ungarn und Jugoslawien* (Klartext, 1999), p. 22.
35. Gebhardt, 'Migrationsbewegungen', p. 21.
36. See, for instance, Ladisdlav Deak, *Viedenska arbitráz – 'Mnichov pre Slovensko'* (Nadacia Korene, 1998), p. 43.
37. The Hungarian census did not include those members of the armed forces and public servants who had moved to the region from the Trianon Territory. Thus the figures of the censuses held in 1930 and in 1938 are comparable. On Czechoslovakian censuses, see Gyula Popély, *Népfogyatkozás: A csehszlovákiai magyarság a népszámlálások tükrében, 1918–1945* (Régio, 1991), pp. 116–19.
38. Károly Kocsis, 'Teleptések és az etnikai térszerkezet a Kárpát-Medence határvidékein, 1944–1950', in Sándor Illés and Pal Peter Toth (eds) *Migráció, Tanulmánygyüjtemény*, vol. 1 (KSH Népességtudományi Kutató Intézet, 1998), p. 126. See also Kálmán Janics, *A hontalanság évei* (Europai Protestáns Magyar Szabadegyetem, 1979), p. 206.
39. On the fate of Slovak colonists, see Lóránt Tilkovszky, *Revizió és nemzetiségpolitika Magyarországon, 1938–1941* (Akadémia Kiadó, 1967), pp. 74–5.
40. Károly Kocsis and Eszter Kocsis-Hodosi, *Ethnic Geography of the Hungarian*

Minorities in the Carpathian Basin (Geographical Research Institute, 1998), p. 64. Igor Daxner estimates the number of expelled Czechs at 120,000. See Igor Daxner, *L'udáctvo pred Národným śdom 1945–1947* (Akademia, 1961), p. 73.

41. The records of the Central National Bureau for the Control of Foreigners are cited by Béni L. Balogh, 'Az erdélyi magyar menekültkérdés', in *Régió*, vol. 10, no. 3–4 (1999), p. 250.

42. Ibid., p. 251. According to data published in January 1944 by the Romanian General Commissariat for the Refugees from Transylvania, however, 218,000 refugees arrived in Romania from northern Transylvania. See Schechtman, *European Population Transfers*, p. 430.

43. Enikő A. Sajti, *Impériumváltások, Revízió, Kisebbség: Magyarok a Délvidéken, 1918–1947* (Napvilág Kiadó, 2004), p. 198.

44. Ibid.

45. The figure of about 35,000 expatriated Serbs originated from Karl Frahne, the second secretary of the German legation in Budapest. Enikő A. Sajti gives a detailed analysis of the contemporary German and Serb sources in her book *Délvidék, 1941–1944* (Kossuth Könyvkiadó, 1987), p. 43.

46. On Hungarian occupation policies see Péter Gosztonyi, *A magyar honvédség a második világháborúban* (Európa Könyvkiadó, 1992), p. 55. See also Carlile A. Macartney, *October Fifteenth, vol. II* (Edinburgh University Press, 1961), p. 13. About the directives of the Hungarian army see János Csima, *Adalékok a Horthy hadsereg szervezetének és háborús tevékenységének a tanulmányozásához, 1938–1945* (Honvédelmi Minisztérium Központi Irattár Kiadása, 1961), p. 59.

47. The source of the lower estimate is Slobodan D. Milošević, *Izbeglice i preseljenici na teritoriji okupirane Jugoslavije 1941–1945* (Narodna knjiga: In-t za savremenu istoriju, 1981), p. 276. For the higher estimates see Aleksandar Kasas, *Madari u Vojvodini 1941–1946* (Filozofski Fakultet u Novom Sadu, 1996), p. 39.

48. György Ránki, Ervin Pamlényi, Lóránt Tilkovszky and Gyula Juhász (eds), *A Wilhelmstrasse és Magyarország: Német diplomáciai iratok Magyarországról 1933–1944* (Kossuth Könyvkiadó, 1968), p. 581.

49. Archives of the Hungarian Central Statistical Office (Központi Statisztikai Hivatal Levéltára, KSH Levéltár), Gyula Barsy's papers. The relevant documents of the Department for Refugees, Prisoners of War and Deportees in the Ministry of Public Welfare are in the possession of Tamás Stark.

50. József Ősi Oberding, 'A bukovínai székelyek dunántúli letelepítése', *Agrártörténeti Szemle*, vol. 10, no. 1–2 (1967), p. 185; Schechtman, *European Population Transfers*, p. 436.

51. Sajti, *Impériumváltások*, p. 228.

52. Despite its short period in power, the Cuza–Goga government introduced a series of discriminative measures. The gravest was the law to review the citizenship of Jews. It resulted in a loss of citizenship for about 250,000, one third of the total Jewish population.

53. Viorel Achim, 'The Romanian Population Exchange Project Elaborated by Sabin Manuilă in October 1941', *Annali dell'Istituto storico italo-germanico in Trento*, XXVII (2001), p. 605.

54. Aurică Simion, *Dictatul de la Viena* (Albatros, 1996), pp. 217–18.

55. Schechtman, *European Population Transfers*, p. 184.
56. Ibid., p. 227.
57. Dov Levin, *The Lesser of the Two Evils: Eastern European Jewry under Soviet Rule, 1939–1941* (The Jewish Publication Society, 1995), p. 336.
58. Pavel Polian, *Against Their Will: The History and Geography of Forced Migrations in the USSR* (Central European University Press, 2004), p. 121.
59. Ibid., p. 123.
60. Stéphane Courtois, Nicolas Werth, Jean-Louis Panné, Karel Bartosek, Jean-Louis Margolin and Andrzej Paczkowski, *A kommunizmus fekete könyve* (Nagyvilág, 2000), p. 221. See also Gabriel Gherasim, 'Românii din Ucraina', online at http://noinu.rdscj.ro/article.php?articleID=149.
61. Achim, 'The Romanian Population Exchange Project', p. 599.
62. Manuilă's memorandum is cited in ibid., p. 610. See also Zoltán Szász, 'Tévutak keresése', *História*, vol. 22, no. 8 (1999), pp. 17–19.
63. Achim, 'The Romanian Population Exchange Project', p. 616.
64. Ibid., p. 607.
65. On 12 October 1943 Dr Wilhelm Filderman, President of the Federation of Romanian Jews in Romania, informed Michail Antonescu that 77,000 deported Jews were still alive in Transnistria. See Jean Ancel (ed.), *Documents Concerning the Fate of Romanian Jewry during the Holocaust, Vol. 4* (The Beate Klarsfeld Foundation, 1987), p. 355.
66. On 10 February 1944 General Vasiliu, General Inspector of Gendarmerie, informed the Jewish Center in Bucharest that there were only 42,000 Jews in Transnistria. See Jean Ancel (ed.), *Documents Concerning the Fate*, p. 393. This figure is backed by the documents of the Romanian Ministry of the Interior, USHMM, Washington, DC, SRI RG 25004M, reel 10, vol. 20.
67. Dalia Ofer, 'The Holocaust in Transnistria: A Special Case of Genocide', in Lucjan Dobroszycki and Jeffry S. Gurock (eds), *The Holocaust in the Soviet Union* (M.E. Sharpe, 1993), p. 138; Joseph B. Schechtman, 'The Transnistria Reservation', in Michael R. Marrus (ed.), *The Final Solution outside Germany, Vol. 1* (Meckler, 1989), p. 376; Alexander Dallin, *Odessa, 1941–1944* (The Rand Corporation, 1957), p. 308.
68. Joseph B. Schechtman, 'The Transnistria Reservation', p. 387.
69. Viorel Achim (ed.), *Documente privind deportarea tiganilor în Transnistria – Documents Concerning the Deportation of Gypsies to Transnistria* (Editura Enciclopedică, 2004), p. XXIV.
70. Ibid., p. XXXVII.
71. Lya Benjamin (ed.), *Evreii din România între anii 1940–1944, Vol. I* (Editura Hasefer, 1993), p. LXXXIV.

4 Population Movements at the End of the War and in Its Aftermath

1. United States Congress, Senate Committee on Foreign Relations (ed.), *A Decade of American Foreign Policy: Basic Documents, 1941–1949* (United States Government Printing Office, 1950), p. 2.
2. The Allies propagated openly anti-German propaganda from the start of the war,

aimed in good part at their own populations. In his infamous pamphlet of 1942 entitled 'The German', Ilya Ehrenburg wrote: 'We remember everything. Now we know. The Germans are not human. Now the word 'German' has become the most terrible swear word. Let us not speak. Let us not be indignant. Let us kill.' Source: *Krasnaya Zvezda*, 14 August 1942, cited by Alexander Werth, *Russia at War, 1941–1945* (Avon Books, 1964), p. 388. In the United States the anti-German propaganda campaign was led by a semi-official organization called the Writers' War Board, founded by Secretary of the Treasury, Henry J. Morgenthau. See Richard Overy, *Why the Allies Won* (Norton & Company, 1996), pp. 287–98.

3. Winston S. Churchill, *The Second World War, vol. V: Closing the Ring* (Cassel & Co., 1952), p. 252.

4. Ibid., p. 355.

5. Senate Committee on Foreign Relations (ed.), *A Decade of American Foreign Policy*, p. 36.

6. Gyula Juhász (ed.), *Magyar-brit titkos tárgyalások 1943–ban* (Kossuth Könykiadó, 1978), p. 158.

7. Péter Gosztonyi, *Háború az háború* (Népszava, 1989), p. 26.

8. Katalin Vadkerty, *A belső telepítések és a lakosságcsere* (Kalligram, 1999), p. 82.

9. Joseph B. Schechtman, *Postwar Population Transfers in Europe 1945–1955* (University of Pennsylvania Press, 1962), pp. 55–6.

10. The Benes–Molotov meeting of 9 June 1942. Papers of Sir Robert Hamilton Bruce Lockhardt, Hoover Institution Archives (Stanford, California), Box 5, cited by András D. Bánd, 'Föderációs és Konföderációs tervek Kelet-Közép- és Délkelet-Európáról 1939–1947', in Ignác Romsics (ed.), *Interegrációs tő rekvések Közép- és Kelet-Európában a 19. és a 20. században* (Teleki László Alapítvány, 1997), p. 147.

11. Vadkerty, *A belső telepítések*, p. 83.

12. Alfred M. de Zayas, *Nemesis at Potsdam: The Anglo-Americans and the Expulsion of the Germans* (Henley and Routledge & Kegan Paul, 1977), p. 34.

13. Ibid., p. 34.

14. Vadkerty, *A belső telepítések*, p. 83.

15. Béla Zselicki, 'Benes, a magyar kérdés és a Szovjetunió, 1943–1948', *Múltunk*, vol. 17, no. 2 (2005), pp. 46–7.

16. Gottwald's text is cited by Kálmán Janics, *A hontalanság évei* (Hunnia Kiadó, 1989), p. 85.

17. The memorandum is cited by László Szarka, *Jogfosztó jogszabályok Csehszlovákiában, 1944–1949* (MTA Etnikai-Nemzeti Kisebbségkutató Intézet, 2005), p. 14. The Czech version of the memorandum was published by Milan Churan, *Potsdam a Československo: M tus a skutečnost* (Libri, 2001), pp. 105–6.

18. Ibid.

19. Zselicki, 'Benes', p. 47.

20. Moljević essentially repeated the Serbian territorial claims of the First World War. For a more detailed description see Lajos Pándy (ed.), *Köztes Európa, 1763–1993: Térképgyűsjtemány* (Osiris Kiadó, 1997), p. 464. See also John R. Schindler, 'Yugoslavia's First Ethnic Cleansing', in Steven Béla Várdy and T. Hunt Tooley (eds), *Ethnic Cleansing in 20th-century Europe* (Boulder, CO, 2003), p. 364.

21. Čubrilović's plan was published in Hungarian by Béla Csorba (ed.), *Források a Délvidék történetéhez, III* (Hatodik Síp Alapítvány, 1999), p. 180.

22. According to Hungarian and Serbian scholarly literature, the Hungarian authorities killed about 3,500 Serbs and Jews in the course of anti-partisan raids. See Sajti, *Impériumváltások*, p. 282, and Aleksandar Kasaš, *Mađ]arí u Vojvodini 1941–1946* (Filozofski Fakultet u Novom Sadu, 1996), p. 91.
23. Csorba, *Források*, p. 182.
24. Milošević, *Izbeglice i preseljenici*, p. 276.
25. Csorba, *Források*, p. 185.
26. Ibid., p. 187.
27. Ibid., p. 185.
28. Ibid.
29. Zdenek Zeman and Edvard Beneš, *Politicky zivotopis* (Malada Fronta, 2002), pp. 261f.
30. Viorel Achim, 'Romania and the Refugees from Bessarabia and Northern Bucovina after 1944', *Annali dell'Istituto storico italo-germanico in Trento*, vol. XXIX (il Mulino, 2003), p. 679. The author refers to two sources: Veaceslav Stăvilă, 'Populaţia Basarabiei în perioda celui de al doilea război mondial', *Revista de Istorie a Moldovei*, no. 3 (1993); Ioan Scurtu and Constantin Hlihor, *Complot împotriva României 1939–1947* (Ed. Academiei de Înalte Studii Militare, 1994).
31. Géza Lakatos, *Ahogy én láttam* (Aurora, 1981), pp. 126–7.
32. John F. Cadzow, Andrew Ludanyi and Louis J. Elteto (eds), *Transylvania: The Roots of Ethnic Conflict* (Kent State University Press, Ohio, 1983), p. 340. See also László Szenczei, *Magyar román kérdés* (Officina, 1947), p. 171.
33. *Az 1949 évi népszámlálás, IX*, Vol. 9 (Központi Statisztikai Hivatal, 1950), p. 13.
34. Norbert Spannenberger, *A magyarországi Volksbund Berlin és Budapest között* (Lucidus Kiadó, 2005), p. 378.
35. Paul Georgescu, '"Volksdeutsche" in der Waffen-SS – Die Deutschen aus Romänien als Testfall, 1938–1945', *Südostdeutsche Vierteljahresblätter*, vol. 53, no. 2 (2004), pp. 117–23.
36. Schechtman, *Postwar Population Transfers*, p. 267. On the basis of the registration data on Germans in Romania, collected by the Romanian authorities at the beginning of 1945, Schechtman estimated the number of the refugees and evacuees at about 200,000. See ibid., p. 269.
37. Archives of Hungarian Central Statistical Office (Központi Statisztikai Hivatal Levéltára, KSH Levéltár), Gyula Barsy's papers.
38. *Az 1949 évi népszámlálás, IX*, p. 13.
39. Josip Mirnić, a Serbian scholar, and Enikő A. Sajti, a Hungarian historian, estimate the number of Germans who fled from Backa at 70,000. See Sajti, *Impériumváltások*, p. 315, and Josip Mirnić, *Nemci u Bačkoj u drugom svetskom ratu* (Institut za izučavanje istorije Vojvodine, 1974), pp. 325–32. The German–Hungarian historian Norbert Spannanberger wrote about 120,000 German refugees in his book: Spannenberger, *A magyarországi Volksbund*, p. 378.
40. Sajti, *Impériumváltások*, p. 315.
41. Schindler, 'Yugoslavia's First Ethnic Cleansing', p. 365.
42. Tamás Stark, 'Hungary's Casualties in World War II', in György Lengyel (ed.), *Hungarian Economy and Society during World War II* (Boulder, CO, 1993), p. 225.
43. According to György Gyarmati, a Hungarian historian, 20,000 Germans fled from Hungary with the German and Hungarian armies. Gyarmati György, 'Modern

népvándorlás, nemzeti kérdés', in Ferenc Glatz (ed.), *Magyarok a Kárpát-medencében* (Pallas Lap- és Könyvkiadó Vállalat, 1988), p. 317. Michael Kroner writes about 50,000–60,000 refugees: Michael Kroner, 'Umsiedlung und Flucht von Südostdeutschen im Zweiten Weltkrieg', *Südostdeutsche Vierteljahresblätter*, vol. 53, no. 4. (2004), pp. 344–5. See also Bundesministerium für Vertriebene, Flüchtlinge und Kriegsgeschädigte – BVFK (ed.), *Das Schicksal der Deutschen in Ungarn* (Dtv, 1984), p. 40.

44. On the number of Hungarian emigrants, see Julianna Puskás, 'Elvándorlások Magyarországról 1945 óta és a magyar diaszpóra néhány jellegzetessége az 1970-es években', in János Molnár-Sándor Orbán-Károly Urbán (eds), *Tanulmányok a magyar népi demokrácia negyven évéről* (Kossuth Könyvkiadó, 1985) pp. 236–60.

45. Mihály Korom, 'Az Atlanti Chartától a potsdami kollektív büntetésig', *Századok*, vol. 132, no. 3 (1998), p. 557.

46. Soňa Gabzdilová, 'Situácia nemeckej menšiny na Slovensku pri návrate z evakuácie na jar a v lete 1945', *Historický časopis*, vol. 49, no. 3 (2001), pp. 453–76.

47. Maksim M. Zagorul'ko (ed.), *Voennoplennye v SSSR 1939–1956: Dokumenty i materialy* (Logos, 2000), p. 26.

48. Jochen Laufer, 'Die Reparationsplanungen im sowjetischen Außenministerium während des Zweiten Weltkrieges', in Christoph Buchheim (ed.), *Wirtschaftliche Folgelasten des Krieges in der SBZ/DDR* (Nomos, 1995), pp. 21–43.

49. Polian, *Against Their Will*, p. 123.

50. Zbigniew S. Siemaszko, *W sowieckim osaczeniu* (Polska Fundacja Kulturalna, 1991); Władysław Wielhorski, *Los Polakow w niewoli sowieckiej, 1939–1956* (n.p., 1956); Keith Sword, *Deportation and Exile: Poles in the Soviet Union 1939–1948* (Macmillan, 1994). Up until June 1942, 1.2 million Germans were deported to Central Asia and Siberia, and the number of those who were taken to the camps of GUPVI and GULAG by force can be put at several tens of thousands. Accused of cooperation with the German invaders, about 900,000 Karachais, Kalmyks, Ingush, Chechens, Balkarians and Crimean Tartars were removed from their homelands and resettled in the Asian regions of the Soviet Union between November 1943 and June 1944. In November 1944 the Meshets, Kurds and Hemchins living close to the Turkish border were targeted as well. They were also resettled in Siberia because of internal and external security fears.

51. Of them, 38,352 were Bessarabians, 8,198 Bukovinians and 9,900 originated from the area east of the Dniester River. See Achim, 'Romania and the Refugees from Bessarabia', p. 686.

52. Ibid., p. 683.

53. Polian, *Against Their Will*, pp. 250–2.

54. Zalán Bognár, 'Egy csata utóélete', *Studia Carolinensia*, vol. 1, no. 1 (2000), pp. 78–81; Krisztián Ungváry, *Budapest ostroma* (Corvina Kiadó, 1998), p. 274.

55. On the statistical sources, see Tamás Stark, *Magyarok szovjet fogságban* (Lucidus Kiadó, 2006), pp. 91–9.

56. Polian, *Against Their Will*, p. 44.

57. Ibid., p. 259; Schindler, 'Yugoslavia's First Ethnic Cleansing', p. 367.

58. Nicolae Harsányi, 'Deportation of Germans from Romania', in Várdy and Hunt Tooley, *Ethnic Cleansing*, p. 391.

59. Polian, *Against Their Will*, p 260. The number of deportees was 75,000, according to

the following German sources: Bundesministerium für Vertriebene, Flüchtlinge und Kriegsgeschädigte – BVFK (ed.), *Das Schicksal der Deutschen in Rumänien* (Weltbild Verlag, 1994), p. 80E; Georg Weber, *Die Deportation von Siebenbürger Sachsen in die Sowjetunion 1945–1949*, vol. 1 (Böhlau, 1995). The number of deportees was between 75,000 and 80,000, according to Günter Schödl, Werner Conze and Hartmut Boockmann (eds), *Land an der Donau* (Siedler, 1995), p. 596.

60. The best documentary book on the history of early post-war internment in Romania is Zoltán Nagy Mihály and Gábor Vincze (eds), *Autonomisták és Centristák, Észak-Erdély a két román bevonulás között, 1944 szeptember-1945 március* (Erdélyi Múzeum Egyesület – Pro-Print Könyvkiadó, 2004).

61. Ibid., p. 296.

62. Sajti, *Impériumváltások*, p. 322.

63. Sándor Mészáros, 'A járeki haláltábor', in Csorba, *Források*, p. 204.

64. Sajti, *Impériumváltások*, p. 322.

65. Schindler, 'Yugoslavia's First Ethnic Cleansing', p. 366.

66. On the German sources see ibid., pp. 366–8.

67. Kasaš, *Maďʃarí u Vojvodini*, p. 178.

68. Sándor Mészáros, *Holttá nyilvánítva, I. Bácska* (Hatodik Síp Alapítvány Kiadás, 1995), pp. 200–3. The best summary of the research by Hungarian scholars in Serbia on the revenge campaign is the following collection of essays: Béla Csorba, Márton Matuska and Béla Ribár (eds), *Rémuralom a Délvidéken, Tanulmányok, Elemzések, Helyzetértékelések az 1944/45 évi magyarellenes atrocitásokról* (Atlantis, 2004).

69. Hungarian National Archives, *Külügyminisztérium, Békeelőkészítő Osztály Iratai, II./28. Magyar Országos Levéltár*.

70. Ágnes Tóth, *Telepítések Magyarországon 1945–1948 között: A németek kitelepítése, a belső népmozgások és a szlovák-magyar lakosságcsere összefüggései* (BKMÖL, 1993), p. 78. German edition: *Migrationen in Ungarn 1945–1948: Vertreibung der Ungarndeutschen, Binnenwanderungen und slowakisch-ungarischer Bevölkerungsaustausch* (Oldenbourg, 2001).

71. Soňa Gabzdilová and Milan Olejnik, 'Proces internácie nemeckého obyvateľstva na Slovensku v rokoch 1945–1946', *Historický časopis*, vol. 50, no. 3 (2002), p. 435.

72. The decree is cited in Szarka, *Jogfosztó*, pp. 93–4.

73. Ibid.

74. These were the decree numbers 4, 50, 104 and 64.

75. Gabzdilová and Olejnik, 'Proces internácie', p. 433.

76. Károly Kocsis and Eszter Kocsis-Hodosi, *Ethnic Geography of the Hungarian Minorities in the Carpathian Basin* (Geographical Research Institute, 1998), p. 56.

77. In general, Czech, Slovak and Hungarian scholars give similar figures on the consequences of population movements between the two countries. See Juraj Zvara, *Maďarská menšina na Slovensku po roku 1945* (Epocha, 1969), p. 64; Eva Irmanová, *Maʃarsko a versailleský mírový systém* (Albis International, 2002), p. 357; Sándor Balogh, *A népi demokratikus Magyarország külpolitikája 1945–1947* (Kossuth Könyvkiadó, 1982), p. 131; Vadkerty, *A belső telepítések*, pp. 166–7.

78. Stefan Šutaj, 'A Déli akció', *Regió*, vol. 3, no. 2 (1992), p. 92.

79. Vadkerty, *A belső telepítések*, p. 49.

80. Marjan Gajdos, Ivan Szjuszko and Ivan Vovkanics, 'Lakosságcsere Csehszlovákia és Szovjetunió között a háború utáni években', in Ferenc Nagy (ed.), *Tanulmányok a*

Kárpátalja, Erdély és a Felvidék múltjából (Szabolcs-Szatmár-Bereg Megyei Levéltár, 1999), p. 148.

81. Ibid.

82. In 1947 the Statistical Department of the Association of Jewish Religious Communities in Czechoslovakia registered 8,455 Jews who had arrived from Carpatho-Ruthenia after the Holocaust. See Tamás Stark, *Hungarian Jews during the Holocaust and after the Second World War, 1939–1949: A Statistical Review* (Boulder, CO, 2000), p. 108.

83. László Szűcs (ed.), *Dálnoki Miklós Béla kormányának minisztertanácsi jegyző könyvei, 1944. december 23.–1945. november 15. B. kötet* (Magyar Országos Levéltár, 1997), p. 58.

84. Tóth, *Telepítések Magyarországon*, p. 121.

85. Ibid., p. 186.

86. Zoltán Czibulka, Ervin Heinz and Miklos Lakatos (eds), *A magyarországi németek kitelepítése és az 1941. évi népszámlálás* (Központi Statisztikai Hivatal, 2004), p. 35.

87. On the wartime plans for the expulsion of Germans from Poland and Czechoslovakia, see especially Detlef Brandes, *Der Weg zur Vertreibung 1938–1945* (Oldenbourg, 2001). See also Václav Kural, 'Tschechen, Deutsche und die sudetendeutsche Frage während des Zweiten Weltkrieges', in Detlef Brandes et al., *Erzwungene Trennung*, pp. 71–94.

88. For the estimate of some 7.5 million expellees from Poland, see BVFK (ed.), *Dokumentation der Vertreibung der Deutschen aus Ost-Mitteleuropa*, vol. 1: *Die Vertreibung der deutschen Bevölkerung aus den Gebieten östlich der Oder–Neiße* (Munich, 1984), p. 78. For a lower estimate of some 6 million, see Bernadetta Nitschke, *Vertreibung und Aussiedlung der deutschen Bevölkerung aus Polen 1945 bis 1949* (Munich, 2003), p. 82; Emilia Hrabovec, *Vertreibung und Abschub: Deutsche in Mähren 1945–1947* (Frankfurt, 1995), esp. pp. 319–21.

89. Nitschke, *Vertreibung*, p. 83.

90. BVFK (ed.), *Die Vertreibung der Deutschen Bevölkerung aus der Tschechoslowakei*, vol. 1 (Munich, 1984), pp. 19–27; Hrabovec, *Vertreibung*, pp. 57–61.

91. Anna Magierska's 1978 study of the Polish border regions, cited in Nitschke, *Vertreibung*, p. 88.

92. Most of the remaining ethnic German population in Slovakia was subsequently expelled to Germany during the summer and autumn of 1946. See BVFK (ed.), *Tschechoslowakei*, vol. 1, pp. 166–78; Dušan Kováč, 'Die "Aussiedlung" der Deutschen aus der Slowakei', in Brandes et al. (eds), *Erzwungene*, pp. 231–6.

93. K. Erik Franzen, *Die Vertriebenen: Hitlers letzte Opfer* (Propyläen, 2001), p. 173.

94. Nitschke, *Vertreibung*, p. 170.

95. BVFK (ed.), *Oder–Neiße*, vol. 1, pp. 62–8; Ingo Eser's introduction in Włodzimierz Borodziej and Hans Lemberg (eds), *'Unsere Heimat ist uns ein fremdes Land geworden ...': Die Deutschen östlich von Oder und Neiße 1945–1950. Dokumente aus polnischen Archiven*, vol. 2: *Zentralpolen, Wojwodschaft Schlesien* (Herder, 2003), pp. 38, 375–6.

96. Beneš in May 1945, as cited in Johann Wolfgang Brügel, *Tschechen und Deutsche*, vol. 2 (Munich, 1974), p. 147; Hrabovec, *Vertreibung*, pp. 57–104.

97. Brandes et al. (eds), *Erzwungene*, pp. 396–7; Nitschke, *Vertreibung*, pp. 89–110.

98. Jerzy Kochanowski, 'Verräter oder Mitbürger? Staat und Gesellschaft in Polen zum

Problem der Volksdeutschen vor und nach 1945', in Jerzy Kochanowski and Maike Sachs (eds), *Die 'Volksdeutschen' in Polen, Frankreich, Ungarn und der Tschechoslowakei: Mythos und Realität* (fibre Verlag, 2006), pp. 333–52.

99. See, for example, Eagle Glassheim, 'The Mechanics of Ethnic Cleansing: The Expulsion of Germans from Czechoslovakia, 1945–1947', in Philipp Ther and Ana Siljak (eds), *Redrawing Nations: Ethnic Cleansing in East-Central Europe, 1944–1948* (Rowman & Littlefield), pp. 197–219.

100. For good accounts, see Nitschke, *Vertreibung*, pp. 65–122; Hrabovec, *Vertreibung*, pp. 57–104; Claudia Kraft's introduction to Włodzimierz Borodziej and Hans Lemberg (eds), *'Unsere Heimat ist uns ein fremdes Land geworden ...': Die Deutschen östlich von Oder und Neiße 1945–1950. Dokumente aus polnischen Archiven, Bd 4* (Herder, 2004), esp. pp. 358–79.

101. See Nitschke, *Vertreibung*, pp. 181–7.

102. For the best account of the international context and planning, see Brandes et al. (eds), *Erzwungene*.

103. For good accounts of the 'wild expulsions', see Nitschke, *Vertreibung*, pp. 169–87; Hrabovec, *Vertreibung*, pp. 61–139; Benjamin Frommer, *National Cleansing: Retribution against Nazi Collaborators in Postwar Czechoslovakia* (Cambridge University Press, 2005), chapter 1; and the introductory essays to each of the four volumes in the series *'Unsere Heimat ist uns ein fremdes Land geworden...': Die Deutschen östlich von Oder und Neiße 1945–1950. Dokumente aus polnischen Archiven* (Herder, 2000–4).

104. On Potsdam, see Brandes et al. (eds), *Erzwungene*, pp. 401–17.

105. Articles VIIIB and XIII of the Potsdam Protocols, in Ingo von Münch (ed.), *Dokumente des geteilten Deutschland* (DVA, 1968), pp. 42–3.

106. Ibid.

107. Hrabovec, *Vertreibung*, pp. 144–5.

108. Nitschke, *Vertreibung*, esp. pp. 190–2; Kraft's introduction to Borodziej and Lemberg (eds), *'Unsere Heimat'*, *Bd 4*, pp. 393–9.

109. Hrabovec, *Vertreibung*, p. 146.

110. One example was Danzig, where free train tickets were available for Germans willing to leave for the Soviet occupation zone of Germany during the autumn of 1945.

111. Franzen, *Die Vertriebenen*, pp. 145–8; Nitschke, *Vertreibung*, pp. 187–99; Hrabovec, *Vertreibung*, pp. 144–91; Ingo Eser's and Witold Stankowski's introduction to Borodziej and Lemberg (eds), *'Unsere Heimat'*, *Bd 4*, pp. 58–61.

112. Hrabovec, *Vertreibung*, pp. 371–420. For the figures see p. 416. See also Manfred Wille, 'Die "freiwillige Ausreise" sudetendeutscher Antifaschisten in die sowjetische Besatzungszone Deutschlands – erfüllte und enttäuschte Hoffnungen und Erwartungen', in Manfred Wille (ed.), *Die Sudetendeutschen in der Sowjetischen Besatzungszone Deutschlands* (Magdeburg, 1993).

113. Nitschke, *Vertreibung*, pp. 199–203; Hrabovec, *Vertreibung*, pp. 144–90.

114. For good accounts of the details, see Hrabovec, *Vertreibung*, pp. 157–90; Nitschke, *Vertreibung*, pp. 199–253.

115. See *Europa Archiv* (August 1947), p. 823.

116. BVFK (ed.), *Tschechoslowakei*, p. 118 and appendix 31, pp. 328–33.

117. For the Polish–British agreement of 14 February 1946, see ibid., p. 824. On the

Soviet–Polish and Soviet–Czechoslovak agreements, see, respectively, Nitschke, *Vertreibung*, p. 215, and BVFK (ed.), *Tschechoslowakei*, vol. 1, p. 124.

118. At this stage, the Soviet occupation zone was only receiving small contingents of the so-called anti-fascists.

119. Nitschke, *Vertreibung*, pp. 207, 216, 219; BVFK (ed.), *Tschechoslowakei*, vol. 1, p. 123.

120. For good accounts, see Nitschke, *Vertreibung*, pp. 206–32; Hrabovec, *Vertreibung*, pp. 221–312.

121. Franzen, *Die Vertriebenen*, p. 183.

122. Nitschke, *Vertreibung*, pp. 225–6; Franzen, *Die Vertriebenen*, p. 184; BVFK (ed.), *Tschechoslowakei*, pp. 124–5.

123. Nitschke, *Vertreibung*, pp. 223–4.

124. Franzen, *Die Vertriebenen*, pp. 183–4. For more detail see Hrabovec, *Vertreibung*, esp. pp. 313–22.

125. See especially Hrabovec, *Vertreibung*, pp. 313–26.

126. Nitschke, *Vertreibung*, p. 276.

127. This estimate is from Franzen, *Die Vertriebenen*, p. 183. For a longer discussion, see Hrabovec, *Vertreibung*, pp. 322–36.

128. Gerhard Reichling, *Die deutschen Vertriebenen in Zahlen*, Vol. II (Bonn, 1989), p. 30. Here and below, the figure for territories under Polish rule also includes northern-east Prussia, which had been annexed by the Soviet Union.

129. Nitschke, *Vertreibung*, p. 333.

130. Hrabovec, *Vertreibung*, pp. 322–36; Nitschke, *Vertreibung*, esp. p. 280.

131. Nitschke, *Vertreibung*, pp. 280–1; Hrabovec, *Vertreibung*, esp. pp. 329–30.

132. According to Nitschke, *Vertreibung*, p. 283, the Polish estimate of the extant German minority in Poland at the end of the 1950s was 3,000, whereas West Germans projected figures as high as 87,425. See also Klaus J. Bade, 'Fremde Deutsche: "Republikflüchtlinge" – Übersiedler – Aussiedler', in Klaus J. Bade (ed.), *Deutsche im Ausland – Fremde in Deutschland: Migration in Geschichte und Gegenwart* (C.H. Beck, 1992), pp. 401–10.

133. Piotr Eberhardt, *Polska granica wschodnia 1939–1945* (Spotkania, 1993).

134. Ciesielski, *Przesiedlenie ludności polskiej*, p. 14.

135. The terminology used with respect to the relocation of the Poles in the years 1944–6 is still debated. Instead of the terms 'evacuation' and 'repatriation' used in the 1940s (which are incorrect with respect to the Polish nationals in the eastern parts of pre-war Poland), the terms 'relocation', 'enforced relocation', 'transfer' or – in extreme situations such as in the Ukraine – 'expulsion' seem more appropriate.

136. *Dokumenty i materiały do historii stosunków polsko-radzieckich*, vol. VIII (Książka i Wiedza, 1974), pp. 221–2.

137. Włodzimierz Borodziej, 'Sprawa polska i przemieszczenia ludności w czasie II wojny światowej', in Włodzimierz Borodziej and Hans Lemberg (eds), *Niemcy w Polsce 1945–1950: wybór dokumentów*, vol. 1 (Neriton, 2000), pp. 43, 109–14.

138. Leszek Olejnik, *Polityka narodowościowa Polski w latach 1944–1960* (Wydawn. Uniwersytetu Łódźkiego, 2003); Leszek Olejnik, 'Rozwiązanie przez władze polskie w latach 1945–1946 kwestii grup narodowościowych uprzywilejowanych w czasie okupacji niemieckiej', in Ryszard Sudziński and Włodzimierz Jastrzębski (eds), *Wrzesień 1939 roku i jego konsekwencje dla ziem zachodnich i północnych Drugiej*

Rzeczypospolitej (Wydawn. Uniwersytetu Mikołaja Kopernika w Toruniu-Akademia Bydgoska im. Kazimierza Wielkiego, 2001); Leszek Olejnik, *Zdrajcy narodu? Losy volksdeutschów w Polsce po II wojnie światowej* (Trio, 2006); Andrzej Pasek, *Przestępstwa okupacyjne w polskim prawie karnym z lat 1944–1956* (Wydawn. Uniwersytetu Wrocławskiego, 2002), pp. 111ff. (with ample bibliography).

139. Cf. Mirosław Dymarski, *Ziemie postulowane (ziemie nowe) w prognozach i działaniach polskiego ruchu oporu 1939–1945* (Wydawn. Uniwersytetu Wrocławskiego, 1997).

140. Włodzimierz Bonusiak, 'Rekrutacja, rozmieszczenie i struktura polskich robotników przymusowych do pracy w Rzeszy', in Włodzimierz Bonusiak (ed.), *Polscy robotnicy przymusowi w Trzeciej Rzeszy* (Wydaw. Uniw. Rzeszowskiego, 2005), pp. 69–77.

141. Dorota Sula, *Działalność przesiedleńczo-repatriacyjna Państwowego Urzędu Repatriacyjnego w latach 1944–1951* (Red. Wydawnictw Katolickiego Uniwersytetu Lubelskiego, 2002), p. 77.

142. See Orest Subtelny, 'Expulsion, Resettlement, Civil Strife: The Fate of Poland's Ukrainians, 1944–1947', in Ther and Siljak, *Redrawing Nations*, pp. 155–72; Eugeniusz Misiło (ed.), *Repatriacja czy deportacja: Przesiedlenie Ukraińców z Polski do USSR 1944–1946, vol. 1: Dokumenty 1944–1945* (Oficyna Wydawn. Archiwum Ukrai'nskie, 1996); Jurij Szapował and Jędrzej Tucholski (eds), *Przesiedlenia Polaków i Ukraińców 1944–1946* (Rytm, 2000).

143. Sula, *Działalność*, p. 78.

144. Olga W. Buźko, 'Przesiedlenia ukraińsko-polskie 1944–1946', in Jan E. Zamojski (ed.), *Migracje polityczne XX wieku (Migracje i Społeczeństwo 4)* (Instytut Historii PAN, 2000), pp. 142–7; Sula, *Działalność*, pp. 78–9. See also Misiło, *Repatriacja*; Subtelny, 'Expulsion, Resettlement, Civil Strife'.

145. Some 36,400 Belorussians and 1,000 Lithuanians were also relocated by the end of 1946. This gives a number that exceeds the commonly accepted figure of 518,718 by about 1,500, which is within the admissible margin of calculation error. Stanisław Ciesielski (ed.), *Kresy Wschodnie II Rzeczypospolitej: Przekształcenia struktury narodowościowej 1931–1948* (Wrocław 2006), p. 11.

146. Sula, *Działalność*, pp. 120–1; Eugeniusz Misiło (ed.), *Akcja 'Wisła': Dokumenty* (Zakład Wydawn. Tyrsa, 1993), p. 65; Subtelny, 'Expulsion, Resettlement, Civil Strife', pp. 166–8; Marek Jasiak, 'Overcoming Ukrainian Resistance: The Deportation of Ukrainians within Poland in 1947', in Ther and Siljak, *Redrawing Nations*, pp. 173–94. See also Roman Drozd, *Droga na zachód: Osadnictwo ludności ukraińskiej na ziemiach zachodnich i północnych Polski w Ramach akcji 'Wisła'* (Tyrsa, 1997).

147. For the State Office for Repatriation see Ciesielski, *Przesiedlenie ludności polskiej*, pp. 15–16.

148. Jan Czerniakiewicz, *Repatriacja ludności polskiej z ZSRR 1944–1948* (Państwowe Wydawn. Nauk., 1987), p. 54.

149. Ibid., p. 43.

150. Mieczysław Motas, 'Niektóre kwestie dotyczące przesiedlania ludności polskiej z USRR do Polski w latach 1944–1948', in *Z dziejów stosunków polsko-radzieckich: Studia i materiały*, vol. X–XI (Książka i Wiedza, 1975), p. 227.

151. Julian Siedlecki, *Losy Polaków w ZSRR w latach 1939–1986* (Gryf, 1987), p. 335.

152. The city of Vilna/Vilnius was the site of a conflict between the Poles and the Lithuanians which had a symbolic dimension. The Constitution of the Republic of Lithuania decreed Vilnius the capital of the country. On the basis of the Annex to the Ribbentrop–Molotov Pact, signed on 28 September 1939, the region of Vilnius was handed over to Lithuania, whereby Vilnius became its capital. Until Lithuania's incorporation into the USSR in August 1940, the whole region, and the city in particular, was subject to forced Lithuanization.

153. Czerniakiewicz, *Repatriacja ludności polskiej*, p. 43.

154. Ciesielski, *Przesiedlenie ludności polskiej*, p. 304.

155. Ibid., pp. 18–24.

156. Ibid., pp. 24, 30; Małgorzata Ruchniewicz, *Repatriacja ludności polskiej z ZSRR w latach 1955–59* (Volumen, 2000), p. 34.

157. Ruchniewicz, *Repatriacja*.

158. On 13 February 1945 the Polish government passed a resolution stating that 'immediate measures must be taken to start mass repatriation of the Polish people, notwithstanding the technical difficulties resulting from war damage', quoted in Ciesielski, *Przesiedlenie ludności polskiej*, p. 32.

159. An example of such an attempted prohibition was the directive of Minister of Public Administration Władysław Wolski issued in mid-1946. On 11 December 1945 Prime Minister Edward Osóbka-Morawski openly stated that 'all the repatriated persons should be directed to the western regions, and they should not be provided with quarters in the city of Łódź' (Ciesielski, *Przesiedlenie ludności polskiej*, p. 324).

160. Elio Apih, *Italia, fascismo e antifascismo nella Venezia Giulia (1918–1943)* (Laterza, 1966). See also Anna Vinci, 'Il fascismo al confine orientale', in *Storia d'Italia: Le regioni dall'unità a oggi. Il Friuli-Venezia Giulia* (Einaudi, 2002), vol. I, pp. 377–513.

161. See Milica Kacin-Wohinz, 'I programmi di snazionalizzazione degli solveni e croati nella Venezia Giulia', *Storia contemporanea in Friuli*, vol. 18, no. 19 (1988), pp. 9–33.

162. Raoul Pupo, *Il lungo esodo. Istria: le persecuzioni, le foibe, l'esilio* (Rizzoli, 2005), p. 33.

163. Marco Cuzzi, *L'occupazione italiana della Slovenia (1941–1943)* (Ufficio Storico Stato Maggiore Esercito, 1998). Of fundamental importance is the collection of documents edited by Ferenc Tone, *La provincia 'italiana' di Lubiana: Documenti 1941–1943* (Istituto Regionale per la storia del movimento di liberazione nel Friuli-Venezia Giulia, 1994).

164. See Capogreco, *I campi del duce*.

165. Nevenka Troha, 'Il Movimento di liberazione sloveno e i confini occidentali sloveni', *Qualestoria*, vol. 31, no. 2 (2003).

166. One of the most balanced and most recent studies of this phenomenon is the short book by Raoul Pupo and Roberto Spazzali, *Foibe* (Bruno Mondadori, 2003), annotated with useful documents.

167. Karl Stühlpfarrer, *Le zone d'operazione Prealpi e Litorale Adriatico 1943–1945* (Editrice Goriziana, 1979; original edition 1969). One should not underestimate the hegemonic ambitions towards this region, especially in National Socialist Austria. See Enzo Collotti, *Il Litorale Adriatico nel Nuovo Ordine Europeo* (Vangelista, 1974).

168. Galliano Fogar, *Sotto l'occupazione nazista nelle provincie orientali*, 2nd rev. edn (Del Bianco, 1968).

169. Roberto Gualtieri, *Togliatti e la politica estera italiana: Dalla Resistenza al trattato di pace 1943–1947* (Editori Riuniti, 1995).

170. For an accurate analysis of the Trieste question, see Giampaolo Valdevit, *La questione di Trieste 1941–1954: Politica internazionale e contesto locale* (Angeli, 1986). These events ended in 1954, with the return of Trieste and zone 'A' to Italian rule.

171. Raoul Pupo, 'L'esodo degli italiani da Zara, da Fiume e dall'Istria. Un quadro fattuale', in Cattaruzza, Dogo, Pupo, *Esodi*, p. 186.

172. Cristiana Colummi, 'Guerra, occupazione nazista e resistenza', in Cristiana Columni, Liliana Ferrari, Gianna Nassisi and Germano Trani (eds), *Storia di un esodo: Istria 1945–1956* (Istituto Regionale per la storia del movimento di liberazione nel Friuli-Venezia Giulia, 1980), pp. 44f.

173. There was strong support for Bishop Comozzo, including from the majority of Rijeka's working class; ibid., p. 83.

174. See Alfredo Bonelli, *Fra Stalin e Tito: Cominformisti a Fiume 1948–1956* (Istituto Regionale per la storia del movimento di liberazione nel Friuli-Venezia Giulia, 1994).

175. Columni et al. (eds), *Storia di un esodo*, pp. 158f. But the strong Italian Communist Party did not participate in the group, which it strongly opposed.

176. Ibid., pp. 355f.

177. Ibid., p. 495.

178. Antonio Colella (ed.), *L'esodo dalle terre adriatiche: Rilevazioni statistiche* (Opera profughi giuliani e dalmati, 1958).

179. Pupo, 'L'esodo degli italiani', p. 190.

180. On the most recent developments in Slovenian and Croatian historiography, see the papers by Marta Verginella and Luciano Giuricin, in Cattaruzza, Dogo and Pupo, *Esodi*, pp. 269–85.

181. Roberto Spazzali and Orietta Moscarda, 'L'Istria epurata (1945–1948): Ragionamenti per una ricerca', in Cattaruzza, Dogo and Pupo, *Esodi*, p. 239.

5 The Experience of Forced Migration

1. Lumans, *Himmler's Auxiliaries*, passim; Jürgen von Hehn, *Die Umsiedlung der baltischen Deutschen: Das letzte Kapitel baltisch-deutscher Geschichte* (Herder-Institut, 1982), pp. 88–104.

2. Latvian-German Werner Sticinsky, in Hehn, *Umsiedlung*, p. 96; S.K. from North Bukovina, in BVFK (ed.), *Rumänien*, p. 30.

3. Alois Kirsch from Yugoslavia, in BVFK (ed.), *Das Schicksal der Deutschen in Jugoslawien* (Dtv, 1984), p. 13.

4. Otto Klett from Dobrudja, in BVFK (ed.), *Rumänien*, p. 20.

5. BVFK (ed.), *Rumänien*, p. 7; Lumans, *Himmler's Auxiliaries*; Koehl, *RKFDV*; Rainer Schulze, 'Forgotten Victims or Beneficiaries of Genocide? The Mass Resettlement of Ethnic Germans "heim ins Reich"', *Annali dell'Istituto storico italo-germanico in Trento*, XXVII (2001): esp. pp. 544–8; Karl Stühlpfarrer, *Umsiedlung Südtirol 1939–1940*, 2 vols (Oldenbourg, 1985).

6. Lumans, *Himmler's Auxiliaries*, pp. 161–5; Schechtman, *Population Transfers*, pp. 159–62.
7. Koehl, *RKFDV*, p. 103.
8. Otto Klett in BVFK (ed.), *Rumänien*, p. 20; Dirk Jachomowski, *Umsiedlung der Bessarabien-, Bukowina- und Dobrudschadeutschen* (Oldenbourg, 1984); Aly, *Endlösung*.
9. The only other group that received similarly speedy resettlement comprised the roughly 30,000 ethnic Germans moved within the Reich's borders from the Lublin-Cholm region of the General Government to the Warthegau in September 1940. See Koehl, *RKFDV*, pp. 100–1.
10. Von Hehn, *Umsiedlung*, pp. 192–9; Schechtman, *Transfers*, pp. 317–33.
11. Gottlob Enslen in Theodor Schieder (ed.), *Documents on the Expulsion of the Germans from Eastern Central Europe, Vol II/III: The Expulsion of the German Population from Hungary and Rumania* (German Federal Ministry for Expellees, Refugees and War Victims, 1961), p. 188.
12. K.R. from Yugoslavia, in BFVK (ed.), *Jugoslawien*, p. 36.
13. Schechtman, *Transfers*, esp. pp. 354–63.
14. Alois Kirsch, in BFVK (ed.), *Jugoslawien*, p. 13.
15. Rutowska, *Wysiedlenia*, p. 65.
16. Rutowska, *Wysiedlenia*, p. 78.
17. Ludwik Landau, *Kronika lat wojny i okupacji*, vol. 1 (Państwowe Wydawn. Naukowe, 1962), p. 80.
18. Landau, *Kronika*, vol. 1, pp. 133, 149.
19. Browning, *Entfesselung*, pp. 148–9; Czesław Łuczak (ed.), *Położenie ludności polskiej w tzw. Kraju Warty w okresie hitlerowskiej okupacji: Wybór źródeł* (Instytut Zachodni, 1990), pp. 133–9.
20. Cf. Sławomir Abramowicz, 'Obozy przejściowe i przesiedleńcze', in Albin Głowacki and Sławomir Abramowicz (eds), *Obozy hitlerowskie w Łodzi: praca zbiorowa* (Instytutu Pamięci Narodowej, 1998), pp. 101–32.
21. Maria Wardzyńska, 'Obozy hitlerowskie i ich rola w polityce okupacyjnej III Rzeszy', in Głowacki and Abramowicz (eds), *Obozy*.
22. Aly, *Endlösung*, pp. 187–95.
23. Koehl, *RKFDV*, p. 139; Lumans, *Himmler's Auxiliaries*, pp. 186–95; Schulze, 'Forgotten Victims', pp. 548–52.
24. S.K. in Schieder (ed.), *Documents*, p. 195.
25. Ibid., p. 196.
26. Lumans, *Himmler's Auxiliaries*, pp. 189–91; Koehl, *RKFDV*, pp. 105–7.
27. Otto Schmidt in Schieder (ed.), *Documents*, p. 199.
28. Ibid., pp. 198–9.
29. Lumans, *Himmler's Auxiliaries*, pp. 189–95; Schulze, 'Forgotten Victims', pp. 549–52.
30. Otto Klett, in BVFK (ed.), *Rumänien*, p. 23.
31. Aly, *Endlösung*, p. 320; Lumans, *Himmler's Auxiliaries*, p. 197.
32. Rutowska, *Wysiedlenia*, p. 210.
33. Landau, *Kronika*, vol. I, p. 131.
34. Bogdan Kroll, *Rada Główna Opiekuńcza 1939–1945* (Książka i Wiedza, 1985), p. 120.

35. Marian Woźniak (ed.), *Encyklopedia konspiracji wielkopolskiej 1939–1945* (Instytut Zachodni, 1998), pp. 535–6, 614–16.
36. Ibid., pp. 607–8, 616–18, 618–20.
37. Rutowska, *Wysiedlenia*, p. 221.
38. AAN, Delegatura Rządu na Kraj, call no. 202/I-32, f. 15, in Czeslaw Madajczyk (ed.), *Zamojszczyzna – Sonderlaboratorium SS*, 2 vols (Ludowa Spółdzielnia Wydawn., 1977), vol. I, p. 229.
39. Kiełboń, *Migracje*, p. 46; Henryk Kajtel, *Hitlerowski obóz przesiedleńczy w Zamościu: UWZ Lager Zamość* (Zarząd Stowarzyszenia Dzieci Zamojszczyzny, 2003).
40. Kiełboń, *Migracje*, p. 51.
41. Madajczyk, *Zamojszczyzna*, vol. I, p. 333.
42. Some people signed the German National List or converted to the Orthodox Church. Anna Glińska (ed.), *Zamojszczyzna w okresie okupacji hitlerowskiej (relacje wysiedlonych i partyzantów)* (Pax, 1968), p. 14.
43. Ibid., pp. 16–24.
44. Theodor Schieder (ed.), *Documents on the Expulsion of the Germans from Eastern Central Europe*, Vol. 1: *The Expulsion of the German Population from the Territories East of the Oder–Neiße Line* (Federal Ministry for Expellees, Refugees and War Victims, 1958), pp. 62–8; Nitschke, *Vertreibung*, pp. 84–6; BVFK (ed.), *Rumänien*, pp. 75–80; BVFK (ed.), *Ungarn*, pp. 41–4; BVFK (ed.), *Jugoslawien*, pp. 93–7.
45. Ciesielski et al., *Masowe deportacje*, p. 40.
46. Ibid., p. 41.
47. Ibid., p. 57; Ciesielski et al., *Represje sowieckie*, pp. 16–17.
48. Ciesielski et al., *Masowe deportacje*, p. 49.
49. Kowalska, *Przeżyć*, p. 124.
50. Kowalska, *Przeżyć*, pp. 133–4; Ciesielski et al., *Masowe deportacje*, p. 61; Ciesielski et al., *Represje sowieckie*, pp. 19–20.
51. Ciesielski et al., *Masowe deportacje*, p. 70.
52. Kowalska, *Przeżyć*, p. 161.
53. Głowacki, *Ocalić*, pp. 28–9.
54. Ibid.
55. Sula, *Działalność*, pp. 129, 133–4.
56. Ibid., p. 140.
57. This excludes 10,000 to 20,000 demobilized soldiers from units formed in the USSR in 1942–4.
58. Estimates reach 60,000–65,000. Ciesielski et al., *Represje sowieckie*, pp. 29–30.
59. Some 20,700 repatriates were registered during that period. Ruchniewicz, *Repatriacja*, p. 44.
60. Ciesielski, *Przesiedlenie ludności polskiej*, p. 19.
61. Czerniakiewicz, *Repatriacja*, p. 43.
62. Ciesielski, *Przesiedlenie ludności polskiej*, p. 304.
63. Jerzy Kochanowski (ed.), *Protokoły posiedzeń Prezydium Krajowej Rady Narodowej 1944–1947* (Sejmowe, 1995), pp. 273–8.
64. Kochanowski, *Protokoły*, p. 274.
65. Czerniakiewicz, *Repatriacja*, p. 56.
66. APW, Państwowy Urząd Repatriacyjny (PUR), call no. 411, f. 2.

67. AAN, GPRR, call no. 46, f. 243.
68. Ciesielski, *Przesiedlenie ludności polskiej*, p. 330.
69. AAN, MIP, vol. 785, f. 24–6.
70. AAN, GPRR, call no. 13, f. 204.
71. AAN, PUR, call no. XIV/29, f. 135.
72. Henryk Słabek, *Polityka agrarna PPR: Geneza, realizacja, konsekwencje* (Książka i Wiedza, 1978), pp. 343–6.
73. Stefan Banasiak, *Działalność osadnicza Państwowego Urzędu Repatriacyjnego na Ziemiach Odzyskanych w latach 1945–1947* (Instytut Zachodni, 1963), p. 123.
74. Jerzy Kochanowski, 'Eine andere Schuldrechnung: Die polnischen Umsiedler und ihr Kampf um Entschädigungen', *Zeitschrift für Geschichtswissenschaft*, vol. 51, no. 1 (2003), pp. 65–73. Because they failed to get compensation from the Polish state, some of the former repatriates, or their ancestors, lodged complaints with the European Tribunal for Human Rights in Strasburg. On 22 June 2004 the Tribunal ruled that Poland has to honour the claims of these repatriates, but they have still not received compensation.
75. Jerzy Kochanowski, 'Lubelskie czarne gabinety: Sprawozdania cenzury wojennej z 1944 r.', in *Polska 1944/45–1989: Studia i materiały*, vol. IV (Instytut Historii PAN, 1998).
76. APW, PUR, call no. 495, f. 21.
77. T. Żochowski, *Notatki z podróży po kraju*, in *'Po Prostu' 1955–1956: Wybór artykułów* (Warsaw, 1956), pp. 136–7.
78. Tomasz Szarota, *Osadnictwo miejskie na Dolnym Śląsku w latach 1945–1948* (Zakład Narodowy im. Ossoliński, 1969), p. 153.
79. Szarota, *Osadnictwo*, p. 152; Banasiak, *Działalność*, pp. 52–3.
80. Natalia Aleksiun, *Dokąd dalej? Ruch syjonistyczny w Polsce (1944–1950)* (Trio, 2002), pp. 66–8; Bożena Szaynok, *Ludność żydowska na Dolnym Śląsku 1945–1950* (Wydawn. Uniw. Wrocławskiego, 2000).
81. Aleksiun, *Dokąd dalej?*, p. 83.
82. BVFK (ed.), *Rumänien*, esp. E85–90, 63–225; BVFK (ed.), *Ungarn*, esp. E34–E40, 5–27; BVFK (ed.), *Jugoslawien*, esp. E85–E90, 91–193; BVFK (ed.), *Tschechoslowakei*, vol. 1, esp. E166–E172; vol. 2, esp. 711–48; Koehl, *RKFDV*, pp. 172–5; Lumans, *Himmler's Auxiliaries*, pp. 250–5; Geza C. Paikert, *The Danube Swabians: German Populations in Hungary, Rumania and Yugoslavia and Hitler's Impact on Their Patterns* (Nijhoff, 1967), pp. 185–91.
83. Franzen, *Vertriebenen*, p. 74.
84. F. Lackner, in Jerzy Kochanowski's introduction to Borodziej and Lemberg, *'Unsere Heimat'*, vol. 2, p. 36.
85. Nitschke, *Vertreibung*, pp. 78–9.
86. Heidemarie Mielack, 'Die wahren Heldinnen', in Hans Jürgen Bömelburg, Renate Stössringer and Robert Traba (eds), *Vertreibung aus dem Osten: Deutsche und Polen erinnern sich* (Borussia, 2000), pp. 314–28.
87. Nitschke, *Vertreibung*, pp. 82–3.
88. Norman Naimark, *The Russians in Germany: A History of the Soviet Zone of Occupation, 1945–1949* (Belknap, 1995), pp. 69–140; Atina Grossman, 'A Question of Silence: The Rape of German Women by Occupation Soldiers', *October*, vol. 72 (1995), pp. 43–65.

89. Testimony of Theodore Grub from East Prussia, in BVFK (ed.), *Oder–Neiße*, vol. 2, p. 9.
90. Testimony of E.P., in ibid., p. 86.
91. Nitschke, *Vertreibung*, pp. 65–84; Manfred Zeidler, *Kriegsende im Osten: Die Rote Armee und die Besetzung Deutschlands östlich von Oder und Neiße 1944/1945* (Oldenbourg, 1996).
92. Franzen, *Vertriebenen*, pp. 168–72; BVFK (ed.), *Tschechoslowakei*, vol. 2, pp. 107–49; BVFK (ed.), *Tschechoslowakei*, vol. 1, E51–E64.
93. F.K., in BVFK (ed.), *Oder–Neiße*, vol. 2, pp. 495–7. See also ibid., p. 380; BVFK (ed.), *Tschechoslowakei*, vol. 2, p. 158; Borodziej and Lemberg, *'Unsere Heimat'*, vol. 4, pp. 565–6.
94. Franzen, *Vertriebenen*, pp. 125–33, 169–82; Nitschke, *Vertreibung*, pp. 65–122; Hrabovec, *Vertreibung*; BVFK (ed.), *Tschechoslowakei*, vol. 1, pp. 51–104; BVFK (ed.), *Tschechoslowakei*, vol. 2; Schieder (ed.), *Documents on the Expulsion of the Germans from Eastern Central Europe*, Vol. IV: *The Expulsion of the German Population from Czechoslovakia*, pp. 68–103; BVFK (ed.), *Oder–Neiße*, vol. 2.
95. Testimonies of B.L., in BVFK (ed.), *Oder–Neiße*, vol. 2, p. 145, and Matthias Krebs, in BVFK (ed.), *Tschechoslowakei*, vol. 2, p. 19.
96. Eagle Glassheim, 'The Mechanics of Ethnic Cleansing: The Expulsion of Sudeten Germans from Czechoslovakia, 1945–1947', in Ther and Siljak (ed.), *Redrawing*, p. 208; BVFK (ed.), *Tschechoslowakei*, vol. 1, pp. 71–2.
97. Glassheim, 'Mechanics', p. 206; BVFK (ed.), *Tschechoslowakei*, vol. 1, p. 66.
98. Nitschke, *Vertreibung*, pp. 172, 185.
99. Article XIII of the Potsdam Agreement, in von Münch, *Dokumente des geteilten Deutschlands*, pp. 42–3.
100. Nitschke, *Vertreibung*, pp. 197, 195.
101. Ibid., p. 197.
102. Ibid., pp. 187–202, 275–6; Franzen, *Vertriebenen*, pp. 176–82; Borodziej and Lemberg, *'Unsere Heimat'*, vol. 4, pp. 393–9.
103. BVFK (ed.), *Ungarn*, pp. 59–66, 71–2.
104. Gerhard Reichling, *Die deutschen Vertriebenen in Zahlen, Teil 1* (Kulturstiftung der deutschen Vertriebenen,1986), p. 27.
105. Rüdiger Overmans, 'Personelle Verluste der deutschen Zivilbevölkerung durch Flucht und Vertreibung', *Dzieje Najnowsze*, vol. 26 (1994), pp. 51–65.
106. In Hungary the conditions were somewhat less harsh. BVFK (ed.), *Ungarn*, pp. 59–66.
107. Nitschke, *Vertreibung*, pp. 206–68; Franzen, *Vertriebenen*, pp. 140–53, 182–4; BVFK (ed.), *Tschechoslowakei, Bd 1*, pp. 115–36; Schieder (ed.), *Documents*, pp. 104–22.
108. Borodziej and Lemberg, *'Unsere Heimat'*, vol. 4, p. 615.
109. BVFK (ed.), *Oder–Neiße*, vol. 2, pp. 686–8, esp. p. 687.
110. Nitschke, *Vertreibung*, p. 204.
111. Testimony of E.M., in BVFK (ed.), *Oder–Neiße*, vol. 2, p. 733.
112. Rainer Schulze, 'Growing Discontent: Relations between Native and Refugee Populations in a Rural District in Western Germany after the Second World War', *German History*, vol. 7, no. 3 (1989), pp. 332–49; Rainer Schulze (ed.), *Unruhige Zeiten: Erlebnisberichte aus dem Landkreis Celle 1945–1949* (Oldenbourg, 1990);

Michael Schwartz, *Vertriebene und 'Umsiedlerpolitik': Integrationskonflikte in den deutschen Nachkriegs-Gesellschaften und die Assimilationsstrategien in der SBZ/DDR 1945 bis 1961* (Oldenbourg, 2004).

113. See Rainer Schulze's work, including 'Die deutsche Titanic und die verlorene Heimat', *Annali dell'Istituto storico italo-germanico in Trento*, vol. XXIX (2003), pp. 577–616; 'Alte Heimat – neue Heimat – oder heimatlos dazwischen? Zur Frage der regionalen Identität deutscher Flüchtlinge und Vertriebene – Eine Skizze', *Nordostarchiv*, New Series, vol. 6 (1997), pp. 759–87.

114. Pertti Ahonen, 'Taming the Expellee Threat in Post-1945 Europe: Lessons from the Two Germanies and Finland', *Contemporary European History*, vol. 14, no. 1 (2005), pp. 1–21.

6 Forced Migrations and Mass Movements in the Memorialization Processes since the Second World War

1. Maurice Halbwachs, *La Mémoire collective* (Presses universitaires de France, 1950). The book was translated into German and Italian in the 1980s as *Das kollektive Gedächtnis* (Fischer, 1985) and *La memoria collettiva* (Unicopli, 1987).

2. Henry Rousso, 'Das Dilemma eines europäischen Gedächtnisses', *Zeithistorische Forschungen*, vol. 1, no. 3 (2004), p. 370.

3. Pierre Nora (ed.), *Les lieux de mémoire*, 3 vols (Gallimard, 1984). English edition: *Realms of Memory: Rethinking the French Past*, 3 vols (Columbia University Press, 1996–8).

4. Mario Isnenghi, *I luoghi della memoria*, 3 vols (Laterza, 1997); Etienne François and Hagen Schulze (eds), *Deutsche Erinnerungsorte*, 3 vols (Beck, 2001). For the Netherlands see Pim den Boer and Willem Frijhoff (eds), *Lieux de mémoire et identités nationales* (Amsterdam University Press, 1993).

5. For Germany see Rudy Koshar, *From Monuments to Traces: Artifacts of German Memory 1870–1990* (California University Press, 2000). On monuments of the camps see Detlef Hoffmann (ed.), *Das Gedächtnis der Dinge: KZ-Relikte und KZ-Denkmäler 1945–1995* (Campus, 1998).

6. Methodologically most relevant are Alessandro Portelli, *L'ordine è già stato eseguito: Roma, le Fosse Ardeatine, la memoria* (Donzelli, 1999); Lutz Niethammer, *Die Jahre weiss man nicht, wo man die heute hinsetzen soll: Faschismuserfahrungen im Ruhrgebiet* (Dietz, 1983); idem, *Die volkseigene Erfahrung: Archäologie des Lebens in der Industrieprovinz der DDR* (Dietz, 1991).

7. 'We forget what we do not want to remember, communities forget what in the opinion of their members is against their interest, and both processes have their, often neglected, moral dimension'; see Sławomir Kapralski, 'Battlefields of Memory: Landscape and Identity in Polish–Jewish Relations', *History & Memory*, vol. 13, no. 2 (2001), p. 38.

8. The usefulness of linking historical and anthropological methods is demonstrated by Catherine Wanner, *Burden of Dreams: History and Identity in Post-Soviet Ukraine* (Penn State University Press, 1998).

9. A recent example was the exhibition 'Mythen der Nationen: 1945: Arena der Erinnerungen' at the Deutsches Historisches Museum Berlin in 2004/2005; see the

catalogue edited by Monika Flacke, *Mythen der Nationen: 1945: Arena der Erinnerungen*, 2 vols (Deutsches Historisches Museum, 2004). See also Jay Winter and Emmanuel Sivan (eds), *War and Remembrance in the Twentieth Century* (Cambridge University Press, 1999).

10. Lawrence L. Langer, *Holocaust Testimonies: Ruins of Memory* (Yale University Press, 1991); Annette Wieviorka, *L'ère du témoin* (Plon, 1998); a more general approach is taken by Clemens Wischermann, *Vom kollektiven Gedächtnis zur Individualisierung der Erinnerung* (Steiner, 2002).

11. See Wulf Kansteiner, 'Finding Meaning in Memory: A Methodological Critique of Collective Memory Studies', *History & Theory*, vol. 41, no. 1 (2002), pp. 179–97.

12. See Pavel Poljan, *Zhertvy dvuch diktatur: Ostarbaitery i voennoplennye v tret'em reikhe i ikh repatriaciya* (Vash vybor TSIRZ, 1996). German edition: *Deportiert nach Hause: Sowjetische Kriegsgefangene im 'Dritten Reich' und ihre Repatriierung* (Oldenbourg, 2001).

13. Nina Tumarkin, *The Living and the Dead: The Rise and Fall of the Cult of World War II in Russia* (Basic Books, 1994).

14. Guido Crainz, *Il dolore e l'esilio: L'Istria e le memorie divisa d'Europa* (Donzelli, 2005). For recent Italian legislative activity on memorialization, see Italian Law no. 92, 30 March 2004.

15. For a comparison between the two countries see Manfred Kittel, *Nach Nürnberg und Tokio: 'Vergangenheitsbewältigung' in Japan und Westdeutschland 1945 bis 1968* (Oldenbourg, 2004); Ian Buruma, *Wages of Guilt: Memories of War in Germany and Japan* (Phoenix, 2002).

16. Pertti Ahonen, *After the Expulsion: West Germany and Eastern Europe 1945–1990* (Oxford University Press, 2003); see also Matthias Beer, 'Im Spannungsfeld von Politik und Zeitgeschichte: Das Großforschungsprojekt "Dokumentation der Vertreibung der Deutschen aus Ost-Mitteleuropa"', *Vierteljahrshefte für Zeitgeschichte*, vol. 46 (1998), pp. 345–89; Bill Niven (ed.), *Germans as Victims: Remembering the Past in Contemporary Germany* (Palgrave Macmillan, 2006).

17. Robert G. Moeller, *War Stories: The Search for a Viable Past in the Federal Republic of Germany* (California University Press, 2001).

18. Philipp Ther, *Deutsche und polnische Vertriebene: Gesellschaft und Vertriebenenpolitik in der SBZ/DDR und in Polen 1945–1956* (Vandenhoeck & Ruprecht, 1998).

19. On the changes in public memory after 1990, see Bill Niven, *Facing the Nazi Past: United Germany and the Legacy of the Third Reich* (Routledge, 2002).

20. See Christoph Cornelißen, Roman Holec and Jiří Pešek (eds), *Diktatur – Krieg – Vertreibung: Erinnerungskulturen in Tschechien, der Slowakei und Deutschland seit 1945* (Klartext, 2005), and the final statement of the Italian-Slovenian historical commission, published in *Qualestoria*, vol. 27, no. 2 (2000), pp. 145–67.

21. Two recent overviews are: Eva Hahn and Hans Henning Hahn, 'Flucht und Vertreibung', in François and Schulze, *Deutsche Erinnerungsorte*, vol. 1, pp. 335–51; Hans Lemberg, 'Geschichten und Geschichte: Das Gedächtnis der Vertriebenen in Deutschland nach 1945', *Archiv für Sozialgeschichte*, vol. 44 (2004), pp. 509–23. They pursue a somewhat different line of argument from that developed here; see also Rainer Schulze, 'The Politics of Memory: Flight and Expulsion of German

Populations after the Second World War and German Collective Memory', *National Identities*, vol. 8 (2006), pp. 367–82.

22. Annerose Rosan, *Das verlorene Gesicht: Lebensbilder 1932–1947* (Donat, 2000), pp. 117–18.

23. Michael Schwartz, 'Tabu und Erinnerung: Zur Vertriebenen-Problematik in Politik und literarischer Öffentlichkeit der DDR', *Zeitschrift für Geschichtswissenschaft*, vol. 51, no. 1 (2003), pp. 85–101; see also Manfred Wille, 'SED und "Umsiedler" – Vertriebenenpolitik der Einheitspartei im ersten Nachkriegsjahrzehnt', in Dierk Hoffmann and Michael Schwartz (eds), *Geglückte Integration? Spezifika und Vergleichbarkeiten der Vertriebenen-Eingliederung in der SBZ/DDR* (Oldenbourg, 1999), pp. 91–104.

24. See, among many others, Pertti Ahonen, *After the Expulsion*; Samuel Salzborn, *Heimatrecht und Volkstumskampf: Außenpolitische Konzepte der Vertrieben-enverbände und ihre praktische Umsetzung* (Offizin, 2001). Still useful are Max Hildebert Boehm, 'Gruppenbildung und Organisationswesen', in Eugen Lemberg and Friedrich Edding (eds), *Die Vertriebenen in Westdeutschland* (Hirt, 1959), vol. 1, pp. 521–605; Hermann Weiß, 'Die Organisationen der Vertriebenen und ihre Presse', in Wolfgang Benz (ed.), *Die Vertreibung der Deutschen aus dem Osten: Ursachen, Ereignisse, Folgen*, rev. edn (Fischer, 1995), pp. 244–64.

25. See Franz Neumann, *Der Block der Heimatvertriebenen und Entrechteten 1950– 1960: Ein Beitrag zur Geschichte und Struktur einer politischen Interessenpartei* (Hain, 1968).

26. Ulrich Tolksdorf, 'Heimatmuseen, Heimtstuben, Heimatecken', *Jahrbuch für ostdeutsche Volkskunde*, vol. 26 (1983), pp. 338–42.

27. See, for example, Instruction of the Minister of Education of *Land* Niedersachsen, 5 February 1952, *Schulverwaltungsblatt für Niedersachsen*, vol. 4, no. 3 (1952). 'East Germany', or 'the eastern territories', in this period referred to the territories east of the Oder–Neiße line, whereas the GDR was to be officially called the 'Soviet Zone' (SBZ).

28. See, for example, Instruction of the Minister of Education of *Land* Niedersachsen, 13 December 1954, *Schulverwaltungsblatt für Niedersachsen*, vol. 6, no. 12 (1952), p. 269. One example: 'Unsere Heimat im Osten: Ostdeutsche Woche der Lutherschule Hannover vom 12. bis 16. Mai 1956' (undated [1956]).

29. Eugen Lemberg, *Ostkunde: Grundsätzliches und Kritisches zu einer deutschen Bildungsaufgabe* (Ch. Jaeger & Co., 1964); Ernst Lehmann (ed.), *Eingliederung der Vertriebenen und Flüchtlinge in Westdeutschland als Unterrichtsaufgabe: Eine Handreichung* (Ch. Jaeger & Co., 1964). See also *Ostkunde im Unterricht: Ein Jahrbuch für Gesamtdeutsche Fragen* (Ch. Jaeger & Co., 1963 and 1964).

30. Only a fraction of these testimonies were published: Bundesministerium für Vertriebene, Flüchtlinge und Kriegsgeschädigte (ed.), *Dokumentation der Vertreibung der Deutschen aus Ost-Mitteleuropa*, 9 vols (Bernard & Graefe, 1953– 1962, reprint dtv 1984). See also Kulturstiftung der deutschen Vertriebenen (ed.), *Vertreibung und Vertreibungsverbrechen 1945–1948: Bericht des Bundesarchivs vom 28. Mai 1974. Archivalien und ausgewählte Erlebnisberichte* (Kulturstiftung der deutschen Vertriebenen, 1989). Abbreviated versions of five volumes were also published in an English translation: Theodor Schieder (ed.), *Documents on the Expulsion of the Germans from Eastern Central Europe: A Selection and Translation*

(Federal Ministry for Expellees, Refugees and War Victims, 1956–60). For a critical discussion of this project, see Mathias Beer, 'Im Spannungsfeld von Politik und Zeitgeschichte: Das Großforschungsprojekt "Dokumentation der Vertreibung der Deutschen aus Ost-Mitteleuropa"', *Vierteljahrshefte für Zeitgeschichte*, vol. 46 (1998), pp. 345–89.

31. Louis Ferdinand Helbig, *Der ungeheure Verlust: Flucht und Vertreibung in der deutschsprachigen Belletristik der Nachkriegszeit*, 3rd rev. edn (Harrassowitz, 1996); Klaus Weigelt (ed.), *Flucht und Vertreibung in der Nachkriegsliteratur: Formen ostdeutscher Kulturförderung* (Knoth, 1986); Jörg Bernhard Bilke, 'Flucht und Vertreibung in der deutschen Belletristik', *Deutsche Studien*, vol. 32 (1995), pp. 177–88. See also Jörg Bernhard Bilke, 'Ausgelöschte Erinnerungen: Auf der Suche nach der verlassenen Heimat', *Kulturpolitische Korrespondenz*, vol. 63 (1995), pp. 4–16, and the other contribution in this special edition on 'Verlorenes Leben, verdrängte Geschichte: Ostdeutsche Autoren in Mitteldeutschland'.

32. One of the best examples of the stereotypical way in which refugees and expellees and their situation were represented in popular culture is the film *Grün ist die Heide* (The Heath Is Green), which was released in 1951 and attracted almost twenty million viewers up to 1960 – perhaps because it had little to do with the historical reality. The only film which tried to present a more realistic picture of the difficulties which refugees faced in the West was *Mamitschka* (1955); it was commercially unsuccessful. For more detail, see Hanno Sowade, 'Das Thema im westdeutschen Nachkriegsfilm', in Stiftung Haus der Geschichte der Bundesrepublik Deutschland (ed.), *Flucht, Vertreibung, Integration* (Kerber, 2005), pp. 124–31; Peter Stettner, '"Sind Sie denn überhaupt Deutsche?" Stereotype, Sehnsüchte und Ängste im Flüchtlingsbild des deutschen Nachkriegsfilm', in Rainer Schulze (ed.), *Zwischen Heimat und Zuhause: Deutsche Flüchtlinge und Vertriebene in (West)Deutschland 1945–2000* (Secolo, 2001), pp. 156–70; Moeller, *War Stories*, pp. 123–70.

33. It is this aspect on which Hahn and Hahn focus in their article 'Flucht und Vertreibung'.

34. Robert G. Moeller, 'War Stories: The Search for a Usable Past in the Federal Republic of Germany', *American Historical Review*, vol. 101, no. 4 (1996), p. 1019. Moeller takes up this argument again in his article 'Sinking Ships, the Lost *Heimat* and Broken Taboos: Günter Grass and the Politics of Memory in Contemporary Germany', *Contemporary European History*, vol. 12, no. 2 (2003), pp. 152–9. More generally on the concept of Germans as victims in post-war West German collective memory, see Michael L. Hughes, '"Through No Fault of Our Own": West Germans Remember Their War Losses', *German History*, vol. 18, no. 2 (2000), pp. 193–213; Robert G. Moeller, 'Germans as Victims? Thoughts on a Post-Cold War History of World War II's Legacies', *History & Memory*, vol. 17, no. 1/2 (2005), pp. 147–94.

35. On the following, see Manfred Kittel, *Vertreibung der Vertriebenen? Der historische deutsche Osten in der Erinnerungskultur der Bundesrepubublik (1961–1982)* (Oldenbourg, 2006); Mathias Beer, 'Verschlusssache, Raubdruck, autorisierte Fassung: Aspekte der politischen Auseinandersetzung mit Flucht und Vertreibung in der Bundesrepublik (1949–1989)', in Cornelißen et al., *Diktatur – Krieg – Vertreibung*, pp. 369–401; Hans-Werner Rautenberg, 'Die Wahrnehmung von Flucht und Vertreibung', *Aus Politik und Zeitgeschichte*, issue 53 (1997), pp. 34–46; Bernd Faulenbach, 'Flucht und Vertreibung in der individuellen und kollektiven Erinnerung

und als Gegenstand von Erinnerungspolitik', in *Flucht und Vertreibung: Europa zwischen 1939 und 1948* (Ellert & Richter, 2004), pp. 224–31. See also Moeller, *War Stories*, pp. 175–93, or Moeller, 'Sinking Ships', pp. 159–68.

36. The first major survey with this focus was Eugen Lemberg amd Friedrich Edding (eds), *Die Vertriebenen in Westdeutschland*, 3 vols (Hirt, 1959). Flight and expulsion did not diasappear altogether from public discourse, of course; notable examples are Siegfried Lenz's novel *Heimatmuseum* (Hoffmann und Campe, 1978) and a three-part TV documentary shown in 1981 and a book to go with it: Rudolf Mühlfenzl (ed.), *Geflohen und vertrieben: Augenzeugen berichten* (Athenäum, 1981).

37. This found its most powerful expression in the speech by the then West German President, Richard von Weizsäcker, at a commemorative ceremony on 8 May 1985 in the German Bundestag: 'Der 8. Mai 1945 – vierzig Jahre danach', in Eberhard Jäckel (ed.), *Demokratische Leidenschaft: Reden des Bundespräsidenten* (Deutsche Verlagsanstalt, 1994), pp. 39–56.

38. This motto was changed to 'Silesia Remains Ours in the Europe of Free Peoples' when Chancellor Kohl personally intervened and threatened not to attend the meeting. For more detail, see Dietrich Strothmann, '"Schlesien bleibt unser": Vertriebenenpolitiker und das Rad der Geschichte', in Benz, *Die Vertreibung der Deutschen*, pp. 265–76 (originally published in the German weekly *Die Zeit*).

39. This is strongly expressed in narrative interviews conducted with more than sixty refugees and expellees since 1997 (Collection Rainer Schulze, University of Essex). All of those interviewed were born east of the Oder–Neiße line, forced to leave their homes – either by flight or expulsion – at the end of the Second Word War, and eventually settled in Landkreis Celle. See Rainer Schulze, 'Alte Heimat – neue Heimat – oder heimatlos dazwischen? Zur Frage der regionalen Identität deutscher Flüchtlinge und Vertriebener – Eine Skizze', *Nordost-Archiv*, vol. 6, no. 2 (1997), pp. 759–87; Rainer Schulze, '"Wir leben ja nun hier": Flüchtlinge und Vertriebene in Niedersachsen – Erinnerung und Identität', in Klaus J. Bade and Jochen Oltmer (eds), *'Hier geblieben!' Zuwanderung und Integration in Niedersachsen von 1945 bis heute* (Universitätsverlag Rasch, 2002), pp. 69–100. See also Albrecht Lehmann, *Im Fremden ungewollt zuhaus: Flüchtlinge und Vertriebene in Westdeutschland 1945–1990* (C.H. Beck, 1991).

40. Albrecht Lehmann, 'Flüchtlingserinnerungen im Erzählen zwischen den Generationen', *Bios*, vol. 2 (1989), pp. 189–206; Torsten Koch and Sabine Moller, 'Flucht und Vertreibung im Familiengedächtnis', in Schulze, *Zwischen Heimat und Zuhause*, pp. 216–28.

41. See Lutz Niethammer, 'Flucht ins Konventionelle? Einige Randglossen zu Forschungsproblemen der deutschen Nachkriegsmigration', in Rainer Schulze, Doris von der Brelie-Lewien and Helga Grebing (eds), *Flüchtlinge und Vertriebene in der westdeutschen Nachkriegsgeschichte: Bilanzierung der Forschung und Perspektiven für die künftige Forschungsarbeit* (August Lax, 1987), pp. 317–18.

42. Rainer Voss, 'Ortsgeschichten: Flucht und Vertreibung im Spiegel der Heimatgeschichtsschreibung', in Schulze, *Zwischen Heimat und Zuhause*, pp. 184–200. For a very illuminating example, see Christoph Lerch, *Duderstädter Chronik von der Vorzeit bis zum Jahre 1973* (Mecke, 1979), p. 198.

43. Kathrin Panne, 'Erinnerungspolitik – Erinnerungsspuren: Zur Funktion symbolischer Erinnerung an Flucht und Vertreibung im öffentlichen Raum. Eine Skizze', in Schulze, *Zwischen Heimat und Zuhause*, pp. 201–15.

44. Schulze et al., *Flüchtlinge und Vertriebene*.
45. See, for example, Regine Just, 'Zur Lösung des Umsiedlerproblems auf dem Gebiet der DDR 1945 bis Anfang der fünfziger Jahre', *Zeitschrift für Geschichtswissenschaft*, vol. 35, no. 11 (1987), pp. 971–84; Wolfgang Meinicke, 'Zur Integration der Umsiedler in die Gesellschaft, 1945–1952', *Zeitschrift für Geschichtswissenschaft*, vol. 36, no. 10 (1988), pp. 867–78. Most studies before 1989 were in the form of (unpublished) MA dissertations.
46. Niethammer, 'Flucht ins Konventionelle?', p. 323. For a similar agrument, see Arnold Sywottek, '"Umsiedlung" und "Räumung", "Flucht" und "Ausweisung" – Bemerkungen zur deutschen Flüchtlingsgeschichte', in Schulze et al., *Flüchtlinge und Vertriebene*, pp. 79–80. See also Friedemann Bedürftig, 'Eichendorff spricht wieder lauter: Die deutschen Vertriebenen und die Linke', *Freibeuter: Vierteljahreszeitschrift für Kultur und Politik*, no. 63 (1995), pp. 73–80.
47. For the following, see Helga Hirsch, 'Flucht und Vertreibung: Kollektive Erinnerung im Wandel', *Aus Politik und Zeitgeschichte*, issue 40–41 (2003), pp. 14–26; Bernd Faulenbach, 'Die Vertreibung der Deutschen aus den Gebieten jenseits von Oder und Neiße: Zur wissenschaftlichen und öffentlichen Diskussion in Deutschland', *Aus Politik und Zeitgeschichte*, issue 51–52 (2002), pp. 44–54; Rautenberg, 'Die Wahrnehmung', pp. 41–6.
48. Ulrich Tolksdorff, 'Zum Stand der ostdeutschen Volkskundeforschung', in Schulze et al., *Flüchtlinge und Vertriebene*, pp. 199–200.
49. To name just a few: Ralph Giordano, *Ostpreußen ade: Reise durch ein melancholisches Land* (Kiepenheuer & Witsch, 1994); Ulla Lachauer, *Ostpreußische Lebensläufe* (Rowohlt, 1998); Petra Reski, *Ein Land so weit* (List, 2000); K. Erik Franzen, *Die Vertriebenen: Hitlers letzts Opfer* (Propyläen, 2001); Guido Knopp, *Die große Flucht: Das Schicksal der Vertriebenen* (Econ, 2001).
50. These activities resulted in a number of publications and, probably even more importantly for the redefinition of collective memory, in exhibitions. One of them was the exhibition 'Fremde – Heimat – Niedersachen' in Celle; see Reinhard Rohde, Rainer Schulze and Rainer Voss, *Fremde – Heimat – Niedersachsen: Begleitheft zur Ausstellung '50 Jahre Flüchtlinge und Vertriebene in Stadt und Landkreis Celle' im Bomann-Museum Celle vom 20.3.1999 bis 29.8.1999* (Landkreis Celle, 1999).
51. One recent publication on this is Helga Hirsch, *Schweres Gepäck: Flucht und Vertreibung als Lebensthema* (Körber-Stiftung, 2004). Early examples are Lehmann, *Im Fremden ungewollt zuhaus*, and Alena Wagnerová, *1945 waren sie Kinder: Flucht und Vertreibung im Leben einer Generation* (Kiepenheuer & Witsch, 1990).
52. Günter Grass, *Crabwalk*, translated by K. Winston (Faber and Faber, 2003), p. 103. In *Mein Jahrhundert* (English translation: *My Century*) Grass had noted that he found it impossible to write about these events in an appropriate way: 'Describing misery was something I hadn't been trained to do. I lacked the words. So I learned silence.' Günter Grass, *My Century*, translated by M.H. Heim (Harcourt, 1999), p. 115.
53. See also Moeller, 'Sinking Ships'. At around the same time, a number of other novels took up this theme as well, among them Jörg Bernig, *Niemandszeit* (Deutsche Verlags-Anstalt, 2002); Reinhard Jirgl, *Die Unvollendeten* (Hanser, 2003); Tanja Dückers, *Himmelskörper* (Aufbau-Verlag, 2003); Olaf Müller, *Schlesisches Wetter* (Berlin Verlag, 2003); Michael Zellner, *Die Reise nach Samosch* (ars vivendi, 2003).

54. Hans Rothfels, 'Zehn Jahre danach', *Vierteljahrshefte für Zeitgeschichte*, vol. 3 (1955), p. 234. Hans Rothfels had taught at the University of Königsberg in East Prussia until 1934, when he lost his teaching licence because of his Jewish origins. He managed to flee from Germany in 1939, first to Britain, then to the United States. He returned to (West) Germany in 1951 to take a chair at the University of Tübingen.

55. Hartmut Boockmann, 'Die Geschichte Ostdeutschlands und der deutschen Siedlungsgebiete im östlichen Europa', in Deutsches Historisches Museum Berlin (ed.), *Deutsche im Osten: Geschichte, Kultur, Erinnerungen (Ausstellung Lokschuppen Rosenheim 15. Juli bis 1. November 1994)* (Koehler & Amelang, 1994), p. 12; see also his 'Historische, politische und kulturelle Traditionen der Herkunftsgebiete: Bemerkungen zur Einführung in den Forschungsgegenstand', in Schulze et al., *Flüchtlinge und Vertriebene*, p. 88. Boockmann was born in 1934 in Marienburg (today Malbork) in West Prussia and became one of the leading experts on German history in Eastern Europe; he was one of the editors of the highly respected series 'Deutsche Geschichte im Osten Europas', to which he contributed the first volume: *Ostpreußen und Westpreußen* (Siedler, 1992).

56. Following the publication of Grass's novella, *Der Spiegel* ran a four-part series on flight and expulsion and the aftermath (Nos. 13–16/2002), later expanded and published as a book: Stefan Aust and Stephan Burgdorff (eds), *Die Flucht: Über die Vertreibung der Deutschen aus dem Osten* (Deutsche Verlags-Anstalt, 2002). In 2004 the periodical *GEO* published a special issue on 'Flucht und Vertreibung: Europa zwischen 1939 und 1948'.

57. A lavishly illustrated book accompanied the exhibition: Stiftung Haus der Geschichte der Bundesrepublik Deutschland, *Flucht, Vertreibung, Integration*.

58. Jörg Lau, 'Ein deutscher Abschied', *Die Zeit*, 8 December 2005. Similarly, Michael Jeismann, 'Tränen sind nicht aus Blei', *Frankfurter Allgemeine Zeitung*, 5 December 2005. For a more critical review, see Martin Fochler, 'Verschobene Perspektiven: Zur Ausstellung "Flucht, Vertreibung, Integration, Heimat"', *Deutsch-Tschechische Nachrichten*, no. 70, 25 January 2006.

59. See, among others, Klaus Bachmann and Jerzy Kranz (eds), *Verlorene Heimat: Die Vertreibungsdebatte in Polen* (Bouvier, 1998); Cornelißen et al., *Diktatur – Krieg – Vertreibung*. See also the speech of the then Polish foreign minister and historian Władysław Bartoszewski on 28 April 1995 before a special joint session of both houses of the German parliament, cited in Bachmann and Kranz, *Verlorene Heimat*, p. 33. An early literary example of this reassessment outside of Germany is Stefan Chwin's novel *Hanemann*, published in Poland in 1995 (Marabut). It focuses on events in Danzig/Gdańsk in the period from summer 1944 to *c.*1946, dealing with the exodus of the German population and the influx of Poles who took over the town.

60. For a brief overview, see Thomas Urban, 'Vertreibung als Thema in Polen', Jiří Pešek, 'Vertreibung als Thema in Tschechien' and Bernd Faulenbach, 'Vertreibungen – Ein europäisches Thema', in Stiftung Haus der Geschichte der Bundesrepublik Deutschland, *Flucht, Vertreibung, Integration*, pp. 156–65, 166–73 and 189–95.

61. Bund der Vertriebenen – Vereinigte Landsmannschaften und Landesverbände e.V., Konzeption für ein 'Zentrum gegen Vertreibungen – Stiftung der Deutschen Heimatvertriebenen', Berlin, typescript, Bonn 2000. For further and updated information, see the *Zentrum*'s official webpage: www.z-g-v.de.

62. 'Internationaler wissenschaftlicher Aufruf gegen ein "Zentrum gegen Vertreibungen": Für einen kritischen und augeklärten Vergangenheitsdiskurs', 10 August
2003, online at www.vertreibungszentrum.de. Within four months, more than 300
signatures had been collected. See also Deutsches Kulturforum östliches Europa
(ed.), *Ein Zentrum gegen Vertreibungen: Nationales Gedenken oder europäische
Erinnerung? Podiumsgespräch in der Französischen Friedrichstadtkirche Berlin mit
Nawojka Cieslinska-Lobkowicz, Helga Hirsch, Hans Lemberg, Markus Meckel und
Erika Steinbach, Moderation Thomas Urban* (Deutsches Kulturforum östliches
Europa, 2004), or Bernd Faulenbach and Andreas Helle (eds), *Zwangsmigration in
Europa: Zur wissenschaftlichen und politischen Auseinandersetzung um die
Vertreibung der Deutschen aus dem Osten* (Klartext, 2005).
63. See, for example, the interview with Władyslaw Bartoszewski in *Die Welt*, 16 July
2003. The Polish weekly *Wprost* had a photo montage on its front cover of 21
September 2003 depicting the president of the BdV, Erika Steinbach, in SS uniform
and riding on the back of SPD Chancellor Gerhard Schröder, with the caption 'The
German Trojan Horse'.
64. Deutscher Bundestag, 14. Wahlperiode, Drucksache 14/9033 i.V.m. 14/9661.
65. See, for example, Erika Steinbach, 'Berlin darf sich nicht drücken!', *Die Welt*, 18
May 2002; Gabriele Lesser, 'Zentrum gegen Vertreibungen: Zentrum gegen
Versöhnung', *taz – Die Tageszeitung*, 19 September 2003; Konrad Weiß, 'Zutiefst
beunruhigende Töne: Der Streit um das Zentrum gegen Vertreibungen', *Publik-
Forum*, no. 21, 7 November 2003.
66. In her first policy statement after her election, Merkel only declared that her government was committed to the historical reappraisal of forced migrations, flight and
expulsion, and wanted to give an important signal in Berlin in the spirit of reconciliation.
67. Shortly after the opening of the exhibition 'Flucht – Vertreibung – Integration', the
director of the Haus der Geschichte der Bundesrepublik Deutschland, Hermann
Schäfer, was appointed to the Office of the Federal Representative for Culture and
Media in the Chancellor's Office in Berlin.
68. Markus Patzke, 'Kein Ersatz fürs "Zentrum": Bonner Haus der Geschichte zeigt
Ausstellung "Flucht – Vertreibung – Integration"', *Preußische Allgemeine Zeitung:
Das Ostpreußenblatt*, 10 December 2005.
69. There is an exhibition catalogue: *Erzwungene Wege: Flucht und Vertreibung im
Europa des 20. Jahrhunderts – Ausstellung im Kronprinzenpalais, Berlin* (Stiftung
Zentrum gegen Vertreibungen, 2006).
70. See, for example, Regina Mönch, 'Es gibt kein fremdes Leid – "Erzwungene Wege":
Die Berliner Ausstellung des Zentrums gegen Vertreibungen vergleicht, ohne
aufzurechnen', *Frankfurter Allgemeine Zeitung*, 11 August 2006; Jens Jessen, 'Die
Mitschuld der Opfer: Die Berliner Ausstellung "Erzwungene Wege" ist zu Unrecht
umstritten', *Die Zeit*, 17 August 2006.
71. See, for example, Gunter Hoffmann, 'Trübe Wege: Eine Ausstellung über Flucht und
Vertreibung in Berlin entlastet die deutsche Geschichte und erschwert die
Beziehungen zu Polen', *Die Zeit*, 10 August 2006; Thomas Urban, 'Warschau sieht
die Nation in der Berliner Ausstellung über Vertreibung bedroht', *Süddeutsche
Zeitung*, 12 August 2006; see also Emma Bode, '"Erzwungene Wege" –
Revanchismus light: Zur Ausstellung der Vertriebenenverbände', Word Socialist

Web Site, 5 October 2006 (see online at www.wsws.org/de2006/okt2006/vert-o05.shtml.)

72. It was perhaps a coincidence, but one of a highly symbolic nature, that at the time of the opening of the exhibition 'Erzwungene Wege' at the Kronprinzenpalais, the Bonn exhibition 'Flucht – Vertreibung – Integration' had moved to Berlin and was being shown at the German Historical Museum directly opposite the Kronprinzenpalais.

73. Stefan Chwin, 'Das Geheimnis der Vetreibung', *Die Welt*, 21 August 1999.

74. Müller, *Schlesisches Wetter*, p. 197.

75. Polish émigré publications estimate the number of deportees from the years 1939–41 at between 960,000 and 1,270,000. Those figures were attained on the basis of memoirs and reports collected by the intelligence services of the Polish Armed Forces. At the end of the 1980s some Polish historians accepted these approximations uncritically and even raised the numbers further. Piotr Żaroń, for instance, states that around two million Polish citizens found themselves in the USSR after 1939: Piotr Żaroń, *Ludność polska w Związku Radzieckim w czasie II wojny światowej* (Państwowe Wydawn. Nauk, 1990), p. 132. Jan Czerniakiewicz repeated similar errors fifteen years later. See his *Przesiedlenia ludności w Europie 1915–1959* (Wydawn. Wyższej Szkoły Pedagogicznej TWP, 2005) p. 15.

76. Zdzisław Grot and Wincenty Ostrowski (eds), *Wspomnienia młodzieży wielkopolskiej z lat okupacji niemieckiej 1939–1945* (Instytut Zachodni, 1946); Edward Serwański (ed.), *Dulag 121., Pruszków – sierpień-październik 1944 roku* (Wydawnictwo Zachodnie, 1946).

77. Chiefly the works of: Włodzimierz Jastrzębski, Czesław Łuczak, Czesław Madajczyk, Karol Marian Pospieszalski, Edward Serwański, Janusz Sobczak, Andrzej Szefer, Jan Szyling, Stanisław Waszak, Janusz Wróbel.

78. Feature films are characteristic in this respect. The relocations from the territories incorporated into the Reich were shown directly only in one of the episodes – episode no. 4 – of the serial *Polskie drogi*, directed by Janusz Morgenstern and first released in 1977.

79. In Poznań, for instance, only one place connected with the relocations is honoured by a commemorative plaque, set up in 1962: the location of the main interim camp at 7 Bałtycka Street. See Zbysław Wojtkowiak, *Napisy pamiątkowe miasta Poznania* (Kurpisz, 2004).

80. Stefan Chwin, *Kartki z dziennika* (Tytuł, 2004), pp. 68–9.

81. See Edward Kołodziejczyk, *Tryptyk warszawski* (Wydawn. Ministerstwa Obrony Narodowej, 1984), or the multi-volume primary source edition *Exodus Warszawy: Ludzie i miasto po powstaniu 1944*, vols 1–2: Małgorzata Berezowska (ed.), *Pamiętniki. Relacje* (Państwowy Instytut Wydaw., 1992–3); Józef Kazimierski (ed.), vols 3–4: *Archiwalia* (Państwowy Instytut Wydaw., 1994); Jan Górski (ed.), vol. 5: *Prasa* (Państwowy Instytut Wydaw., 1995).

82. During the ceremonies commemorating the sixtieth anniversary of the end of the Warsaw Uprising, for example, the Society of the Friends of Warsaw organized a special 'memorial tour along the route of the inhabitants of Warsaw expelled after the Uprising'.

83. See, for example, Ferdynand Goetel, *Czasy wojny* (Arcana, 2005), p. 193, who recalls here his impressions of the 'exodus' of the inhabitants of Żoliborz (the

northern quarter of Warsaw): 'Looking at them I somehow regained confidence that Warsaw was not just a heap of ashes. For they would return.'

84. The discussions and the research projects of the first half of the 1990s are summarized in Klaus Bachmann and Jerzy Kranz (eds), *Przeprosić za wypędzenie? Wypowiedzi oficjalne oraz debata prasowa o wysiedleniu Niemców po II wojnie światowej* (Znak, 1997) and Włodzimierz Borodziej and Artur Hajnicz (eds), *Kompleks wypędzenia* (Znak, 1998). On 21 May 1997 the presidents of Poland and Ukraine, Aleksander Kwaśniewski and Leonid Kuczma, signed a declaration of reconciliation in Kiev. The Polish side condemned 'Akcja Wisła' and related forced relocations; on the Ukrainian side there was no similar condemnation of the so-called Volhynian massacres.

85. Text in Borodziej and Hajnicz, *Kompleks wypędzenia*, pp. 478–95.

86. Since then about half a million people have received compensation from the Foundation for Polish–German Reconciliation.

87. 'The Resolution of the Polish Parliament of 10 September 2004 on the rights of Poland to war reparations from Germany and on the unlawful claims against Poland and Polish citizens forwarded in Germany', *Monitor Polski*, no. 39 (2004), p. 678. German demands for compensation were countered by Polish studies on the destruction suffered during the Second World War; see Witold M. Góralski (ed.), *Transfer, obywatelstwo, majątek: Trudne problemy stosunków polsko-niemieckich. Studia i dokumenty* (Polski Instytut Spraw Międzynarodowych, 2005); Witold M. Góralski (ed.), *Problem reparacji, odszkodowań i świadczeń w stosunkach polsko-niemieckich 1944–2004*, vol. 1: Witold M. Góralski (ed.), *Studia* (Polski Instytut Spraw Międzynarodowych, 2004), vol. 2: Sławomir Dębski and Witold M. Góralski (eds), *Dokumenty* (Polski Instytut Spraw Międzynarodowych, 2004); Wojciech Fałkowski (ed.), *Straty Warszawy 1939–1945: Raport* (Miasto Stołeczne Warszawa, 2005). On the German side, see also Pertti Ahonen, 'German Expellee Organisations: Between Revisionism and Reconciliation', *Archiv für Sozialgeschichte*, vol. 45 (2005), esp. pp. 361–72.

88. See note 63 for a description.

89. See the anthology of the Polish, Czech and German publicists Piotr Buras and Piotr M. Majewski (eds), *Pamięć wypędzonych: Grass, Beneš i środkowoeuropejskie rozrachunki* (Biblioteka Więzi, 2003).

90. The Society of the Deported from the Łódź Region established in January 1990, for example, has some 4,500 members to date. According to the Society's Statute, its aims encompass 'documenting the historical truth about the relocations of Polish society in Warthegau and undertaking activities aimed at securing compensation for the persecutions and the damage caused to life and limb'. It helped to secure combatant privileges for children who were in the holding camps during the war.

91. The Society of the Deported from the Łódź Region initiated the publication of Lucjusz Włodkowski (ed.), *Czas przeszły – ciągle obecny: Z dziejów wysiedleń – historia, wspomnienia, dokumenty* (Związek Wysiedlonych Ziemi Łódzkiej, 1998). The activities of the Society for the Solidarity of Polish Combatants of Wielkopolska are also very important; see Zenon Czesław Wartel, *Wysiedlenia niemieckie 1939–1945: Losy mieszkańców powiatu Nowy Tomyśl-Grodzisk* (Wielkopolski Związek Solidarności Polskich Kombatantów w Poznaniu, 2002); Zenon Czesław Wartel (ed.), *Niemiecki obóz przesiedleńczy w Gnieźnie w latach 1939–1940* (Wielkopolski Zw. Solidarności Pol. Kombatantów, 2003).

92. Agnieszka Jaczyńska, 'Dzieci Zamojszczyzny', *Biuletyn Instytutu Pamięci Narodowej*, no. 9 (2001), pp. 49–54; Sławomir Abramowicz, 'Wypędzeni z osiedla "Montwiłła" Mareckiego w Łodzi', *Biuletyn Instytutu Pamięci Narodowej*, no. 12–1 (2003–4), pp. 28–32; Monika Tomkiewicz, 'Wysiedlenia z Gdyni w 1939 r.', ibid., pp. 33–7; almost all of the *Biuletyn IPN* published in May 2004 was devoted to relocations.
93. The Museum of Martyrology in Żbików near Poznań is a good example. Between October 2003 and March 2004 it housed a photo-exhibition of the camp at Główna Street in Poznań (1939–40). There are also plans to set up a permanent exhibition concerning the war relocations in Wielkopolska. I am indebted to Dr Anna Ziółkowska for this information.
94. Włodzimierz Borodziej, 'Der Umgang mit der Vertreibung der Deutschen in Polen – gestern und heute', in Christoph Kleßmann, Burghard Ciesla and Hans-Hermann Hertle (eds), *Vertreibung, Neuanfang, Integration: Erfahrungen in Brandenburg* (Brandenburgische Landeszentrale für Politische Bildung, 2001), p. 37; idem, 'Historiografia polska o "wypędzeniu" Niemców', in *Polska 1944/45–1989*, vol. 2 (1997), p. 251.
95. Piotr Madajczyk, *Na drodze do pojednania: Wokół orędzia biskupów polskich do biskupów niemieckich z 1965 roku* (Wydawn. Naukowe PWN, 1994).
96. Herbert Czaja and Hubert Hupka, two prominent activists of the German expellee organization BdV, became the prime targets. They were frequently attacked by the press and were favourite characters of anti-German cartoonists. Rafał Fuks, *Przywódcy ziomkostw w Niemieckiej Republice Federalnej: hitlerowska i zbrodnicza przeszłość* (Głowna Komisja Badania Zbrodni Hitlerowskich w Polsce, 1973); Krzysztof Ruchniewicz, 'Groźni wypędzeni', *Karta*, no. 38 (2003), pp. 89–93.
97. Borodziej, 'Historiografia', p. 151.
98. Eugeniusz Cezary Król, 'Wizerunek Niemca etnicznego w polskim filmie po II wojnie światowej', *Przegląd Historyczny*, vol. XCVI (2005), Fasc. 1.
99. Borodziej, 'Historiografia', p. 255.
100. See Krzysztof Skubiszewski, *Wysiedlenie Niemców po II wojnie światowej* (Książka i Wiedza, 1968), and Stefan Banasiak, *Przesiedlenie Niemców z Polski w latach 1945–1950* (Biblioteka Uniwersytetu Łódźskiego, 1968).
101. Copy in the possession of the author.
102. The historical works published in the 1990s are summarized in Borodziej, 'Historiografia', pp. 262–9. Of the subsequent works not covered there, one should mention: Bernadetta Nitschke, *Wysiedlenie ludności niemieckiej z Polski w latach 1945–1999* (Wyższa Szkoła Pedagogiczna im. Tadeusza Kotarbińskiego, 1999); idem, *Wysiedlenie czy wypędzenie? Ludność niemiecka w Polsce w latach 1945–1949* (Marszałek, 2000), German edn: Nitschke, *Vertreibung*; Stanisław Jankowiak, *Wysiedlenie i emigracja ludności niemieckiej w polityce władz polskich w latach 1945–1970* (Instytut Pamięci Narodowej, Komisja Ścigania Zbrodni przeciwko Narodowi Polskiemu, 2005). A detailed bibliography on German prisoners of war can be found in Jerzy Kochanowski, *W polskiej niewoli: Niemieccy jeńcy wojenni w Polsce 1945–1950* (Neriton, 2001), and on the *Volksdeutsche* in Olejnik, *Zdrajcy narodu?*. There is a four-volume primary source edition concerning Germans in Poland in the years 1945–50: Włodzimierz Borodziej and Hans Lemberg (eds), *Niemcy w Polsce 1945–1950: Wybór dokumentów* (Neriton, 2000–1); vol. 1:

Włodzimierz Borodziej and Claudia Kraft (eds), *Władze i instytucje centralne: Województwo olsztyńskie* (Neriton, 2000); vol. 2: Ingo Eser and Jerzy Kochanowski (eds), *Polska Centralna: Województwo śląskie* (Neriton, 2000); vol. 3: Stanisław Jankowiak and Karin Steffen (eds), *Województwa poznanskie i szczecińskie* (Neriton, 2001); vol. 4: Ingo Eser, Witold Stankowski, Claudia Kraft and Stanisław Jankowiak (eds), *Pomorze Gdańskie i Dolny Śląsk* (Neriton, 2001). The collection is also available in a German language version: Borodziej and Lemberg, *'Unsere Heimat ist uns ein fremdes Land geworden …'.*

103. Borodziej and Hajnicz, *Kompleks wypędzenia*, pp. 439–77. See also the results of an opinion poll conducted in 2004 by the German Institut für Demoskopie on deportations in general, which showed changes in attitude in particular among the younger generation in Poland, but also revealed how persistent some misconceptions are, for example about the number of Germans deported from Poland; Thomas Petersen, *Flucht und Vertreibung aus Sicht der deutschen, polnischen und tschechischen Bevölkerung* (Stiftung Haus der Geschichte der Bundesrepublik Deutschland, 2005).

104. The following is based to a large extent on my own previously published articles ('Paradoksy kresowej pamięci', *Borussia*, no. 35 (2004), pp. 111–23; 'Paradoxien der Erinnerung an die Ostgebiete', *Inter Finitimos: Jahrbuch zur deutsch-polnischen Beziehungsgeschichte*, no. 3 (2005), pp. 61–76), and footnotes have therefore been kept to a minimum here.

105. Some of these emigrants were refugees from 1939 who reached the West after the outbreak of the war via Rumania, Hungary or Lithuania. The largest group consisted of those deported in the years 1940–41, who left the USSR in 1942 with the Polish army and remained in the West after the war. Relatively few 'Borderland emigrants' managed to leave Poland after 1945. Hence, the chief collective memories of the occupation were connected with the 1940–41 deportations, not with the 'repatriations' of 1944–6.

106. Rafał Habielski, *Życie społeczne i kulturalne emigracji* (Biblioteka Więzi, 1999), p. 97.

107. See Bolesław Klimaszewski, Ewa R. Nowakowska and Wojciech Wyskiel, *Słownik pisarzy polskich na obczyźnie 1939–1980* (Interpress, 1993); Tymon Terlecki (ed.), *Literatura polska na obczyznie, 1940–1960: Praca zbiorowa wydana staraniem Związku Pisarzy Polskich na Obczyznie*, vols 1–2 (B. Świderski, 1964–5); Józef Bujnowski (ed.), *Literatura polska na obczyźnie* (Veritas, 1988).

108. In 1986 the London-based Lwów Circle passed a resolution that ended with the appeal: 'The aims of independent Polish politics must encompass the return of the Eastern Territories, with Lwów and Vilnius, and the reinstallation of national sovereignty over the entire territory of the state between the rivers Oder and Neiße in the west, and the Riga Peace Treaty in the east.' Quoted in: Sławomir Dąbrowski, 'Kresowiacy', *Karta*, no. 4 (1991), p. 137.

109. One of the most important statements in the history of the Parisian Literary Institute in this respect was a letter by Father Józef Majewski, a Polish activist in the USA, published in *Kultura*, vol. 11, no. 61 (1952), pp. 157–8. On this, see also Jerzy Giedroyć, *Autobiografia na cztery ręce*, edited and with a foreword by Krzysztof Pomian (Czytelnik, 1994), p. 153.

110. Paweł Machcewicz, *Emigracja w polityce międzynarodowej* (Biblioteka Więzi, 1999), pp. 195–6.

111. Andrzej Friszke, *Życie polityczne emigracji* (Biblioteka Więzi, 1999), pp. 41–3.
112. For one example, see Motas, 'Niektóre kwestie dotyczące przesiedlania ludności polskiej z USRR do Polski', p. 232, who speaks of 'certain irregularities'. Even the title of Motas's article is revealing, stressing that only 'some problems' of the relocations from the Borderlands will be discussed. Of the other pre-1989 works dealing with the 'repatriation', see above all: Czerniakiewicz, *Repatriacja ludności polskiej*; Tadeusz Bugaj, *Dzieci polskie w ZSRR i ich repatriacja 1939–1952* (Prace Karkonoskiego Towarzystwa Naukowego, 1982); Albin Głowacki, *Przemieszczenie obywateli polskich w Związku Radzieckim w 1944* (Wydawn. Uniwersytetu Łódzkiego, 1989).
113. Tadeusz Kukiz, *Madonny Kresowe i inne obrazy sakralne z Kresów z diecezjach Polski* (Bagiński, 2002), pp. 9–10.
114. The short story 'Dwa miasta' ('The Two Cities'), published in 1991 by Adam Zagajewski, is a good illustration of this 'migration schizophrenia'. The two cities in question are Lwów, where the author was born in 1945, and Gliwice, where he was relocated with his parents shortly afterwards. The writer's mother treated the Silesian city as their ancestral Lwów. The park where little Adam was taken for walks was called after their local park in Lwów; the streets in the neighborhood had the same names as the ones that once surrounded their house in Lwów. The modest belongings brought over from Lwów were the most prized possessions in the apartment taken over from a German family.
115. *Dziennik Polski* (London), 9 September 1953.
116. *Słowo Powszechne*, no. 254, 27 October 1954.
117. Zbigniew Siedlecki, 'Sprawy wileńskie', *Trybuna Ludu*, no. 66, 7 March 1956.
118. Paweł Machcewicz, *Polski rok 1956* (Oficyna Wydawn. Mówią Wieki, 1993), pp. 170–71.
119. Eugeniusz Czaplejewicz, 'Czym jest literatura kresowa?', in Eugeniusz Czaplejewicz and Edward Kasperski (eds), *Kresy w literaturze: Twórcy dwudziestowieczni* (Wiedza Powszechna, 1996), pp. 7–73.
120. Roman Graczyk, 'Drugie dno kresowej nostalgii', *Gazeta Wyborcza*, no. 185, 10 August 1994 (KOR = Komitet Obrony Robotnikow, Committee for the Defence of the Workers, an organization established by anti-communist protesters in 1976).
121. Grunt pod nogami', *Tygodnik Powszechny*, no. 30, 24 July 1966.
122. Piotr Skrzynecki (pseudonym), 'Stosunek opozycji w PRL do polskiej granicy wschodniej', *Dziennik Polski* (London), 7 May 1986.
123. *Katalog druków zwartych wydanych w Polsce poza cenzurą w latach 1976–1990 w zbiorach Ośrodka KARTA* (Ośrodek KARTA, 1999); *Katalog zbiorów Archiwum Opozycji (do 1990 roku)* (Ośrodek KARTA, 2001).
124. Bohdan Dydenko, 'Rekompensata', *Słowo Powszechne*, 15 September 1981.
125. Stanisław Sławomir Nicieja, *Cmentarz Łyczakowski we Lwowie w latach 1786–1986* (Zakład Narodowy im. Ossolińskich, 1988). Some 150,000 copies of this book have been sold.
126. Aleksandra Garlicka, 'Kresy i mit Lwowa piętnaście lat później' (manuscript in the possession of the author).
127. See Alicja Paczoska, *Dzieci Jałty: exodus ludności polskiej z Wileńszczyzny w latach 1944–1947* (Wydawn. Adam Marszałek, 2002); Sula, *Działalność*.
128. Ryszard Terlecki, 'Rozstanie ze Lwowem', *Tygodnik Powszechny*, no. 2, 9 January 2000.

7 Forced Labourers in the Third Reich

1. Ulrich Herbert, *Fremdarbeiter: Politik und Praxis des 'Ausländer-Einsatzes' in der Kriegswirtschaft des Dritten Reiches* (Berlin/Bonn, 1985). This chapter emerged within the framework of APART (Austrian Programme for Advanced Research and Technology) of the Austrian Academy of Sciences, conducted at the Ludwig Boltzmann-Institut für Kriegsfolgen-Forschung, Geschichte-Cluster, in Graz. I would like to thank Alex J. Kay for translating the text into English.
2. Herbert, *Fremdarbeiter*, p. 11.
3. Mark Spoerer, *Zwangsarbeit unter dem Hakenkreuz: Ausländische Zivilarbeiter, Kriegsgefangene und Häftlinge im Deutschen Reich und im besetzten Europa 1939–1945* (Stuttgart/Munich, 2001), p. 9.
4. Spoerer, *Zwangsarbeit unter dem Hakenkreuz*, p. 33.
5. Ulrich Herbert, 'Arbeit und Vernichtung: Ökonomische Interesse und Primat der "Weltanschauung" im Nationalsozialismus', in Ulrich Herbert (ed.), *Europa und der 'Reichseinsatz': Ausländische Zivilarbeiter, Kriegsgefangene und KZ-Häftlinge in Deutschland 1938–1945* (Essen, 1991), pp. 384–426, here pp. 415–17.
6. Herbert, 'Arbeit und Vernichtung', pp. 388f.
7. Helga Roswitha Gatterbauer, 'Arbeitseinsatz und Behandlung der Kriegsgefangenen in der Ostmark während des Zweiten Weltkrieges', Dr. Phil. thesis, Salzburg, 1975, p. 56.
8. Ernst Klee and Willi Dreßen, *'Gott mit uns': Der deutsche Vernichtungskrieg im Osten 1939–1945* (Frankfurt am Main, 1989), p. 142.
9. Pavel Poljan, *Zhertvy dvuch diktatur: Ostarbaitery i voennoplennye v tret'em reikhe i ikh repatriaciya* (Moscow, 1996), pp. 151f.
10. Christian Zentner and Friedemann Bedürftig, *Das große Lexikon des Dritten Reiches* (Munich, 1985), p. 660; *Meyers Taschenlexikon Geschichte*, vol. 6 (Mannheim, 1982), p. 295.
11. BGBl. I 74/2000 vom 8.8.2000. Bundesgesetz über den Fonds für freiwillige Leistungen der Republik Österreich an ehemalige Sklaven- und Zwangsarbeiter des nationalsozialistischen Regimes (Versöhnungsfonds-Gesetz). See also Hubert Feichtlbauer, *Fonds für Versöhnung, Frieden und Zusammenarbeit: Späte Anerkennung. Geschichte. Schicksale. 1938–1945. Zwangsarbeit in Österreich* (Vienna, 2005), pp. 325–30.
12. Spoerer, *Zwangsarbeit unter dem Hakenkreuz*, pp. 23f.
13. Spoerer, *Zwangsarbeit unter dem Hakenkreuz*, p. 17.
14. Stefan Karner and Peter Ruggenthaler, 'Kategorien der Zwangsarbeit und deren NS-rechtliche Grundlagen', in Stefan Karner and Peter Ruggenthaler (in collaboration with Harald Knoll, Peter Pirnath, Arno Wonisch, Wolfram Dornik, Jens Gassmann, Gerald Hafner, Herbert Killian, Reinhard Möstl, Nikita Petrov, Edith Petschnigg and Barbara Stelzl-Marx), *Zwangsarbeit in der Land- und Forstwirtschaft auf dem Gebiet Österreichs 1939 bis 1945*, Veröffentlichungen der Österreichischen Historikerkommission, vol. 26/2 (Vienna/Munich, 2004), pp. 33–89, here p. 34.
15. RGBl, 1942 I, p. 419: 'Ordinance Regarding Deployment Conditions for Eastern Workers', 30.6.1942.
16. The district of Lwów was attached to the General Government on 1 August 1941. It

essentially comprised today's Ukrainian provinces of L'viv, Ternopil and Ivano-Frankivsk.

17. Stefan Karner and Peter Ruggenthaler, 'Einleitung', in Karner et al., *Zwangsarbeit in der Land- und Forstwirtschaft*, p. 34.

18. Peter Ruggenthaler, *'Ein Geschenk für den Führer': Sowjetische Zwangsarbeiter in Kärnten und der Steiermark*, Veröffentlichungen des Ludwig Boltzmann-Instituts für Kriegsfolgen-Forschung, vol. 5 (Graz, 2001), pp. 21–33.

19. Gerald Hafner, Edith Petschnigg and Peter Ruggenthaler, 'Zur Zwangsarbeit im "Dritten Reich": NS-Rassentheorien und Kategorisierungen', in Stefan Karner, Peter Ruggenthaler and Barbara Stelzl-Marx (eds), *NS-Zwangsarbeit in der Rüstungsindustrie: Die Lapp-Finze AG in Kalsdorf bei Graz 1939–1945*, Veröffentlichungen des Ludwig Boltzmann-Instituts für Kriegsfolgen-Forschung, vol. 8 (Graz, 2004), pp. 15–46, here p. 28; Spoerer, *Zwangsarbeit unter dem Hakenkreuz*, pp. 35–88.

20. RGBl, 1934 II, Geneva Convention, pp. 233–5.

21. On the fate of Soviet prisoners of war see especially Christian Streit, *Keine Kameraden: Die Wehrmacht und die sowjetischen Kriegsgefangenen 1941–1945*, 4th edn (Bonn, 1997); Reinhard Otto, *Wehrmacht, Gestapo und sowjetische Kriegsgefangene im deutschen Reichsgebiet 1941/42*, Schriftenreihe der Vierteljahrshefte für Zeitgeschichte, vol. 77 (Munich, 1998).

22. Karner and Ruggenthaler, 'Einleitung', in Karner et al., *Zwangsarbeit in der Land- und Forstwirtschaft*, p. 36.

23. Gabriele Hammermann, *Zwangsarbeit für den 'Verbündeten': Die Arbeits- und Lebensbedingungen der italienischen Militärinternierten in Deutschland 1943–1945*, Bibliothek des Deutschen Historischen Instituts in Rome, vol. 99 (Tübingen, 2002); Gabriele Hammermann, 'Zur Situation der italienischen Militärinternierten aus sozialhistorischer Perspektive', in Günter Bischof, Stefan Karner and Barbara Stelzl-Marx (eds), *Kriegsgefangene des Zweiten Weltkrieges: Gefangennahme – Lagerleben – Rückkehr. Zehn Jahre Ludwig Boltzmann-Institut für Kriegsfolgen-Forschung*, in collaboration with Edith Petschnigg, Kriegsfolgen-Forschung, vol. 4 (Vienna/Munich, 2005), pp. 438–59, here p. 438; Brunello Mantelli, 'Von der Wanderarbeit zur Deportation: Die italienischen Arbeiter in Deutschland 1938–1945', in Herbert (ed.), *Europa und der 'Reichseinsatz'*, pp. 51–89.

24. Herbert, 'Arbeit und Vernichtung', p. 387; Spoerer, *Zwangsarbeit unter dem Hakenkreuz*, p. 17; Karner and Ruggenthaler, 'Einleitung', pp. 37f.; Florian Freund and Bertrand Perz, 'Die Zahlenentwicklung der ausländischen Zwangsarbeiter und Zwangsarbeiterinnen auf dem Gebiet der Republik Österreich 1939–1945', in *Zwangsarbeiter und Zwangsarbeiterinnen auf dem Gebiet der Republik Österreich 1939–1945*, with contributions from Florian Freund, Bertrand Perz and Mark Spoerer, Veröffentlichungen der Österreichischen Historikerkommission. Vermögensentzug während der NS-Zeit sowie Rückstellungen und Entschädigungen seit 1945 in Österreich, vol. 26 (Vienna/Munich, 2004), pp. 7–274, here p. 220.

25. Quoted in Rolf-Dieter Müller, 'Die Rekrutierung sowjetischer Zwangsarbeiter für die deutsche Kriegswirtschaft', in Herbert (ed.), *Europa und der 'Reichseinsatz'*, pp. 234–50, here p. 237.

26. Quoted in Peter Ruggenthaler and Barbara Stelzl-Marx, 'Fern der Heimat: Ostarbeiterinnen in Graz', in *Gedenkdienst*, vol. 4 (2000), p. 5.

27. The passages in italics were said in German, as opposed to Russian, during the interview.

28. AdBIK, Oral History Interview Antonina Kopylova, Novocherkassk 3.7.2001. Quoted in Harald Knoll, Peter Ruggenthaler and Barbara Stelzl-Marx, 'Zwangsarbeit bei der Lapp-Finze AG', in Karner et al. (eds), *NS-Zwangsarbeit in der Rüstungsindustrie*, pp. 103–78, here p. 112.

29. AdBIK, Interview Kopylova. Quoted in Knoll et al., 'Zwangsarbeit bei der Lapp-Finze AG', p. 112.

30. AdBIK, Interview Kopylova. Quoted in Knoll et al., 'Zwangsarbeit bei der Lapp-Finze AG', p. 113.

31. AdBIK, Oral History Interview Maria Viets, Graz 9.10.2002. Quoted in Knoll et al., 'Zwangsarbeit bei der Lapp-Finze AG', pp. 113f.

32. Herbert, *Fremdarbeiter*, p. 88.

33. Karner and Ruggenthaler, 'Kategorien der Zwangsarbeit', pp. 46–9.

34. Spoerer, *Zwangsarbeit unter dem Hakenkreuz*, p. 116.

35. Spoerer, *Zwangsarbeit unter dem Hakenkreuz*, pp. 117f.; Knoll et al., 'Zwangsarbeit bei der Lapp-Finze AG', pp. 126f.; Karner and Ruggenthaler, 'Kategorien der Zwangsarbeit', p. 53.

36. AdBIK, Oral History Interview Zinaida Fomenko, Novocherkassk 3.7.2001. Quoted in Knoll et al., 'Zwangsarbeit bei der Lapp-Finze AG', p. 131.

37. Knoll et al., 'Zwangsarbeit bei der Lapp-Finze AG', p. 131.

38. Spoerer, *Zwangsarbeit unter dem Hakenkreuz*, pp. 124f.

39. Karner et al., *Zwangsarbeit in der Land- und Forstwirtschaft*; Ela Hornung, Ernst Langthaler and Sabine Schweitzer, *Zwangsarbeit in der Landwirtschaft in Niederösterreich und dem nördlichen Burgenland*, Veröffentlichungen der Österreichischen Historikerkommission, vol. 26/2 (Vienna/Munich, 2004).

40. Edith Petschnigg, *Von der Front aufs Feld: Britische Kriegsgefangene in der Steiermark 1941–1945*, Veröffentlichungen des Ludwig Boltzmann-Instituts für Kriegsfolgen-Forschung, vol. 7 (Graz, 2003), pp. 164f.

41. Spoerer, *Zwangsarbeit unter dem Hakenkreuz*, p. 136; Knoll et al., 'Zwangsarbeit bei der Lapp-Finze AG', pp. 136f.

42. Hornung et al., *Zwangsarbeit in der Landwirtschaft*, pp. 259–61.

43. AdBIK, Interview Fomenko. Quoted in Knoll et al., 'Zwangsarbeit bei der Lapp-Finze AG', p. 136.

44. Spoerer, *Zwangsarbeit unter dem Hakenkreuz*, p. 140.

45. Spoerer, *Zwangsarbeit unter dem Hakenkreuz*, pp. 138–41.

46. Wolfgang Benz, 'Zwangsarbeit im nationalsozialistischen Staat: Dimensionen – Strukturen – Perspektiven', *Dachauer Hefte: Studien und Dokumente zur Geschichte der nationalsozialistischen Konzentrationslager*, vol. 16 (2000), pp. 3–17, here p. 3.

47. Herbert, *Fremdarbeiter*, p. 45; Hornung et al., *Zwangsarbeit in der Landwirtschaft*, p. 13.

48. Benz, 'Zwangsarbeit im nationalsozialistischen Staat', p. 5.

49. Spoerer, *Zwangsarbeit unter dem Hakenkreuz*, pp. 154–61.

50. AdBIK, Oral History Interview Ekaterina Khalitova, Krasnyi Sulin 13.7.2002. Quoted in Knoll et al., 'Zwangsarbeit bei der Lapp-Finze AG', p. 144.

51. Quoted in Herbert, *Fremdarbeiter*, p. 286.

52. Hornung et al., *Zwangsarbeit in der Landwirtschaft*, pp. 308–11.

53. Quoted in Herbert, *Fremdarbeiter*, p. 90.
54. Herbert, *Fremdarbeiter*, p. 90.
55. Spoerer, *Zwangsarbeit unter dem Hakenkreuz*, pp. 173–5.
56. Hornung et al., *Zwangsarbeit in der Landwirtschaft*, pp. 347–60.
57. Spoerer, *Zwangsarbeit unter dem Hakenkreuz*, pp. 196f.
58. Karner and Ruggenthaler, 'Kategorien der Zwangsarbeit', p. 78.
59. Spoerer, *Zwangsarbeit unter dem Hakenkreuz*, p. 198; Karner and Ruggenthaler, 'Kategorien der Zwangsarbeit', p. 77.
60. Knoll et al., 'Zwangsarbeit bei der Lapp-Finze AG', p. 152.
61. Knoll et al., 'Zwangsarbeit bei der Lapp-Finze AG', p. 150.
62. Barbara Stelzl-Marx, *Zwischen Fiktion und Zeitzeugenschaft: Amerikanische und sowjetische Kriegsgefangene im Stalag XVII B Krems-Gneixendorf* (Tübingen, 2000), pp. 107–208; Andreas Kusternig, 'Zwischen "Lageruniversität" und Widerstand: französische kriegsgefangene Offiziere im Oflag XVII A Edelbach', in Bischof et al. (eds), *Kriegsgefangene des Zweiten Weltkrieges*, pp. 352–97.
63. Tamara Frankenberger, *Wir waren wie Vieh: Lebensgeschichtliche Erinnerungen ehemaliger sowjetischer Zwangsarbeiterinnen* (Münster, 1997), pp. 195f.; Wolfram Dornik, 'Besatzungsalltag in Wien. Die Differenziertheit von Erlebniswelten: Vergewaltigungen – Plünderungen – Erbsen – Straußwalzer', in Stefan Karner and Barbara Stelzl-Marx (eds), *Die Rote Armee in Österreich. Sowjetische Besatzung 1945–1955: Beiträge*, Veröffentlichungen des Ludwig Boltzmann-Instituts für Kriegsfolgen-Forschung, special vol. 4 (Graz/Vienna/Munich, 2005), pp. 449–68, here p. 462.
64. Spoerer, *Zwangsarbeit unter dem Hakenkreuz*, p. 212.
65. Russian State Archive for Social-Political History, Moscow (RGASPI), F. 17, op. 125, d. 314, p. 2.
66. Ulrike Goeken, 'Von der Kooperation zur Konfrontation: die sowjetischen Repatriierungsoffiziere in den westlichen Besatzungszonen', in Klaus-Dieter Müller, Konstantin Nikischkin and Günther Wagenlehner (eds), *Die Tragödie der Gefangenschaft in Deutschland und in der Sowjetunion 1945–1956*, Schriften des Hannah-Arendt-Instituts für Totalitarismusforschung, vol. 5 (Cologne/Weimar, 1998), pp. 315–34, here p. 333.
67. Bernd Bonwetsch, 'Ein Sieg mit Schattenseiten: Die Sowjetunion im Zweiten Weltkrieg', in Haus der Geschichte (ed.), *Kriegsgefangene – Voennoplennye. Sowjetische Kriegsgefangene in Deutschland: Deutsche Kriegsgefangene in der Sowjetunion* (Düsseldorf, 1995), pp. 135–40, here p. 138.
68. Goeken, 'Von der Kooperation zur Konfrontation', pp. 316f.; Wolfgang Jacobmeyer, *Vom Zwangsarbeiter zum Heimatlosen Ausländer: Die displaced persons in Westdeutschland 1945–1951*, Kritische Studien zur Geschichtswissenschaft, vol. 65 (Göttingen, 1985), pp. 123ff.; Ulrike Goeken-Haidl, 'Repatriierung in den Terror? Die Rückkehr der sowjetischen Zwangsarbeiter und Kriegsgefangenen in ihre Heimat 1944–1956', *Dachauer Hefte: Studien und Dokumente zur Geschichte der nationalsozialistischen Konzentrationslager. Zwangsarbeit*, vol. 16 (2000), pp. 190–209.
69. Stefan Karner and Peter Ruggenthaler, '(Zwangs-)Repatriierung sowjetischer Staatsbürger aus Österreich in die UdSSR', in Karner and Stelzl-Marx (eds), *Die Rote Armee in Österreich*, pp. 243–74; Harald Stadler, Martin Kofler and Karl C.

Berger, *Flucht in die Hoffnungslosigkeit: Die Kosaken in Osttirol* (Innsbruck/Vienna/Bozen, 2005).

70. Jacobmeyer, 'Vom Zwangsarbeiter zum Heimatlosen Ausländer', p. 124.
71. State Archive of the Russian Federation (GARF), Moscow, F. 9526, op. 1, d. 75, p. 26.
72. Nikita Petrov, Peter Ruggenthaler and Barbara Stelzl-Marx, 'Repatriierung oder Verbleib in Österreich? Entscheidung nach Kriegsende', in Karner et al., *Zwangsarbeit in der Land- und Forstwirtschaft*, pp. 455–78; Stefan Karner, *Im Archipel GUPVI: Kriegsgefangenschaft und Internierung in der Sowjetunion*, Kriegsfolgen-Forschung, vol. 1 (Vienna/Munich, 1995), p. 55.
73. Vladimir Naumov and Leonid Rešin, 'Repressionen gegen sowjetische Kriegsgefangene und zivile Repatrianten in der UdSSR 1941 bis 1956', in Müller et al. (eds), *Die Tragödie der Gefangenschaft*, pp. 335–64, here p. 344.
74. An example of an MGB (Ministry of State Security) filtration file for a female 'eastern worker' is to be found in: Ludwig Boltzmann-Institut für Kriegsfolgen-Forschung, National Archive of the Republic of Belarus, Weißrussischer Republikanischer Fond 'Verständigung und Versöhnung' (ed.), *'Ostarbeiter' – 'Ostarbaitery'. Weißrussische Zwangsarbeiter in Österreich: Dokumente und Materialien. Prinuditel'nyi trud belorusskogo naseleniya v Avstrii: Dokumenty i materialy*, Veröffentlichungen des Ludwig Boltzmann-Instituts für Kriegsfolgen-Forschung, special vol. 2 (Graz/Minsk, 2003), pp. 230–9.
75. Naumov and Rešin, 'Repression gegen sowjetische Kriegsgefangene', p. 344; Petrov et al., 'Repatriierung oder Verbleib in Österreich?', pp. 465f.; Spoerer, *Zwangsarbeit unter dem Hakenkreuz*, p. 213.
76. Petrov et al., 'Repatriierung oder Verbleib in Österreich?', p. 468.
77. M.I. Semiryaga, *Sovetskie lyudi v evropeiskom dvizhenii soprotivleniya* (Moscow, 1970), p. 327.
78. Upravlenie upolnomochennogo sovnarkoma SSSR po delam repatriacii sovetskikh grazhdan, *Repatriaciya sovetskikh grazhdan* (Moscow, 1945), p. 40.
79. Goeken-Haidl, 'Repatriierung in den Terror?', p. 208.
80. V.N. Zemskov, 'K voprosu o repatriacii sovetskikh grazhdan 1944–1951 gody', *Istoriya SSSR*, vol. 4 (1990), pp. 26–43, here p. 36. Also with reference to this number: Pavel Polian, *Deportiert nach Hause: Sowjetische Kriegsgefangene im 'Dritten Reich' und ihre Repatriierung*, Kriegsfolgenforschung, vol. 2. (Munich/Vienna, 2001), p. 166.
81. Aleksandr F. Bichekhvost, 'Repatriaciya sovetskikh i inostrannykh grazhdan: vnutripoliticheskie i mezhdunarodnye aspekty (1944–1953)', postdoctoral thesis, Saratov, 1996, p. 210; Spoerer, *Zwangsarbeit unter dem Hakenkreuz*, p. 212.
82. Petrov et al., 'Repatriierung oder Verbleib in Österreich?', p. 470.
83. Barbara Stelzl-Marx, 'Der Krieg der Bilder: Plakate der sowjetischen Regierungsverwaltung 1944–1945', in Harald Knoll, Peter Ruggenthaler and Barbara Stelzl-Marx (eds), *Konflikte und Kriege im 20. Jahrhundert: Aspekte ihrer Folgen*, Veröffentlichungen des Ludwig Boltzmann-Instituts für Kriegsfolgen-Forschung, special vol. 3 (Graz/Vienna/Klagenfurt, 2002), pp. 317–34; Barbara Stelzl-Marx, '"Die Heimat wartet auf Euch …": Zur politisch-agitatorischen Arbeit unter ehemaligen weißrussischen Zwangsarbeitern', in Ludwig Boltzmann-Institut für Kriegsfolgen-Forschung (ed.), *'Ostarbeiter' – 'Ostarbaitery'*, pp. 44–61.

84. Aleksandr Solzhenitsyn, 'Ein Frühjahr der russischen Kriegsgefangenen', in Dieter Bach and Jochen Leyendecker (eds), *Ich habe geweint vor Hunger: Deutsche und russische Gefangene in Lagern des Zweiten Weltkrieges* (Wuppertal, 1993), p. 174.
85. GARF, F. 9526, op. 4a, d. 1, pp. 21ff.; RGASPI, F. 17, op. 116, d. 225, pp. 11–15. On the realization of this ordinance by October 1945 also see RGASPI, F. 17, op. 125, d. 314, pp. 76–80.
86. *Propaganda i agitaciya v resheniyakh i dokumentakh VKP(b)* (Moscow, 1947), pp. 486f.
87. RGASPI, F. 17, op. 125, d. 314, pp. 1–2.
88. RGASPI, F. 17, op. 125, d. 314, pp. 2f.
89. GARF, F. 9526, op. 1, d. 1124, pp. 147f.; Stelzl-Marx, 'Die Heimat wartet auf Euch'.
90. GARF, F. 9526, op. 4a, d. 1, pp. 126f.
91. Bichekhvost, *Deyatel'nost' repatriacionnykh organov*, p. 217.
92. Upravlenie upolnomochennogo sovnarkoma SSSR, *Repatriaciya sovetskikh grazhdan*, pp. 6f.
93. GARF, F. 9526, op. 4a, d. 1, pp. 126f.
94. GARF, F. 9526, op. 1, d. 42, p. 118; GARF, F. 9526, op. 4a, d. 1, p. 128.
95. Stelzl-Marx, 'Der Krieg der Bilder'.
96. GARF, F. 9526, op. 4, d. 32, p. 69; *Za chest' Rodiny*, 10.7.1945, no. 1, p. 1.
97. GARF, F. 9526, op. 4, d. 58.
98. GARF, F. 9526, op. 4, d. 32, pp. 51f.
99. GARF, F. 9526, op. 4a, d. 1, p. 130.
100. GARF, F. 9526, op. 4, d. 61, pp. 93ff.
101. GARF, F. 9526, op. 4, d. 32, pp. 54ff.
102. GARF, F. 9526, op. 4, d. 61, pp. 89ff.
103. GARF, F. 9526, op. 4a, d. 1, p. 130.
104. N. Brychev, *Domoy, na rodinu!*, 2nd extended edn (Moscow, 1945).
105. GARF, F. 9526, op. 4a, d. 1, pp. 128f.
106. GARF, F. 9526, op. 1, d. 42, p. 117; GARF, F. 9526, op. 4a, d. 1, p. 129.
107. Barbara Stelzl-Marx, '"Kommt schnellstens in die Heimat zurück!" Broschüren und Plakate für sowjetische Repatrianten', *Annali dell'Istituto italo-germanico in Trento*, vol. XXIX (2003), pp. 517–40.
108. RGASPI, F. 17, op. 125, d. 314, p. 19; RGASPI, F. 17, op. 125, d. 391, pp. 148–67; GARF, F. 9526, op. 1, d. 460. An example of a radio transmission for repatriates in the Estonian language can be found in: GARF, F. 9526, op. 1, d. 460, pp. 73ff.
109. National Archive of the Republic of Belarus (NARB), Minsk, F. 4, op. 47, d. 56, pp. 51f. Printed in: Ludwig Boltzmann-Institut für Kriegsfolgen-Forschung et al., *'Ostarbeiter'–'Ostarbaitery'*, pp. 226–9.
110. Goeken-Haidl, 'Repatriierung in den Terror?', p. 209.
111. NARB, F. 7, op. 3, d. 1941, p. 29. Printed in: Ludwig Boltzmann-Institut für Kriegsfolgenforschung et al., *'Ostarbeiter'–'Ostarbaitery'*, pp. 246f.
112. RGASPI, F. 17, op. 121, d. 541, p. 82.
113. RGASPI, F. 17, op. 125, d. 391, pp. 148–50.
114. Stelzl-Marx, 'Die Heimat wartet auf Euch', p. 58.
115. RGASPI, F. 17, op. 132, d. 101, pp. 1–3.
116. RGASPI, F. 17, op. 143, d. 101, pp. 4–6.

117. Archive of the President of the Russian Federation (APRF), Moscow, F. 3, op. 50, d. 509, pp. 27–31. I would like to thank Nikita Petrov, Moscow, for this information.
118. Herbert, *Fremdarbeiter*, p. 11.
119. Wolfram Dornik, '"Sie wurden durchwegs gut behandelt"? NS-Sklavenarbeiterinnen im Kollektiven Gedächtnis der II. Republik', *eForum*, vol. 3, no. 4 (2001), pp. 1–16.
120. Quoted in Stelzl-Marx, *Zwischen Fiktion und Zeitzeugenschaft*, p. 61.
121. Heidemarie Uhl (ed.), *Steinernes Bewusstsein: Die öffentliche Repräsentation staatlicher und nationaler Identität Österreichs in seinen Denkmälern* (Vienna/Cologne/Weimar, 2001).
122. Dornik, 'Sie wurden durchwegs gut behandelt', pp. 2–4.
123. For example, the Prisoner of War Museum in Lamsdorf in Poland or the memorials in Zeithain and Bergen-Belsen in Germany. There is so far nothing comparable in Austria.
124. On Sandbostel see Werner Borgsen and Klaus Volland, *Stalag X B Sandbostel: Zur Geschichte eines Kriegsgefangenen- und KZ-Auffanglagers in Norddeutschland, 1939–1945* (Edition Temmen, 1991).
125. An exact documentation of these burial grounds is to be found in Peter Sixl, *Sowjetische Kriegsgräber in Österreich. Sovetskie mogily Vtoroi mirovoi voiny v Avstrii*, Veröffentlichungen des Ludwig Boltzmann-Instituts für Kriegsfolgen-Forschung, special vol. 6 (Graz/Vienna/Klagenfurt, 2005).
126. Dornik, 'Sie wurden durchwegs gut behandelt', p. 4.
127. On this see Barbara Stelzl-Marx, 'Das Oflag XVIII B/Stalag XVIII A Wolfsberg 1939–1945', in Robert Gratzer, *Wolfsberg* (Wolfsberg, 2001), pp. 182–206, here p. 199; Stelzl-Marx, *Zwischen Fiktion und Zeitzeugenschaft*, pp. 103–5.
128. Dornik, 'Sie wurden durchwegs gut behandelt', p. 3.
129. Ulrich Herbert, 'Zwangsarbeit im "Dritten Reich": Kenntnisstand, offene Fragen, Forschungsprobleme', in Wilfried Reininghaus and Norbert Reimann (eds), *Zwangsarbeit in Deutschland 1939–1945: Archiv- und Sammlungsgut, Topographie und Erschließungsstrategien* (Bielefeld, 2001), pp. 16–37, here p. 29.
130. Herbert, 'Zwangsarbeit im "Dritten Reich"', pp. 29f.
131. Ibid., p. 30; Barbara Hopmann, Mark Spoerer, Birgit Weitz and Beate Brüninghaus, *Zwangsarbeit bei Daimler-Benz* (Stuttgart, 1994); Hans Mommsen and Manfred Grieger, *Das Volkswagenwerk und seine Arbeiter im Dritten Reich* (Düsseldorf, 1995).
132. Freund and Perz, 'Die Zahlenentwicklung der ausländischen Zwangsarbeiter und Zwangsarbeiterinnen'; Karner et al., *Zwangsarbeit in der Land- und Forstwirtschaft*; Hornung et al., *Zwangsarbeit in der Landwirtschaft*.
133. Wolfram Dornik, 'Zwangsarbeiterinnen im Kollektiven Gedächtnis der II. Republik', D.Phil. thesis, Graz, 2001, pp. 75–92.
134. On the studies examining company histories see among others Oliver Rahtkolb (ed.), *NS-Zwangsarbeit: Der Standort Linz der 'Reichswerke Hermann Göring AG Berlin' 1938–1945*, 2 vols (Vienna/Cologne/Weimar, 2001); Oliver Rathkolb and Florian Freund (eds), *NS-Zwangsarbeit in der Elektrizitätswirtschaft der 'Ostmark' 1938–1945: Enndwerke – Kaprun – Draukraftwerke – Ybbs-Persenbeug – Ernsthofen* (Vienna/Cologne/Weimar, 2002); Karner et al. (eds), *NS-Zwangsarbeit in der Rüstungsindustrie*.
135. Hubert Feichtlbauer, *Fonds für Versöhnung*, pp. 325–30.

136. Wolfgang Schüssel, 'Geste des Respekts und der Solidarität', in Hubert Feichtlbauer, *Fonds für Versöhnung*, pp. 6f.

137. Feichtlbauer, *Fonds für Versöhnung*, p. 325.

138. Maria Schaumayer, 'Wir wollten niemanden vergessen', in Feichtlbauer, *Fonds für Versöhnung*, pp. 8f.

139. Richard Wotava, 'Mit einem jungen, engagierten Team', in Feichtlbauer, *Fonds für Versöhnung*, pp. 12–14.

140. Peter Ruggenthaler and Barbara Stelzl-Marx, 'Menschenbilder: Biographische Spurensuche', in Karner et al. (eds), *NS-Zwangsarbeit in der Rüstungsindustrie*, p. 191.

141. http://www.zukunftsfonds-austria.at/ accessed 15.2.2007, Mozilla Firefox.

142. Viktor Rodinow, 'In den Mythen der Kriegsgefangenen gefangen', in Bach and Leyendecker (eds), *Ich habe geweint vor Hunger*, pp. 170–3, here p. 171.

143. Michail Šolochov, 'Sud'ba cheloveka', in *Pravda*, 31.12.1956, 1.1.1957.

144. Stepan Pavlovich Zlobin, *Propavščie bez vesti*, 2 vols (Moscow, 1962).

145. Stelzl-Marx, *Zwischen Fiktion und Zeitzeugenschaft*, pp. 252f.

146. *Sud'ba cheloveka*, Mosfil'm 1959, 103 minutes, black and white. Director: Sergei Bondarchuk.

147. *Čistoe nebo*, Mosfil'm 1961, 110 minutes, colour. Director: Grigori Chukhrai.

148. Stelzl-Marx, *Zwischen Fiktion und Zeitzeugenschaft*, pp. 282–92.

149. Jörn Borchert, 'Dokumente des Leids: Was von 5,7 Millionen sowjetischen Kriegsgefangenen übrigblieb …', in Haus der Geschichte der Bundesrepublik Deutschland (ed.), *Kriegsgefangene – Voennoplennye*, pp. 167–91, here p. 191.

150. Stelzl-Marx, *Zwischen Fiktion und Zeitzeugenschaft*, pp. 217–22.

151. Barbara Stelzl-Marx, '"Das Schweigen brechen": Briefe ehemaliger sowjetischer Zwangsarbeiter an Memorial Moskau', in Reininghaus and Reimann (eds), *Zwangsarbeit in Deutschland 1939–1945*, pp. 217–25.

152. Polian, *Deportiert nach Hause*, p. 205; Barbara Stelzl-Marx, 'Kriegsgefangenschaft in der Retrospektive: Kontext, Entstehung und Merkmals von Dmitrij Čirovs "Unter den Verschollenen"', in Barbara Stelzl-Marx (ed.), *Unter den Verschollenen: Erinnerungen von Dmitrij Čirov an das Kriegsgefangenenlager Krems-Gneixendorf 1941 bis 1945* (Horn/Waidhofen, Thaya, 2003), pp. 13–48, here pp. 32f.

Select Bibliography

Collections of Documents

Berezowska, Małgorzata (ed.), *Exodus Warszawy: Ludzie i miasto po powstaniu 1944*, vols 1–2: *Pamiętniki. Relacje* (Warsaw, Państwowy Instytut Wydaw., 1992–3); Józef Kazimierski (ed.), vols 3–4: *Archiwalia* (Warsaw, Państwowy Instytut Wydaw., 1994); Jan Górski (ed.), vol. 5: *Prasa* (Państwowy Instytut Wydaw., 1995).

Borodziej, Włodzimierz and Lemberg, Hans (eds), *'Unsere Heimat ist uns ein fremdes Land geworden ...': Die Deutschen östlich von Oder und Neiße 1945–1950. Dokumente aus polnischen Archiven*, vols 1–4 (Marburg, Herder-Institut, 2000–4). Polish edition: *Niemcy w Polsce 1945–1950: Wybór dokumentów* (Warsaw, Neriton, 2000–1).

Bundesministerium für Vertriebene, Flüchtlinge und Kriegsgeschädigte (BVFK) (ed.), *Dokumentation der Vertreibung der Deutschen aus Ost-Mitteleuropa*, 9 vols (Bundesminister für Vertriebene, Flüchtlinge und Kriegsgeschädigte 1953–62, reprint Munich, Dtv, 1984). English abridged edition: Schieder, Theodor (ed.), *Documents on the Expulsion of the Germans from Eastern Central Europe: A Selection and Translation* (Bonn, Federal Ministry for Expellees, Refugees and War Victims, 1956–60).

Ciesielski, Stanisław (ed.), *Przesiedlenie ludności polskiej z Kresów Wschodnich do Polski 1944–1947* (Warsaw, Neriton, 1999). German edition: *Umsiedlung der Polen aus den ehemaligen polnischen Ostgebieten nach Polen in den Jahren 1944–1947* (Marburg, Herder-Institut, 2006).

Csorba, Béla (ed.), *Források a Délvidék történetéhez, III* [Sources of the History of Voivodina, vol. 3] (Budapest, Hatodik Síp Alapítvány, 1999).

Grudzińska-Gross, Irena and Gross, Jan Tomasz (eds), *War through Children's Eyes: The Soviet Occupation of Poland and the Deportations, 1939–1941* (Palo Alto, CA, Hoover Institution Press, 1981)

Gust, Wolfgang (ed.), *Der Völkermord an den Armeniern 1915/16: Dokumente aus dem politischen Archiv des deutschen Auswärtigen Amts* (Springe, zu Klampen, 2005).

Kaden, Helma and Schumann, Wolfgang (eds), *Die faschistische Okkupationspolitik in Österreich und in der Tschekoslowakei (1938–1945)* (Cologne, Pahl-Rugenstein, 1988).

Kárný, Miroslav, Milotova, Jaroslava and Karna, Margita (eds), *Deutsche Politik im Reichsprotektorat Böhmen und Mähren unter Reinhard Heydrich* (Berlin, Metropol, 1997).

Knat'ko, Galina D. (ed.), *'Ostarbeiter' – 'Ostarbaitery'. Weißrussische Zwangsarbeiter in Österreich: Dokumente und Materialien. Prinuditel'nyi trud belorusskogo naseleniya v Avstrii: Dokumenty i materialy* (Graz, Verein zur Förderung [der Forschung] von Folgen nach Konflikten und Kriegen, 2003).

Kochanowski, Jerzy (ed.), *Protokoły posiedzeń Prezydium Krajowej Rady Narodowej 1944–1947* (Warsaw, Scjmowe 1995).

Komogorov, Viktor et al. (eds) *Deportacje obywateli polskich z Zachodniej Ukrainy i Zachodniej Białorusi w 1940 roku* (Warsaw and Moscow, Instytut Pamięci Narodowej, Ministerstwo Spraw Wewnętrznych i Administracji Rzeczypospolitej Polskiej with Federal'naja Služba Besopanosti RF, 2003).

Kulturstiftung der deutschen Vertriebenen (ed.), *Vertreibung und Vertreibungsverbrechen 1945–1948: Bericht des Bundesarchivs vom 28. Mai 1974. Archivalien und ausgewählte Erlebnisberichte* (Bonn, Kulturstiftung der deutschen Vertriebenen, 1989).

Loeber, Dietrich A., *Diktierte Option: Die Umsiedlung der Deutsch-Balten aus Estland und Lettland* (Neumünster, Karl Wachholtz Verlag, 1972).

Madajczyk, Czeslaw (ed.), *Zamojszczyzna – Sonderlaboratorium SS*, 2 vols (Warsaw, Ludowa Spóldzielnia Wydawn., 1977).

Misiło, Eugeniusz (ed.), *Akcja 'Wisła': Dokumenty* (Warsaw, Zaklad Wydawn. Tyrsa, 1993).

Misiło, Eugeniusz (ed.), *Repatriacja czy deportacja: Przesiedlenie Ukraińców z Polski do USSR 1944–1946*, vol. 1: *Dokumenty 1944–1945* (Warsaw, Oficyna Wydawn. Archiwum Ukrai'nskie, 1996), vol. 2: *Dokumenty 1946* (Warsaw, Oficyna Wydawn. Archiwum Ukrai'nskie, 1999).

Röhr, Werner (ed.), *Die faschistische Okkupationspolitik in Polen (1939–1945)* (Berlin, Deutscher Verlag der Wissenschaften, 1989).

Schulze, Rainer (ed.), *Unruhige Zeiten: Erlebnisberichte aus dem Landkreis Celle 1945–1949* (Munich, Oldenbourg, 1990).

Szarka, László (ed.), *Jogfosztó jogszabályok Csehszlovákiában, 1944–1949* [Unlawful Rules in Czechoslovakia, 1944–1949] (MTA Etnikai-Nemzeti Kisebbségkutató Intézet, Budapest, 2005).

Tone, Ferenc, *La provincia 'italiana' di Lubiana: Documenti 1941–1943* (Udine: Istituto Friulano per la storia del movimento di liberazione, 1994).

Włodkowski, Lucjusz (ed.), *Czas przeszły – ciągle obecny: Z dziejów wysiedleń – historia, wspomnienia, dokumenty* (Lódź, Związek Wysiedlonych Ziemi Lódźkiej, 1998).

Zagorul'ko, Maksim M. (ed.), *Voennoplennye v SSSR 1939–1956: Dokumenty i materialy* (Moscow, Logos, 2000).

General Literature

Beer, Mathias (ed.), *Auf dem Weg zum ethnisch reinen Nationalstaat?* (Tübingen, Attempto, 2004).

Béla Várdy, Steven and Tooley, T. Hunt (eds), *Ethnic Cleansing in 20th-Century Europe* (New York, Boulder, 2003).

Bömelburg, H.-J. and Troebst, S., 'Zwangsmigrationen in Nordosteuropa im 20. Jahrhundert', *Nordost-Archiv. Zeitschrift für Regionalgeschichte*, n.s., XIV (2005).

Cattaruzza, Marina, Dogo, Marco and Pupo, Raoul (eds), *Esodi: Trasferimenti forzati di popolazione nel Novecento europeo* (Naples, Edizioni Scientifiche Italiane, 2000).

Ferrara, Antonio, 'Esodi, deportazioni e stermini: la "guerra-rivoluzione" europea', *Contemporanea*, vol. 9 (2006), pp. 449–75 and 653–79.

Mann, Michael, *The Dark Side of Democracy: Explaining Ethnic Cleansing* (Cambridge, Cambridge University Press, 2005).

Marrus, Michael R., *The Unwanted: European Refugees in the Twentieth Century* (New York, Oxford University Press, 1985).

Melville, Ralph, Pešek, Jiří and Scharf, Claus (eds), *Zwangsmigrationen im mitteleren und östlichen Europa: Völkerrecht – Konzeptionen – Praxis (1938–1950)* (Mainz, Philipp von Zabern, 2007).

Naimark, Norman, *Fires of Hatred: Ethnic Cleansing in Twentieth-century Europe* (Cambridge, MA, Harvard University Press, 2001).

Proudfoot, Malcom J., *European Refugees 1939–1952: A Study in Forced Population Movement* (London, Faber & Faber, 1957).

Schechtman, Joseph B., *European Population Transfers, 1939–1945* (New York, Oxford University Press, 1946).

Schechtman, Joseph B., *Postwar Population Transfers in Europe 1945–1955* (Philadelphia, University of Pennsylvania Press, 1962).

Snyder, Thomas, *The Reconstruction of Nations: Poland, Ukraine, Lithuania, Belarus* (New Haven, Yale University Press, 2003).

Suny, Ronald G. and Martin, Terry (eds), *A State of Nations: Empire and Nation-making in the Age of Lenin and Stalin* (New York/Oxford, Oxford University Press, 2001).

Ther, Philip and Siljak, Ana (eds), *Redrawing Nations: Ethnic Cleansing in East-Central Europe, 1944–1948* (Lanham, MD, Rowman & Littlefield, 2001).

1 Introduction

Akçam, Taner, *From Empire to Republic: Turkish Nationalism and the Armenian Genocide* (London, Zed Books, 2004).

Dadrian, Vahakn N., *The History of the Armenian Genocide: Ethnic Conflict from the Balkans to Anatolia to the Caucasus*, 6th rev. edn (New York, Berghahn Books, 2004).

Hirschon, Renée, *Heirs of the Greek Catastrophe: The Social Life of Asia Minor Refugees in Piraeus* (New York, Berghahn Books, 1998).

Hirschon, Renée (ed.), *Crossing the Aegean: An Appraisal of the 1923 Compulsory Population Exchange between Greece and Turkey* (New York, Berghahn Books, 2003).

Ladas, Stephen P., *The Exchange of Minorities: Bulgaria, Greece and Turkey* (London, Macmillan, 1932).

Lewy, Günter, *The Armenian Massacres in Ottoman Turkey: A Disputed Genocide* (Salt Lake City, University of Utah Press, 2005).

Pentzopoulos, Dimitri, *The Balkan Exchange of Minorities and Its Impact on Greece*, 2nd edn (London, Hurst & Company, 2002).

Raitz von Frentz, Christian, *A Lesson Forgotten: Minority Protection under the League of Nations. The Case of the German Minority in Poland 1920–1934* (New York, St Martin's Press, 1999).

2 Forced Migration Plans and Policies of Nazi Germany

Aly, Götz, *Endlösung: Völkerverschiebung und der Mord an den europäischen Juden* (Frankfurt am Main, Fischer, 1995).

Aly, Götz and Heim, Susanne, *Vordenker der Vernichtung: Auschwitz und die deutschen Pläne für eine neue europäische Ordnung* (Hamburg, Hoffmann und Campe, 1991).

Bergen, Doris L., 'The Nazi Concept of "Volksdeutsche" and the Exacerbation of Anti-Semitism in Eastern Europe, 1939–1945', *Journal of Contemporary History*, vol. 29, no. 4 (1994), pp. 569–82.

Bergen, Doris L., 'The Volksdeutsche of Eastern Europe and the Collapse of the Nazi Empire 1944–1945', in Alan E. Steinweis and Daniel E. Rogers (eds), *The Impact of Nazism: New Perspectives on the Third Reich and Its Legacy* (Lincoln, University of Nebraska Press, 2003).

Berkhoff, Karel C., *Harvest of Despair: Life and Death in Ukraine under Nazi Rule* (Cambridge, MA, Belknap Press, 2004).

Browning, Christopher R., *The Origins of the Final Solution: The Evolution of Nazi Jewish Policy, September 1939–March 1942* (Lincoln, University of Nebraska Press, 2004).

Burleigh, Michael, *Germany Turns Eastward: A Study of Ostforschung in the Third Reich* (Cambridge, Cambridge University Press 1988).

Corni, Gustavo, *Hitler's Ghettos: Voices from a Beleaguered Society 1939–1944* (London, Arnold, 2002).

Esch, Michael G., *'Gesunde Verhältnisse': Die deutsche und polnische Bevölkerungspolitik in Ostmitteleuropa* (Marburg, Herder-Institut, 1998).

Fahlbusch, Michael, *Wissenschaft im Dienst der nationalsozialistischen Politik: Die 'Volksdeutschen Forschungsgemeinschaften' von 1939–1945* (Baden-Baden, Nomos, 1999).

Gross, Jan Tomasz, *Polish Society under German Occupation: The General-gouvernement 1939–1944* (Princeton, Princeton University Press, 1979).

Haar, Ingo and Fahlbusch Michael (eds), *German Scholars and Ethnic Cleansing 1920–1945* (New York, Berghahn Books, 2005).

Hartenstein, Michael A., *Neue Dorflandschaften: Nationalsozialistische Siedlungsplanung in den 'eingegliederten' Ostgebieten 1939–1944* (Berlin, Dr. Köster Verlag, 1998).

Hartungen, Christoph von, Miori, Fabrizio and Rosani, Tiziano (eds), *Le lettere aperte: 1939–1943 l'Alto Adige delle opzioni*, 2 vols (Bolzano-Bozen, La Fabbrica del tempo, 2006).

Harvey, Elizabeth, *Women and the Nazi East: Agents and Witnesses of Germanization* (New Haven, Yale University Press, 2003).

Heinemann, Isabel, *'Rasse, Siedlung, deutsches Blut': Das Rasse- und Siedlungshauptamt der SS und die rassenpolitische Neuordnung Europas* (Göttingen, Wallstein, 2002).

Jachomowski, Dirk, *Umsiedlung der Bessarabien-, Bukowina- und Dobrudschadeutschen* (Munich/Vienna, Oldenbourg, 1984).

Koehl, Robert L., *RKFDV: German Resettlement and Population Policy 1939–1945. A History of the Reich Commission for the Strengthening of Germandom* (Cambridge, MA, Harvard University Press, 1957).

Kowalska, Ewa, *Przeżyć, aby wrócić! Polscy zesłańcy lat 1940–1941 w ZSRR i ich losy do roku 1946* (Warsaw, Neriton, 1998).

Levine, Herbert S., 'Local Authority and the SS State: The Conflict over Population Policy in Danzig-West Prussia 1939–1945', *Central European History*, vol. 2 (1969), pp. 331–55.

Lower, Wendy, 'Hitler's "Garden of Eden" in Ukraine', in Jonathan Petropoulos and John K. Roth (eds), *Gray Zones: Ambiguity and Compromise in the Holocaust and Its Aftermath* (New York, Berghahn Books, 2005).

Lukas, Richard C., *Forgotten Holocaust: The Poles under German Occupation 1939–1944*, 2nd rev. edn (New York : Hippocrene Books, 1997).

Lumans, Valdis O., *Himmler's Auxiliaries: The Volksdeutsche Mittelstelle and the German National Minorities of Europe 1933–1945* (Chapel Hill, North Carolina University Press, 1993).

Müller, Rolf-Dieter, *Hitlers Ostkrieg und die deutsche Siedlungspolitik* (Frankfurt am Main, Fischer, 1991).

Pohl, J. Otto, *Ethnic Cleansing in the USSR, 1937–1949* (Westport, CT, Greenwood Press, 1999).

Poljan, Pavel, *Ne po svoej vole... Istoriia i geografiia prinuditelnykh migracii v SSSR* (Moscow, OGI-Memorial, 2001); English edn: *Against Their Will: The History and Geography of Forced Migrations in the USSR* (Budapest/New York, Central European University Press, 2004).

Rössler, Mechtild and Schleiermacher, Sabine (eds), *Der 'Generalplan Ost': Hauptlinien der nationalsozialistischen Planungs- und Vernichtungspolitik* (Berlin, Akademie, 1993).

Rutowska, Maria, *Wysiedlenia ludności polskiej z Kraju Warty do Generalnego Gubernatorstwa 1939 1941* (Poznań, Instytut Zachodni, 2003).

Stuhlpfarrer, Karl, *Umsiedlung Südtirol 1939–1940*, 2 vols (Munich/Vienna, Oldenbourg, 1985).

Wambaugh, Sarah, *Plebiscites since the World War* (Stanford, CA, Carnegie Endowment for International Peace, 1933).

Zimmermann, Volker, *Die Sudetendeutschen im NS-Staat* (Essen, Klartext, 1999).

3 The Population Policies of the 'Axis' Allies

Achim, Viorel, 'The Romanian Population Exchange Project Elaborated by Sabin Manuilă in October 1941', *Annali dell'Istituto storico italo-germanico in Trento*, XXVII (2001).

Ben-Ghiat, Ruth, *Fascist Modernities: Italy 1922–1945* (Berkeley, University of California Press, 2001).

Burgwyn, H. James, *Empire on the Adriatic: Mussolini's Conquest of Yugoslavia 1941–1943* (New York, Enigma Books, 2005).

Collotti, Enzo, *Il Litorale Adriatico nel Nuovo Ordine Europeo* (Milan, Vangelista, 1974).

Cuzzi, Marco, *L'occupazione italiana della Slovenia (1941–1943)* (Rome, Ufficio Storico Stato Maggiore Esercito, 1998).

Gentile, Emilio, *La Grande Italia: Ascesa e declino del mito della nazione nel ventesimo secolo* (Milan, Mondadori, 1997).

Kacin-Wohinz, Milica, 'I programmi di snazionalizzazione degli sloveni e croati nella Venezia Giulia', *Storia Contemporanea in Friuli*, vol. 18, no. 19 (1988), pp. 9–33.

Kocsis, Károly and Kocsis-Hodosi, Eszter, *Ethnic Geography of the Hungarian Minorities in the Carpathian Basin* (Budapest, Geographical Research Institute, 1998).

Rodogno, Davide, *Il nuovo ordine mediterraneo: Le politiche d'occupazione dell'Italia in Europa 1940–1943* (Turin, Bollati Boringhieri, 2001); English translation: *Fascism's European Empire: Italian Occupation during the Second World War* (Cambridge, Cambridge University Press, 2006).

Sajti, Enikő A., *Impériumváltások, Revízió, Kisebbség: Magyarok a Délvidéken, 1918–1947* [Domination-changes, Revision, Minority: Hungarians in the Southernland, 1918–1947] (Budapest, Napvilág Kiadó, 2004).
Tóth, Ágnes, *Migrationen in Ungarn 1945–1948: Vertreibung der Ungarndeutschen, Binnenwanderungen und slowakisch-ungarischer Bevölkerungsaustausch* (Munich/Vienna, Oldenbourg, 2001).

4 Population Movements at the End of the War and in Its Aftermath

Brandes, Detlef, Ivaničkova, Edita and Pešek, Jiří (eds), *Erzwungene Trennung, Vertreibungen und Aussiedlungen in und aus der Tschechoslowakei 1938–1947 im Vergleich mit Polen, Ungarn und Jugoslawien* (Essen, Klartext, 1999).
Ciesielski, Stanisław (ed.), *Przesiedlenie ludności polskiej z Kresów Wschodnich do Polski 1944–1947* (Warsaw, Neriton, 1999).
Crainz, Guido, *Il dolore e l'esilio: L'Istria e le memorie divisa d'Europa* (Rome, Donzelli, 2005).
Czerniakiewicz, Jan, *Repatriacja ludności polskiej z ZSRR 1944–1948* (Warsaw, Państwowe Wydawnictwo Naukowe, 1987).
Nitschke, Bernadetta, *Wysiedlenie czy wypędzenie? Ludność niemiecka w Polsce w latach 1945–1949* (Toruń, Marszałek, 2000); German edn: *Vertreibung und Aussiedlung der deutschen Bevölkerung aus Polen 1945 bis 1949* (Munich/Vienna, Oldenbourg, 2003).
Olejnik, Leszek, *Polityka narodowościowa Polski w latach 1944–1960* (Łódź, Wydawn. Uniwersytetu Łódźkiego, 2003).
Olejnik, Leszek, *Zdrajcy narodu? Losy volksdeutschów w Polsce po II wojnie światowej* (Warsaw, Trio, 2006).
Pupo, Raoul, *Il lungo esodo. Istria: le persecuzioni, le foibe, l'esilio* (Milan, Rizzoli, 2005).
Pupo, Raoul and Spazzali, Roberto, *Foibe* (Milan, Bruno Mondadori, 2003).
Ruchniewicz, Małgorzata, *Repatriacja ludności polskiej z ZSRR w latach 1955–59* (Warsaw, Volumen, 2000).
Stark, Tamás, *Magyarok szovjet fogságban* [Hungarians in Soviet Custody] (Budapest, Lucidus Kiadó, 2006).
Sula, Dorota, *Działalność przesiedleńczo-repatriacyjna Państwowego Urzędu Repatriacyjnego w latach 1944–1951* (Lublin, Red. Wydawnictw Katolickiego Uniwersytetu Lubelskiego, 2002).
Vadkerti, Katalin, *A belső telepítések és a lakosságcsere* [Interior Settlement and Population Transfer] (Pozsony/Bratislava, Kalligram, 1999).

5 The Experience of Forced Migration

Ahonen, Pertti, *After the Expulsion: West Germany and Eastern Europe 1945–1990* (New York/Oxford, Oxford University Press, 2003).

Brandes, Detlef, *Der Weg zur Vertreibung 1938–1945: Pläne und Entscheidungen zum 'Transfer' der Deutschen aus der Tschechoslowakei und aus Polen* (Munich/Vienna, Oldenbourg, 2001).

Ciesielski, Stanisław, Hryciuk, Grzegorz and Srebrakowski, Aleksander, *Masowe deportacje radzieckie w okresie II wojny światowej* (Wrocław, Instytut Historyczny, 1994).

Ciesielski, Stanisław, Materski, Wojciech and Paczkowski, Andrzej, *Represje sowieckie wobec Polaków i obywateli polskich* (Warsaw, Ośrodek KARTA, 2000).

Connor, Ian, *Refugees and Expellees in Post-war Germany* (Manchester, Manchester University Press, 2007).

Franzen, K. Erik, *Die Vertriebenen: Hitlers letzte Opfer* (Munich, Propyläen, 2001).

Grossman, Atina, 'A Question of Silence: The Rape of German Women by Occupation Soldiers', *October* (1995), pp. 43–63.

Hrabovec, Emilia, *Vertreibung und Abschub: Deutsche in Mähren 1945–1947* (Frankfurt am Main/Berlin, Lang, 1995).

Jankowiak, Stanisław, *Wysiedlenie i emigracja ludności niemieckiej w polityce władz polskich w latach 1945–1970* (Warsaw, Instytut Pamięci Narodowej, Komisja Ścigania Zbrodni przeciwko Narodowi Polskiemu, 2005).

Kiełboń, Janina, *Migracje ludności w dystrykcie lubelskim w latach 1939–1944* (Lublin, Państwowe Muzeum na Majdanku, 1995).

Kowalska, Ewa, *Przeżyć, aby wrócić! Polscy zesłańcy lat 1940–1941 w ZSRR i ich losy do roku 1946* (Warsaw, Neriton, 1998).

Madajczyk, Czesław (ed.), *Vom Generalplan Ost zum Generalsiedlungsplan* (Munich, Saur, 1994).

Olejnik, Leszek, *Polityka narodowościowa Polski w latach 1944–1960* (Łódź, Wydawn. Uniwersytetu Łódź,kiego, 2003).

Schulze, Rainer, 'Growing Discontent: Relations between Native and Refugee Populations in a Rural District in Western Germany after the Second World War', *German History*, vol. 7, no. 3 (1989), pp. 332–49.

Schulze, Rainer, 'Forgotten Victims or Beneficiaries of Genocide? The Mass Resettlement of Ethnic Germans "heim ins Reich"', *Annali dell'Istituto storico italo-germanico in Trento*, XXVII (2001): 533–63.

Schwartz, Michael, *Vertriebene und 'Umsiedlerpolitik': Integrationskonflikte in den deutschen Nachkriegs-Gesellschaften und die Assimilationsstrategien in der SBZ/DDR 1945 bis 1961* (Munich/Vienna, Oldenbourg, 2004).

Szapował, Jurij and Tucholski, Jędrzej (eds), *Przesiedlenia Polaków i Ukraińców 1944–1946* (Warsaw, Rytm, 2000).

Ther, Philipp, *Deutsche und polnische Vertriebene: Gesellschaft und Vertriebenenpolitik in der SBZ/DDR und in Polen 1945–1956* (Göttingen, Vandenhoeck & Ruprecht, 1998).

6 Forced Migrations and Mass Movements in the Memorialization Processes since the Second World War

Assmann, Aleida, *Der lange Schatten der Vergangenheit: Erinnerungskultur und Geschichtspolitik* (Munich, C.H. Beck, 2006).

Assmann, Aleida and Frevert, Ute, *Geschichtsvergessenheit – Geschichtsversessenheit: Vom Umgang mit deutschen Vergangenheiten nach 1945* (Stuttgart, Deutsche-Verlags-Anstalt, 1999).

Bingen, Dieter, Borodziej, Włodzimierz and Troebst, Stefan (eds), *Vertreibung europäisch erinnern? Historische Erfahrungen – Vergangenheitspolitik – Zukunftskonzeptionen* (Wiesbaden, Harrassowitz, 2003).

Cornelißen, Christoph, Holec, Roman and Pešek, Jiří (eds), *Diktatur – Krieg – Vertreibung: Erinnerungskulturen in Tschechien, der Slowakei und Deutschland seit 1945* (Essen, Klartext, 2005).

Den Boer, Pim and Frijhoff, Willem (eds), *Lieux de mémoire et identités nationales* (Amsterdam, Amsterdam University Press, 1993).

Faulenbach, Bernd, 'Die Vertreibung der Deutschen aus den Gebieten jenseits von Oder und Neiße: Zur wissenschaftlichen und öffentlichen Diskussion in Deutschland', *Aus Politik und Zeitgeschichte*, B 51–52 (2002), pp. 44–54.

Faulenbach, Bernd and Helle, Andreas (eds), *Zwangsmigration in Europa: Zur wissenschaftlichen und politischen Auseinandersetzung um die Vertreibung der Deutschen aus dem Osten* (Essen, Klartext, 2005).

Herf, Jeffrey, *Divided Memory: The Nazi Past in the Two Germanys* (Cambridge, MA, Harvard University Press, 1997).

Hirsch, Helga, 'Flucht und Vertreibung: Kollektive Erinnerung im Wandel', *Aus Politik und Zeitgeschichte*, B 40–41 (2003), pp. 14–26.

Isnenghi, Mario, *I luoghi della memoria*, 3 vols (Rome-Bari, Laterza, 1997).

Kansteiner, Wulf, 'Finding Meaning in Memory: A Methodological Critique of Collective Memory Studies', *History & Theory*, vol. 41, no. 1 (2002), pp. 179–97.

Kittel, Manfred, *Vertreibung der Vertriebenen? Der historische deutsche Osten in der Erinnerungskultur der Bundesrepublik (1961–1982)* (Munich, Oldenbourg, 2006).

Kochanowski, Jerzy, 'Eine andere Schuldrechnung: Die polnischen Umsiedler und ihr Kampf um Entschädigungen', *Zeitschrift für Geschichtswissenschaft*, vol. 51, no. 1 (2003), pp. 65–73.

Kochanowski, Jerzy, 'Paradoksy kresowej pamięci', *Borussia*, no. 35 (2004), pp. 111–23; German translation: 'Paradoxien der Erinnerung an die Ostgebiete', *Inter Finitimos. Jahrbuch zur deutsch-polnischen Beziehungsgeschichte*, no. 3 (2005).

Lagrou, Pieter, *The Legacy of Nazi Occupation: Patriotic Memory and National Recovery in Western Europe 1945–1965* (Cambridge, Cambridge University Press, 2000).

Lehmann, Albrecht, *Im Fremden ungewollt zuhaus: Flüchtlinge und Vertriebene in Westdeutschland 1945–1990* (Munich, C.H. Beck, 1991).

Lemberg, Eugen and Edding, Friedrich (eds), *Die Vertriebenen in Westdeutschland*, 3 vols, (Kiel, Hirt, 1959).

Lemberg, Hans, 'Geschichten und Geschichte: Das Gedächtnis der Vertriebenen in Deutschland nach 1945', *Archiv für Sozialgeschichte*, 44 (2004), pp. 509–23.

Moeller, Robert G., *War Stories: The Search for a Usable Past in the Federal Republic of Germany* (Berkeley and Los Angeles, University of California Press, 2001).

Rautenberg, Hans-Werner, 'Die Wahrnehmung von Flucht und Vertreibung in der deutschen Nachkriegsgeschichte bis heute', *Aus Politik und Zeitgeschichte*, B 53 (1997), pp. 34–46.

Rousso, Henry, 'Das Dilemma eines europäischen Gedächtnisses', *Zeithistorische Forschungen*, vol. 1, no. 3 (2004), pp. 363–78.

Schulze, Rainer, 'The Politics of Memory: Flight and Expulsion of German Populations after the Second World War and German Collective Memory', *National Identities*, 8 (2006), pp. 367–82.

Schulze, Rainer (ed.), *Zwischen Heimat und Zuhause: Deutsche Flüchtlinge und Vertriebene in (West) Deutschland 1945–2000* (Osnabrück, Secolo, 2001).

Schulze, Rainer, Brelie-Lewien, Doris von der and Grebing, Helga (eds), *Flüchtlinge und Vertriebene in der westdeutschen Nachkriegsgeschichte: Bilanzierung der Forschung und Perspektiven für die künftige Forschungsarbeit* (Hildesheim, August Lax, 1987).

Urban, Thomas, *Der Verlust: Die Vertreibung der Deutschen und Polen im 20. Jahrhundert* (Munich, C.H. Beck, 2004).

Wieviorka, Annette, *L'ère du témoin* (Paris, Plon, 1998).

Wolfrum, Edgar, *Geschichtspolitik in der Bundesrepublik Deutschland: Der Weg zur bundesrepublikanischen Erinnerung 1948–1990* (Darmstadt, Wissenschaftliche Buchgesellschaft, 1999).

7 Forced Labourers in the Third Reich

Benz, Wolfgang, 'Zwangsarbeit im nationalsozialistischen Staat: Dimensionen – Strukturen – Perspektiven', *Dachauer Hefte: Studien und Dokumente zur Geschichte der nationalsozialistischen Konzentrationslager*, vol. 16 2000).

Bischof, Günter, Karner, Stefan and Stelzl-Marx, Barbara (eds), *Kriegsgefangene des Zweiten Weltkrieges: Gefangennahme – Lagerleben – Rückkehr. Zehn Jahre Ludwig Boltzmann-Institut für Kriegsfolgen-Forschung* (Munich/Vienna, Oldenbourg, 2005).

Dornik, Wolfram, 'Besatzungsalltag in Wien. Die Differenziertheit von Erlebniswelten: Vergewaltigungen – Plünderungen – Erbsen – Straußwalzer', in Stefan Karner and Barbara Stelzl-Marx (eds), *Die Rote Armee in Österreich: Sowjetische Besatzung 1945–1955. Beiträge* (Graz/Vienna/Munich, Oldenbourg, 2005).

Feichtlbauer, Hubert, *Fonds für Versöhnung, Frieden und Zusammenarbeit: Späte Anerkennung. Geschichte. Schicksale. 1938–1945. Zwangsarbeit in Österreich* (Vienna, Braintrust, 2005).

Frankenberger, Tamara, *Wir waren wie Vieh: Lebensgeschichtliche Erinnerungen ehemaliger sowjetischer Zwangsarbeiterinnen* (Münster, Westfälisches Dampfboot, 1997).

Freund, Florian, Perz, Betrand and Spoerer, Mark (eds), *Zwangsarbeiter und Zwangsarbeiterinnen auf dem Gebiet der Republik Österreich 1939–1945* (Munich/Vienna, Oldenbourg, 2004).

Goeken-Haidl, Ulrike, 'Repatriierung in den Terror? Die Rückkehr der sowjetischen Zwangsarbeiter und Kriegsgefangenen in ihre Heimat 1944–1956', *Dachauer Hefte: Studien und Dokumente zur Geschichte der nationalsozialistischen Konzentrationslager. Zwangsarbeit*, vol. 16 (2000).

Hammermann, Gabriele, *Zwangsarbeit für den 'Verbündeten': Die Arbeits- und Lebensbedingungen der italienischen Militärinternierten in Deutschland 1943–1945* (Tübingen, Niemeyer, 2002).

Herbert, Ulrich (ed.), *Europa und der 'Reichseinsatz': Ausländische Zivilarbeiter, Kriegsgefangene und KZ-Häftlinge in Deutschland 1938–1945* (Essen, Klartext, 1991).

Herbert, Ulrich, *Fremdarbeiter: Politik und Praxis des 'Ausländer-Einsatzes' in der Kriegswirtschaft des Dritten Reiches* (Berlin/Bonn, Dietz, 1985).

Hornung, Ela, Langthaler, Ernst and Schweitzer, Sabine, *Zwangsarbeit in der Landwirtschaft in Niederösterreich und dem nördlichen Burgenland* (Munich/Vienna, Oldenbourg, 2004).

Jacobmeyer, Wolfgang, *Vom Zwangsarbeiter zum Heimatlosen Ausländer: Die displaced persons in Westdeutschland 1945–1951* (Göttingen, Vandenhoeck & Ruprecht, 1985).

Karner, Stefan, *Im Archipel GUPVI: Kriegsgefangenschaft und Internierung in der Sowjetunion* (Munich/Vienna, Oldenbourg, 1995).

Karner, Stefan and Ruggenthaler, Peter (in collaboration with Harald Knoll, Peter Pirnath, Arno Wonisch, Wolfram Dornik, Jens Gassmann, Gerald Hafner,

Herbert Killian, Reinhard Möstl, Nikita Petrov, Edith Petschnigg and Barbara Stelzl-Marx), *Zwangsarbeit in der Land- und Forstwirtschaft auf dem Gebiet Österreichs 1939 bis 1945* (Munich/Vienna, Oldenbourg, 2004).

Karner, Stefan and Ruggenthaler, Peter, '(Zwangs-)Repatriierung sowjetischer Staatsbürger aus Österreich in die UdSSR', in Stefan Karner and Barbara Stelzl-Marx (eds), *Die Rote Armee in Österreich: Sowjetische Besatzung 1945–1955. Beiträge* (Graz/Vienna/Munich, Oldenbourg, 2005).

Müller, Klaus-Dieter, Nikischkin, Konstantin and Wagenlehner, Günther (eds), *Die Tragödie der Gefangenschaft in Deutschland und in der Sowjetunion 1945–1956* (Cologne, Böhlau, 1998).

Otto, Reinhard, *Wehrmacht, Gestapo und sowjetische Kriegsgefangene im deutschen Reichsgebiet 1941/42*, Schriftenreihe der Vierteljahrshefte für Zeitgeschichte, vol. 77 (Munich/Vienna, Oldenbourg, 1998).

Petschnigg, Edith, *Von der Front aufs Feld: Britische Kriegsgefangene in der Steiermark 1941–1945* (Graz, Verein zur Förderung der Forschung von Folgen nach Konflikten und Kriegen, 2003).

Polian, Pavel, *Deportiert nach Hause: Sowjetische Kriegsgefangene im 'Dritten Reich' und ihre Repatriierung* (Munich/Vienna, Oldenbourg, 2001).

Speckner, Hubert, *In der Gewalt des Feindes: Kriegsgefangenenlager in der 'Ostmark' 1939 bis 1945* (Vienna/Munich, Oldenbourg, 2003).

Spoerer, Mark, *Zwangsarbeit unter dem Hakenkreuz: Ausländische Zivilarbeiter, Kriegsgefangene und Häftlinge im Deutschen Reich und im besetzten Europa 1939–1945* (Stuttgart/Munich, Deutsche Verlag-Anstalt, 2001).

Stelzl-Marx, Barbara, 'Der Krieg der Bilder: Plakate der sowjetischen Repatriierungsverwaltung 1944–1945', in Harald Knoll, Peter Ruggenthaler and Barbara Stelzl-Marx (eds), *Konflikte und Kriege im 20. Jahrhundert: Aspekte ihrer Folgen* (Graz/Vienna/Klagenfurt, Verein zur Förderung der Forschung von Folgen nach Konflikten und Kriegen, 2002).

Stelzl-Marx, Barbara, *Zwischen Fiktion und Zeitzeugenschaft: Amerikanische und sowjetische Kriegsgefangene im Stalag XVII B Krems-Gneixendorf* (Tübingen, Narr, 2000).

Streit, Christian, *Keine Kameraden: Die Wehrmacht und die sowjetischen Kriegsgefangenen 1941–1945*, 4th edn (Bonn, Dietz, 1997).

Zemskov, V.N., 'K voprosu o repatriacii sovetskikh grazhdan 1944–1951 gody', *Istoriya SSSR*, vol. 4 (1990).

Index